Communications
in Computer and Information Science   724

Commenced Publication in 2007
Founding and Former Series Editors:
Alfredo Cuzzocrea, Dominik Ślęzak, and Xiaokang Yang

More information about this series at http://www.springer.com/series/7899

Gülen Çağdaş · Mine Özkar
Leman Figen Gül · Ethem Gürer (Eds.)

Computer-Aided Architectural Design

Future Trajectories

17th International Conference, CAAD Futures 2017
Istanbul, Turkey, July 12–14, 2017
Selected Papers

 Springer

Editors
Gülen Çağdaş
Istanbul Technical University
Istanbul
Turkey

Mine Özkar
Istanbul Technical University
Istanbul
Turkey

Leman Figen Gül
Istanbul Technical University
Istanbul
Turkey

Ethem Gürer
Istanbul Technical University
Istanbul
Turkey

ISSN 1865-0929   ISSN 1865-0937 (electronic)
Communications in Computer and Information Science
ISBN 978-981-10-5196-8   ISBN 978-981-10-5197-5 (eBook)
DOI 10.1007/978-981-10-5197-5

Library of Congress Control Number: 2017943845

Printed on acid-free paper

This Springer imprint is published by Springer Nature
The registered company is Springer Nature Singapore Pte Ltd.
The registered company address is: 152 Beach Road, #21-01/04 Gateway East, Singapore 189721, Singapore

Preface

The Computer-Aided Architectural Design Foundation was established in 1985, and ever since, has encouraged state-of-the-art research and practice of computing in architectural design through conferences and publications. Istanbul, the vibrant metropolis that lies between Asia and Europe, was the host of the 17th CAADFutures Conference.

For the designer in the multidisciplinary world of the 21st century, computation provides a powerful medium for the extension of understanding other disciplines. In accordance with this global change in the field of design, CAADFutures 2017 called for papers around the theme of "Future Trajectories of Computation in Design." In fostering a multidisciplinary discourse for the future of computation in design, the conference aimed at not only gathering the latest research, design practice, and pedagogies but also revealing the possible phenomena, factors, and forces that will influence these trajectories in design with an exploratory perspective.

From the initial 184 abstracts received in the first stage of paper evaluations from 27 different countries, only 22 papers were selected for this book in a two-tier double-blind review process. Each paper was reviewed by at least three experts from an international committee of 80 experienced researchers. In the same process, 46 other papers were selected for publication in the conference proceedings and in Cumincad (cumincad. scix.net), where the abstracts of papers in this book are also indexed.

The papers in this book have been organized under five headings: (1) Modeling Urban Design, (2) Support Systems for Design Decisions, (3) Studying Design Behavior in Digital Environments, (4) Materials, Fabrication, Computation, and (5) Shape Studies. The first group provides examples of various applications of computation in the study of the urban environment. The second represents a broad range of studies in optimizing the creation and sustaining the built environment. The third comprises papers that describe research into individual or group design processes. The fourth group offers research into new ways of making, which incorporate materials and computational thinking. Finally, the fifth group includes research on mathematics of shapes in design. Contributors of the book are researchers from the fields of architecture, design, urban design, computer science, engineering, and other disciplines that address issues of computational design.

As editors of this volume, and organizers of the conference, we thank Professors Bauke de Vries and Tom Kvan, the chairs of the CAADFutures Foundation for their continuing support in the process of organizing the conference and the preparation of this book. Gabriela Celani, the chair of the 2015 conference, was extremely resourceful and helpful to us from the very beginning. We also thank all members of the Scientific Committee for their diligent reviews that paved the way to match the high academic standards CAADFuture conferences are known for. We are also grateful to each member of the conference Organizing Committee. Finally, the conference would not have been possible without the support of Istanbul Technical University Rectorate, the Faculty of Architecture, and our generous sponsors.

It has been a great honor and pleasure to organize and host the CAAD Futures Conference in Istanbul. We hope that this great selection of papers is an indication of the contribution of the conference to the field and that you enjoy the book.

July 2017

Gülen Çağdaş
Mine Özkar
Leman Figen Gül
Ethem Gürer

Organization

CAAD Futures Board

Bauke de Vries	Eindhoven University of Technology, The Netherlands
Tom Kvan	University of Melbourne, Australia
Mark Gross	Carnegie Mellon University, USA

Organizing Committee

Gülen Çağdaş (Conference Chair)
Mine Özkar (Conference Co-chair)
Leman Figen Gül (Workshops Coordinator)
Ethem Gürer
Birgül Çolakoğlu
Ömer Halil Çavuşoğlu
Saadet Zeynep Bacınoğlu
Begüm Hamzaoğlu

Scientific Program Committee

Henri Achten	Czech Technical University in Prague, Czech Republic
Fulya Akipek	Bilgi University, Turkey
Meltem Aksoy	Istanbul Technical University, Turkey
Sema Alaçam	Istanbul Technical University, Turkey
José Nuno Beirão	University of Lisbon, Portugal
Henriette Bier	TU Delft, The Netherlands
Nimish Biloria	TU Delft, The Netherlands
Gabriela Celani	Unicamp, Brazil
Gülen Çağdaş	Istanbul Technical University, Turkey (Conference Chair)
Birgül Çolakoğlu	Istanbul Technical University, Turkey
Yüksel Demir	Istanbul Technical University, Turkey
İpek Gürsel Dino	Middle East Technical University, Turkey
Fehmi Doğan	Izmir Institute of Technology, Turkey
Dirk Donath	Bauhaus-Universität Weimar, Germany
Jose Duarte	Penn State University, USA
Özgür Ediz	Uludağ University, Turkey
Halil Erhan	Simon Fraser University, Canada
Tomohiro Fukuda	Osaka University, Japan
John Gero	UNCC And GMU, USA
Thomas Grasl	Swap/Plus, Austria
Leman Figen Gül	Istanbul Technical University, Turkey

Contents

Modeling Urban Design

An Experimental Methodology for Urban Morphology Analysis 3
  Anetta Kepczynska-Walczak and Anna Pietrzak

Interactive Urban Synthesis: Computational Methods for Fast Prototyping
of Urban Design Proposals 23
  Reinhard Koenig, Yufan Miao, Katja Knecht, Peter Buš,
  and Chang Mei-Chih

CIM-St: A Parametric Design System for Street Cross Sections 42
  Rui de Klerk and José Nuno Beirão

Integration of a Structure from Motion into Virtual and Augmented Reality
for Architectural and Urban Simulation: Demonstrated in Real Architectural
and Urban Projects 60
  Tomohiro Fukuda, Hideki Nada, Haruo Adachi, Shunta Shimizu,
  Chikako Takei, Yusuke Sato, Nobuyoshi Yabuki, and Ali Motamedi

Support Systems for Design Decisions

CAMBRIA: Interacting with Multiple CAD Alternatives 81
  Siniša Kolarić, Halil Erhan, and Robert Woodbury

A Matter of Sequence: Investigating the Impact of the Order of Design
Decisions in Multi-stage Design Processes 100
  Julia Tschetwertak, Sven Schneider, Alexander Hollberg, Dirk Donath,
  and Jürgen Ruth

Why Do We Need Building Information Modeling (BIM) in Conceptual
Design Phase? 121
  Ömer Halil Çavuşoğlu and Gülen Çağdaş

Challenges in Raising Digital Awareness in Architectural Curriculum 136
  Guzden Varinlioglu, Lale Basarir, Ozgur Genca, and Zeynep Vaizoglu

SILVEREYE – The Implementation of Particle Swarm Optimization
Algorithm in a Design Optimization Tool 151
  Judyta M. Cichocka, Agata Migalska, Will N. Browne,
  and Edgar Rodriguez

Solar Collection Multi-isosurface Method: Computational Design
Advanced Method for the Prediction of Direct Solar Access
in Urban Environments   170
    Francesco De Luca and Hendrik Voll

Studying Design Behavior in Digital Environments

Making Sense of Design Space: What Designers Do with Large Numbers
of Alternatives?   191
    Naghmi Shireen, Halil Erhan, Robert Woodbury, and Ivy Wang

Studying Co-design: How Place and Representation Would Change
the Co-design Behavior?   212
    Leman Figen Gül, Can Uzun, and Süheyla Müge Halıcı

Association Rule Mining to Assess User-Generated Content in Digital
Heritage: Participatory Content Making in 'The Museum of Gamers'   231
    Serdar Aydin, Marc Aurel Schnabel, and Iman Sayah

Computing with Watercolor Shapes: Developing and Analyzing
Visual Styles   252
    Onur Yüce Gün

Materials, Fabrication, Computation

Robot-Aided Fabrication of Interwoven Reinforced Concrete Structures   273
    Elif Erdine, Alexandros Kallegias, Angel Fernando Lara Moreira,
    Pradeep Devadass, and Alican Sungur

Computing Stitches and Crocheting Geometry   289
    Özgüç Bertuğ Çapunaman, Cemal Koray Bingöl, and Benay Gürsoy

Discrete Heuristics: Digital Design and Fabrication Through Shapes
and Material Computation   306
    Diego Pinochet

Shape Studies

EthnoComputation: An Inductive Shape Grammar on Toraja Glyph   329
    Rizal Muslimin

Shape Computations Without Compositions   348
    Iestyn Jowers, Chris Earl, and George Stiny

The Marching Shape: Extensions to the Ice-Ray Shape Grammar   366
    Alexandros Tsamis

Outlining Terragni: A Riddle Reworked.   381
   Hayri Dortdivanlioglu and Athanassios Economou

Rectilinear Floor Plans.   395
   Krishnendra Shekhawat and José P. Duarte

Author Index   413

Modeling Urban Design

An Experimental Methodology for Urban Morphology Analysis

Anetta Kepczynska-Walczak[iD] and Anna Pietrzak[(⊠)] [iD]

Lodz University of Technology, Lodz, Poland
anetta@p.lodz.pl, a.pietrzak@dokt.p.lodz.pl

Abstract. The paper presents results of a research conducted in 2015 and 2016 at Lodz University of Technology. It proposes a purpose and context fit approach towards the automation of urban data generation based on GIS tools and New Urbanism typologies. First, background studies of methods applied in urban morphology analysis are revealed. Form-based Code planning, and subsequently Transect-based Code are taken into account. Then, selected examples from literature are described and discussed. Finally, the research study is presented and the outcomes compared with more traditional methodology.

Keywords: GIS · Urban morphology · Spatial analysis · Decision support systems · Urban design · Data analytics · Modelling and simulation

1 Introduction

The paper presents results of a research conducted in 2015 and 2016 at Lodz University of Technology. It focuses on selected studies of most adequate methodologies applied in urban morphology analysis. The research problem, and the main task, was to propose a purpose and context fit approach towards automation of urban data generation based on GIS tools and the New Urbanism typologies. That is why, the main goal of the conducted analysis and research was to verify if GIS tools could be applied in Form-Based Code planning. What is more, the aim was to identify whether transect zones were well chosen according to the urban planning policy of the analysed city. The results are evaluated and discussed in the paper.

2 Background

The first key concept, which formed the basis for this research, is New Urbanism – a postmodern urban design movement which promotes environmentally friendly habits by creating walkable neighbourhoods containing a wide range of housing and job types. Originated in the United States in the early 1980s by Elizabeth Plater–Zyberk and Andreas Duany, it has gradually influenced many aspects of real estate development, urban planning, and municipal land-use strategies [1]. According to its foundational text, The Charter of the New Urbanism, the metropolitan region is a fundamental economic unit of the contemporary world. Governmental cooperation, public policy, physical planning, and economic strategies must reflect this new reality [2].

© Springer Nature Singapore Pte Ltd. 2017
G. Çağdaş et al. (Eds.): CAAD Futures 2017, CCIS 724, pp. 3–22, 2017.
DOI: 10.1007/978-981-10-5197-5_1

As the idea of zoning prescribes to segregate residential from commercial and industrial development has been replaced by multi-use concept, it has evoked new strategies and tools. One of the widely discussed recently is Form-based Code. This approach contrasts with conventional zoning and is a land development regulation that fosters predictable built results and a high-quality public realm by using physical form (rather than separation of uses) as the organizing principle for the code. Form-based Code is a regulation, not a mere guideline, adopted into city, town, or county law. Form-Based Code offers a powerful alternative to the conventional zoning regulation [3].

Table 1. The impacts of various forms of planning policies.

How zoning defines a one-block parcel	How design guidelines define a one-block parcel	How form-based codes define a one-block parcel
Density, use, FAR (floor-area ratio), setbacks, parking requirements and maximum building height(s) specified	Density, use, FAR (floor-area ratio), setbacks, parking, requirements, maximum buildings height(s), frequency of openings, and surface articulation specified	Street and building types (or mix of types), build-to lines, number of floors, and percentage of built site frontage specified

(Source: Authors' work based on http://www.sig.msstate.edu/publications/research/smartgrowth/SC1.pdf [4])

Table 1 illustrates the impacts of various forms of planning policies. Use-based or Euclidean Zoning only regulate the use of the property, setbacks, and parking requirements. Euclidean Zoning is primarily concerned with the private realm and the use of the land rather than the form and character of the buildings. Design guidelines in combination with Euclidean Zoning allow communities to guide the aesthetics and character of a new development. Finally, Form-Based Codes allow for mixed uses while guiding the form of the buildings. Form-Based Codes focus on the public realm heavily rather than on the use of the land [4].

One of the types of Form-Based Codes is Transect-Based Code which describes zones, from rural to urban structures. In this respect, zones should be defined according to the local character and form [5].

Consequently, it is worth to mention the idea of SmartCode and Smart Growth in intelligent planning. SmartCode gives an opportunity to implement growth sectors (Table 2).

Table 2. Growth sectors defined in SmartCode.

Symbol	Name	Description
O-1	Preserved open sector	Shall consist of Open Space that is protected from development in perpetuity. The Preserved Open Sector includes areas under environmental protection by law or regulation, as well as land acquired for conservation through purchase, by easement, or by past Transfer of Development Rights
O-2	Reserved open sector	Shall consist of Open Space that should be, but is not yet, protected from development
G-1	Restricted growth sector	Shall be assigned to areas that have value as Open Space but nevertheless are subject to development, either because the zoning has already been granted or because there is no legally defensible reason, in the long term, to deny it
G-2	Controlled growth sector	Shall be assigned to those locations that can support Mixed Use by virtue of proximity to an existing or planned Thoroughfare
G-3	Intended growth sector	Shall be assigned to those locations that can support substantial Mixed Use by virtue of proximity to an existing or planned regional Thoroughfare and/or transit
G-4	Infill growth sector	Shall be assigned to areas already developed, having the potential to be modified, confirmed or completed in the pattern of Infill Traditional Neighbourhood Developments or Infill Regional Centre Developments
SD	Special district	Shall be assigned to areas that, by their intrinsic size, Function, or Configuration, cannot conform to the requirements of a Clustered Land Development, a Traditional Neighbourhood Developments, or an Regional Centre Developments

(Source: Own work based on SmartCode 9.2. [6])

3 Examples of Best Practices

For the purpose of the research Form-Based Codes documents from different countries were analysed. One of the most complex zoning code was adapted in Miami, in the state of Florida. The Miami 21 Code was implemented in reaction to suburbanisation and urban sprawl. Authorities have decided to change a development policy and to build compact and walkable city instead of placing wide and busy thoroughfares in it. Urban marketing was crucial to encourage people to return to the city centre. In Miami 21 Code, a city is divided into twelve different zones and each of them was being described with different urban parameters, for example lot coverage, density, building height or frontage buildout [7].

The next example worth mentioning is Transect Code Manual [8] which is a step-by-step guide for how to delineate transect zones using the GIS-based method. On the example of Phoenix city (Arizona), the document describes what data is required to perform analysis and how to verify characteristics for each transect zone according to the local conditions. In this manual, the city was analysed in five categories i.e. thoroughfare types, residential density, land use mix, environmental sensitivity and block sizes. It was stressed that there were some areas which did not fit to any of transect zones and ultimately they were called 'transitional'. The preliminary transect zone was assigned to each of the urban blocks based on a proper parameter combination.

American cities were not the only cities considered as examples of good practice. For instance, Gdynia, a seaside city in Poland, is another location where Form-Based Codes principles were applied. In 2008, it was planned to build an eight line expressway and another artery with a high traffic flow through Gdynia West district which represents 20% of entire city area [9]. Such planning policy would divide district into four separated parts. Thanks to charrette workshops, in which citizens, investors and local administration participated, a new concept and optimization of six Local Spatial Management Plans were adopted. According to this shift in thinking, Gdynia West has become a walkable residential district with a sustainable transport. The district has been delineated into five transect zones, from T1 to T5 with different building types, urban parameters and mixed uses.

Such critical review preceded and allowed for defining the objectives of the research.

4   Urban Planning in the Analysed City

The analyses were performed for the city of Lodz – a city which is located in the central part of Poland with the population of approx. 700 thousands residents. In last years, the processes of suburbanization and de-urbanization were observed. Local authorities recognised problems of urban sprawl and, as a result, a new strategic document was enacted in 2012. According to this document, the analysed city was divided into three zones (Fig. 1) and the growth scenario was presented for each.

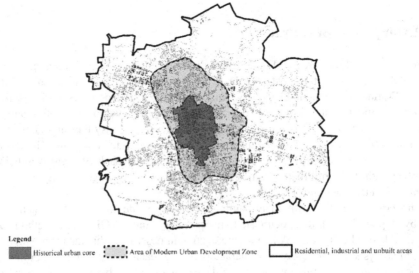

Legend

Historical urban core   Area of Modern Urban Development Zone   Residential, industrial and unbuilt areas

Fig. 1. Development zones in the city of Lodz (Source: Own work based on Spatial Strategy for Lodz 2020+ [10])

Defined scenarios for the analysed city can be compared to the Growth sectors previously described in *SmartCode*. For instance, the way of development and re-development in historical city core is similar to infill growth sector in *SmartCode*. Intended growth sector can represent scenario for the second zone which consists of compact single-family houses, incomplete urban structures, factories and villas. The last zone of the analysed city is the most diversified one. There are housing estates, sparse single-family houses, industries, stores, non-urban and rural areas present. The growth within this zone is planned to be similar to that in a controlled growth sector, restricted growth sector, preserved open sector and reserved open sector. The main idea of the document is to encourage people to return to the city center. After changes in planning strategy for the city of Lodz, the planning documents need to be adjusted.

Seeing similarity between SmartCode and the strategy adopted in Lodz, it was decided to perform further spatial multi-criteria decision analyses which focused on urban structures based on the New Urbanism methods mainly.

Following the collection of the designers' actions, a thorough investigation has taken place using the protocol analysis method.

5 Methodologies

The first step was the selection of appropriate urban parameters which were being considered in further analyses. Therefore, it focused on the form of the urban structures and mixed-uses. Parameters selection was preceded by literature studies. Afterwards, two methods of calculation and presentation of spatial data were applied simultaneously – the regular grid of square blocks (100 m side) and irregular urban blocks (areas surrounded by streets with perimeters from around ~ 200 m to even 10000 m). The grid of square method is increasingly used in spatial analysis and it allows to observe a continuity of analysed phenomena, whereas urban blocks method is usually used in transect zone analysis and also in drawing-up Local Spatial Management Plans which are urban planning documents in Poland. First, each parameter was presented on separate maps using both methods, and subsequently, all parameters were combined as a multi-criteria analysis.

- Floor-area ratio
- Height of built-up areas
- Lot coverage
- Residential density
- Frontage buildout
- Lot proportions and size
- Block size (only in irregular urban blocks method)
- Land use mix.

To conduct the analysis, the following vector layers were used:

- Buildings with number of floors
- Parcels
- Subdivision of Lodz with population

- Public transport stops
- Grocery stores
- Pharmacies
- Clinics
- Educational Establishments
- Churches
- Libraries
- Urban blocks
- Grid of square blocks.

5.1   Floor Area Ratio

The floor-area ratio (FAR) is not defined in SmartCode but it is widely used in urban planning documents and commonly used in Local Spatial Management Plans in Poland. Conventional Zoning uses such parameter but New Urbanists consider it as hard to visualise and they believe that developers would interpret values improperly. In consequence, the form of designed buildings would have inadequate impact on urban structures [11]. It was agreed at the very early stage of the research that FAR should not be used as a standalone measure in planning but in combination with other parameters it can help with identifying urban structures.

The main difference in calculating floor-area ratio in both methods lies in the fact that one building is always located in one urban block only but a grid of squares can intersect with the buildings. In such cases, while working on analyses, a building was divided and each part of it was calculated separately, and subsequently, using the location, joined with a proper square (Fig. 2).

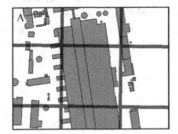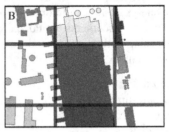

Fig. 2. A division of the buildings located in more than one square into parts. ((A) Buildings before division; (B) Divided buildings based on the grid of blocks)

Having regard to a local condition, the parameter was defined for transect zones from T1 to T6 (Table 3). The results in both methods appeared very similar, but the grid of squares allowed to recognize incompleteness of structures more precisely.

Table 3. The value of floor-area ratio in accordance with transect zones.

Zone	Floor-area ratio
T1	0
T2	0,01–0,2
T3	0,21–0,4
T4	0,41–0,8
T5	0.81–1,2
T6	>1,2

5.2 Height of Built-Up Areas

As it was shown in SmartCode, a building's height was measured as a maximum number of floors. It was hard to unambiguously determine this parameter because Lodz city center is relatively low – townhouses are usually 5 floors high. Outside of the centre there are also housing estates where typical blocks of flats are 5 floors high. However, those multifamily buildings can be sometimes even 11 floors high and this has indicated a broad range of values for this zone (Table 4). The analysis showed there were buildings found with more than 6 floors high within a city centre in both methods. As this parameter was measured as the maximum height within a unit, in urban blocks method such buildings influenced a whole unit area, whereas in grid of squares method, which turned out to be more detailed, there were only spots with such height.

Table 4. Building's height in accordance with transect zones.

Zone	Number of floors
T1	0
T2	1–2
T3	2
T4	3–4
T5	4–5
T6	4–6
Housing estates	>5

5.3 Lot Coverage

The lot coverage is a typical criterion used in SmartCode to delimit the transect zones. This parameter was also calculated per analysed units and, in the combination with the maximum number of floors, appeared really important in identifying special structures such as industrial areas within the city boundaries. The values assigned to each zone are presented below in Table 5. This parameter was calculated more accurately in the urban blocks method. In these units, areas of roads and railways were not taken into account, while in grid of squares they were included.

Table 5. Lot coverage in accordance with transect zones.

Zone	Lot coverage [%]
T1	0
T2	0,1–10
T3	10,1–20
T4	20,1–35
T5	35,1–50
T6	>50
Special districts	>70

5.4 Residential Density

In SmartCode, density is defined as a number of dwelling units per standard measure of land area [6]. The available population data for Lodz were presented in transport units which were basically used to frame a transport strategy. In the city centre most of these units are equal to one or two urban blocks but outside the city core their size depends on the function of a specific area. Usually a whole housing estate or industrial area is assigned to one transport unit. The first step was to estimate the population per urban block and per square in grid. According to the governmental portal, the Local Data Bank, on average 2.23 persons live in one dwelling unit in Lodz. The population was divided by this value in each transport unit and, in effect, the count of dwelling units in a distinguished transport unit was extracted. Afterwards, this value was divided by the sum of gross floor areas of residential buildings for each transport unit. Owing to performed calculations, the dwelling unit per 1 m^2 floor area was estimated. The centroids of urban blocks and squares in grid were generated and, using spatial join, the values were assigned to the properly analysed units. The gross floor area in each unit was multiplied by the count of dwelling units per 1 m^2. The results were presented as an amount of dwelling units per 1 ha (Table 6). The results for both methods were very similar in the city core, but on the outskirts grid of square method results were more relevant.

Table 6. Residential density in accordance with transect zone

Zone	Amount of dwelling units per 1 ha
T1 and special districts	0
T2	1
T3	2–10
T4	11–30
T5	31–80
T6 and housing estates	>80

5.5   Frontage Buildout

The frontage buildout is a minimum percentage of the primary setback that shall be built-up. This parameter is defined for the principal frontage buildings only. In case of these analyses, the frontage buildout was calculated differently for both methods. Taking into account that grid of squares is regular and can be located in a middle of an urban block, it will be inappropriate to identify transect zones based on percentage of a building facade at primary setback (e.g. no principal building will be located inside the square in quite big urban blocks in Lodz city core). It was decided that squares could only have two values: true or false (Table 7). In the urban blocks method, the parameter was calculated as a percentage for the whole block (Table 8).

Table 7. Frontage buildout in grid of squares method in accordance with transect zones.

Zone	Frontage buildout
T1, T2, T3	False
T4, T5, T6	True

Table 8. Frontage buildout in urban blocks method in accordance with transect zones.

Zone	Frontage buildout [%]
T1	N/A
T2	N/A
T3	N/A
T4	10–25
T5	25,1–50
T6	>50

5.6   Lot Proportions and Size

Referring to New Urbanism, it is important to describe how a building should be situated on a parcel. What is more, in SmartCode requirements the proposal of the lot width for each transect zone is given. It was decided to combine two values: lot proportions and size. In the analytical part, these two parameters would be helpful to assert if the lot was qualified as a building plot. The lot proportions were measured by calculating the minimum of bounding geometry – each lot was outlined with the smallest, feasible rectangle. In both methods, the areas of roads, railways, airport with associated infrastructure, green areas, parks and cemeteries were discounted. The grade was assigned to each combination of these parameters. According to the Polish law, it is easier to divide a big plot into smaller parts than merge a few small plots into one. Too big lots were graded higher than too small ones. It was assumed that the best proportions were estimated between 0,3 and 0,7. The best size of a lot was evaluated from 400 to 1000 m^2. The ascription of the grade to the spatial units was based on the mode – the most frequent value. Grades assigned to the transect zones are presented in a Table 9. In both methods results were discontinuous – this parameter was the most valid in the recognition of T2 zone.

Table 9. Proportions and a lot size with grades in accordance with transect zones.

Lot proportions and size	Grade	Zone
Too narrow and too small	1	N/A
Too wide and too small	2	N/A
With optimal proportions and too small	3	N/A
Too narrow and with optimal size	4	N/A
Too narrow and too big	5	T2
Too wide and too big	6	T4, T5, T6
Too wide and with optimal size	7	T4, T5, T6
With optimal proportions and too big	8	T4, T5, T6
With optimal proportions and with optimal size	9	T4, T5, T6

5.7   Block Size

The block size is also a typical parameter in New Urbanists documents and it is defined as a maximum block perimeter. It was calculated this way for irregular urban blocks method (Table 10). This parameter turns out to be unmeasurable in the grid of squares method.

Table 10. Blocks' size in accordance with transect zones.

Zone	Blocks' size [m]
T1/T2	>2000
T3/T4	1200,1–2000
T4/T5	800,1–1200
T5/T6	≤ 800

5.8   Land Use Mix

Having in mind the importance of walkability in the cities, distances to the following amenities were analysed: public transport stops, groceries, clinics, pharmacies, nurseries, kindergartens, primary schools, junior high schools, libraries and churches. It is generally considered that average walking speed is 5 km per h. In the conducted analysis, the isochrones from 5 to 35 min were assumed using buffers analysis. The buffers were created for each amenity and afterwards spatial analytical units have proper values assigned. Depending on a distance and priority of each amenity grades between 0 and 10 were added. The algorithm with grades and weight for each amenity is presented below in Table 11.

Table 11. Algorithm of calculation walkability.

Isochrones [min]	Grade	Category	Subcategory	Weight
5	10	Grocery	–	1
10	5			
15	2			
20	1			
>20	0			
5	10	Public transport	–	1
10	5			
15	2			
20	1			
>20	0			
5	10	Health	Clinic	0,8
10	9			
15	7,5			
20	5			
25	2,5		Pharmacy	0,2
30	1,5			
35	1			
>35	0			
5	10	Education	Nursery	0,25
10	9			
15	7		Kindergarten	0,25
20	4			
25	2		Primary school	0,25
30	1,5			
35	1		Junior high school	0,25
>35	0			
5	10	Culture	Library	0,8
10	9			
15	7,5			
20	4			
25	2		Church	0,2
30	1,5			
35	1			
>35	0			

The grades were aggregated and assigned to transect zones – the highest grade was 50 (Table 12). More useful results were given in grid of squares method because of the depth of this analysis, especially on the outskirts where big urban blocks are located.

Table 12. Walkability grades in accordance with transect zones.

Zone	Aggregated grade
T1	0–5
T2	5,1–15
T3	15,1–25
T4	25,1–35
T5	35,1–45
T6	45,1–50

6   Research Synthesis

6.1   Transect Zones Assignment

In order to assign appropriate transect zones for both analytical methods, particular results from each of conducted analyses were spatially joined and copied to one vector layer. In effect, the attributes table was containing a full range of the attributes and thanks to that proper queries were applied. Due to the incompleteness of certain structures, units were identified on the grounds of predominant values. Not all parameters were counted in the same way for each transect zone, for instance proportions and plots' sizes were the most important in identifying rural structures. Besides, the frontage buildout was the most significant in zones T4, T5 and T6. Additionally, if the special district (other than housing estates) was detected, the buildings function analysis were subsumed. Cognately, if T1 was detected in the regular grid of squares method, then the layers with land use were subsumed – the T1 zone was identified within all unbuilt areas i.e. roads, parks, cemeteries, farmlands, however, not all of them should be classified as a natural transect zone.

The examples of applied queries are presented below:

- *If FAR equals T6, building height equals T6, lot coverage equals T6, proportions and size equal T6, frontage buildout equals at least T5, block size equals T6, walkability equals T6,* then transect zone equals T6
- *If FAR equals at least T3, building height equals T4, lot coverage equals T4, proportions and size equal T4, frontage buildout equals at least T4, block size equals T4, walkability equals T6,* then transect zone equals T4
- *If FAR equals at least T3, building height equals at least T6, lot coverage equals T4, residential density equals T6, frontage buildout equals T1, walkability equals at least T5,* then transect zone equals SD – Housing estate
- *If FAR equal at least T3, building height equals T2 or less, lot coverage equals at least T5, proportions and size equals T4/T5/T6, frontage buildout equals T1, block size equals T1/T2, walkability equals T3 or T4,* then transect zone equals SD - Industries.

6.2   Generalization

The grid of squares method turned out to be deeply detailed and, to reach more legible results, it needed to be generalized. Such step was crucial in order to improve the readability of the maps. For instance, sometimes squares were located in the middle of a crossroad and it did not mean that zone T1 should be recognized. Using a neighbourhood of each square, the prevalent values were assigned. The generalization was performed in two stages. The second stage of generalization was performed using the neighbourhood from the first stage of generalization. An example of a result is presented below in the Fig. 3.

Fig. 3. Grid of squares generalization ((A) Orthophoto map; (B) Grid of squares; (C) First stage of generalization; (D) Second stage of generalization).

7   Results and Conclusions

The following maps (Figs. 4, 5, 6 and 7) present results of analyses for the city of Lodz using both methods and generalizations of the grid of squares.

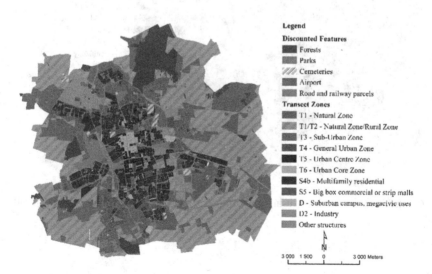

Legend

Discounted Features
- Forests
- Parks
- Cemeteries
- Airport
- Road and railway parcels

Transect Zones
- T1 - Natural Zone
- T1/T2 - Natural Zone/Rural Zone
- T3 - Sub-Urban Zone
- T4 - General Urban Zone
- T5 - Urban Centre Zone
- T6 - Urban Core Zone
- S4b - Multifamily residential
- S5 - Big box commercial or strip malls
- D - Suburban campus, megacivic uses
- D2 - Industry
- Other structures

3 000 1 500   0   3 000 Meters

Fig. 4. Identified transect zones using urban blocks method.

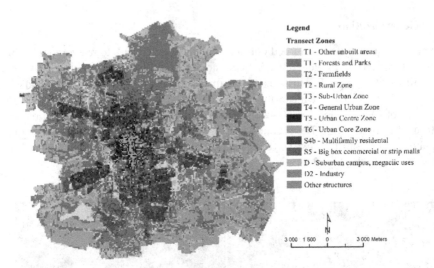

Fig. 5. Identified transect zones using grid of squares method.

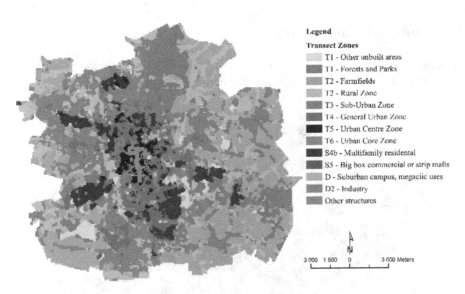

Fig. 6. Identified transect zones using grid of squares method – the first stage of generalization.

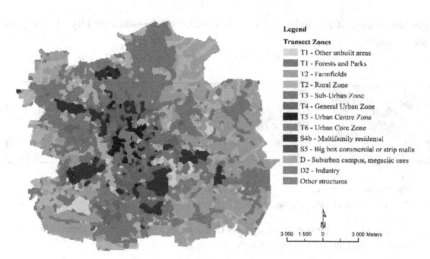

Legend

Transect Zones

- T1 - Other unbuilt areas
- T1 - Forests and Parks
- T2 - Farmfields
- T2 - Rural Zone
- T3 - Sub-Urban Zone
- T4 - General Urban Zone
- T5 - Urban Centre Zone
- T6 - Urban Core Zone
- S4b - Multifamily residenial
- S5 - Big box commercial or strip malls
- D - Suburban campus, megaciic uses
- D2 - Industry
- Other structures

Fig. 7. Identified transect zones using grid of squares method – the second stage of generalization.

The urban transect as an idea of spatial structures identification is increasingly taken into account by authorities responsible for urban planning. The research has verified that GIS tools are appropriate for recognizing cities' spatial forms automatically. As a result, two applied methodologies were compared. The automated analytical process has indicated characteristics of spatial forms in the case-study city. In both methods all transect zones and special districts were identified. The results emphasized the incompleteness of forms in the urban core as well as in urban centre zones. Analysis highlighted the need of infill in Lodz city centre. Using urban blocks and regular grid of squares approaches, the zones T3 – sub-urban zone and T4 – general urban zone were delimited. However, to unambiguously delineate those zones, the additional analysis of street furniture should be conducted. In the urban block method the zones T1 and T2 were aggregated, because borders between those two zones were not explicit – commonly, the urban blocks in the suburbs are sizeable. Not only anthropological barriers but also the natural borders, for instance river valleys, should be taken into account in delimiting blocks borders in the outskirts. It is observed the rural structures were identified more precisely in the grid of squares method. Using both methods allows to classify housing estates properly. What is more, the research has revealed the scale of modernistic structures in the city. Industrial areas have been recognized better in the urban blocks approach since the grid of squares turns out to be too detailed in this case – the spaces between buildings were classified as T2 and T4 zones incorrectly. Strip malls, such as shopping centres, were properly identified in the urban blocks method, as well as in the regular grid of squares. They are usually located in a separate urban block and are deployed as spots within city borders in contrast to industrial buildings which are usually clustered.

Figures below (from 8, 9, 10, 11, 12, and 13) present examples of results for selected zones. In these terms, the outcomes proved a success of a chosen and applied methodology since it has delivered rich and meaningful results for city planning and decision making.

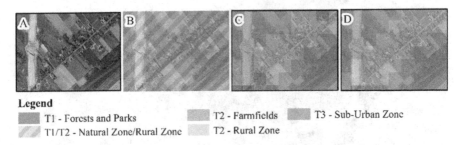

Legend

   T1 - Forests and Parks   T2 - Farmfields   T3 - Sub-Urban Zone

   T1/T2 - Natural Zone/Rural Zone   T2 - Rural Zone

Fig. 8. Rural zone. (A) Orthophoto map; (B) Urban blocks; (C) Grid of squares; (D) Grid of squares after the first stage of generalization.

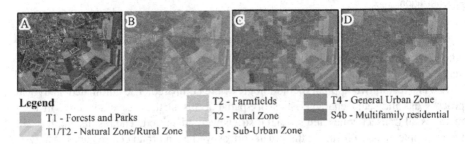

Legend

                              T2 - Farmfields   T4 - General Urban Zone

   T1 - Forests and Parks   T2 - Rural Zone   S4b - Multifamily residential

   T1/T2 - Natural Zone/Rural Zone   T3 - Sub-Urban Zone

Fig. 9. Sub-Urban structures. (A) Orthophoto map; (B) Urban blocks; (C) Grid of squares; (D) Grid of squares after the first stage generalization.

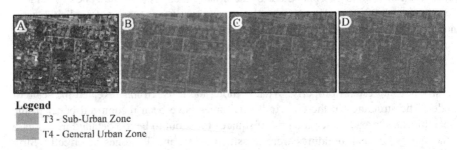

Legend

   T3 - Sub-Urban Zone

   T4 - General Urban Zone

Fig. 10. Sub-Urban Zone. (A) Orthophoto map; (B) Urban blocks; (C) Grid of squares; (D) Grid of squares after the first stage of generalization.

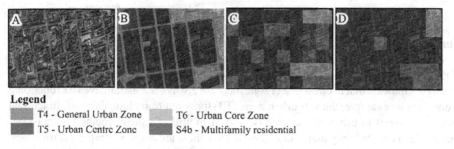

Legend
- T4 - General Urban Zone
- T5 - Urban Centre Zone
- T6 - Urban Core Zone
- S4b - Multifamily residential

Fig. 11. Urban Centre Zone. (A) Orthophoto map; (B) Urban blocks; (C) Grid of squares; (D) Grid of squares after the first stage of generalization.

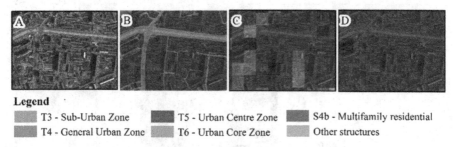

Legend
- T3 - Sub-Urban Zone
- T4 - General Urban Zone
- T5 - Urban Centre Zone
- T6 - Urban Core Zone
- S4b - Multifamily residential
- Other structures

Fig. 12. Multifamily residential. (A) Orthophoto map; (B) Urban blocks; (C) Grid of squares; (D) Grid of squares after the first stage of generalization.

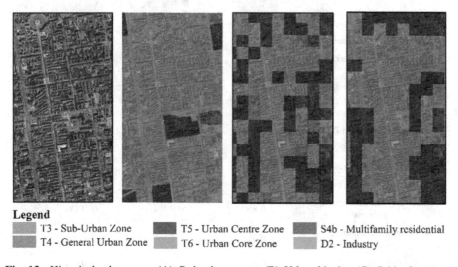

Legend
- T3 - Sub-Urban Zone
- T4 - General Urban Zone
- T5 - Urban Centre Zone
- T6 - Urban Core Zone
- S4b - Multifamily residential
- D2 - Industry

Fig. 13. Historical urban core. (A) Orthophoto map; (B) Urban blocks; (C) Grid of squares; (D) Grid of squares after the first stage of generalization.

The next step was to compare the results with currently effective planning and strategical documents. A comparison between recognized transect zones and traditional functional zones defined in Study of the Conditions and Directions of the Spatial Management for the city of Lodz has been performed. This planning document is obligatory for each commune and, based on it, Local Spatial Management Plans are compiled. Analyses indicate that in one transect zone there are always at least 4 to even 31 functional zones. As an example, the sub-urban zone (T3) turns out to include the most functional zones: 26 zones in urban blocks method and 31 in grid of squares method were recognized. Such results imply that in one transect zone there are neighbouring areas for which separate planning guidelines are produced. This leads to functional segregation and may

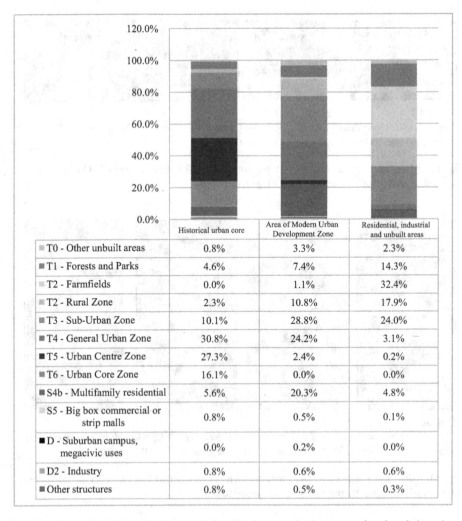

	Historical urban core	Area of Modern Urban Development Zone	Residential, industrial and unbuilt areas
■ T0 - Other unbuilt areas	0.8%	3.3%	2.3%
■ T1 - Forests and Parks	4.6%	7.4%	14.3%
■ T2 - Farmfields	0.0%	1.1%	32.4%
■ T2 - Rural Zone	2.3%	10.8%	17.9%
■ T3 - Sub-Urban Zone	10.1%	28.8%	24.0%
■ T4 - General Urban Zone	30.8%	24.2%	3.1%
■ T5 - Urban Centre Zone	27.3%	2.4%	0.2%
■ T6 - Urban Core Zone	16.1%	0.0%	0.0%
■ S4b - Multifamily residential	5.6%	20.3%	4.8%
■ S5 - Big box commercial or strip malls	0.8%	0.5%	0.1%
■ D - Suburban campus, megacivic uses	0.0%	0.2%	0.0%
■ D2 - Industry	0.8%	0.6%	0.6%
■ Other structures	0.8%	0.5%	0.3%

Fig. 14. Zones identified within borders defined in the strategic document of analysed city using grid of squares method.

also have an impact on spatial order - it can be difficult to prevent building development that will not fit harmoniously into existing urban landscape.

According to another comparison between delimited transect zones with Lodz strategical zones, it was also possible to assess decisions concerning in which direction the city should be developed. The charts (Figs. 14 and 15) present recognized zones area percentage within the zones depicted in Lodz strategic document. To continue the urban policy in the city of Lodz, the existing urban fabric in Urban Core Zone and Urban Centre Zone needs to be transformed and infilled. New building functions should help in creating liveable spaces and, in consequence, the citizens will be encouraged to return to the centre of the city. According to the *SmartCode*, the development in the Area of Modern Urban Development Zone needs to be controlled and restricted. The unbuilt areas existing in residential, industrial and unbuilt areas zone need to be protected from further urban sprawl process.

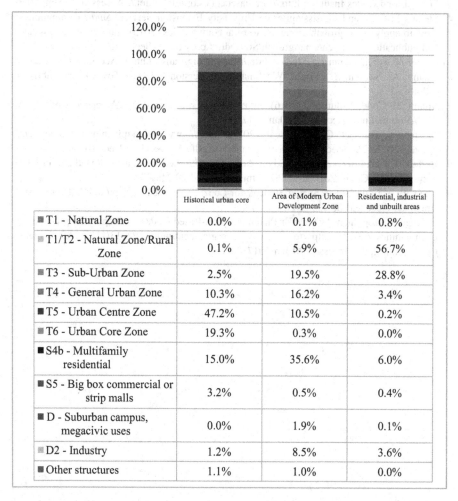

	Historical urban core	Area of Modern Urban Development Zone	Residential, industrial and unbuilt areas
■ T1 - Natural Zone	0.0%	0.1%	0.8%
■ T1/T2 - Natural Zone/Rural Zone	0.1%	5.9%	56.7%
■ T3 - Sub-Urban Zone	2.5%	19.5%	28.8%
■ T4 - General Urban Zone	10.3%	16.2%	3.4%
■ T5 - Urban Centre Zone	47.2%	10.5%	0.2%
■ T6 - Urban Core Zone	19.3%	0.3%	0.0%
■ S4b - Multifamily residential	15.0%	35.6%	6.0%
■ S5 - Big box commercial or strip malls	3.2%	0.5%	0.4%
■ D - Suburban campus, megacivic uses	0.0%	1.9%	0.1%
■ D2 - Industry	1.2%	8.5%	3.6%
■ Other structures	1.1%	1.0%	0.0%

Fig. 15. Zones identified within borders defined in the strategic document of analysed city using urban blocks method.

Summing up, the GIS-based method as a way of urban morphology analyses and automatic recognition of transect zones allowed to detect problematic areas and to determine how the city should evolve. Such calculations can help to preserve a harmoniousness in urban structures. Having appropriate data, it is possible to repeat analysis in different cities. Depending on the particular results, the most important step is to adjust ranges of parameters to the local conditions.

References

1. Boeing, G., et al.: LEED-ND and livability revisited. Berkeley Plan. J. **27**, 31–55 (2014)
2. The Congress for the New Urbanism, Charter of the New Urbanism (1996). https://www.cnu.org/sites/default/files/charter_english.pdf. Accessed 19 Sept 2016
3. Form_Based Codes Institute: http://formbasedcodes.org/definition/. Accessed 19 Sept 2016
4. Stennis Institute and Mississippi State University Extension Service: *Smart* Communities: How to apply smart growth principles to rural communities (2015). http://www.sig.msstate.edu/publications/research/smartgrowth/SC1.pdf. Accessed 19 Sept 2016
5. Center of Applied Transect Studies. http://transect.org/transect.html. Accessed 6 Oct 2016
6. Duany, A., Sorlien, S., Wright, W.: SmartCode Version 9.2. The Town Paper Publisher (2008)
7. Miami 21 Code: Volume 1 (2016). http://www.miami21.org/PDFs/Amended_Codes/May 2016-VolumeI.pdf. Accessed 20 Jan 2017
8. Talen, E.: Transect Code Manual (2013). http://www.design4planning.org/wpcontent/uploads/2013/12/transectmanualDec13smallersize.pdf. Accessed 13 Dec 2016
9. Budnik, E.: Jaka przyszłość dla Gdyni Zachód? http://www.trojmiasto.pl/wiadomosci/Jaka-przyszlosc-dla-Gdyni-Zachod-n58623.html. Accessed 29 May 2016
10. The City of Lodz Office: Spatial Strategy for Lodz 2020+ (2013). http://uml.lodz.pl/miasto/strategia/. Accessed 06 Jan 2017
11. Chicago Metropolitan Agency for Planning: Form-Based Codes: A Step-by-Step Guide for Communities (2013). http://formbasedcodes.org/content/uploads/2013/11/CMAP-Guidefor Communities.pdf. Accessed 20 Jan 2017

Interactive Urban Synthesis

Computational Methods for Fast Prototyping of Urban Design Proposals

Reinhard Koenig[1,2,3(✉)] ⓘ, Yufan Miao[4] ⓘ, Katja Knecht[4,5],
Peter Buš[3] ⓘ, and Chang Mei-Chih[3]

[1] Center for Energy, Austrian Institute of Technology, Graz, Austria
reinhard.koenig@ait.ac.at
[2] Faculty of Architecture and Urbanism, Bauhaus-University Weimar,
Weimar, Germany
[3] Department of Architecture ETH Zürich, Zurich, Switzerland
{bus,chang}@arch.ethz.ch
[4] Future Cities Laboratory, Singapore-ETH Centre, Singapore, Singapore
{miao,katja.knecht}@arch.ethz.ch
[5] Queen Mary University of London, London, UK

Abstract. In this paper, we present a method for generating fast conceptual urban design prototypes. We synthesize spatial configurations for street networks, parcels and building volumes. Therefore, we address the problem of implementing custom data structures for these configurations and how the generation process can be controlled and parameterized. We exemplify our method by the development of new components for Grasshopper/Rhino3D and their application in the scope of selected case studies. By means of these components, we show use case applications of the synthesis algorithms. In the conclusion, we reflect on the advantages of being able to generate fast urban design prototypes, but we also discuss the disadvantages of the concept and the usage of Grasshopper as a user interface.

Keywords: Procedural grammars · Artificial intelligence in design · Urban synthesis · Generative design · Grasshopper plugin · Cognitive design computing

1 Introduction and Aims

Modern cities exhibit growing complexities and dynamics where traditional urban design methods, which still rely on static and sectorial approaches, reach their limits for fast adaptation. At the same time, with the advent of big data and the improvement of our abilities to process large amounts of data as well as advances in artificial intelligence such as cognitive computing, new opportunities emerge for future-oriented computational design. Inspired by IBM's Watson, cognitive computing provides a productive combination of human cognition and computing power to support automated problem solving [1].

© Springer Nature Singapore Pte Ltd. 2017
G. Çağdaş et al. (Eds.): CAAD Futures 2017, CCIS 724, pp. 23–41, 2017.
DOI: 10.1007/978-981-10-5197-5_2

The integration of cognitive computing in computational design assistance systems could revolutionize the urban design and planning process by allowing to model urban complexities and changing urban dynamics and thus helping to address and respond to these challenges in the urban design and planning processes. A framework for this approach called 'cognitive design computing' has been proposed by Koenig and Schmitt [2]. The framework rests on four pillars: data analysis, user interaction and learning, geometry synthesis, and evolutionary multi-criterion optimization (EMO).

Following this research track, we present in this paper a computational method for the third pillar, a fast synthesis of urban planning prototypes. The main idea of the method is that the designer can define certain restrictions and the corresponding spatial configurations are generated automatically. To allow a systematic design space exploration, the designer needs to interact with the generative procedure by changing the design framework as well as manipulating the initial geometric elements that are used as the starting point for the urban synthesis process. In this paper we focus on i) the technical description of the methods used for the generation of urban fabric, ii) the presentation of first exemplary case studies, and iii) the long-term idea of our approach concerning the data structure used.

2 State of the Art

For the integration of optimization techniques in design or planning processes, we build on the methodology described by Radford and Gero [3], which describes a concept of how problem representation, generative methods, simulation methods, and decision-making can be combined to form a design-oriented optimization method. Similar concepts have been presented in other research fields, for example the concept of Design Synthesis in engineering [4].

Current commercial solutions for generative or procedural modeling, for example CityEngine, exemplify the difficulties of integrating them in the early stages of planning processes: the results of generative or procedural algorithms are based on a set of rules, which are very technical, abstract and not related to a planning problem. As a result, planners don't understand the control mechanism of the system and its possible benefit. In other words, *"we have a model that can generate designs but has no means of establishing whether those designs are any good"* [3]. With the methods and components we present in this paper we want to improve this situation.

According to Weber, Müller, Wonka, and Gross [5] the modeling of urban structures consists of a sequence of several processes: the creation of a road network, the definition of land use areas, parceling and building placement. In this context, additive processes are relevant for the generation of road networks and the placement of buildings. Systems have been developed, for example, for procedural creation of road networks based on L-systems [6] and tensor fields [7]. In particular, the system CityEngine facilitates the planning and three-dimensional, rule-based modelling of cities and urban structures to the level of building details [5, 8].

Some components of CityEngine use subdivision methods, for example, for the creation of plots. Using subdivision methods, spatial configurations are generated from the division of a predetermined shape outline in smaller parts. Early work using so-called subdivision trees as subdivision method originates from Mitchell, Steadman, and Liggett [9] as well as Stiny and Mitchell [10]. A more recent application of this procedure can be found in the work of Duarte et al, who used it to generate floor plan layouts [11] and urban structures [12]. In these examples, both constraints and rules for the creation of a solution have to be specified a priori in detail. The combination of subdivision trees with genetic programming [13] results in promising formal options [14]. The Kaisersrot project [15] employs a different approach creating plots and road network using Voronoi diagrams.

3   Methods

In contrast to other more experimental [16, 17] or established [6] urban procedural methods, we introduce a new data structure, which makes it possible to realize computational design that is based on the Backcasting approach [2]. Backcasting allows to define what performance a design solution should achieve and to automatically synthesize a set of best possible solutions.

Our urban synthesis method is composed of three procedural steps, as described by Weber et al. [5]. Firstly, street networks are initialized and extended. Secondly, blocks are defined and extracted from the street networks. Lastly, blocks are sliced into parcels, onto which buildings are placed on.

For the implementation, the urban synthesis is realized in CPlan, an open source library for computational urban design proposed by Koenig and colleges [18, 19], whereas interaction functionalities are provided by the built-in functions of Rhino3D. Based on CPlan, we developed new components for the visual programming interface Grasshopper to connect CPlan to Rhino3D.

For the generation of street networks, instruction trees are proposed (Fig. 1) to represent instructions of how a street network should grow from initial nodes by defining three key characteristic parameters: the deviation angles of street segments α_i, the lengths of street segments l_i, and the possible arms at a crossroad κ [20]. The advantage of this data structure is that it can easily parameterize both the geometric and topological structures of the street networks into tree structures, which provide convenience for the mutation and crossover in evolutionary algorithms.

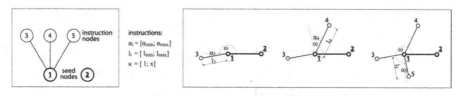

Fig. 1. Mapping process from an instruction tree to a street network. Figure adapted from Koenig et al. [20].

For the extraction of the blocks, street networks are converted into their dual directed graphs. In this graph representation, edge rings are searched and labeled for transformation into their geometric representation as polygons.

For the generation of parcels and buildings, the blocks are subdivided based on parameters specified by the planners. For their representation, a slicing tree structure is adopted given the resulting parcels possess the desired sizes (geometry) and neighborhood relationships (topology) [21, 22]. As is illustrated in Fig. 2, the slicing tree on the left is an abstract representation of the parcels on the right. After the generation of the parcels, buildings are placed inside each parcel according to the characteristics of different building typologies. In our program, we provide four typologies, namely, 'row', 'column', 'freestanding', and 'block'.

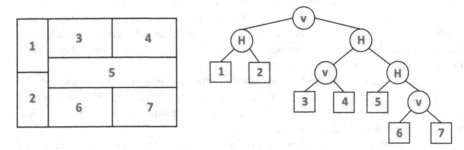

Fig. 2. The slicing tree representation of the parcels. The tree on the left is the abstract representation of the sliced parcels on the right. 'H' and 'V' represent horizontal slicing and vertical slicing respectively. The leaves are indexed identical to their geometric counterpart as parcel on the right. Indices also reflect the branch generating order in the program [22].

The slicing procedure, which generates the parcel layout, is limited to ensure that all the parcels have a direct connection to a street. This is illustrated exemplary in Fig. 2, in which parcel 5 is longer than the others but not sliced further because there is only one edge on the street, whose length is not long enough for further slicing. However, in reality the shapes of street blocks are not always as regular as represented in Fig. 2. To deal with this, we use a rectangular bounding box for the polygon as

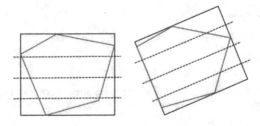

Fig. 3. Slicing based on the boundary box of irregular shapes. On the left, the slicing uses the edges of a normal bounding box whereas on the right, the slicing is oriented on the minimum bounding box [23].

shown on the left in Fig. 3 [23]. This strategy keeps the slicing process working consistently. However, it often generates parcels with irregular shape, which are not suitable for urban design purposes. To improve this, we use a minimum bounding box as base shape for slicing as shown on the right side of Fig. 3.

4 New Grasshopper Components

For the development of the components in Grasshopper for Rhino 3D, each step in the generative process is implemented as one component (Fig. 4) including the generation of street networks, extracting street blocks from the street network, slicing the blocks into parcels and generating buildings inside the parcels. Grasshopper is currently a compromise interface for the CPlan framework given its popularity among designers and architects and the existing abundant and versatile add-ons. Its drawback are its limitations in allowing direct user interaction with generated urban configurations.

The street network component (Fig. 4A) has the following input parameters, which control the morphology of the resulting network. The algorithm works iteratively so that one segment is added after the others in an additive process. The input parameters for the component (Fig. 4A) are:

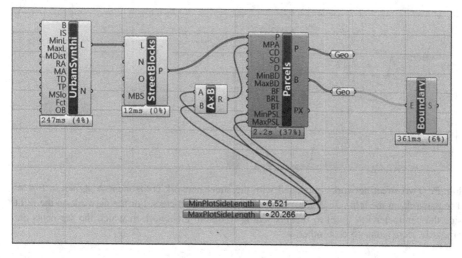

Fig. 4. The new grasshopper components. From left to right the components are used for creating A) a street network, B) street blocks, and C) parcels and buildings.

- *B:* A border polygon, which defines the border for the street network to be generated.
- *IS:* The initial street segment, from which the network starts to grow.
- *MinL:* The minimum length of a new street segment l_{min}.
- *MaxL:* The maximum length of a new street segment l_{max}.

- *MDist*: The minimum distance between two nodes of the network (between start and end points of the street segments).
- *RA*: Random value that is added to a regular angle to define the direction angle α_i of a new street segment.
- *MA*: Maximum number of arms (streets) at crossroads κ.
- *TD*: Tree depth defines the size of the resulting street network. This means it defines the branch-levels for adding control-nodes as described in Fig. 1, on the left side.
- *TP*: Topography points represent the points of a topography surface. This input data may be used for custom functions how new street segments shall react to a given topography.
- *MSlo*: Maximum slope for a street segment (using topography information).
- *Fct*: A list of custom functions to define rules of how new street segments are added.

The output L of the street network component (Fig. 4A) returns a list of line segments that represent the network. The second output N is the raw data of the street network, which is useful for later optimization purposes. Figure 5 shows two exemplary resulting networks as output of the street network component.

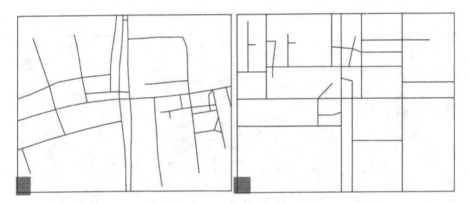

Fig. 5. Two street networks generated with the street network component A shown in Fig. 4. The network on the left side is generated using default parameters. For the network on the right side the parameter RA is set to 0. This setting results in a network in which the segments are primarily rectangular to each other.

The line segments from output L can now been used as an input for the street blocks component (Fig. 4B), which allows the generation of street blocks based on the street network. The other parameters of the street blocks component are:

- *N*: Raw data of the street network generation process.
- *O*: Offset of the street blocks from the street segments.
- *MBS*: Minimum block size. If the area of a polygon representing the block is smaller than this value, the block is not created.

The output P is a list of polygons, which represent the street blocks. To visualize the street blocks, we extrude the street blocks by using a boundary surface component that returns the green colored polygons on the right in Fig. 6.

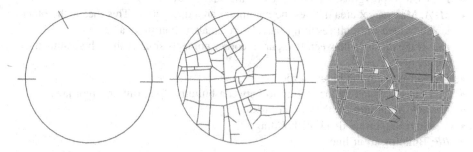

Fig. 6. From a generated street network (component A shown in Fig. 4) with a custom border input B and three custom initial street segments IS, the street blocks are generated on the right side using the component B shown in Fig. 4

To show the possible effect of the topography input parameter TP of the street network component (Fig. 4A), we import data from the EarthExplorer website (http:// earthexplorer.usgs.gov), and import the GeoTIFF with the help of the Grasshopper component $Elk2$. Based on the topography we can now restrict the network by adding new street segments only if the slope between start and end point is less than the $MSlope$ parameter values (20 degrees by default). An exemplary street network reacting to a topography is illustrated in Fig. 7.

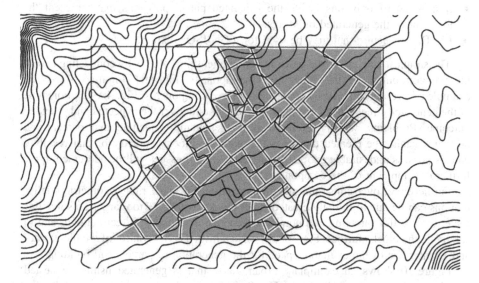

Fig. 7. Street network generated with a topographicsl input, a custom border B, and initial street segments IS. New street segments are only added if the slop of the segment is below the threshold value $MSlope$ of 20°.

Finally, the third component generates parcels and buildings (Fig. 4C). It takes the street block polygons as input and subdivides them following the procedure illustrated in Figs. 2 and 3. The input parameters of the parcel and building component are:

- *P*: A list of polygons, which represent the street blocks.
- *MPA*: Max parcel area defines the maximum area of a parcel. This means the block is subdivided until all resulting parcels are smaller than this value.
- *CD*: If the distance between two parcel corner points is smaller than this value, they are merged.
- *SO*: Offset from the block border.
- *D*: Density, which defines the ratio between building footprint and plot area.
- *MinBD*: Minimum depth of buildings.
- *MaxBD*: Maximum depth of buildings.
- *BF*: Building front-line.
- *BRL*: Building restriction line, which defines the distance to the backside parcel border edge.
- *BT*: Building type - so far four types have been implemented: rows, columns, blocks, and freestanding houses [24].
- *MinPSL*: Minimum length of a side of a parcel.
- *MaxPSL*: Maximum length of a side of a parcel.

Some of the input parameters may contradict each other or result in an over constraint configuration. At the current stage of the development of the algorithm, not all of these issues are solved. Therefore, the output geometry generated by the component may give unsatisfactory results. As output parameters the component delivers:

- *P*: A list of polygons representing the generated parcels.
- *Bld*: A list of polygons inside the generated parcel polygons that represent the footprint of the generated buildings.
- *PX*: Data structure that may be used for a GeoJSON export.

The simplest way to use the parceling component (Fig. 4C) is by connecting it with the polygon output of the street block component (Fig. 4B). Figure 8 shows an example of a result obtained by connecting all tree components (Fig. 4A–C). For some of the generated street blocks, the algorithm does not deliver the expected and intended outcome. Problems, which can be seen in the example, include that parcels and buildings cannot be created due to issues with the block geometry or that resulting parcels possess undesirable geometric properties. These issues will be addressed in the further development of the components.

Furthermore, over-constraint situations resulting in undesirable geometric configurations can be due to initially created street blocks, which are too large. To solve this issue, we use the parceling component to generate a secondary street network and to subdivide the blocks further (Fig. 9). This also allows a better control of the block sizes and a better use of the available space for the generation of parcels and buildings.

Figure 10 shows an exemplary urban fabric that is generated using the nested parceling component as shown in Fig. 9. The secondary streets generated by the parceling component C' in Fig. 9 produce street blocks with similar depth, which results in a relatively regular parceling structure.

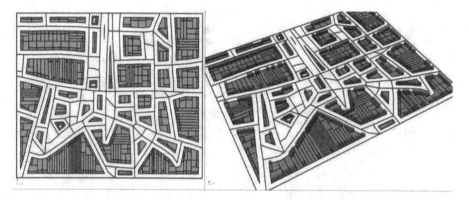

Fig. 8. Urban fabric generated by combining the street network, street blocks, and parceling components.

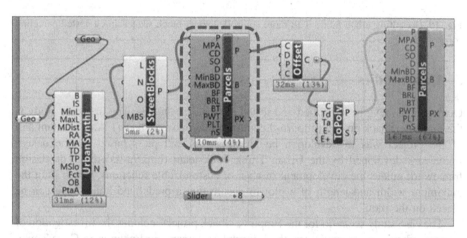

Fig. 9. A second parceling component is added to deal with large street blocks. Street blocks are firstly partitioned into smaller ones with the component marked as C' and then partitioned into the final parcels by the green component. (Color figure online)

The generated urban fabric can be controlled by the input parameters of the components shown in Figs. 4 and 9. In addition, the urban fabric can be controlled more directly and interactively by changing its border geometry and the initial street segments that are used as reference-inputs for the components. After moving or rotating one of these elements, the fabric is re-computed immediately. The main drawback of using Grasshopper and Rhino3D as a user interface is that it is not possible to directly manipulate the geometry, which is generated by the components, and have an inter-active feedback loop, which would then adapt the remaining elements. The generated geometry can only be manipulated after finishing the algorithmic design process by "baking" the geometry permanently.

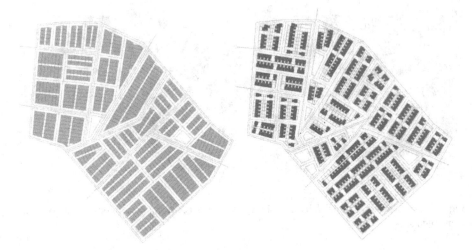

Fig. 10. Resulting urban fabric with more controlled street block sizes using a nested parceling component (Fig. 9).

5 Case Studies

Our methods have been applied and tested in two case studies. The first case study is the EmpowerShack project (http://u-tt.com/project/empower-shack/). An important aim of the project was to develop a layout of streets and plots based on the design framework developed by the Urban Think Tank team (http://u-tt.com/). The design framework guides the development of a set of customizable functions, which limit the maximum width and length of a plot to ensure that a predefined house type can be placed on the plot.

The case study scenario for the EmpowerShack project includes the investigation of a larger urban area, in particular, the informal settlements in Enkanini in Cape Town. Three smaller selected neighborhoods were selected. Outline polygons representing the borders of the neighborhoods were defined as initial empty shapes for a new urban layout generation (first column in Fig. 11). According to the specific design require- ments from the urban designers, each plot within the new urban block should be defined by its precise dimensions. This was achieved by an extension of the basic street network algorithm with new separate algorithms for the plot generation allowing for the definition of precise plot dimensions and taking into account specific predefined models of building prototypes. The plot generation approach combines the developed street network components with standard Grasshopper components. The results, as can be seen in Fig. 11, fulfill the requirements of the urban designers precisely in respect to the accuracy of the plots dimensions. The algorithm provides the necessary flexibility to incorporate other building prototypes and typologies.

In addition, the urban layout generation and building placement algorithm was enriched with a clustering feature (Fig. 12). The building units were assigned to certain households taking into account their preferences for a unit size, a specific location, and

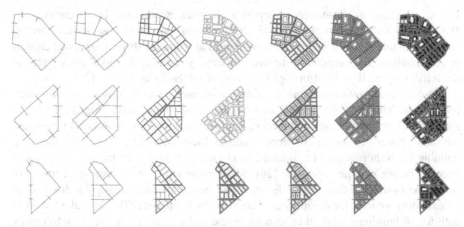

Fig. 11. Various urban scenarios for different shapes of initial input polygons representing three different neighborhoods. The tool provides fast results and the designer can modify the initial positions of axis for the street network generation. The layout of streets and blocks rearranges accordingly. For more details on the generative process, see also the video-links listed in the acknowledgement.

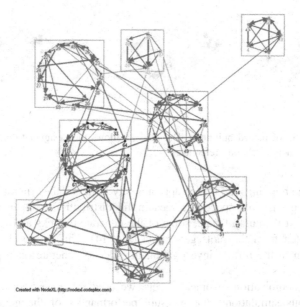

Created with NodeXL (http://nodexl.codeplex.com)

Fig. 12. Clusters of neighborhood preferences. Each household was asked for the preferred other households it would like to live nearby. Cluster computation and visualization created with NodeXL (http://nodexl.codeplex.com).

the proximity to other households. The aim of this approach was to ensure that people living in the neighbourhoods could create or preserve communities. For this, we proposed a social network and integrated cognitive analysis to help arrange how people live together and in consequence support an intimate relationship in the community. We use the collected information of the preferred proximities as social network structure. In this network, we can identify groups and arrange them in so called clusters or communities. For computing the clusters from given neighborhood preferences of the inhabitants as illustrated in Fig. 12, we used the NodeXL library [25].

Each cluster shows a network consisting of densely connected residents with their preferences. The difficulty was to transfer the household clusters from Fig. 12 to a spatial distribution of houses that form corresponding spatial communities. Distributing the same cluster of residents in proper building locations needed to confirm that each building had a shortest path between them. The measurement of distance in urban space depends on the cognitive distance [26], which represents a better empirical model of pedestrian movement than metric distance. For the computation of angular distances in Grasshopper we used the components developed by Fuchkina [27]. The ranked-shortest path for all buildings allowed to map the household clusters from Fig. 12 into nearby buildings (Fig. 13). The optimized cluster layout was limited by the minimum total metric area size, which allowed to create a more dense living arrangement. This method assisted the urban planner in allocating residents close to each other according to preferences in combination with an efficient plot packing strategy (Fig. 13).

Fig. 13. Clustering of placed buildings. The method allows the designer to allocate residents according to their neighborhood preferences.

Although the buildings are placed appropriately based on the criteria introduced so far, limitations persist in respect to a meaningful distribution of open public spaces across the site. At the current state, some of the generated blocks are randomly taken out and exempted from the plots generation (Fig. 14). This aspect should be given serious attention in the further investigation in order to generate open public spaces with higher qualities.

For a later optimization of other aspects, we used the generated urban fabric as input for various simulations that measure performances of the generated spatial configurations. Whereas the optimizations methods are not presented in this paper, we consider possible performance measures. We use an Isovist field analysis as shown in Fig. 15 to derive perceived security (measured by the Isovist properties compactness, occlusivity or control), potentials for community spaces (by the Isovist property area), and potentials for pedestrian traffic (measured by the Isovist property view-through). These performance measures shall be used in a later stage of this research for optimizing them at certain locations. For example, we can maximize the maximum area

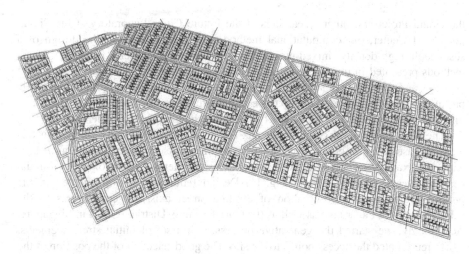

Fig. 14. The larger urban scenario test. The definition incorporates unique building prototypes defined by the designers and they are being placed on the site according to the generated street and plots layout.

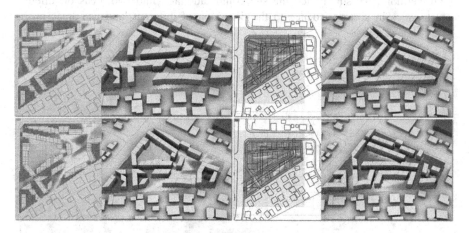

Fig. 15. Four variations for a synthesized neighborhood in Cape Town. The plots are limited to a defined size. The colors in the layouts show an Isovist field analysis. In this case the area that can be seen from one location is encoded by the colors (red maximum area, green minimum area).

values for creating bigger community spaces. Alternatively, we may maximize the average compactness values in order in increase perceived security. This approach has been exemplified by Schneider and Koenig [28].

The second case study regards the redevelopment of the Singapore container terminal in Tanjong Pagar, which will be relocated by 2027 freeing 325ha of land for a high-profile waterfront development [33]. In collaboration with urban designers from the Grand Projet and other researchers at the Future Cities Laboratory at the Singapore ETH Center, our computational method is applied to support the design of a sustainable high-density, mixed-use urban waterfront development. In particular, the methods presented in this paper are applied to test and explore different urban design concepts and development strategies for the site, as they allow generating urban fabric prototypes quickly and to easily explore and evaluate design alternatives. There is a link to a video provided at the end of this article, which shows the generative process.

The functionalities of our components are further developed and adapted in this ongoing case study to better respond to the requirements of the collaborating design team. An example and proof of concept, which was generated based on a given initial design concept, can be seen in Fig. 16. Design requirements implemented in the prototype includes the observation of existing street axis and connections to the existing Tanjong Pagar area as well as the Core Business District (CBD) in Singapore. Accordingly, we started the generative process with a set of initial street segments, which represented the access points to the site. The good selection of the position of the initial street also guarantees the generation of relatively regular and realistic plots, as can be seen in Fig. 16. The further generation of blocks, parcels and buildings followed the nested approach describe in Sect. 4 to create a hierarchical street pattern with primary and secondary streets.

Furthermore, we subdivided the site computationally into two areas of different characteristics in correspondence to the definition of different land use areas in the

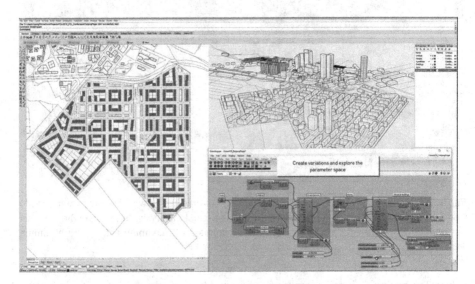

Fig. 16. Example for a fast urban fabric prototyping for the Tanjong Pagar container terminal in Singapore. The data of the environment including the 3D information of the buildings are imported from open street maps via the Grasshopper plugin Elk2. For generating the urban fabric, we used the components introduced in Sect. 4. For more details on the generative process, see also the video-links listed in the acknowledgement.

design brief. To exemplify different land uses, different minimum block widths, parcel widths and building heights were defined, with larger blocks and higher buildings in the area towards the CBD and smaller blocks and lower buildings in the area towards the waterfront (Fig. 17).

For the performance evaluation of the generated street patterns, we used the DecodingSpaces Grasshopper components for spatial analysis, which allows to cal-

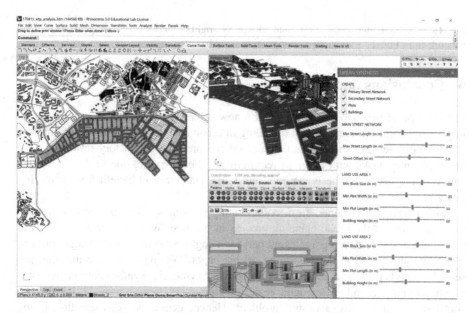

Fig. 17. Exemplary definition of different land use areas for the Tanjong Pagar site with larger blocks and parcels as well as higher buildings towards the CBD area and smaller blocks and parcels as well as lower buildings towards the waterfront.

culate and evaluate centrality measures and thus evaluate the integration and accessibility of the generated urban area [27, 32]. Figure 18 shows the calculated global betweenness centrality of an exemplary generated urban network for the Tanjong Pagar site in relation to the existing neighborhoods in its vicinity on the left and its calculated global closeness centrality on the right. Analysis methods can be easily integrated into the design workflow, as respective components can be integrated into the generative parametric definition. Thus, they can help provide immediate feedback on the performance of a solution based on which the designer can adjust the parameters and adapt the solution accordingly.

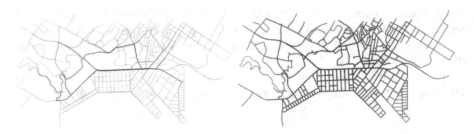

Fig. 18. Global betweenness (left) and closeness (right) centrality of the generated urban network from Fig. 17 in relation to the existing neighborhood.

6 Conclusions and Outlook

In the scope of this paper, we presented a new urban synthesis method as well as its implementation for the procedural modeling of urban designs. Based on two exemplary case studies, we have shown that this method can produce satisfactory results [30] for urban planning tasks with different requirements. Furthermore, due to the interactive nature of our urban synthesis methods and tools, planners can benefit from exploring many possible solutions quickly.

Initial feedback obtained from collaborating designers suggests that our components can support the urban planning process in practice. Whereas our main aim with this research was to develop a relevant part for a cognitive design computing approach, which we introduced in the beginning of this paper. We may conclude that the presented methods provide a good basis for geometry synthesis. Synthesizing geometry is in turn an important pillar for cognitive design computing, since it provides the specific contribution for solving a design problem. Hence, geometric representation is the primary basis for a productive combination of human cognition and computing power. How we may use our geometry synthesis methods in a next step for optimization is described later in this section.

Towards our cognitive design computing approach our geometry synthesis implementation still comes with a few limitations. For example, the generation and desirable distribution of the plots are very much dependent on the generated layout of the street network, which itself is dependent on the defined control parameters and the placement of initial street segments. Even though the nesting of the parceling component (Fig. 9) helped to alleviate the precise plot dimension problem encountered in the Empower Shack case study, it does not solve it fundamentally. A more general issue we are facing is that the rules that generate the spatial configurations cannot be saved. As the generative algorithms use in part random values or behaviors, all parts of a generated solution are changed if a user changes a control parameter or manipulates the initial geometry. Furthermore, the user interaction capabilities of Grasshopper are limited to changes of the referenced geometry and to the manipulation of control parameter values. A more sophisticated user interaction during the generative process, which includes the direct interaction with and manipulation of generated geometries, and for later during an optimization process is not possible. The addition of such features would require a separate user interface on top of Grasshopper or a standalone implementation as exemplified by Koenig and Schmitt [2, 31].

Moreover, for the time being, we have not integrated components for data analysis and evolutionary multi-criterion optimization (EMO) to achieve our final goal: the realization of a system based on the cognitive design computing framework as described in [2, 29]. For more advanced data analysis, the capabilities to process big data still need to be introduced into the system. One big data application could be the collection and analysis of existing urban patterns and their deployment as a library, which can be utilized for the generation and evaluation of urban layouts. For EMO, an abstract data representation has to be developed, which can parameterize all urban features for unified optimization. Existing approaches and plugins for Grasshopper like Galapagos or Octopus.E (http://www.food4rhino.com/app/octopuse) are limited to numerical representations but cannot compute complicated data structures as used in our approach in form of the instruction tree (Fig. 1). However, for example, spatial analysis components, which are available as Grasshopper plugins [27, 32], can be used and integrated to compute the fitness of generated urban designs.

In consequence, further investigation will address the development of a more comprehensive data structure, which will allow to represent generated urban fabrics in a way that they can be used for evolutionary optimization. In a subsequent step, we will then be looking at extending the Grasshopper Octopus.E component to work with our newly developed data structure. Finally, the combination of user-friendly interaction strategies with easy to understand problem representations and intuitively navigable solution spaces as a basis for integrated computational planning and design is an issue that is still unresolved.

Acknowledgement. The research presented in this paper was partially conducted at the Future Cities Laboratory at the Singapore-ETH Centre, which was established collaboratively between ETH Zurich and Singapore's National Research Foundation (FI 370074016) under its Campus for Research Excellence and Technological Enterprise program. Some methods presented in the paper were developed as part of the research project ESUM: Analyzing trade-offs between the energy and social performance of urban morphologies funded by the German Research Foundation (DFG) and the Swiss National Science Foundation (SNF, project number 100013L_149552).

There is a demo video for the generative process illustrated in Fig. 16 at https://vimeo.com/191807352 and https://vimeo.com/212540621. The process for generating the urban fabrics shown in Figs. 11, 12, 13 and 14 is shown in this video: https://www.youtube.com/watch?v=ELUKfsx89og&feature=youtu.be

The Rhino3D/Grasshopper components can be downloaded from the website of the Computational Planning Group: http://cplan-group.net/

References

1. Rouse, M.: Cognitive computing. In: WhatIs.com. http://whatis.techtarget.com/definition/cognitive-computing (2014). Accessed 15 March 2016
2. Koenig, R., Schmitt, G.: Backcasting and a new way of command in computational design. In: CAADence Archit, Budapest, pp. 15–25 (2016)

3. Radford, A., Gero, J.S.: Design by Optimization in Architecture, Building and Construction. Van Nostrand Reinhold, New York, Wokingham (1988)
4. Cagan, J., Campbell, M.I., Finger, S., Tomiyama, T.: A framework for computational design synthesis: model and applications. J. Comput. Inf. Sci. Eng. 5, 171–181 (2005). doi:10.1115/1.2013289
5. Weber, B., Müller, P., Wonka, P., Gross, M.: Interactive geometric simulation of 4D cities. In: Eurographics, pp. 481–492 (2009)
6. Parish, Y., Müller, P.: Procedural modeling of cities. SIGGRAPH, pp. 301–308. ACM, Los Angeles, CA (2001)
7. Chen, G., Esch, G., Wonka, P., et al.: Interactive procedural street modeling. ACM Trans. Graph. 27, 10 (2008). doi:10.1145/1360612.1360702
8. Müller, P., Wonka, P., Haegler, S., et al.: Procedural modeling of buildings. In: (TOG) ACMT on G (ed) ACM SIGGRAPH, pp. 614–623. ACM Press, Boston (2006)
9. Mitchell, J., Steadman, P., Liggett, R.S.: Synthesis and optimization of small rectangular floor plans. Environ. Plan. B Plan. Des. 3, 37–70 (1976)
10. Stiny, G., Mitchell, J.: The palladian grammar. Environ. Plan. B Plan. Des. 5, 5–18 (1978)
11. Duarte, J.P.: A discursive grammar for customizing mass housing: the case of Siza's houses at Malagueira. Autom. Constr. 14, 265–275 (2005). doi:10.1016/j.autcon.2004.07.013
12. Duarte, J.P., de Rocha, J.M., Soares, G.D.: Unveiling the structure of the Marrakech Medina: A shape grammar and an interpreter for generating urban form. Artif. Intell. Eng. Des. Anal. Manuf. 21, 317–349 (2007)
13. Doulgerakis, A.: Genetic Programming + Unfolding Embryology in Automated Layout Planning. University College London (2007)
14. O'Neill, M., McDermott, J., Swafford, J.M., et al.: Evolutionary design using grammatical evolution and shape grammars: designing a shelter. Int. J. Des. Eng. 3, 4–24 (2010)
15. Braach, M.: Programmieren statt Zeichnen: Kaisersrot. archithese (2002)
16. Braach, M.: Solutions you cannot draw. Archit. Des. 84, 46–53 (2014). doi:10.1002/ad.1807
17. Coates, P., Derix, C.: The deep structure of the picturesque. Archit. Des. 84, 32–37 (2014). doi:10.1002/ad.1805
18. Koenig, R.: CPlan: an open source library for computational analysis and synthesis. In: Martens, B., Wurzer, G.T.G., et al. (eds.) Real Time—Proceedings of the 33rd eCAADe Conference on Vienna University of Technology, Vienna, pp. 245–250 (2015)
19. Koenig, R.: CPlan Group (2015). http://cplan-group.net/. Accessed 28 May 2015
20. Koenig, R., Treyer, L., Schmitt, G.: Graphical smalltalk with my optimization system for urban planning tasks. In: Stouffs, R., Sariyildiz, S. (eds.) Proceedings of the 31st eCAADe Conference—vol. 2, Delft, Netherlands, pp. 195–203 (2013)
21. Knecht, K., Koenig, R.: Generating floor plan layouts with k-d trees and evolutionary algorithms. In: GA2010—13th Generative Art Conference (2010)
22. Koenig, R., Knecht, K.: Comparing two evolutionary algorithm based methods for layout generation: dense packing versus subdivision. Artif. Intell. Eng. Des. Anal. Manuf. 28, 285–299 (2014). doi:10.1017/S0890060414000237
23. Miao, Y., Koenig, R., Bus, P., et al.: Empowering urban design prototyping: a case study in Cape Town with interactive computational synthesis methods. In: Janssen, P., Loh, P., Atomic, A., Schnabel, M.A. (eds.) Protoc. Flows Glitches, Proceedings of the 22nd International Conference on Association Computers in Architecture Design and Research in Asia, Hong Kong, pp. 407–416 (2017)
24. Knecht, K., Koenig, R.: Automatische Grundstücksumlegung mithilfe von Unterteilungsalgorithmen und typenbasierte Generierung von Stadtstrukturen. Bauhaus-Universität Weimar, Weimar (2012)

25. Hansen, D.L., Shneiderman, B., Smith, M.A.: Analyzing Social Media Networks with NodeXL: Insights from a Connected World. Morgan Kaufmann, Burlington (2011)
26. Turner, A.: From axial to road-centre lines: a new representation for space syntax and a new model of route choice for transport network analysis. Environ. Plan. B Plan. Des. **34**, 539–555 (2007)
27. Fuchkina, E.: Pedestrian Movement Graph Analysis. Weimar (2016)
28. Schneider, S., Koenig, R.: Exploring the generative potential of isovist fields: the evolutionary generation of urban layouts based on isovist field properties. In: 30th International Conference on Education Research in Computer Aided Architectural Design in Europe, Prague, pp. 355–363 (2012)
29. König, R., Schmitt, G., Standfest, M.: Cognitive computing for urban design. Virtual real plan. Urban Des. Perspect. Pract. Appl. (2017)
30. Simon, H.A.: The Sciences of the Artificial, 3rd edn. MIT Press, Cambridge (1969)
31. Koenig, R.: Urban design synthesis for building layouts urban design synthesis for building layouts based on evolutionary many-criteria optimization. Int. J. Archit. Comput. **13**, 257–270 (2015). doi:10.1260/1478-0771.13.3-4.257
32. Bielik, M., Schneider, S., Koenig, R.: Parametric urban patterns: exploring and integrating graph-based spatial properties in parametric urban modelling. In: eCAADe 2012 (2012)
33. URA: Master Plan Greater Southern Waterfront (2014). https://www.ura.gov.sg/uol/master-plan/View-Master-Plan/master-plan-2014/master-plan/Regional-highlights/central-area/central-area/Greater-southern-waterfront.aspx. Accessed 15 Feb 2017

CIM-St

A Parametric Design System for Street Cross Sections

Rui de Klerk$^{(\boxtimes)}$ ⓘ and José Nuno Beirão ⓘ

Faculdade de Arquitetura, Universidade de Lisboa,
Rua Sá Nogueira, Pólo Universitário, Alto da Ajuda, 1349-055 Lisbon, Portugal
{ruideklerk, jnb}@fa.ulisboa.pt

Abstract. City environment is very much determined by the design of its streets and in particular by the design of its cross section. This paper shows a street cross section design interface where designs are controlled by an ontology and a parametric design system. The system keeps its semantic structure through the ontology and provides a design interface that understands the computer interaction needed by the urban designer. Real time visual analytics are used to support the design decision process, allowing designers to objectively compare designs and measure the differences between them, in order to make informed decisions.

Keywords: Parametric design · Ontologies · Compound grammars · Street cross section · Urban design systems

1 Introduction

CIM-St is a parametric design system dedicated to the (semi-)automatic generation of street cross sections of street types selected by the designer. It is an extension to a City Information Modelling (CIM) tool, complementing it with more specific and detailed representations of the urban networks.

To generate meaningful solutions, this design system combines computational ontologies [1] with a compound grammar [2], an extension of the shape grammar formalism [3]. The first describes and structures knowledge about a specific knowledge domain (in this case, the city) and are used to inform and control the design generation process, ensuring the feasibility and accuracy of the final product. The compound grammar, on the other hand, combines generic shape rules [4] with description functions [5] that, informed by the ontologies, select which rule to apply and when to apply it, thus controlling the design derivation process.

Ontologies (knowledge bases) and shape grammars (generative design systems) have been combined in the past, aiming to introduce semantic control over the generative design process. Similarities between ontologies and shape grammars (both contain design rules) have been identified by Grobler et al. [6], who then used ontologies in parallel with shape grammars to inform shape rule application. Trescack, Esteva and Rodriguez [7] used ontologies to define the relevant concepts for a generative process and shape grammars to generate the designs, with heuristics guiding the

© Springer Nature Singapore Pte Ltd. 2017
G. Çağdaş et al. (Eds.): CAAD Futures 2017, CCIS 724, pp. 42–59, 2017.
DOI: 10.1007/978-981-10-5197-5_3

generation process and validations evaluating the designs. More recently, Stouffs and Tunçer [8] used an ontology as a meta-model for the generation of an historical architectural type, using description rules to generate an instance of the typology described in the ontology.

This work takes as a reference the City ontology described in [9]. The ontologies in use contain particular features from a specific domain and are a part of the Networks ontology, which is, itself, a sub-ontology of the City ontology. Besides defining the taxonomic structure of the elements they represent, these ontologies also store ranges of values and admissible parameters specific to the elements.

The parametric design system proposed should facilitate the work of the urban designer when it comes to specifying the composition of streets, allowing him/her to quickly test and evaluate different solutions, such as the recommendations offered by street design guides [10, 11]. By relieving the repetitive workload of the designers, the design system allows them to focus on the qualities of their choices instead, supported by an interface with visual analytics and metrics.

Current Parametric Design Systems for Street Cross Sections. There are currently a few parametric systems focused on the design of street cross sections. The ones identified here are all web based and freely available to everyone. The first, and more complete, is the Abu Dhabi Urban Street Utility Design Tool [12]. Developed by the Abu Dhabi Urban Planning Council (UPC), it allows users to create street cross section arrangements using the "drag and drop" paradigm to place and adjust modules corresponding to street components. The interface presents the cross section of the street as well as its plan, dimensions, types of components and utilities (such as the sewage system). Street designs can be then exported to either DXF, PDF, CSV or USDT (the design system's file) formats.

Streetplan [13] follows the same strategy to place and adjust the components of the street. An interesting feature of its interface is the possibility to work on two street cross sections simultaneously, comparing different options between two designs. However, it doesn't offer the same number of features and detailing as the previous design system and only supports exporting to image files (JPG or PNG).

Finally, we would like to mention Streetmix [14], a simpler interface directed towards urban communities, inviting everyone to test and propose their own solutions for any street they would like to change. It also features drag-and drop operations and both cross section and plan views of the designs. Users can either save the design to a PNG image file or print it. All of these systems allow users to share their designs using social networks.

2 Methodology

Each street can be considered as a particular arrangement of street components, such as sidewalks, bicycle lanes or car lanes. The number and type of street components, as well as their arrangement, vary from one street type to another, though they are not necessarily exclusive to a specific type. A boulevard will necessarily have a large width and varied number of street components, with its arrangement defining spatial qualities attributed to that type of street, while an alley, much narrower, will have a small number of components (maybe only one) allowing for little arrangements.

This arrangement of street components is represented as a street description and each street type has a minimum arrangement of these components. The resulting street cross section will be a formal representation of a street description, considering the street type chosen, the parameters selected for each component, the available street width and additional constraints specified by the designer.

Our design system takes advantage of the taxonomic structure of the *City* ontology mentioned above, more specifically of the sub-ontologies that compose it, to drive and control the design generation process. These sub-ontologies represent different levels of abstraction of the concept of 'city', describing features from specific domains that compose the city and its structure.

For the generation of street cross sections, CIM-St uses a combination of specific sub-ontologies of the *Networks* ontology, a sub-ontology itself of the global *City* ontology. The sub-ontologies used are: *Street Nomenclature* (SN), *Street Descriptions* (SD) and *Street Components* (SC). Figure 1 illustrates the relations between these sub-ontologies, which will guide the implementation of the CIM-St parametric design system.

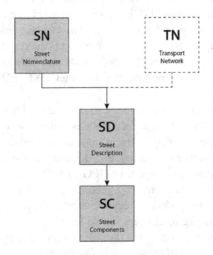

Fig. 1. Structure of the sub-ontologies used in the CIM-St design system.

The *Transportation Network* (TN) sub-ontology is also considered here to illustrate its role in the hierarchy of the knowledge base, even though it will be the focus of future development (see Sect. for more details).

The SN ontology, for instance, represents a collection of representative street types: Street (st), Avenue (av), Boulevard (bv), Main Street (ms), Promenade (pr), Grove (gr), Lane (la), Alley (al), Cul-de-Sac (cs) and Ring Roads (rr). This establishes the set of street name abbreviations {st, av, bv, ms, pr, gr, la, al, cs, rr}, which will be used to filter street descriptions allowed for the street type chosen by the designer.

The choice of elements from the SN ontology will have a direct influence on the arrangement of the street description, defined by the SD ontology, and consequently on the selection of the adequate street components from the SC ontology.

Components in SC refer to parts of the street section or profile, for instance, sidewalks, car lanes, bicycle lanes, bus lanes, green stripes (vegetation distributed along a street either for separating car lanes in different directions or for creating a buffer zone between sidewalk and traffic lanes), tree alignments, parking lanes, tram lanes, a canal (for the case of Dutch or Venetian streets) and other. The large variety of street sections produced by the code is based on compositions of these components.

The ontologies are structured as external XML[1] files which are fed into Grasshopper 3D[2], a Visual Programming Interface (VPI) for Rhinoceros 3D[3], through a XML parser developed for this purpose. The XML parser is a component developed to read external XML files which allows the designer to input XPath[4] queries to its content, returning either the names of XML nodes or their values, according to the choice of the designer. The overall structure of the XML document is also displayed in the VPI for user reference, presenting the nodes and their hierarchies. This allows designers who are not familiar with the ontology, or with its structure, to easily understand the hierarchy of its elements, facilitating the writing of new XPath queries to the XML document.

The XML format was selected to represent the ontologies, instead of RDF/S[5,6] or OWL[7] languages, due to its widespread use and familiarity. By externalising the ontologies as independent files, instead of having them hard-coded into the design system, these can be shared with the community, which may then modify and/or increment them with new knowledge about the subject. Street types specific to certain regions or cultures, such as the underlying structure of Marrakech Medina [15], may be added to the *City* ontology in this way, extending the knowledge regarding these objects and the global concept of City itself. This way, the design system remains flexible and promotes its extension by the people in a community using it.

These ontologies not only describe the hierarchical relations between its elements but also contain information regarding their values and parameters, such has their *id*, the range of admissible widths, differences between particular instances of the same type of element (lateral or central sidewalks, for instance), etc. This makes them an active part in the generative process, providing information to the system at different levels: from general descriptions to their parameters.

This methodology may be extended to grammar-based design systems where semantic control is vital, such as the generative design of architectural types within a design language.

---

[1] https://www.w3.org/XML/.

[2] http://www.grasshopper3d.com/.

[3] https://www.rhino3d.com/.

[4] https://www.w3schools.com/xml/xpath_syntax.asp.

[5] https://www.w3.org/RDF/.

[6] https://www.w3.org/TR/rdf-schema/.

[7] https://www.w3.org/OWL/.

3   CIM-St Framework

The framework of CIM-St is composed of four main parts: a knowledge base, a grammar engine, an evaluation module and a user interface. We begin by giving an overview of the framework, illustrated in Fig. 2, and proceed to a more detailed explanation about the mechanisms behind the system, following the diagram from Fig. 3.

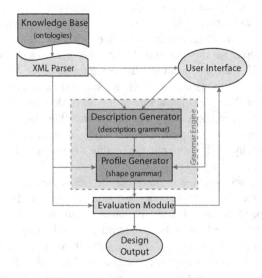

Fig. 2. CIM-St system overview.

The knowledge base consists of the SN, SD and SC ontologies mentioned above and communicates with the design system through an XML parser, using XPath queries. The knowledge base is ubiquitous throughout the system, informing and controlling it, with a direct relation to the user interface, the grammar engine and the evaluation module.

The grammar engine is the core of the design system, consisting of two modules that operate in sequence: a generator of street descriptions, based on a description grammar, and a generator of the resulting shape of the street profile, based on a (compound) shape grammar. The output of the grammar engine is then evaluated according to the knowledge represented by the ontologies, informing the user about the validity and properties of the design via the user interface (described in more detail in Sect. 5).

Figure 3 shows the workflow of a design session in CIM-St, illustrating the most relevant steps behind the parametric generation of a street profile and the relations between the different parts of the design system.

A design session starts with the input of a street width and the choice of a street type (from the SN ontology) to be used as a base upon which the final street profile will be created. To each street type corresponds (at least) one minimum description of street

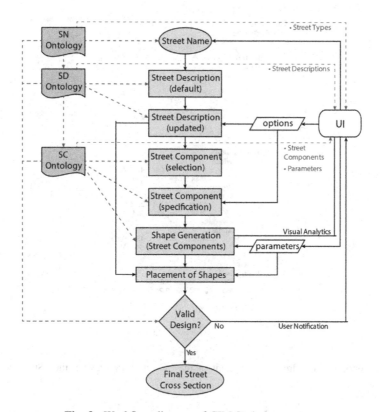

Fig. 3. Workflow diagram of CIM-St design system.

components, which is loaded from the SD ontology by default. The user may then customize the profile of the street by updating its default description, either picking from a set of options from the user interface or by manually altering the indices of the street components in the description. This triggers description rules that modify the indices of the street components in the default description.

Indices in a street description are then mapped to their corresponding street component, selecting them from the SC ontology. Each SC is then specified, according to either its placement in the description or to the options selected. An example of SC positional specification would be the differentiation between "Lateral Sidewalks" and "Central Sidewalks", or the case of sidewalks with trees, specified by the adjacency of the "id" number "8" (tree) to and "id" number "2" (sidewalk) ("…2 8…" or "…8 2…") in the description. Street Components may also be specified from the inputs given by the user, when s/he selects a "two-way" Bicycle Lane instead of a "one-way" Bicycle Lane or when choosing if the Street Parking will be parallel or not.

For every specification of a component, the SC ontology provides a set of parameters, feeding them into the user interface, to the shape generation process and to the shape placement process. Below, in Fig. 4, we can see the taxonomic structure of the "Street Parking" component with its sub-components (specifications) "Parallel" and "Not Parallel", and their respective parameters, taken from Table 1.

```
<Street_Components>
    <Street_Parking>
        <id type="integer">1</id>
        <Valid_For type="string">S3 - S2</Valid_For>
        <Prefered_For type="string">S2.5 - S2</Prefered_For>
        <Parallel>
            <Width>
                <Min type="float">2.0</Min>
                <Max type="float">2.4</Max>
            </Width>
            <Length>
                <min type="float">4.7</min>
                <max type="float">5.5</max>
            </Length>
        </Parallel>
        <Not_Parallel>
            <Width>
                <Min type="float">4.8</Min>
                <Max type="float">5.5</Max>
            </Width>
            <Length>
                <Min type="float">2.25</Min>
                <Max type="float">2.5</Max>
            </Length>
            <Angle unit="deg">
                <Min type="float">45</Min>
                <Max type="float">90</Max>
            </Angle>
        </Not_Parallel>
        <h adj_id="">
            <Min type="float">0.0</Min>
            <Max type="float">0.2</Max>
        </h>
        <h adj_id="10" type="float">0</h>
    </Street_Parking>
    <Sidewalks> [...] </Sidewalks>
    [...]
</Street_Components>
```

Fig. 4. Taxonomic structure of a fragment of the SC ontology (XML), the "Street Parking" component.

Table 1. Partial representation of the SC object class (Street Parking).

Street Components (SC)	Profile Schema		Profile Parameters
	Parallel	Not Parallel	Parallel
			$2.0 \le w \le 2.4$
			$4.7 \le l \le 5.5$
① - Street Parking			Not Parallel
			$4.8 \le w \le 5.5$
			$2.25 \le l \le 2.5$
			$45° \le \alpha \le 90°$
			$0 \le h \le 0.2$
	⑪⑩② ① ③④⑤	⑪⑩② ① ③④⑤	If ⑩ $h = 0$
② - Sidewalks			
[...]			
⑫ - Protection Rails			

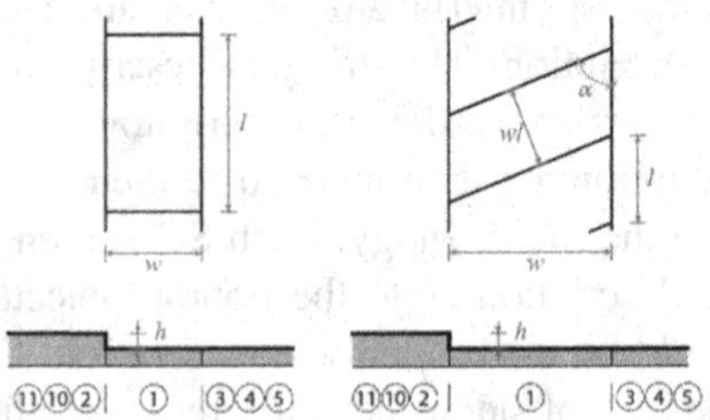

It is from the specification of the street components that their shape representation will be generated, considering the specific properties and parameters of each one of them. Street component shapes are generated using very simple generic shape rules, following a tree derivation process from a simple rectangular shape to a more detailed representation. Variations to the parameters of the component will result in changes to the parameters in the shape rules that produce the shape representation of the component, processed in real time by the profile generator.

The last step in the generative process is the correct placement of the shapes of the street components, following the up-to-date description of the street. Since the representations of the components are generated at the center of the street, they need to be correctly displaced according to the order established in the street definition, placing one component after another to create the representation of the street profile. This, in turn, needs to be relocated so its center matches the center of the street, resulting in a properly allocated street profile, which may or not need to be corrected if it doesn't fit the street width.

Before returning the design output to the user, the profile is evaluated by the system with the support of the knowledge base, informing the user on the development of the design. This information is presented in real time, such as the amount of space left to complete the profile of the street, the number of car/bus/tram lanes in the design, etc., not hindering the workflow of the session. If, however, there is something wrong with the design, warnings and error will be raised, asking the user to solve them. This occurs, for instance, when the design proposal is larger than the total width of the street (the solution is invalid) or if any of the buildings adjacent to the street has a height larger than the width of the street (see Sect. 5).

The evaluation module will also retrieve the data to be used in visual analytics, providing information to support both quantitative and qualitative design decisions (further detailed in Sect. 6).

In the end, the resulting street profile is returned to the user, accompanied by relevant information regarding the components that compose it and warnings/errors if there is some (quantitative) inconsistency in the design.

4 User Interface

The user interface was created using Human UI[8] plugin for Grasshopper 3D and consists of a main window with information and controls distributed over three tabs ("Street Type", "Definition" and "Extras"), a pop-up window with visual analytics and metrics of the design ("Analysis" window) and the Rhinoceros 3D "Front" viewport, where the geometric representation of the street cross-section will be drawn (Fig. 5).

The most relevant options and parameters to generate a design are grouped under the "Street Type" tab, the first of the main window and the one which is displayed by default. There, the designer will start by selecting a street type from the SN ontology and defining the width of the street. The geometric representation of the minimum description for the chosen street type, defined in the Street Description (SD) ontology, will be automatically drawn in the "Front" viewport. From then on, the designer is free to easily introduce changes to the design in several ways.

---

[8] http://www.food4rhino.com/app/human-ui.

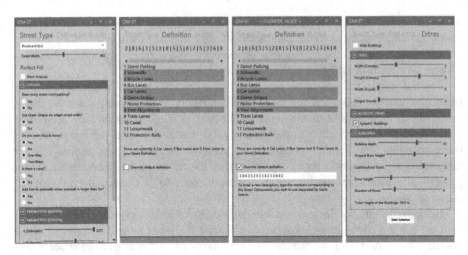

Fig. 5. CIM-St Main Window. Tabs available from left to right: "Street Type", "Definition", "Definition + description override and "Extras". (Color figure online)

The first way to customize the design of a street would be by answering a few simple questions, such as "Do you want bicycle lanes?" or "Use Green Stripes to adapt street width?" Affirmative answers to these questions will automatically add specific Street Components to the original definition ("Street Parking", "Green Stripes", "Bicycle Lanes", "Canal" or "Trees"). In case of affirmative answers to the existence of bicycle lanes or a canal, new options appear, requiring the designer to choose between one-way or two-way bicycle lanes, if the canal is centered on the street or (if not) where it is positioned.

These simple questions allow the designer to quickly test solutions in a natural fashion, rapidly assessing different designs with just a few clicks on the radio buttons available.

The second means of customization focus on fine-tuning the parameters of each Street Component, according to their definition in the respective ontology. To improve user interaction with the system, the "width" parameter sliders are grouped together, allowing the designer to focus first on defining how much space a Street Component takes on the street before setting its details. The sliders for the remaining parameters are packed into a secondary group, collapsed by default in the interface so not to daunt nor confuse the user with too many options.

Relevant notifications regarding the development of the design, as well as warnings and error messages, are displayed at the top of the window, still under the "Street Type" tab. Notifications inform the user on how much space is still left to fill to complete the design of the street and are displayed in black. Warnings and error messages, like the design overshooting the total width of the street, are displayed in bright red. When the design matches the total width of the street, a bright green "Perfect Fit" message is displayed in a larger font size.

Still under the first tab, we find a check box to display the "Analysis" window, hidden by default, which will be discussed in the next topic.

Under the "Definition" tab of the main window, as the name suggests, the user will find the Street Definition of the current design, highlighting the components in use. Towards the bottom of the window, a short summary informs on the amount of "Car Lanes", "Bus Lanes" and "Tram Lanes" in the design.

If the user wishes to further customize the design, introducing bus or tram lanes or producing asymmetric solutions, an "Override default definition" at the bottom of the window will enable a hidden text box with the current definition, which the user can override by typing in the indices of Street Components desired in the order they should appear in the design. The pairing of some components will result on the combination of their geometries; sidewalks with trees will result from pairing their indices ("2" and "8"), as will for green stripes with trees ("6" and "8"). To avoid conflicts of apparent pairing of one component with two other (like the case of "2 8 6"), precedence is given to the most common Street Component (resulting in a sidewalk with trees next to a green stripe, in this case).

The "Override default description" provides a way around the symmetric rigidity of the system, allowing designers to play freely with the composition of the profile of the street and even test absurd solutions.

Lastly, we have the "Extras" tab of the main window. Here the user will find the controls for the parameters of additional elements, such as trees, acoustic panels and buildings, whose representation may be hidden at will. By default, the system will generate symmetric buildings at each end of the street; the user has the possibility to specify asymmetric building, by unchecking the corresponding checkbox, and setting different parameters for each building. If the height of the buildings is larger than the total width of the street, the system raises a warning and displays the corresponding message in red at the top of the window in both the "Street Type" and "Extras" tabs.

At the very bottom of the windows we have a "Bake Solution" button, which will bake the geometry of the design, as well as its dimensions and description onto Rhinoceros 3D.

The geometry generated using the system is displayed at the origin of the "Front" viewport of the Rhinoceros 3D canvas, consisting of the design of the street, the surrounding buildings, the dimensions of the design and the final definition of the street.

During the generation process, the cross section of the street may be displayed in three different colours, yellow, green or red, which work as a visual clue to designer (Fig. 6). If the profile is yellow, then the width of the current design is less than the total width of the street, meaning that the design is incomplete and requires either additional Street Components to be added to the Street Definition or different parameters. If the design is displayed in red, then the final definition of the new street overshoots the total width of the street, making it unfeasible for that space. Finally, if the design fits perfectly in the total width of the street, the solution is displayed in green.

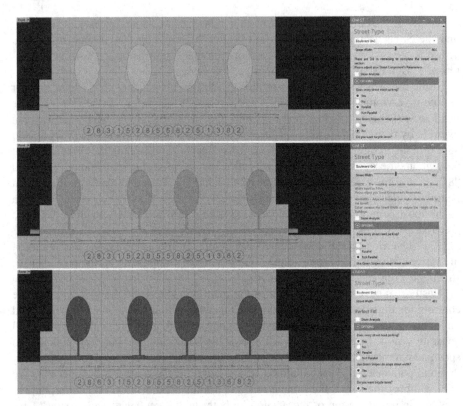

Fig. 6. CIM-St profile visual clues and notifications. From top to bottom: incomplete design (*yellow*), over dimensioned design with buildings taller than the width of the street (*red*) and a valid design (*green*). (Color figure online)

5 Design Objectives and Criteria

Design systems are great tools to reduce repetitive tasks from designers' workload and to quickly produce a large set of design solutions to a given problem. Choosing the best solution from a large set of candidates, however, might prove to be a little harder, especially when multiple players with different backgrounds are involved in the decision process.

To support the design decision process, CIM-St provides an interface with visual analytics, where designers can automatically visualise and measure the impact of their choices. As of this point, the visual analytics available consist of two pie-charts and a summary of the total widths of the components of the street.

The first pie-chart shows the impact (in percentage) of each Street Component (SC) in the cross section of the street, relating the total width of each SC with to total width of the street. Designers can immediately and dynamically visualize the impact of their choices, comparing the weights of the different Street Components with each other.

Since each SC has a different colour, grouping types of uses under different tones (bicycle lanes and sidewalks under light green, vehicular traffic under warm tones and greeneries under darker greens), designers may have a "feel" of the street profile's qualities while they are experimenting different design solutions.

The second pie chart measures the sidewalk tree coverage: that is, the ratio between the total width of the canopies of the trees and the total width of the sidewalks in a street cross section. As before, this graph gives the designers a responsive visual feedback to their settings, in this case how much of the sidewalks will be covered by the canopies of the trees. A simple change in the initial options (for example, "Add tree to sidewalks when sidewalk is larger than 5 m?") may have a big impact on the sidewalk tree coverage chart, as we can see in the images below (Figs. 7 and 8).

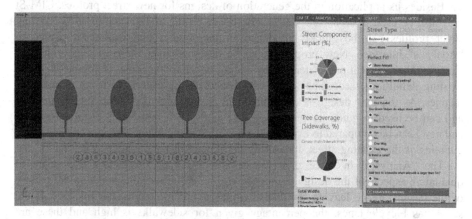

Fig. 7. CIM-St analysis of a Boulevard favoring green spaces and walkable space.

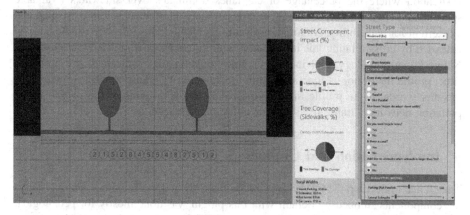

Fig. 8. CIM-St analysis of a Boulevard not favoring green spaces nor walkable space.

Comparing the "Street Component Impact" graph in the Analysis windows of Figs. 7 and 8, we can immediately notice the impact of the decision to change from parallel parking to angular parking ("Not Parallel"). The space reserved for car parking changes drastically from one tenth to a quarter of the street width. We can also notice that the Boulevard design on Fig. 8 has less diversity of Street Components than the design on Fig. 7, after the removal of the Bicycle Lanes and of the Green Stripes adjacent to the lateral sidewalks. In the second design, priority is given to vehicular traffic, with Car Lanes taking occupying thirty percent (30%) of the street width, contrary to fifteen percent (15%) in the first design. Looking at both the "Street Component Impact" and the "Tree Coverage (Sidewalks)" graphs, it is easy to notice a reduction on both the sidewalk space (10%) and the tree coverage of the sidewalks (17.1%), form the first street profile (Fig. 7) to the second (Fig. 8).

Besides its application in the generation of designs for new street profiles, CIM-St may also be used in urban renewal as a design re-profile and evaluation tool. Existing street profiles can be quickly modelled in the system and evaluated, using the "Analysis" interface. New proposals can be designed over these models, either by changing their current parameters, or by adding or removing Street Components to the existing definitions, according to pre-established design criteria or in an exploratory manner. As the new design is configured, the visual analytics automatically updates and can be used to guide its generation. The analysis of both street profiles (original and new) can be compared to evaluate the qualities of the renewal proposed against the qualities of the existing street, measuring the impact of the changes to it.

The "Analysis" interface gives measurable evidence on factors that relate to qualitative aspects of the design without providing definitive statements on the quality of the design, hence leaving the analysis open to interpretation. For instance, if the street has bicycle lanes, the percentage given for sidewalks is high and these are protected from traffic lanes by trees, this may be interpreted as a street that is people oriented and that has some of the necessary qualities for walkability. On the contrary, in a situation where the percentage of car lanes dominates over sidewalks (walkable space) and there are no bicycle lanes, that design may interpreted as traffic oriented and a deterrent for walkability. Although not yet implemented, this interface can be later on extended by cross-relating this information with inputs taken from the "Transportation Network" sub-ontology (TN in Fig. 1). Such relation may indicate if the proposed street profile fits or not its function within the domain of "Transportation Network", or in other words, if the profile fits its expected function in terms of the overall transportation network – traffic feasibility or traffic performance.

6   Implementation and Outputs

The choice to develop the CIM-St in Grasshopper 3D and to use (almost entirely only) the components shipped by default with this plugin was done mostly for pedagogical purposes. This Visual Programming Interface (VPI) has been taught in optative classes at our Faculty for some years, to both Masters and Doctorate students, and has a growing community in both design education and design practice. Despite its limitations [16], it is found to be an easy way to introduce programming to designers [17], allowing them to quickly develop and test parametric designs and to easily redesign their algorithms with new objectives in mind. Using this VPI, any user with a little of experience can customize and/or extend CIM-St to fit his/her needs with a simple twist to the code.

Another reason why this VPI was chosen was to integrate it in the existing CIM tool that CIM-St comes to extend, since it was developed in Grasshopper 3D as well. The end goal is to produce a set of components for Grasshopper 3D dedicated to parametric urban design, addressing different levels of detail in the generation of urban plans.

One of the most relevant parts of the implementation was to create a custom XML parser to access the content of the ontologies and query it using XPath syntax. This allows the user to access, for instance, the Street Components sub-ontology and retrieve all types of components and, if they exist, their sub-types as well as all necessary parameters and/or restrictions (Fig. 9).

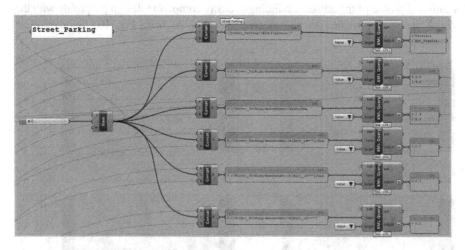

Fig. 9. Retrieving Street Parking Parameters from the SC ontology using XPath queries to the XML parser (Grasshopper 3D).

Elements and parameters are parsed in this way from the ontologies to the UI, to the Grammar engine and to the evaluation module, as described previously in Fig. 2. A short script is used to adjust the limit values of the sliders in the UI, matching them with the minimum and maximum values of the parameters parsed from the ontologies. Updates to the parameters on the ontologies, as a result from a change in legislation, for example, are therefore automatically propagated to the UI, adapting the design system to a new context.

A shortcoming from implementing the system in Grasshopper 3D, without resorting to extensive textual scripting, is the rigidity of the algorithm when it comes to incrementing the content of the sub-ontologies with new types (e.g., adding a new type of street component to the SC ontology). The lack of recursion in the VPI forces every repetitive set of operations to be coded a priori, meaning that additions to the ontology need to be followed by some (sometimes extensive) editing to the algorithm, copying blocks of components and creating new links (at best).

Also regarding the implementation, one of the main difficulties was to prevent the algorithm from entering into infinite feedback loops - an abnormality when programming in Grasshopper 3D. This occurred due to the user interface, particularly when the user chose to override the street description (see third panel, from left to right, from Fig. 5). This was a consequence of using an editable field to both present information to the user and use the information entered in the field in the generative process, feeding the end result of the calculations back as an update to the same field in the UI. The end result was then read by the UI as if it were new information input from the user, thus resulting in an infinite feedback loop. The issue was solved with the use of conditional triggers that operate automatically to control the flow of information at different places in the algorithm.

Regarding the outputs of the design system, as we can see from Fig. 10 it is possible to test multiple and diverse configurations for the same street setup (street width and profile of the adjacent buildings), easily comparing design proposals with the visual analytics provided by the system. Solution A, from Fig. 10, favors a clear

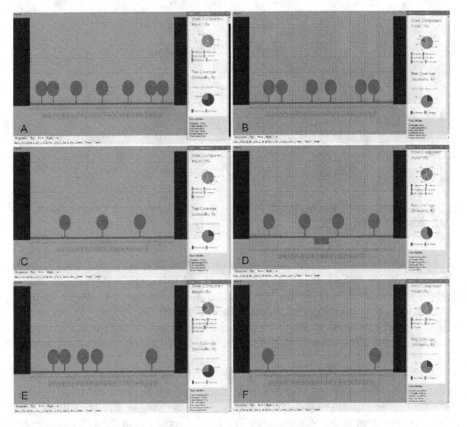

Fig. 10. Examples of different boulevards created using CIM-St.

compartmentalization of the street uses, separating car lanes from public transportation (bus and tram) from bicycle lanes and from sidewalks, while investing in a lot of tree coverage for the walkable areas. This solution doesn't consider, however, any street parking spaces. An opposite solution to design A would be design E, which introduces little or no separations between different types of uses, mixing bus lanes with car lanes and placing bicycle lanes between sidewalks, while tree coverage of the sidewalks is kept to a minimum (and not on the wider sidewalks).

It is easy to see these aspects almost immediately from the street cross section when the differences are explicit, but when they aren't the visual analytics introduces an additional layer of information with visual clues and metrics that may help sustain the choice of a design or disambiguate between similar choices (like solutions A and B).

Variety of street profiles extends beyond the type of street and the components that define it. A crucial part of the street profile is its boundaries; these affect the way we perceive streets and some of their qualities. Because of this, the design system allows users to customize the abstract representation of buildings that limit the street, either making them symmetric or not, or removing them altogether from the cross section. The last case is particularly useful when the user needs to design a Ring-Road (Fig. 11, right).

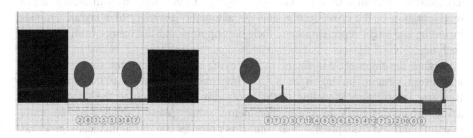

Fig. 11. Examples of different street profiles created using CIM-St (left side – Avenue; right side – Ring-Road).

Complementing the street cross section, the system automatically generates the main dimensions and provides the end description of the components of the street. When satisfied with the result, the user can 'bake' the design into the Rhinoceros interface, where she may carry on further detailing it or finalize its production.

7 Conclusions and Future work

This paper presented a parametric design system for street cross sections (CIM-St), where designs are generated by a grammar engine controlled by a knowledge base composed of three ontologies (SN – "Street Nomenclature"; SD – "Street Descriptions" and SC – "Street Components"). The combination of computational ontologies and shapes grammars ensures semantic control over the shape generation process, resulting in the production of meaningful design solutions. A detailed description of the compound grammar used in the system, consisting of shape and description rules, and its articulation with the knowledge base will be the object of a future publication.

The system is composed of four main modules: knowledge base in XML format, user interface, grammar engine and evaluation. Generating the cross section of a street using CIM-St is as simple as selecting a street type and a street width from the user interface and making simple adjustments to it, using the options and controls available in the interface. Each type of street has a minimum set of street components (sidewalks, roads, bicycle lanes, street parking, etc.) that identifies it, which is presented to the user as a description (an ordered set of street components IDs). An alternative way to customize a street is by directly editing its description, manually overriding the automatically generated set.

To aid the user during the design process, CIM-St provides a set of visual analytics, allowing for the automatic comparison between different options during a design session. This tool empowers designers by supporting their decisions with objective metrics and visual clues of their impact on the design. This way, the user can easily explore multiple scenarios in a short period of time, quickly assessing their qualities, and make objective distinctions between design proposals.

At the current stage of development, the system only generates the cross section of the street with the adjacent buildings, with all of its components dimensioned, alongside with its final description. The next stage of development will include a plan representation of the cross section and the automatic assembly of a layout template, including the street representations, their descriptions and the results from the visual analytics.

Future development will focus on improving and extending the functionalities of the design system, linking it to a City Information Modeling (CIM) tool and to Building Information Modeling (BIM) tools. Linking CIM-St to the CIM tool will allow urban designers to create parametric urban plans (which may be easily re-configured and readapted) so that valid street profiles can be automatically generated whenever the plan changes. With the introduction of the Transport Network (TN) ontology in the knowledge base, additional levels of control and accuracy are added to the generation process, improving the semantics of the design system.

Linking CIM-St to BIM technologies will allow designers to quickly detail the construction elements of the street profile, easily updating them when necessary, and produce all necessary documentation for accurate material quantification, budgeting and construction of the street. This would make the current CIM platform plus CIM-St a complete package for parametric urban design, from conception to construction.

Acknowledgments. This work is integrated in the "Measuring Urbanity: densities and performance of extensive urban fabrics. The Portuguese case" research project at the Research Center for Architecture, Urbanism and Design (CIAUD) at the Faculty of Architecture, University of Lisbon (FA/ULisboa). The first author would like to thank for the research grant CIAUD_BI_09/EAT/04008, which made this work possible.

References

1. Gruber, T.R.: Toward principles for the design of ontologies used for knowledge sharing? Int. J. Hum.-Comput. Stud. **43**, 907–928 (1995)
2. Knight, T.: Computing with emergence. Environ. Plan. B Plan. Des. **30**, 125–155 (2003). doi:10.1068/b12914
3. Stiny, G., Gips, J.: Shape grammars and the generative specification of painting and sculpture. Inf. Process. **71**, 1460–1465 (1972)
4. Beirão, J., Duarte, J. and Stouffs, R.: An urban grammar for Praia: towards generic shape grammars for urban design. In: 27th eCAADe Conference Proceedings, pp. 575–584 (2009)
5. Stiny, G.: A note on the description of designs. Environ. Plan. B Plan. Des. **8**, 257–267 (1981). doi:10.1068/b080257
6. Grobler, F., Aksamija, A., Kim, H., Krishnamurti, R., Yue, K., Hickerson, C.: Ontologies and shape grammars: communication between knowledge-based and generative systems. In: Gero, J.S., Goel, A.K. (eds.) Design Computing and Cognition 2008, pp. 23–40. Springer, Netherlands (2008)
7. Trescak, T., Esteva, M., Rodriguez, I.: A virtual world grammar for automatic generation of virtual worlds. Vis. Comput. **26**, 521–531 (2010). doi:10.1007/s00371-010-0473-7
8. Stouffs, R., Tunçer, B.: Typological descriptions as generative guides for historical architecture. Nexus Netw. J. 785–805 (2015). doi:10.1007/s00004-015-0260-x
9. Beirão, J.: CityMaker: Designing Grammars for Urban Design, Ph.D. thesis, TU Delft (2012). doi:10.7480/abe.2012.5
10. National Association of City Transportation Officials: Urban Street Design Guide. Island Press (2013). ISBN: 978-1-61091-494-9
11. National Association of City Transportation Officials and Global Designing Cities Initiative: Global Street Design Guide. Island Press (2016). ISBN: 978-1-61091-494-9
12. Abu Dhabi Urban Street and Utility Design Tool. https://usdm.upc.gov.ae/USDM/. Accessed 24 April 2017
13. Streetplan. http://streetplan.net. Accessed 24 Apr 2017
14. Streetmix. https://streetmix.net. Accessed 24 Apr 2017
15. Duarte, J.P., Rocha, J.M., Soares, G.D.: Unveiling the structure of the Marrakech Medina: a shape grammar and an interpreter for generating urban form. AI EDAM: Artif. Intell. Eng. Des. Anal. Manuf. **21**(04), 317–349 (2007). doi:10.1017/S0890060407000315
16. Leitão, A., Santos, L.: Programming languages for generative design: visual or textual? In: 29th eCAADe Conference Proceedings, pp. 549–557 (2011)
17. Celani, G., Vaz, C.E.V.: CAD scripting and visual programming languages for implementing computational design concepts: a comparison from a pedagogical point of view. Int. J. Archit. Comput. **10**(1), 121–137 (2012). doi:10.1260/1478-0771.10.1.121

Integration of a Structure from Motion into Virtual and Augmented Reality for Architectural and Urban Simulation

Demonstrated in Real Architectural and Urban Projects

Tomohiro Fukuda[1(✉)], Hideki Nada[2], Haruo Adachi[2],
Shunta Shimizu[3], Chikako Takei[3], Yusuke Sato[1],
Nobuyoshi Yabuki[1], and Ali Motamedi[1]

[1] Osaka University, Suita, Osaka, Japan
{fukuda, yabuki}@see.eng.osaka-u.ac.jp,
u391398i@gmail.com, alimot@gmail.com
[2] Sakaiminato City Office, Sakaiminato, Tottori, Japan
{h-nada, h-adachi}@city.sakaiminato.lg.jp
[3] Forum8 Co., Ltd., Minato, Tokyo, Japan
{simizu, chikako}@forum8.co.jp

Abstract. Computational visual simulations are extremely useful and powerful tools for decision-making. The use of virtual and augmented reality (VR/AR) has become a common phenomenon due to real-time and interactive visual simulation tools in architectural and urban design studies and presentations. In this study, a demonstration is performed to integrate structure from motion (SfM) into VR and AR. A 3D modeling method is explored by SfM under real-time rendering as a solution for the modeling cost in large-scale VR. The study examines the application of camera parameters of SfM to realize an appropriate registration and tracking accuracy in marker-less AR to visualize full-scale design projects on a planned construction site. The proposed approach is applied to plural real architectural and urban design projects, and results indicate the feasibility and effectiveness of the proposed approach.

Keywords: Architectural and urban design · Visual simulation · Virtual reality · Augmented reality · Structure from motion

1 Introduction

Visual simulations are extremely useful and powerful tools in decision-makings involved in architectural and urban design [1]. Recently, significant improvements have characterized visual simulation technology using a computer. Virtual reality (VR) is widely used because it constructs past and future virtual spaces with three-dimensional (3D) Computer graphics (CG) objects and provides interactive movies by real-time rendering processing. The value of VR in large-scale architectural and urban design is demonstrated by using the functions such as walk-through, a comparison of design alternatives, and dynamic simulation in real time [2–6]. However, typically, considerable amount of time

© Springer Nature Singapore Pte Ltd. 2017
G. Çağdaş et al. (Eds.): CAAD Futures 2017, CCIS 724, pp. 60–77, 2017.
DOI: 10.1007/978-981-10-5197-5_4

and expense is entailed on an urban scale to construct and integrate a 3D object for all virtual spaces. However, these costs in creating a building object are reduced owing to the spread of Building Information Modeling (BIM). Additionally, a VR environment created by 3DCG objects is disconnected from the reality and does not allow design stakeholders to experience the feelings of the real world.

Augmented reality (AR) overlays images or 3D virtual objects on real world images with computer-generated data by using video or photographic displays. Specifically, AR can help visualize full-scale design projects on a planned construction site. Diminished reality (DR) is a similar technology that removes the image of an existing object from a real scene, replacing it with the background image of the object's area. Outdoor AR typically requires tracking in unprepared environments [7]. To accurately render the outdoor AR, we must precisely track the geometric registration between a live video and the 3D object, which remains a challenging problem. In the case of the onsite visualization of full-scale design objects by AR, a high real distance tends to exist between AR users and 3D virtual objects that should be visualized. The reference point for geometric registration corresponds to the position of the sensor in sensor-based methods (such as GPS or 3D sensors) [7–9] or the position of an artificial marker in marker-based methods (that is an example of vision-based methods) [7, 10]. In sensor-based methods, the reference point of geometric registration is normally positioned near an AR user, and thus the sensing error significantly influences the error of a 3D object registration. In artificial marker-based methods, it is possible to place large markers near target objects. However, it is necessary for the marker to be properly captured by the AR camera, and this imposes limitations on the user's movability range and requires the installation of large markers. Therefore, many studies continue to focus on developing marker-less AR systems that do not require sensors and artificial markers [11–13]. A study developed a robust geometric registration method of a marker-less outdoor AR that corresponds point cloud data to natural features of the real world [14]. However, the system requires special equipment such as a 3D laser scanner to detect these point clouds.

Recently, redeveloping or renovating existing buildings and urban facilities to improve their safety and strength or adding new functions are common processes to enhance the quality of life. The 3D objects of existing structures in architectural and urban design processes are generally created and used. Structure from motion (SfM) is a photogrammetry technology that estimates 3D structures from two-dimensional sequential images that may be coupled to local motion signals [15, 16]. SfM is becoming increasingly popular for 3D modeling, as it requires only familiar equipment (such as digital cameras or smart phones) and free or low-cost software [17]. Previous studies that recorded historical buildings by SfM instead of CAD/BIM have been presented in architecture and urban fields [18–20]. However, these studies do not focus on real-time calculations such as VR and AR.

This study explores a novel approach by integrating SfM into VR and AR to solve some challenges of VR and AR in architectural and urban design fields. In order to solve the problem of modeling cost in large-scale VR, the study explores an appropriate 3D modeling method by SfM for real-time rendering. When generating 3D objects by SfM, a point cloud is generated from the feature quantities of the input photographic group, and the points are then connected into triangle meshes. A large number of generated meshes will reduce the frame rate (frames per second; fps) which is a metrics for real-time rendering. A suitable SfM-based 3D modeling method for real-time rendering has not been discussed. The camera parameters of SfM are explored for marker-less AR registration and tracking to solve the problem of appropriate registration and tracking accuracy in AR to visualize full-scale design projects on a planned construction site. Previous studies realized marker-less AR using SfM technology that was subsequently extended to a marker-less DR system [21, 22]. However, there is a paucity of extant research that examines the uses and limitations of applying SfM-based AR to real architectural design projects.

2   SfM-Based Modeling for VR

In order to solve the problem of modeling cost in large-scale VR, a sufficient 3D modeling method by SfM is explored in the context of real-time rendering.

2.1   Urban Design Project: Mizuki Shigeru Road Renewal

Sakaiminato is the hometown of Shigeru Mizuki, one of Japan's leading manga artists. The shopping district Mizuki Shigeru Road from JR Sakaiminato station to Honmachi archade shopping street (Extension: 800 m), named after the bronze statues of Yokai monsters created by Mizuki, has been earmarked for downtown revitalization. After ceaseless efforts, the number of Yokai statues in this district has increased from 23 in 1992 to 153 today. Sakaiminato City has a population of 34000, but Mizuki Shigeru Road receives more than two million visitors per year (Fig. 1).

Fig. 1. Photographs of Mizuki Shigeru Road ©MIZUKI Productions

To ensure the future prosperity of Mizuki Shigeru Road, a schematic renovation plan with five main goals was constructed based on the basic renewal philosophy of "creating a hospitable and entertaining road that everyone would like to visit" in 2014. The goals included the following: (1) creation of a one-way and S-shaped roadway, (2) creation of a wider sidewalk space, (3) re-accommodation of the bronze statues within the new zone concept, (4) improvement of cityscape with a sense of unity, and (5) night landscape design. The VR was created for the construction design study and public meeting to build consensus for construction.

In the VR production process, a 3D digital model of bronze statues and buildings along Mizuki Shigeru Road are needed. With respect to the bronze statues, 153 existing statues possessed different shapes and included complicated shapes with holes. Additionally, artists began to create 18 new statues. In order to create a mold for a bronze statue, the artists constructed a 3D plaster model (with a styrofoam interior) from a 2D illustration created for the Mizuki Shigeru road without creating a drawing. The 3D digital object is conventionally created by 3DCG software (e.g. Autodesk 3ds MAX, Trimble SketchUp). However, the surveying and modeling of many statues in 3DCG demands enormous time and cost resources. To alleviate these restrictions, we applied SfM technology.

2.2 Photography for SfM

In order to shoot an object for SfM, if it is possible to shoot an entire object, such as a bronze statue, then the position is determined from eight directions with respect to the bronze statue by viewing the bronze statue from the sky. Subsequently, the height of the camera position in each of the eight directions is set to three points, namely high, medium, and low. That is, the total number of photographed points is 24. In contrast, if it is not possible to shoot the entire object, such as a building, then noisy objects other than the building are excluded to the maximum possible extent, and images are continuously obtained from multiple points to the maximum possible extent.

The shooting was performed on a cloudy day to ensure the optical consistency between the VR virtual space and the 3D object created by SfM. In order to add shadow effects of the whole VR virtual space on the VR system at a later stage, it is desirable to generate a shadowless texture at the stage of 3D modeling by SfM. The shooting was performed at times in which less tourists were present to shoot the complete bronze statue to the maximum possible extent and to not to shoot noise elements apart from the bronze statue.

Project experts, such as designers and VR engineers, worked in Tokyo and Osaka that are located away from the project site (Sakaiminato-city). Thus, significant time and costs are involved if experts are required to visit the site to obtain a number of photographs for SfM. Therefore, staff members of the Sakaiminato city office were asked to photograph the same. As a result, a total of more than 10000 photos could be shot in a month (June 10–July 11, 2016). Thus, this confirmed that non-experts could capture photographs for SfM by using a normal digital camera and a simple technical know-how of photography and that it was possible to perform sharing work.

2.3 SfM-Based Statues Modeling

The following feasibility study was conducted as shown in Fig. 2 to examine the effect of real-time rendering by placing the bronze statues on an object. A target value of the frame rate to realize real-time rendering was set as 30 fps since this is close to that of a digital terrestrial television and a digital video camera. The following steps are involved in the feasibility study:

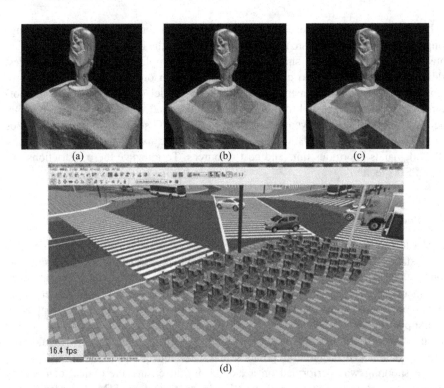

Fig. 2. Feasibility study: (a) high-accuracy, (b) medium-accuracy, (c) low-accuracy, (d) 100 statues are installed in a virtual space of a city

1) Construct the VR virtual space of a city.
2) Model a bronze statue by SfM with a high-accuracy level (4286 polygon), a medium-accuracy level (1025 polygon), and a low-accuracy level (298 polygon).
3) Construct four types of VR virtual space and measure the frame rate when: (a) 100 high-accuracy statues are installed, (b) 100 medium-accuracy statues are installed, (c) 100 low-accuracy statues are installed, and (d) no bronze statues are installed in the constructed VR virtual space of a city.

A feasibility study yielded the following frame rates: (a) 100 high-accuracy statues: 16.4 fps, (b) 100 medium-accuracy statues: 24.1 fps, (c) 100 low-accuracy statues: 27.1 fps, (d) Foundation (No statues): 30.1 fps. The results indicated that it is difficult to realize real-time rendering when all the high-accuracy bronze statues are installed. Additionally, 153 bronze statues were eventually ranked into the following three categories: 27 high-accuracy statues that correspond to famous characters and become landmarks, 46 medium-accuracy statues, and 80 low-accuracy statues.

However, although the number of polygons is reduced for the medium and low accuracy categories, texture mapping data with high accuracy is still used to maintain expression quality.

With respect to the SfM modeling, two commercial softwares (Agisoft PhotoScan ver.1.2.5, Autodesk Remake ver. 17.24.1.4) and a new SfM software developed by the authors (UC-win/Road SfM plug-in) [23] were used. Specifications for SfM include the following:

- Digital camera: CASIO EX-ZS210, EX-ZS190 (standard spec)
- Photos input for SfM (one statue): PhotoScan: 200, Remake: 24, UC-win/Road SfM plug-in: 100
- Image size: 2048 × 1536 pixels
- Photo opportunity (per statue): 10–20 min
- Point clouds created by SfM (a statue): PhotoScan: 60000–70000, Remake: unknown, UC-win/Road SfM plug-in: 19000
- Production time (per statue): 30 min for the automatic calculation from images to 3D polygons, 30 min for adjustment work after the calculation

The results are as follows. Figure 3 shows an example of the created high-accuracy bronze statue. Figure 4 shows the number of polygons and vertices at each accuracy level.

(a)

(b)

Fig. 3. A bronze statue model made by SfM: (a) photographs, (b) 3D model with high-accuracy

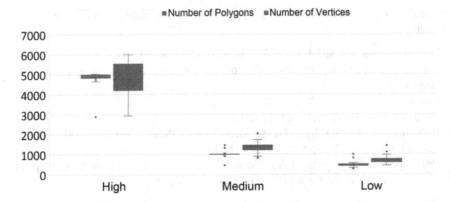

Fig. 4. Number of polygons and vertices at each accuracy level

2.4 SfM-Based Roadside Building Modeling

The 3D modeling of a roadside building by SfM was examined. A conventional method for practical use given the low-cost and small amount of data involved performing 3D manual modeling using 3DCG software based on the building plane information obtained from a map (1/500–1/2500) and elevation information obtained from elevation photographs. The SfM method involved creating other 3D models of the same building from a number of photographs using two types of SfM software (i.e., Agisoft PhotoScan ver.1.2.5, Autodesk Remake ver. 17.24.1.4).

The roadside building object generated by SfM (as shown in Fig. 5) was analyzed. With respect to the amount of data, the number of polygons was 19 and the number of vertices was 48 in the conventional method. Conversely, while creating the roadside building with SfM software (PhotoScan), the number of polygons and number of vertices increased significantly to 2.42 million and 1.12 million, respectively. While creating the roadside building with SfM software (Remake), the number of polygons and number of vertices increased significantly to 790,000 and 420,000. This only corresponds to the data volume of a single building, and there are approximately 120 buildings along the roadside, and thus this can significantly impact real-time rendering. Additionally, SfM software (PhotoScan) includes a polygon reduction function to reduce the number of polygons to be generated. However, it was not possible to reduce this to the number of polygons in the conventional method. Although previous studies attempted to reduce the number of vertices and polygons automatically while preserving the object's features [24], the current situation remains limited.

With respect to a qualitative evaluation, lack of content, inadequate content, and surplus content were observed in the object generated by SfM. The lack of content implies that the elements to be modeled are not modeled by SfM. In the fore-mentioned example, the roof part was absent because it was not photographed from an UAV (Unmanned Aerial Vehicle) or at a high altitude. Inadequate content indicates that the shape is not precisely defined although it is modeled by the SfM. This is related to building signs, arcade features, utility poles, and electric wires in the fore-mentioned example. Surplus content implies that unnecessary objects are modeled. In the

Fig. 5. A roadside building model: (a) photograph, (b) by conventional method, (c) polygons without mask images by SfM (Photoscan), (d) a mask image, (e) polygons with mask images by SfM (Photoscan), (f) polygons by SfM (Remake)

fore-mentioned example, the wire contains several elements of the sky. Following the generation of the 3D object by SfM, it is possible to perform editing work, such as modifying inadequate objects or deleting surplus objects, in SfM software. However, the editing work entailed in the fore-mentioned example involves a considerable amount of time. Therefore, the roadside buildings were finally created by using the conventional method.

A reason for the occurrence of inadequacies and surpluses is that the front of a building includes various noise elements such as arcades and electric wires, which are modeled by SfM. A solution involves using the mask images of the photograph used for the SfM in conjunction with each other. In the mask image, the necessary area in the photograph that is used for SfM is denoted as white, and the unnecessary area is denoted as black. Thus, it is possible to generate 3D objects with fewer inadequacies and surpluses by using mask images. In contrast, it is necessary to create accurate mask images with an image processing software (e.g., Adobe Photoshop). A future study will examine the automatic generation of mask images by image processing or Artificial Intelligence (AI).

2.5   Development of VR Application

Finally, the design proposed for reconfiguring the Mizuki Shigeru road was constructed in the VR application and included the 3D bronze statues model by the SfM as discussed in the previous section (Fig. 6 and Table 1). The VR presents roads (such as road surfaces and markings), road plantings (such as boulevard trees and planting squirrels), traffic lights, 171 bronze statues, lighting poles, utility poles, arcades, and information signs, roadside buildings, advertising signs, open spaces (such as parks), natural elements of the background (such as land forms and seas), artificial elements (such as surrounding buildings), and human activities (such as pedestrians, bicycles, and cars). The traffic flow was reproduced on the VR by inputting data obtained by the pilot program in 2015. The LOD (Level of Detail)-enabled VR application was constructed on UC-win/Road (Ver. 11), and its frame rate exceeded 30 fps. The developed VR could be used standalone or on cloud computing [4].

The constructed VR is applied to events such as public meetings, public symposium, and local elementary school delivery lectures. It is essential to build a consensus between roadside residents, merchants, and tourists prior to the construction, and the conventional method entails considerable time in building a consensus. The developed VR expresses large-scale elements (such as roads) as well as human scale elements (such as bronze statues) and explains a large amount of information simultaneously to the stakeholders. Additionally, consensus with the stakeholders is significantly shortened by an instinctive 3D representation and the functions to change viewpoints and plans based on the demands of stakeholders interactively. Specifically, it is possible to simulate the manner in which citizens and tourists can comfortably spend time in Mizuki Shigeru Road by rearranging the bronze statues on the widened sidewalk with the one-way traffic of vehicles. Furthermore, it was possible to verify features, such as the bronze exhibition position and angle on the sidewalk, the photographing angle of the bronze statue, the illumination irradiation position, and angle to the bronze statue, in a short time. The productivity of the project was significantly improved by using the developed VR.

The developed VR system also included several limitations. All bronze statues by SfM could not be reproduced with high accuracy. Therefore, the bronze statues were classified in advance into three levels, namely high, medium, and low accuracy. A solution is required for real-time rendering while responding to high precision retention and increased data volume.

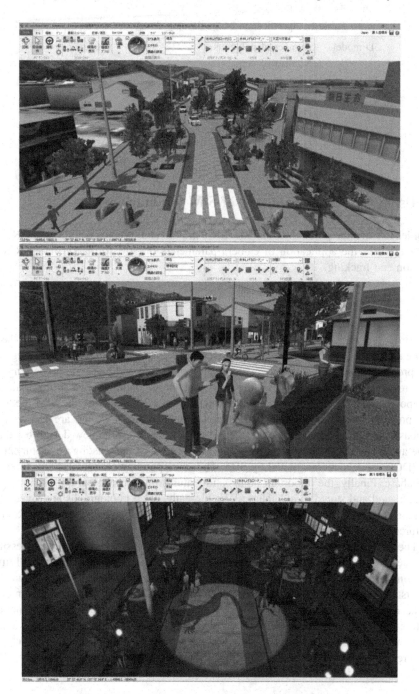

Fig. 6. Developed VR application of Mizuki Shigeru Road renewal

Table 1. Specification of the developed VR application

3D model	Number of polygons	965,472
	Number of vertices	929,325
Texture	Number of textures	885
	Number of texture pixels	65,530,368
	Data amount	1.5 GB
	VRAM use when running VR application	667.4 MB
Total system	Data amount	1.35 GB
	Frame rate	30–50 fps

3 Using Camera Parameters of SfM for Marker-Less AR

In order to solve the problem of sufficient registration and tracking accuracy in AR, the study explores the application of camera parameters of SfM to marker-less AR registration and tracking.

3.1 System Overview

The proposed marker-less system does not require special hardware, such as laser scanners, for the construction of the point cloud data that is used in this system (Fig. 7). The proposed method has two main steps; pre-processing and real-time processing. In the pre-processing step, the existing environment is photographed from multiple viewpoints, and the photographs are constructed into a 3D model by the SfM method. The position and orientation data of all photographs used by SfM are stored in a database. Second, the coordinates of the 3D virtual objects of the new design building to be augmented are defined relative to the coordinates of the existing environment in the 3DCG models, reconstructed by SfM. The corresponding coordinates are stored in a database. Finally, the important points and features of each photograph used in SfM are extracted and stored in a database. The file paths of all photographs are saved in a separate database. The local features are detected and described by Speeded-Up Robust Features (SURF) [25].

The real-time processing step first imports all files created in the pre-processing step. Second, the features in the live video images are extracted by SURF in real time and compared with the features of images stored in the database. Finally, the virtual 3D objects are precisely rendered in an AR display using the position and orientation data of the camera and by finding the most similar image in the database. The motion vectors for tracking are calculated by the optical flow technique. The external parameters are then calculated from the internal parameters, the positions of points on the screen and the corresponding world coordinates of those points.

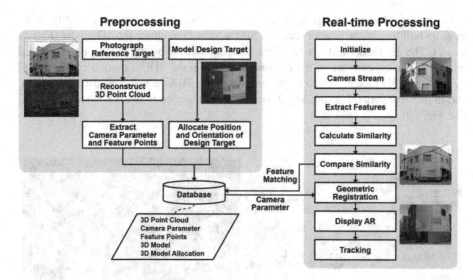

Fig. 7. Overview of the developed AR

3.2 System Implementation

The proposed system was implemented using C++ and by combining multiple open source software applications and libraries. In the preprocessing, OpenMVG (Open Multiple View Geometry. Ver. 0.7), which is an open source software, was used to perform SfM. Additionally, SketchUp2015, 3dsMax2016, and Metasequoia4 that are 3D modeling softwares were used to define the coordinates of 3D virtual objects. In the real-time processing, OpenCV (Open Source Computer Vision Library. Ver. 2.4.9), which is an open source image processing library, was used to capture real-time camera stream and image matching. Additionally, TBB (Threading Building Blocks. Ver. 4.4), which is an open source parallel processing library, was used for parallel processing. FreeGLUT (Ver. 2.8.1), which is a toolkit for OpenGL (Open Graphics Library), was used to draw the 3DCG model on the AR display.

3.3 Application in Building Design Project

The developed AR system was applied to study the facade and entrance of the new office building at the preliminary design stage as opposed to the conventional method of using a photomontage. Based on the request of the owner, the architect designs a new three-story office building to be replaced with the existing two-story office building. The areas of the target site, the building, and the total floor are 109 m^2, 83 m^2, and 243.5 m^2, respectively, and the main structure of the building was composed of steel. The site is located in a commercial district in Osaka City, Japan. The study was implemented from January to March 2016. The authors used a standard spec tablet PC, Microsoft Surface Pro 3 with Intel Core i7-4650U of CPU, 8.0 GB of RAM, and a 2160 × 1440 display operated on a Microsoft Windows 8.1 Pro platform.

In the pre-processing step, approximately 100 photographs were obtained from the existing building in the project site, and SfM was used to create the 3D model (Figs. 8 and 9). The 3D model of the new office building created by the architect was defined relative to the coordinates of the existing building in the 3DCG models reconstructed by SfM. The 3D model created by the architect is in FBX format converted from BIM, and in then converted into the MQO format to be imported to the AR system (Table 2 and Fig. 10).

(a)   (b)

Fig. 8. (a) Images used for SfM, (b) 3D model reconstructed from SfM

Fig. 9. Photography route of SfM and tracking route of experimentation

Table 2. Specification of the 3D model of the new office building

3D model	Number of polygons	1,638,998
	Number of vertices	664,251
Material	Number of materials	7
Total system	Data amount	156 MB

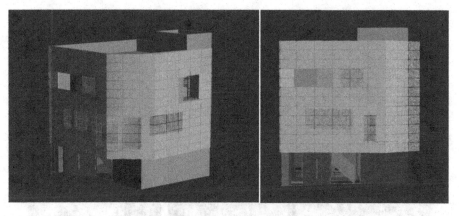

Fig. 10. 3D model of new office building

In the real-time processing step, the building owner and designers studied the facade of the preliminary designed building onsite while performing initial registration and tracking using the AR system (Fig. 11). In order to execute stable AR tracking, the experiment was performed in the morning to avoid backlighting to the web camera. Additionally, in order to avoid the influence of passers-by, vehicles, and sunlight at the

Fig. 11. Experimental photo

time of tracking, points on the AR screen that were focused at the time of tracking by optical flow were placed on the second floor or higher floors of the building wherein significant changes in luminance did not occur.

The results of the experiment verified that accurate representation of the material and texture of the building is possible. Furthermore, it was verified that by using the proposed system, sufficient registration could be realized from the main viewpoints and that it is possible to track the movements of the camera (Fig. 12).

Fig. 12. AR screenshots of new office building simulation

After performing the verification of the experiment onsite, an interview survey of the owner and designers was conducted. The designer evaluated that the size of the building could be intuitively comprehended by using the AR system at the construction site. The owner could also obtain the comments related to the building scale, and it was possible to obtain a more constructive communication when compared with previous communication in the preliminary design stage. The findings also revealed the disadvantages of the proposed system including the difficulty of viewing the exterior as well as the building model through the tablet LCD display of AR. A method to solve this problem involves using HMD (Head Mounted Display). However, walking freely by using a video see-through type HMD is difficult because the surrounding environment is not adequately visible [26]. In addition, when an optical see-through HMD is used, it is difficult to view the AR due to the effect of sunlight [27]. Moreover, although it is important for the size of the rendered 3D model to be accurate, an opinion persisted that this was unsure. In response to this opinion, the validity of the size of the designed building can be explained by comparing it with the size of the adjacent building in the experiment.

4   Conclusions

In this study, an approach to integrate SfM into VR and AR is demonstrated for architectural and urban visual simulations. The usefulness and limitations of the system are confirmed in two case studies. The contributions of this research include the following:

In order to decrease the modeling cost in large-scale VR, an appropriate 3D modeling method by SfM under real-time rendering is explored. A modeling method using SfM is developed to model a number of bronze statues and roadside buildings that correspond to the problems faced in actual urban design projects. Following the consideration under real-time rendering conditions, the total data amount of bronze statues is suppressed by setting three reproduction ranks. The results indicated that the modeling of roadside buildings is characterized by three problems, namely the lack of content, inadequate content, and surplus content. Finally, a large-scale VR application is constructed by integrating the SfM-based model.

In order to realize an appropriate registration and tracking accuracy in marker-less AR, a new AR system is developed to visualize full-scale design objects on a planned construction site using the camera parameters of SfM. The building owner and designers could study the facade of the office building at the preliminary design stage by using the proposed AR. Camera parameters for AR virtual camera could be obtained by the SfM from photographs of the existing office building. The results verified that appropriate registration and tracking could be realized on the proposed AR, and that accurate representation of the material and texture of the building is realized on a tablet PC. The full-scale size of the building could be understood intuitively by using the AR system at the construction site, and it is possible to obtain a more constructive level of communication between the owner and designers when compared to previous approaches.

However, SfM continues to be a developing technology. In future studies, it is important to examine further integration into VR and AR based on the improvement in SfM accuracy to restore a 3D model from photographs and the development of technology to restore a 3D model in real time from camera images (e.g., Simultaneous Localization and Mapping).

Acknowledgements. The research was partly supported by JSPS KAKENHI Grant Number JP25350010 and JP26-04368, and joint research funding between Sakaiminato city office and Osaka University. We would also like to take the opportunity to thank Kyokuyo Electric Co., Ltd. and atelier DoN to apply our proposed AR system to the building design project. We thank all the participants for their generous assistance in conducting projects and experiments.

References

1. Sheppard, S.J.: Visual Simulation: A Users Guide for Architects, Engineers, and Planners. Van Nostrand Reinhold, New York (1989)
2. Dorta, T., LaLande, P.: The impact of virtual reality on the design process, digital design studios: do computers make a difference? In: Proceedings of the 18th Annual Conference of the Association for Computer Aided Design in Architecture, ACADIA, pp. 138–163 (1998)
3. Sun, L., Fukuda, T., Resch, B.: A synchronous distributed cloud-based virtual reality meeting system for architectural and urban design. Front. Archit. Res. **3**(4), 348–357 (2014)

4. Fukuda, T., Ban, H., Yagi, K., Nishiie, J.: Development of high-definition virtual reality for historical architectural and urban digital reconstruction: a case study of Azuchi castle and old castle town in 1581, CAAD Futures 2015 Selected Papers. Commun. Comput. Inf. Sci. **527**, 75–89 (2015)
5. Kieferle, J., Woessner, U.: BIM interactive - about combining BIM and virtual reality - a bidirectional interaction method for BIM models in different environments. In: Proceedings of the 33rd eCAADe Conference, vol. 1, pp. 69–75 (2015)
6. Dokonal, W., Knight, M., Dengg, E.: VR or not VR - no longer a question? In: Proceedings of the 34th eCAADe Conference—vol. 2, pp. 573–579 (2016)
7. Schall, G., Wagner, D., Reitmayr, G., Taichmann, E., Wieser, M., Schmalstieg, D., Hofmann-Wellenhof, B.: Global pose estimation using multi-sensor fusion for outdoor augmented reality. In: ISMAR 2009 (2009)
8. Hii, J.C., Zhou, Z., Karlekar, J., Schneider, M., Lu, W.: Outdoor mobile augmented reality for past and future on-site architectural visualizations. In: CAAD Futures 2009, pp. 557–571 (2009)
9. Fukuda, T., Zhang, T., Yabuki, N.: Improvement of registration accuracy of a handheld augmented reality system for urban landscape simulation. Front. Archit. Res. **3**(4), 386–397 (2014)
10. Yabuki, N., Miyashita, K., Fukuda, T.: An invisible height evaluation system for building height regulation to preserve good landscapes using augmented reality. Autom. Constr. **20** (3), 228–235 (2011)
11. Klein, G., Murray, D.: Parallel tracking and mapping for small AR workspaces. In: ISMAR 2007 Proceedings of the 2007 6th IEEE and ACM International Symposium on Mixed and Augmented Reality, pp. 225–234 (2007)
12. Ventura, J., Hollerer, T.: Wide-area scene mapping for mobile visual tracking. In: Proceedings of the IEEE International Symposium on Mixed and Augmented Reality, pp. 3–12 (2012)
13. Schubert, G., Schattel, D., Tonnis, M., Klinker, G., Petzold, F.: Tangible mixed reality on-site: interactive augmented visualisations from architectural working models in urban design, CAAD Futures 2015 Selected Papers. Commun. Comput. Inf. Sci. **527**, 55–74 (2015)
14. Yabuki, N., Hamada, Y., Fukuda, T.: Development of an accurate registration technique for outdoor augmented reality using point cloud data. In: 14th International Conference on Computing in Civil and Building Engineering (2012)
15. Tomasi, C., Kanade, T.: Shape and motion from image streams under orthography: a factorization method. Int. J. Comput. Vis. **9**(2), 137–154 (1992)
16. Snavely, N., Seitz, M.S., Szeliski, R.: Modeling the world from internet photo collections. Int. J. Comput. Vis. **80**(2), 189–210 (2007)
17. Nagakura, T., Tsai, D., Choi, J.: Capturing history bit by bit—architectural database of photogrammetric model and panoramic video. In: Proceedings of the 33rd eCAADe Conference—vol. 1, pp. 685–694 (2015)
18. Datta, S., Beynon, D.: A computational approach to the reconstruction of surface geometry from early temple superstructures. Int. J. Archit. Comput. **3**(4), 471–486 (2005)
19. Agarwal, S., Snavely, N., Simon, I., Seitz, S.M., Szeliski, R.: Building Rome in a day. In: IEEE 12th International Conference on Computer Vision (ICCV), pp. 72–79 (2009)
20. Verniz, D., Mateus, L., Duarte, J.P., Ferreira, V.: 3D Reconstruction survey of complex informal settlements—towards an understanding of the genesis of form. In: Proceedings of the 34th eCAADe Conference—vol. 2, pp. 365–370 (2016)

21. Sato, Y., Fukuda, T., Yabuki, N., Michikawa, T., Motamedi, A.: A marker-less augmented reality system using image processing techniques for architecture and urban environment. In: Proceedings of the 21st International Conference on Computer-Aided Architectural Design Research in Asia (CAADRIA 2016), pp. 713–722 (2016)

22. Inoue, K., Fukuda, T., Yabuki, N., Motamedi, A., Michikawa, T.: Post-Demolition landscape assessment using photogrammetry-based diminished reality (DR). In: Proceedings of the 16th International Conference on Construction Applications of Virtual Reality, pp. 689–699 (2016)

23. Hanzawa, Y., Torii, A., Okutomi, M.: Practical structure from motion system for online image acquisition. IEICE Trans. Inf. Syst. (Japanese edition) **J96-D**(8), 1753–1763 (2013)

24. Hidaka, N., Michikawa, T., Motamedi, A., Yabuki, N., Fukuda, T.: Polygonization of point cloud of elongated civil infrastructures using lofting operation. In: Proceedings of the 16th International Conference on Construction Applications of Virtual Reality, pp. 677–688 (2016)

25. Bay, H., Ess, A., Tuytelaars, T., Cool, L.: Speeded-up robust feature (SURF). Comput. Vis. Image Underst. **110**, 346–359 (2008)

26. Watanabe, S.: Simulating 3D architecture and urban landscapes in real space. In: Proceedings of the 16th International Conference on Computer Aided Architectural Design Research in Asia, pp. 261–270 (2011)

27. Miyake, M., Fukuda, T., Yabuki, N., Motamedi, A., Michikawa, T.: Outdoor augmented reality using optical see-through HMD system for visualizing building information. In: 16th International Conference on Computing in Civil and Building Engineering, pp. 1644–1651 (2016)

Support Systems for Design Decisions

CAMBRIA: Interacting with Multiple CAD Alternatives

Siniša Kolarić$^{(\boxtimes)}$ (iD), Halil Erhan (iD), and Robert Woodbury (iD)

School of Interactive Arts and Technology,
Simon Fraser University, Surrey, Canada
{skolaric,herhan,rw}@sfu.ca

Abstract. Computer-aided design (CAD) tools aim to assist designers in their professional work, one key aspect of which is devising, evaluating, and choosing among multiple design alternatives. Yet, with few and limited exceptions, current tools handle just a single design model at a time, forcing users to adopt various ad hoc tactics for handling multiple design alternatives. Despite considerable prior work, there are no general, effective strategies for supporting design alternatives. New tools are needed to develop such strategies: to learn how designers' behavior changes with support for multiple alternatives. In this article, we describe CAMBRIA, a multi-state prototype tool we developed for working with multiple 2D parametric CAD models in parallel. We describe the outcomes of an analytical evaluation of CAMBRIA using the Cognitive Dimensions framework.

Keywords: Computer-aided design · CAD · Parametric CAD · Interaction design

1 Introduction

Many designers work with multiple, simultaneously-available design alternatives. We observe this behavior in different domains such as architectural, product, industrial and mechanical design, but also in drawing, painting, sculpting, and fine arts in general. Numerous empirical studies, likewise, report instances of designers developing, and then simultaneously working with multiple design solutions in parallel, in architectural design [1–4], engineering design [5, 6], graphic design [7, 8], and website design [9]. The need for alternatives-enabled work can be further confirmed by instances of expert opinion[1], as well as explained by *theoretical accounts* based on first perceptual principles, such as those governing the human visual system [11] or human perception in general [12].

As an illustration of the use of alternatives in a professional setting (that is, *in the wild*), Fig. 1 shows nine alternative models of the *Elephant House* designed by the architectural firm Foster + Partners, and constructed from 2002–2008 at Copenhagen Zoo in Denmark.

---

[1] For instance, N. Cross wrote that *'consideration of alternative solution concepts might save time and effort in the long run'* [10].

© Springer Nature Singapore Pte Ltd. 2017
G. Çağdaş et al. (Eds.): CAAD Futures 2017, CCIS 724, pp. 81–99, 2017.
DOI: 10.1007/978-981-10-5197-5_5

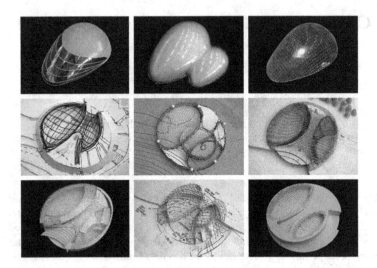

Fig. 1. Example of multiple design alternatives used in the wild in architectural design: *Elephant House* (images by Brady Peters/Buro Happold/Foster + Partners [13]).

Traditional materials, such as wood, corrugated fiberboard, and acrylic, were used to build this collection of physical models or maquettes. The designer can walk around the table stocked with such models, view them, compare them, and evaluate them according to different criteria, including the overall aesthetic impression, the sense of proportion, and their suitability for the environmental context. Based on such comparison and evaluation activities, the designer can then filter-down, prune or recombine the set of alternatives further, ultimately ending up with one or just a few design solutions deemed to be *the best* by the designer [14].

Evidence for alternatives can be found in disciplines beyond design. In fine arts for example, a sketch study *Study for the Trivulzio Equestrian Monument*, made by Leonardo da Vinci in 1508–1510, with a total of four different revisions of the sketch, all drawn by the artist on a single sheet of paper [15]. Different parts of the sketch (such as the rider's head or the horse's hind legs) feature multiple alternative outlines, with different positions and orientations, all superposed on a single sheet of paper. In industrial design, Toyota Corp. famously applies the so-called *set-based* (or *concurrent engineering*) model of designing, which is characterized by the availability of not one but a whole set of design solutions at various stages in the industrial design process, both at the whole car level, and at the subsystem level [16, 17].

Yet, despite the importance of alternatives in design and other disciplines, users of contemporary CAD tools and computational tools in general cannot easily view and handle multiple digital models at once, as they can with analogue models, sketches, and other expressions of design in the physical world. In particular, and as one important special case, current parametric-CAD (pCAD) tools lack adequate support for working with multiple design alternatives in parallel. This forces the users to adopt workflows and methods that do not actually fix the problem, but merely offer alternative ways to avoid it. However, such methods are lengthy, inefficient, and error-prone.

To further explore this as a research problem, in this article we present CAMBRIA, a prototype pCAD tool that aims to allow its users to engage in multi-state work. In Sect. 2 we first describe past research pertinent to computational support for managing and interacting with multiple alternative design solutions. In Sect. 3 we describe the design and implementation of CAMBRIA, a prototype pCAD tool for working with multiple design solutions in parallel. Section 4 presents analytical evaluation of CAMBRIA using the *cognitive dimensions* (CD) framework [18]. We conclude the article in Sect. 5 by a general discussion of CAMBRIA and what it may mean for defining new design task environments augmented by new tools capable of handling multiple alternatives simultaneously.

2 Related Work

In a significant body of work related to alternatives-enabled computational tools (with special emphasis on interaction), that of *subjunctive interfaces*, Lunzer and his colleagues present several approaches to interacting with many computational objects at once, with particular emphasis on the mixed-initiative exploration of n-dimensional parameter spaces[2]. Spanning almost twenty years of research (1996–2014), the authors have applied subjunctive interfaces in many different contexts, such as the problem of exploring Cartesian products of LaTeX editing options [19], of exploring multidimensional spaces [20], conducting exploratory design [21], browsing census data [22, 23], navigating multiple scenarios based on dataflow networks [24–26], exploring online resources [27], clipping and cloning snippets of online resources as well as subjunctive web searching [28, 29], exploratory e-learning [30, 31], text editing [32], and healthcare [33, 34].

In another important body of pertinent work, Michael Terry and his collaborators explore computational support for *set-based interaction* with a number of computational objects (in this case, raster images) in parallel. Subsequent related work has seen the application of set-based interaction in raster image editing [7], *Side Views* and *Parameter Spectrums* interaction techniques [35], *Design Horizon* workspaces that support multiple document versions at once [35], development of multiple design solutions in the area of raster image editing through techniques called *Parallel Paths* and *Parallel Pies* [36], as well as experimental evaluations of the above techniques and approaches [37].

As another important area of multi-state computing, *parallel text editing* provides additional important references to the problem of interacting with multiple objects in parallel [38–40]. Within the general body of work related to ways and approaches to visualize multiple computational objects at once, *small multiples* [41, 42], or scaled-down images, facilitate comparison of multiple (similar) objects, i.e., objects with similar structures repeated across all such objects. Roberts [43, 44] described multiplicity in visualization, where data are shown in separate windows.

---

[2] The adjective 'subjunctive' denotes a condition that permits multiple, contingent, possible, or wished-for outcomes.

Marks et al. [45, 46] introduced *Design Galleries*, an approach to the problem of parameter tweaking involving batch-computing and browsing of a large number of computationally-expensive graphics. Jankun et al. [47] presented a spreadsheet-like interface for exploring and displaying multidimensional parameter spaces and their associated visualizations. Bavoil et al. [48] described *VisTrails*, a scientific visualization system with multiple visualization *pipelines* as well as multiple views with coordinated cameras. In the already mentioned paper by Hartmann et al. [40], the authors described editing and execution of multiple program variations in parallel using an external, hardware-based MIDI board with sliders. In generative design, Zaman et al. [49] presented *GEM-NI*, a system for working with alternatives in generative design, with support for parallel editing, branching, merging, Cartesian products, and history recall.

The CAMBRIA prototype, as described in the next section, builds upon and incorporates many of the aspects of aforementioned tools, systems and approaches. In addition, CAMBRIA introduces several novel pCAD interaction techniques, such as parallelized (*subjunctive*) point snapping.

3 The CAMBRIA Prototype

Based on the outcomes of multiple design sessions, we designed and implemented a sequence of progressively refined interactive prototypes, collectively named CAMBRIA. The choice of this particular name was inspired by the Cambrian Era (lasting from 541 to 485 million years ago) and the corresponding phenomenon of *Cambrian explosion*, or a massive diversification of existing organisms, from simple one-cell to complex, multi-cell ones. Using CAMBRIA, the user should analogously be able to effortlessly copy, duplicate, and modify design models, thus achieving a Cambrian-like diversification and multiplicity of designs.

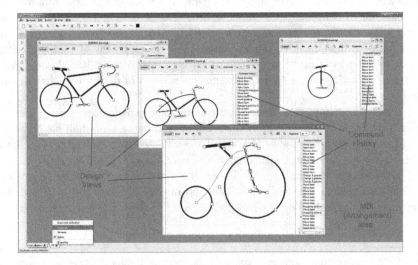

Fig. 2. CAMBRIA screenshot, showing multiple bicycle designs derived from each other.

Figure 2 shows a screenshot of CAMBRIA, along with its main GUI features such as design views (one per each design alternative), command histories (one undo/redo stack per each design alternative), as well as the general area in which those views can be arranged in different ways. As shown in the Fig. 2, users of CAMBRIA can *view and manage multiple models in parallel*. In the following, we describe major features of CAMBRIA.

3.1   Managing Collections of Alternatives

A *collection* serves as a means to organize and gather a set of design alternatives. Collections function as a vehicle to gather a set of designs that are related in some way, using either *objective* criteria (for instance, rank, distance metric, design history, …) or *subjective* criteria (those based on standards and measures idiosyncratic to an individual user). A design project can have multiple collections. In the GUI, in CAMBRIA, each collection is a devoted container. Figure 2 (bottom) illustrates this functionality, with a total of two different collections currently being utilized in the project (one tab per collection).

3.2   Arranging Alternatives

This class of features subsumes the capabilities for displaying (i.e., presenting, laying out) multiple (or just one, as a special case $m = 1$) design alternatives. At any time, the user can manually change the position and size of the view of each alternative in a collection and group them into proximity-based clusters. In the literature, Card et al. [50] claim that grouping can be considered *an elementary form of sensemaking*. In Gestalt theory [12], according to its *Law of Proximity*, objects placed near each other are perceived as a *group*. Available cluster arrangement modes include grid (pack all); slideshow; design history; and randomized arrangement, of which Fig. 3 shows two. To provide continuity and seamless transition in editing, we used animation for transitioning from one arrangement of design alternatives smoothly into the next arrangement. This aims to support users in tracking location changes visually. During transitions, the system interpolates both the *positions* and *sizes* of alternatives' windows.

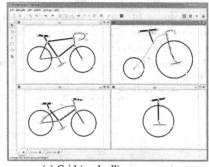   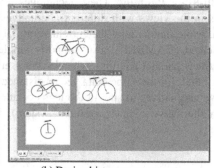

(a) Grid (pack all) arrngement   (b) Design history arrangement

Fig. 3. Two of the arrangement modes available in CAMBRIA

3.3 Navigating Alternatives

Navigation refers to the combination of *wayfinding* (i.e., developing and utilizing a cognitive map of the environment being navigated) and *motion* (i.e. changing the viewpoint within an environment) [51–53]. In CAMBRIA, this environment includes design alternatives, their inner composition and makeup, as well as how those alternatives are grouped into collections within a specific project. The means to navigate collections and alternatives include various *zoom* and *pan* interaction techniques.

Multi-State Zooming. This refers to a class of navigation techniques that are based on a temporal segregation of the overview view and the detailed (zoomed-in) view [54]. CAMBRIA enables both single-state (conventional) zooming and multi-state (synchronized) zooming. The latter is an essential feature of CAMBRIA (and for multi-state tools in general) because it allows the user to maintain analogous *contexts* as well as *zoomed-in details* in parallel, for all the currently active design alternatives shown on screen. Without the multi-state zooming capability, the user may quickly lose the correspondence between said contexts and their contained details. The result is multiple (visually dissociated) views that display different, unrelated parts. Figure 4 shows multi-state zooming in CAMBRIA.

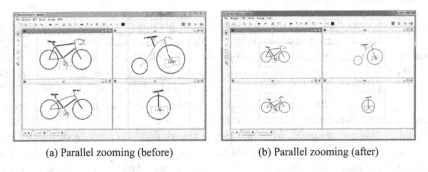

(a) Parallel zooming (before)   (b) Parallel zooming (after)

Fig. 4. Multi-state (interactive) zooming in parallel in CAMBRIA.

Multi-State Panning. These techniques allow the user to synchronously bring the parts in the views with different alternatives that cannot fit into the available display area, while maintaining the current zoom factor of the view. Like zooming techniques presented, CAMBRIA also supports single-state (conventional) panning. Figure 5 illustrates parallel panning, whereby the user has dragged all four canvases to the left, in parallel, for the same delta vector distance. Multi-state (parallel) panning enables all active alternatives to stay in the locus of attention by the same vector (as measured in each alternative's local coordinate system).

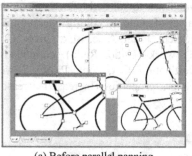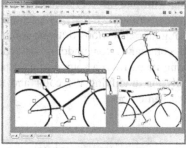

| (a) Before parallel panning | (b) After parrallel panning |

Fig. 5. Panning in parallel across multiple alternatives in CAMBRIA, using mouse press and drag, with the key Alt depressed.

3.4 Parallel (Simultaneous) Editing of Multiple Alternatives

A design challenge for multi-state systems is to keep the data representing content decoupled, but at the same time make their shared parts respond to operations in parallel. For CAMBRIA, consistent with most parametric modelers, we adopted unique identifiers as the means to track correspondences between cognate items contained within separate alternatives, which, in turn, enables the parallel interaction techniques we propose. Outside of parametric modeling, associating unique IDs is commonly used in a number of applications, such as matching, automatic comparison, and differencing [55, 56]. For example, Fig. 6 shows 'brushing' of linked items on mouse-over where the four instances of rear wheels in different alternatives can thus be considered as one subjunctive item.

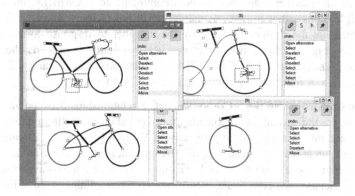

Fig. 6. An illustration of how unique IDs are used in CAMBRIA: brushing of linked (associated) items in CAMBRIA using color coding. (All four rear wheel instances rendered in red.) (Color figure online)

CAMBRIA allows for parallel editing directly within the arrangement view. In other words, standard (i.e. conventional single-state) operations are just a special case of dealing with one ($m = 1$) design alternative. Thus, to start with such conventional, single-state operations, CAMBRIA features a set of standard editing operations, such as choosing among various drawing modes (Select, Point, Line, Box, Circle, Curve), standard commands for undoing or redoing work (Undo, Redo), commands for transferring items from a source to a target destination (Cut, Copy, Paste), as well as commands for modifying the color and thickness properties (Increase/Decrease pen width and Pen color).

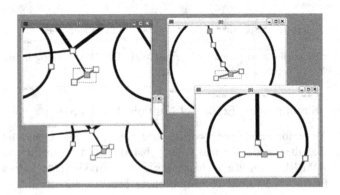

Fig. 7. Parallel (simultaneous, concurrent) selection of linked items in CAMBRIA (cropped screenshot). In this example, bicycle crank has been selected in parallel for three alternatives.

Multi-state (Parallel) Selection Mechanism. For parallel editing the users should be able to select items in one design, and then have CAMBRIA automatically select the corresponding items in other active alternatives. This makes a set of selected items from different alternatives ready for the next command. In CAMBRIA, the user can select multiple items either in one alternative, or all linked items in all 'active' alternatives, which are the designs selected by the designer to response to any change. Parallel select (Fig. 7) takes place if the user is concurrently depressing the Alt-key when normally selecting items. CAMBRIA also supports rubber band (rectangular outline) selection, a functionality common to most CAD tools.

Parametric Constraint Editing. Constraints define relationships between variables in a system and are the essential components of any pCAD tool. Definition and maintenance of constraints in a multi-state parametric CAD tool is more challenging than in systems with single-state models. CAMBRIA provides operations for adding and deleting constraints on any set of items. For example, some constraints available for the point objects include lock coordinate, receive projected coordinate, keep point at delta from another point, mirror point through another point, and parameterize point onto line.

Undo/Redo Functionality. While Undo/Redo is a functionality for recovering from errors, it is also used to experiment with an alternative in the near-term, *what-if?* fashion. A challenge for multi-state systems is to maintain a stack of operations that can both include commands on single and multiple alternatives. The latter has not been seen in conventional tools. In CAMBRIA, each alternative has its own *command* *history*, which is populated whenever a single-state command (for one alternative) or a multi-state command (for multiple alternatives) has been executed. Figure 2 shows multiple design alternatives with their command history views. Similar to the other commands in CAMBRIA, depressing the Alt key on the Undo or Redo operations will result in *parallel undo*, which will move the respective undo stacks' pointers lower by one, for all the currently active alternatives.

Multi-state *Pass Items* and *Pass Item Properties* Mechanisms. In addition to Cut, Copy, Paste commands, CAMBRIA features two novel, parallelized, multi-state transfer mechanisms: (1) *pass items,* and (2) *pass item properties* from a source to a target design alternatives. Figure 8 demonstrates the pass items mechanism, which might be considered a generalization of the standard Paste command, in a sense that it transfers all the selected items into all the currently active alternatives in a collection, not just the current one. The pass property (Fig. 9) allows the user to transfer or propagate a property value (such as position, size, line thickness, color, and so on) to all the linked items in all the other currently linked alternatives, for all selected items in the originating alternative. In this specific example, the pen color of one element (the seat tube) is passed onto all the corresponding elements in other alternatives.

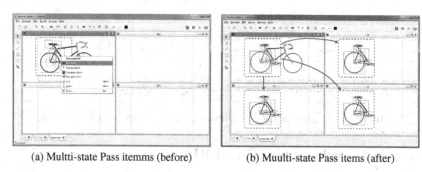

(a) Multti-state Pass itemms (before)   (b) Muulti-state Pass items (after)

Fig. 8. Multi-state *Pass items* mechanism in CAMBRIA, which propagates items that were selected in one alternative, into other active alternatives.

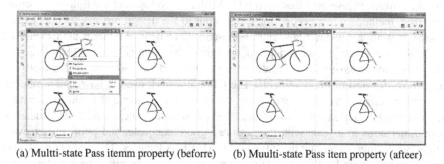

(a) Multti-state Pass itemm property (beforre)   (b) Muulti-state Pass item property (afteer)

Fig. 9. Multi-state *Pass item property* mechanism in CAMBRIA, which propagates attribute values (in this case, pen color of the seat tube) into corresponding items in other visible alternatives.

Parallel (Subjunctive) Point Snapping. Point snapping refers to the interaction where a dragged point automatically moves to a pre-defined position, for instance a position on a grid or a position on a curve defined by an arbitrary $t \in [0, 1]$. The main purpose of snapping is to provide rapid, precise access to common geometric co-incidences in designs. CAMBRIA introduces *subjunctive* point snapping, where a control point snaps to corresponding, matching pre-existing positions in all currently active alternatives in a collection, and not just in the current alternative where the user is dragging a point.

Figure 10 (left) illustrates dragging a control point in alternative#9 in order to snap it onto the curve, while keeping the Alt key depressed at all times, thus dragging the linked control points in the remaining three alternatives as well. Once in position, the user now releases the mouse button. Figure 10 (right) shows how these four linked control points snapped into the respective parametric points on curve with the same t value, although in geometric terms those four positions are different from each other. Therefore, subjunctive matching operates on the basis of identities or semantics of the items involved, instead of on their geometric positions.

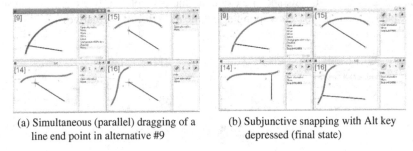

(a) Simultaneous (parallel) dragging of a line end point in alternative #9

(b) Subjunctive snapping with Alt key depressed (final state)

Fig. 10. Point snapping in parallel across multiple alternatives in CAMBRIA.

4 Analytical Evaluation of CAMBRIA

We adapted the Cognitive Dimensions (CD) framework [18] to evaluate the latest version of CAMBRIA. The CD framework is suitable to evaluate almost any kind of cognitive artifact to draw attention to the aspects of user experience when interacting with the artifact. Please note that during CAMBRIA development we followed various evaluation methods when needed for faster input to the design process such as expert reviews, cognitive walkthroughs, and design-consult evaluations. Since, at this stage of CAMBRIA development, we remain focused on discovering new forms for interacting with alternatives, we prefer evaluation techniques such as CD that lead directly to suggestions for design improvements. The CD framework itself is based on a number of *cognitive dimensions* along which the designer can discuss and evaluate a certain aspect of the interaction with the artifacts. Below we discuss how CAMBRIA matches these dimensions in a scale with three scores: good, adequate, and poor. In our evaluation, we distinguish among three types of CAMBRIA features. The first (Type I), and most important, type for this evaluation comprises features specific to interacting with multiple alternatives. The second type (Type II) are features common to other pCAD modelers that are implemented in CAMBRIA largely to provide the pCAD domain in which CAMBRIA works. The third type (Type III) comprises features in which CAMBRIA and pCAD interact, either productively or negatively.

Visibility of states within collection is the *raison d'etre* for CAMBRIA. Its goal is to visualize and interact with the design spaces that conventional pCAD so assiduously hides. With respect to individual design states and individual items within models, visibility is desirable in CAMBRIA to view multiple such states and items at once. In CAMBRIA, design states can be visible either as themselves or superimposed on other states in a composite view. We contend that CAMBRIA's Type I visibility is good. With respect to Type III, the visibility of common components across states is also good, due to the brushing mechanism. On the other hand, in Type II, the visibility of one-way dataflow constraints governing the configuration of geometric items is only adequate to poor, since these elements can be viewed only through the context (pop-up) menu. Other systems, such as *GEM-NI* [51] have attempted to visualize constraints across design states, with resulting very complex interface designs. Possible remedies for low Type II visibility include a) self-standing visual elements ("constraint boxes") that show constraints directly in the model, b) separate views showing the constraint dependency graph, and/or a list of constraints.

Juxtaposability is a goal for modeling alternatives (indeed it is one of the principles of Lunzer and Hornbaek's *subjunctive interfaces* [32]). In CAMBRIA, alternatives can be either arranged in proximity (juxtaposition) or combined in a single view (superposition). Both are instances of CD juxtaposability. Given that juxtaposability is a design goal, it is not surprising that we evaluate it as good for CAMBRIA's Type I features. However, we take the current CAMBRIA implementation of four different automatic layout types for collections, based on simple-to-conceive algorithms, as only a rough prototype for the juxtaposability problem. None is grounded in any deep insight into what alternatives users would actually wish to juxtapose or how they would arrange such alternatives. In this regard, we view CAMBRIA as only defining, rather than definitively addressing, the juxtaposability CD. CAMBRIA introduces a Type III juxtaposability issue from which it provides only an imperfect solution. It is extremely common for pCAD users to divide models into parts, to work on these separately and then combine the parts back into an entire design. Thus juxtaposability of parts of alternatives is important. In CAMBRIA, this is poorly achieved, since the parts cannot be easily displayed side-by-side. Part juxtaposability, while maintaining the contextual relations of parts to wholes (across multiple alternatives), is a design concern new to alternatives-enabled pCAD systems. Possible remedies for aforementioned Type II and III issues include the ability to create smaller views (or *viewlets*) within the view displaying a design alternative.

Hidden dependencies dimension refers to the ability to determine whether an object is controlled by another object. A key feature of pCAD, on which CAMBRIA deeply depends, is the use of unique (and ideally clear and understandable) names within models. CAMBRIA counts on such names to identify common parts across models. In CAMBRIA, common names across the parts of alternatives create a key hidden dependency, which is revealed primarily by brushing, an ephemeral interaction. CAMBRIA lacks facilities to visualize all such links across a collection, for comparing models by their name structures, or for discovering the dependencies given the names themselves. Though brushing appears effective, it is a partial design response, which we label as only adequate. As in the visibility CD, we note that our current handling of one-way constraints via contextual popup menus (a Type II issue) is a poor design for revealing hidden dependencies. Possible design remedies (Type I) include *parallelized focusing* of selected items for revealing linkages, as well as computing the *transitive closure* structure (Type II and III) for determining connectedness between nodes in the associated parametric dependency graphs.

Viscosity questions if there are barriers to change. CAMBRIA's Type I features (design collections, designs and their parts) present extremely low (good) viscosity as there are several quick ways to make collections and add states to them. Indeed, such operations as *pass* item and *pass item properties* are specifically designed for low viscosity. At the level of design states and individual elements, the viscosity score for CAMBRIA can be considered 'good' because the user can edit all active alternatives as well as elements in parallel. In Type II issues, CAMBRIA does less well, as, with one exception, it does not compare well to existing commercial pCAD modelers (nor was it designed to do so). The viscosity of adding, deleting, and modifying constraints in parallel (Type III issue) can be considered to be high, perhaps with the exception of adding *parametric point on line* constraints, which were specifically implemented to demonstrate the subjunctive snapping technique. Possible design remedies include parallel constraint editing, as well as search & replace functionality.

Terseness measures how much content and space is needed to create a result. CAMBRIA's design for collections (a Type I issue) is symbolically terse (items belong to collections) but can be spatially verbose (people can be profligate in arranging collections, though this is a user choice). In terms of design states, CAMBRIA is as terse as pCAD in general, that is good, since the notation in CAMBRIA consists of graphic items (points, lines, curves etc.) on screen, with constraints governing their layout, and is therefore as terse as is possible considering that the notation is in this case equal to the intended final representation (2D parameterized vector drawings).

Proneness to error dimension looks for if the content representation can affect the possibility of making errors. In CAMBRIA, such errors are, in one sense, intentional. When moving an item in parallel for multiple design alternatives, the end positions of the item might not be anticipated by the user, for several or most design alternatives. This discrepancy between the expected and achieved position should probably be characterized as a *divergence* due to the user's inability[3] to effectively track changes in all active alternatives. Accessing such divergent designs is an aim for CAMBRIA-like systems, that is, a Type I issue. The score for this dimension should therefore be considered to be good, since it can be thought of as a tradeoff for increased power along the visibility and viscosity dimensions (because one can view and edit many design states at once).

Hardness of mental operations refers to the cognitive demand needed to work with the content at the representation level, not semantic level. Initial evaluation of Type I features in CAMBRIA shows that (some, or all) parallel editing operations impose high cognitive demands on the user, due to the need to track changes concurrently in multiple places at once, which requires rapid shifts of locus of attention. Increased power along the visibility (for viewing) and viscosity (for editing) dimensions for multi-state tools clearly leads to higher cognitive demands. Although this can

---

[3] Here "inability" denotes the intrinsic limitations of unaided human cognition in general.

be a trade-off for multi-state tools, new techniques can address this challenge. A Type III issue is that edits in parametric model structure itself can only be understood in context of the affected alternative and this requires a user to track that changes have occurred in multiple states and to review each state.

Abstraction gradient dimension refers to the representation level of content and how this level is managed. CAMBRIA introduces a new abstraction: design collections (Type I) and adds no new abstractions otherwise to pCAD system design. We argue that this new abstraction creates a very low abstraction gradient as a collection of one element is essentially identical to conventional pCAD systems and that adding additional elements is a simple operation. The abstraction gradient increases with operations such as pass items and pass item properties and again with subjunctive snapping. However, each of these is a small addition, arguably enabling a *gentle-slope* [57] to abstraction, thus we evaluate this CD as adequate. To improve on this score, possible design remedies include the ability to group and ungroup items, the ability to browse linked items as a single entity, as well as to search & replace items using some set of criteria.

Premature commitment is essentially non-existent in CAMBRIA, beyond that created by its being a pCAD system, where it is innately high. None of CAMBRIA's new operations force particular orders of operation. In particular, collection and state creation and editing are completely independent and do not depend on one being done before (or after) the other.

Progressive evaluation, in CAMBRIA, is supported by collections that can be used to record multiple states through a series of operations. It remains to be seen how users capitalize on this new design feature.

Table 1. Summary of analytical evaluation of CAMBRIA.

Dimension:	Score:	Design intervention(s):
Visibility (alternatives, items) (constraints, linkage)	Adequate to poor Good	– Constraint boxes (II); graph view (II); list of constraints (II)
Juxtaposability (alternatives) (parts of alts.)	Good Poor	– Viewlets (II); parallelized viewlets (III)
Hidden dependencies	Adequate to poor	Focus on linked items (I); transitive closure (II, III)
Viscosity (alternatives, items) (constraints, linkage)	Good Poor	– Parallel constraint/linkage edits (I, III); search & replace (I, II, III)
Terseness	Good	–
Proneness to error	Adequate	(Design tradeoff)
Hardness of mental operations	Adequate	(Design tradeoff)
Abstraction gradient	Adequate	Grouping (I); linked items browser (I); search & replace (I)
Premature commitment	Good	–
Progressive evaluation	Good	–
Secondary notation	Adequate	Visual layout of collections (I)

Secondary notation in CAMBRIA is mainly visual layouts. They have essentially no purpose in representing collections, and exist to make informal and ad hoc layouts to match their work with the tasks they are undertaking. In this sense, a major part of the design of CAMBRIA is devoted to opening a space in which we can observe people use this and other secondary notations, thus we evaluate this CD as adequate. We hope that such observation will better reveal us how to organize collections on the CAMBRIA workspace.

Table 1 summarizes the scores of CAMBRIA along with the set of CD, further split into sub-scores (per aspect of the tool). Scores "poor", "adequate", and "good" in the second column are the analysis for each CD. The last column provides a summary of recommended design interventions for the next iteration of CAMBRIA, along with a type identification (I, II or III) for each.

Due to space constraints for this article, the reader is pointed to [58] for further details on the suggested design interventions, and how they may be implemented in multi-state pCAD tools.

5 Discussion

CAMBRIA aims to address one specific shortcoming of the most contemporary computational tools that support designing: despite the evidence that designers, when using traditional, analogue design media frequently handle multiple design variants in parallel, most computational tools allow their users to effectively work with just one design model at a time.

To illustrate, CAMBRIA, by its very design, affords the process of visual comparison, which "can reveal common structure and combine partial structures and thus promote transfer" [59], and which helps users to direct their attention to *key relations* [60] among the constituent elements of design states. In addition, vision is known to be the sense with the highest bandwidth of all: we "acquire more information through vision than through all of the other senses combined" [11]. Visual comparison, as afforded by CAMBRIA, thus reveals the components of information present in pCAD models: patterns, repetition, change, and surprise [42].

 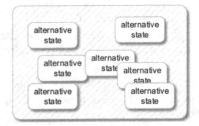

Fig. 11. Left: in single-state systems, users are forced to retrieve states one-by-one. Right: having multiple design alternatives in the field of view facilitates their comparison and recombination.

Another common task in design is the recombination of partial solutions, or *transformation* [61] of design solutions. Having multiple such (partial or whole) design alternatives in the field of view facilitates such a recombination, by eliminating the relatively slow cognitive process of memory retrieval and storage to and from short- and long-term memories, and replacing them with the faster visual scan process [62], thus combatting the *limited transfer problem* [8]. This way, the retrieve-recombine-store process typical of single-state system use, gets replaced by the faster scan-recombine process depicted intuitively to the right of Fig. 11.

As another benefit, CAMBRIA addresses the well-known issue of design fixation, or the phenomenon in which the designer hones the solution incrementally until it satisfies the requirements and constraints of its associated design problem. In the literature, this phenomenon has also been interchangeably called *primary generator, kernel idea, design fixation, solution fixation, premature commitment,* and *early crystallization* [63–66]. However, design fixation presents several problems. First, the designer may commit prematurely to an early design solution that does not address the design problem in the best or adequate manner. And second, the designer may overlook design solutions that address the design problem in much better or fitting fashion. Through its ability to easily duplicate alternatives, create alternative collections, and transfer elements from one alternative to another (such as by means of pass items or pass item properties mechanisms), CAMBRIA allows its users to ameliorate or avoid this problem altogether.

6 Conclusions and Future Work

We have presented CAMBRIA, a novel prototype pCAD platform that allows working with multiple design variants in parallel. The tool addresses one bottleneck of current computational tools, where their users can work with just one design model at a time. The analytical evaluation of CAMBRIA based on the CD framework indicated the strengths of the tool, as well as uncovered areas of potential improvement and refinement.

Future work includes generalizing the approach to other domains of application such as 3D geometric modeling and text editing, quantitative evaluations of mature multi-state tools, and deploying multi-state tools on very large display technologies.

Acknowledgements. One co-author (Siniša Kolarić) was partially supported by the NSERC Discovery and Collaborative Research and Development Programs; Bentley Systems Inc.; and by the GRAND Networks of Centers of Excellence.

References

1. Akin, Ö.: A formalism for problem restructuring and resolution in design. Environ. Plan. B: Plan. Des. **13**(2), 223–232 (1986)
2. Akin, Ö.: Psychology of Architectural Design. Pion, London (1986)
3. Lawson, B.R.: Cognitive strategies in architectural design. Ergonomics **22**(1), 59–68 (1979)

4. Akin, Ö.: Chapter 6 - variants in design cognition. In: Eastman, C.M., McCracken, W.M., Newstetter, W.C. (eds.) Design Knowing and Learning: Cognition in Design Education, pp. 105–124. Elsevier Science, Oxford (2001). https://doi.org/10.1016/B978-008043868-9/50006-1

5. Smith, R.P., Tjandra, P.: Experimental observation of iteration in engineering design. Res. Eng. Des. **10**(2), 107–117 (1998)

6. Atman, C.J., Chimka, J.R., Bursic, K.M., Nachtmann, H.L.: A comparison of freshman and senior engineering design processes. Des. Stud. **20**(2), 131–152 (1999)

7. Terry, M., Mynatt, E.D.: Recognizing creative needs in user interface design. In: Proceedings of the 4th Conference on Creativity & Cognition, pp. 38–44. ACM (2002)

8. Dow, S.P., Glassco, A., Kass, J., Schwarz, M., Schwartz, D.L., Klemmer, S.R.: Parallel prototyping leads to better design results, more divergence, and increased self-efficacy. ACM Trans. Comput.–Hum. Interact. (TOCHI) **17**(4), 18 (2010)

9. Newman, M.W., Landay, J.A.: Sitemaps, storyboards, and specifications: a sketch of web site design practice. In: Proceedings of the 3rd Conference on Designing Interactive Systems: Processes, Practices, Methods, and Techniques, pp. 263–274. ACM (2000)

10. Cross, N.: Design Thinking: Understanding How Designers Think and Work. Bloomsbury Academic (2011)

11. Ware, C.: Information Visualization: Perception for Design. 3rd edn. Morgan Kaufmann Publishers Inc., San Francisco (2012)

12. Wertheimer, M.: Gestalt theory. In: Ellis, W.D (ed.) A Source Book of Gestalt Psychology, chap. 1, pp. 1–11. Kegan Paul, Trench, Trubner & Company, London (1938)

13. Peters, B.: Foster + Partners: Elephant House, Copenhagen Zoo, Copenhagen, Denmark (2008–2010). http://www.bradypeters.com/elephant-house.html. Accessed 15 April 2017

14. Bradner, E., Iorio, F., Davis, M.: Parameters tell the design story: ideation and abstraction in design optimization. In: Proceedings of the Symposium on Simulation for Architecture &Urban Design, Society for Computer Simulation International, p. 26 (2014)

15. Leonardo da Vinci: Study for the Trivulzio equestrian monument (1508–1510). http://www.wga.hu/art/l/leonardo/15sculpt/3trivul1.jpg. Accessed 15 April 2017

16. Ward, A., Liker, J.K., Cristiano, J.J., Sobek, D.K., et al.: The second Toyota paradox: how delaying decisions can make better cars faster. Sloan Manag. Rev. **36**(3), 43–62 (1995)

17. Sobek, D.K., Ward, A.C., Liker, J.K.: Toyota's principles of set-based concurrent engineering. Sloan Manag. Rev. **40**(2), 67–84 (1999)

18. Green, T.R.: Cognitive dimensions of notations. In: A Sutcliffe and Macaulay, editors, People and Computers V, pp. 443–460 (1989)

19. Lunzer, A.: Reconnaissance: A Widely Applicable Approach Encouraging Well-Informed Choices in Computer-Based Tasks. PhD thesis, University of Glasgow (1996)

20. Lunzer, A.: Towards the subjunctive interface: general support for parameter exploration by overlaying alternative application states. In: Late Breaking Hot Topics Proceedings of IEEE Visualization, vol. 98, pp. 45–48 (1998)

21. Lunzer, A.: Choice and comparison where the user wants them: subjunctive interfaces for computer-supported exploration. In: Proceedings of IFIP TC, vol. 13, pp. 474–482 (1999)

22. Lunzer, A., Hornbæk, K.: Side-by-side display and control of multiple scenarios: subjunctive interfaces for exploring multi-attribute data. In: Proceedings of OZCHI 2003, pp. 26–28 (2003)

23. Lunzer, A., Hornbæk, K.: Usability studies on a visualisation for parallel display and control of alternative scenarios. In: Proceedings of the Working Conference on Advanced Visual Interfaces, pp. 125–132. ACM (2004)

24. Lunzer, A.: Interfaces that reduce the cost of examining alternatives. In: Proceedings of the SIGCHI Conference on Human Factors in Computing Systems, ACM, position paper (2004)

25. Lunzer, A., Hornbæk, K.: An enhanced spreadsheet supporting calculation-structure variants, and its application to web-based processing. In: Federation over the Web, pp. 143–158. Springer (2006)
26. Lunzer, A., Hornbæk, K.: RecipeSheet: creating, combining and controlling information processors. In: Proceedings of the 19th Annual ACM Symposium on User Interface Software and Technology, pp. 145–154. ACM (2006)
27. Lunzer, A.: Benefits of subjunctive interface support for exploratory access to online resources. In: Intuitive Human Interfaces for Organizing and Accessing Intellectual Assets, pp. 14–32. Springer (2005)
28. Fujima, J., Lunzer, A., Hornbæk, K., Tanaka, Y.: C3 W: clipping, connecting and cloning for the web. In: Proceedings of the 13th International World Wide Web Conference on Alternate Track Papers & Posters, pp. 444–445. ACM (2004)
29. Fujima, J., Lunzer, A., Hornbæk, K., Tanaka, Y.: Clip, connect, clone: combining application elements to build custom interfaces for information access. In: Proceedings of the 17th Annual ACM Symposium on User Interface Software and Technology, pp. 175–184. ACM (2004)
30. Jantke, K.P., Lunzer, A.: Search, comparison and evaluation in exploratory e-learning with subjunctive interfaces. In: Wissens Management, pp. 140–145 (2005)
31. Jantke, K.P., Lunzer, A., Fujima, J.: Subjunctive interfaces in exploratory e-learning. In: Professional Knowledge Management, pp. 176–188. Springer (2005)
32. Lunzer, A., Hornbæk, K.: Subjunctive interfaces: Extending applications to support parallel setup, viewing and control of alternative scenarios. ACM Trans. Comput.–Hum. Interact. (TOCHI) **14**(4), 17 (2008)
33. Lunzer, A., Belleman, R., Melis, P., Stamatakos, G.: Preparing, exploring and comparing cancer simulation results within a large parameter space. In: 2010 14th International Conference Information Visualisation (IV), pp. 258–264. IEEE (2010)
34. Stamatakos, G., Dionysiou, D., Lunzer, A., Belleman, R., Kolokotroni, E., Georgiadi, E., Erdt, M., Pukacki, J., Rueping, S., Giatili, S., et al.: The technologically integrated oncosimulator: combining multiscale cancer modeling with information technology in the in silico oncology context. IEEE J. Biomed. Health Inform. **18**(3), 840–854 (2014)
35. Terry, M., Mynatt, E.D.: Side views: persistent, on-demand previews for open-ended tasks. In: Proceedings of the 15th Annual ACM Symposium on User Interface Software and Technology, pp. 71–80. ACM (2002)
36. Terry, M., Mynatt, E.D., Nakakoji, K., Yamamoto, Y.: Variation in element and action: supporting simultaneous development of alternative solutions. In: Proceedings of the SIGCHI Conference on Human Factors in Computing Systems, pp. 711–718. ACM (2004)
37. Terry, M.: Set-Based User Interaction. PhD thesis, Georgia Institute of Technology (2005)
38. Miller, R.C., Myers, B.A.: Interactive simultaneous editing of multiple text regions. In: USENIX Annual Technical Conference, General Track, pp. 161–174 (2001)
39. Toomim, M., Begel, A., Graham, S.L.: Managing duplicated code with linked editing. In: 2004 IEEE Symposium on Visual Languages and Human Centric Computing, pp. 173–180. IEEE (2004)
40. Hartmann, B., Yu, L., Allison, A., Yang, Y., Klemmer, S.R.: Design as exploration: creating interface alternatives through parallel authoring and runtime tuning. In: Proceedings of the 21st Annual ACM symposium on User Interface Software and Technology, pp. 91–100. ACM (2008)
41. Tufte, E.R.: Envisioning Information. Graphics Press, Cheshire (1990)
42. Tufte, E.R., Weise Moeller, E.: Visual Explanations: Images and Quantities, Evidence and Narrative, vol. 36. Graphics Press, Cheshire (1997)

43. Roberts, J.: Multiple view and multiform visualization. In: Proceedings of SPIE, vol 3960, p. 176 (2000)
44. Roberts, J.: State of the art: coordinated & multiple views in exploratory visualization. In: Fifth International Conference on Coordinated and Multiple Views in Exploratory Visualization, 2007. CMV 2007, pp. 61–71. IEEE (2007)
45. Marks, J., Andalman, B., Beardsley, P., Freeman, W., Gibson, S., Hodgins, J., Kang, T., Mirtich, B., Pfister, H., Ruml, W. et al.: Design galleries: a general approach to setting parameters for computer graphics and animation. In: Proceedings of the 24th Annual Conference on Computer Graphics and Interactive Techniques, pp. 389–400. ACM Press/Addison-Wesley Publishing Co. (1997)
46. Marks, J., Ruml, W., Andalman, B., Ryall, K., Shieber, S.: Design gallery browsers based on 2d and 3d graph drawing. In: Proceedings of Graph Drawing, vol. 97 (1997)
47. Jankun-Kelly, T., Ma, K.: A spreadsheet interface for visualization exploration. In: Proceedings of the Conference on Visualization 2000, pp. 69–76. IEEE Computer Society Press (2000)
48. Bavoil, L., Callahan, S., Crossno, P., Freire, J., Scheidegger, C., Silva, C., Vo, H.: Vistrails: IEEE Enabling interactive multiple-view visualizations. In: Visualization, 2005. VIS 2005, pp. 135–142. IEEE (2005)
49. Zaman, L., Stuerzlinger, W., Neugebauer, C., Woodbury, R., Elkhaldi, M., Shireen, N., Terry, M.:GEM-NI: a system for creating and managing alternatives in generative design. In: Proceedings of the SIGCHI Conference on Human Factors in Computing Systems. ACM (2015)
50. Card, S.K., Robertson, G.G., York, W.: The WebBook and the Web Forager: an information workspace for the World-Wide Web. In: Proceedings of the SIGCHI Conference on Human Factors in Computing Systems, pp. 111–117. ACM (1996)
51. Waterworth, J.A., Chignell, M.H.: A model of information exploration. Hypermedia 3(1), 35–58 (1991)
52. Passini, R.: Wayfinding in Architecture, vol. 4. Wiley (1992)
53. Darken, R.P., Peterson, B.: Spatial Orientation, Wayfinding, and Representation. Handbook of Virtual Environments, pp. 493–518 (2002)
54. Cockburn, A., Karlson, A., Bederson, B.B.: A review of overview + detail, zooming, and focus + context interfaces. ACM Comput. Surv. (CSUR) 41(1), 2 (2008)
55. Altmanninger, K., Seidl, M., Wimmer, M.: A survey on model versioning approaches. Int. J. Web Inf. Syst. 5(3), 271–304 (2009)
56. Stephan, M., Cordy, J.R.: A survey of model comparison approaches and applications. In: Proceedings of the First International Conference on Model-Driven Engineering and Software Development, MODELWARD 2013, pp. 265–277 (2013)
57. Dertouzos, M.: Gentle slope systems: making computers easier to use. In: ISAT Summer Study, Woods Hole, MA (1992)
58. Kolarić, S.: Interacting with Design Alternatives. PhD thesis, Simon Fraser University (2016)
59. Gentner, D., Loewenstein, J., Thompson, L.: Learning and transfer: a general role for analogical encoding. J. Educ. Psychol. 95(2), 393 (2003)
60. Gentner, D., Markman, A.B.: Structure mapping in analogy and similarity. Am. Psychol. 52(1), 45 (1997)
61. Jones, J.C.: Design Methods. Wiley (1992)
62. Woodbury, R., Kolarić, S., Erhan, H., Guenther, J.: Design Exploration, Configuration Management: Two Sides of the Same Coin? Presented at Maieutic Parataxis, Congress on the Future of Engineering Software (2013)

63. Darke, J.: The primary generator and the design process. Des. Stud. **1**(1), 36–44 (1979)
64. Kant, E.: Understanding and automating algorithm design. IEEE Trans. Softw. Eng. **11**, 1361–1374 (1985)
65. Jansson, D.G., Smith, S.M.: Design fixation. Des. Stud. **12**(1), 3–11 (1991)
66. Visser, W.: Design: one, but in different forms. Des. Stud. **30**(3), 187–223 (2009)

A Matter of Sequence

Investigating the Impact of the Order of Design Decisions in Multi-stage Design Processes

Julia Tschetwertak$^{(\boxtimes)}$ ⓘ, Sven Schneider ⓘ, Alexander Hollberg ⓘ,
Dirk Donath, and Jürgen Ruth

Bauhaus-University Weimar, Weimar, Germany
{julia.tschetwertak, sven.schneider,
alexander.hollberg, dirk.donath,
juergen.ruth}@uni-weimar.de

Abstract. The design as a process is not a new topic in architecture, yet some theories are widely unexplored, such as the multi-stage decision-making (MD) process. This design method provides multiple solutions for one design problem and is characterized by design stages. By adding new building components in every stage, multiple solutions are created for each design solution from the previous stage. If the MD process is to be applied in architectural practice, fundamental and theoretical knowledge about it becomes necessary. This paper investigates the impact of sequence of design stages on the design solutions in the MD process. A basic case study provides the necessary data for comparing different sequences and gaining fundamental knowledge of the MD process. The study contains a parametric model for building generation, a parametric Life Cycle Assessment tool and an optimization mechanism based on Evolutionary Algorithms.

Keywords: Multi-stage decision-making process · Design process · Life Cycle Performance · Design automation

1 Introduction

Over the course of time, numerous design strategies for finding design solutions according to architectural design problems have been developed by theorists like Gero [1], Markus [2], Maver [3], and Rittel [4]. Those strategies aim to structure the design process into manageable chunks which are easier to process for the human mind as design problems can be extremely complex. "The common idea behind all these 'maps' [strategies] of the design process is that it consists of a sequence of distinct and iden- tifiable activities which occur in some predictable and identifiably logical order." [5]. Rittel introduced different methods for solution-finding which are characterized by multiple design stages. In every stage, new features are added to the design, such as windows, circulation cores, etc. The strategies proposed by Rittel range from a linear approach, where one single solution is produced in each design stage and no alternatives are created (Fig. 1a); to a simplified multi-stage decision making approach, where for

© Springer Nature Singapore Pte Ltd. 2017
G. Çağdaş et al. (Eds.): CAAD Futures 2017, CCIS 724, pp. 100–120, 2017.
DOI: 10.1007/978-981-10-5197-5_6

each stage of a design multiple variants are created, and the best one selected for the development in subsequent stages (Fig. 1b); to a multi-stage decision-making (MD) process, where in each stage all design variants are considered for further development (Fig. 1c). The latter method generates a much higher number of designs than the other two strategies. This benefits the solution space exploration and therefore, increases the chance of finding the best performing designs. The solution space contains all possible solutions for a design problem [6]. Additionally, the MD process holds the potential of discovering design variants which have comparatively worse performance in the early stages, although in combination with aspects from the following stages, their performance can improve significantly. Regarding these advantages, the application of the MD process in architectural practice can have a positive impact on the design performance. With this however, fundamental as well as detailed theoretical knowledge of the MD process becomes necessary.

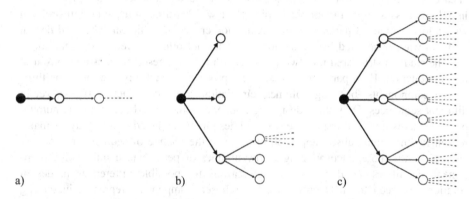

Fig. 1. Linear process (a), simplified multi-stage decision-making process (b), multi-stage decision-making (MD) process (c) [4]

Although Rittel provides the theoretical framework for the design process, he does not make any specific statements concerning the division of a design problem into multiple design stages. Consequently, no guidelines exist for determining the number of design stages and assigning their order in the MD process. In the following, both the stage number and the stage order are summarized under the term 'sequence'. The topic of sequence in the MD process is widely unexplored. This paper investigates the impact of sequence on design solutions in the MD process, in particular on their geometries and performance values. According to the two aspects which make up a sequence, the research is divided into two parts with the following core questions:

(1) How does the fragmentation of a design problem into design stages affect the resulting design solutions?
(2) What impact does the stage order have on design solutions? For arriving at a design solution, it may seem logical to proceed from the general to the detail [5], yet does this strategy lead to the best solutions, or is changing the stage order a useful option for achieving even better results?

These questions are addressed by means of a case study. Findings from the case study should serve as basic theoretical knowledge of MD processes. Conducting an MD process manually can easily become a very time-consuming process due to the numerous design variants that need to be created in every design stage. Therefore, a computational method is required to speed up the process. The application of computational simulation reduces the architectural design process to an optimization process. By integrating optimization into the workflow, the chances of finding design solutions with the highest performance values increase. As a computer-aided application of the MD process that operates completely automatic does not exist yet, a research tool was developed by the authors which enables one to conduct MD processes automatically.

2 Methodology

A case study focuses on the investigation of the impact of sequence on design solutions in MD processes from a theoretical point of view. Therefore, a basic design problem with a low number of parameters and evaluation criteria is sufficient. The used design problem was constructed by the authors and does not refer to a real case scenario.

The study is structured into two parts according to the research questions posed in the introduction. Each part contains two MD processes which involve the same three design components (building volumes, circulation cores, construction types), yet in different sequences. Only three design components, which is a fraction of the number of components involved in practice-oriented design, are included in the study. A major reason for this minimalistic approach is to make the change of sequence reasonably simple. Furthermore, incorporating a low number of performance influencing components facilitates the discovery of the reasons for possible differences in design solutions between the MD processes. The chosen components represent increasing levels of detail in design. The building volumes and their position on the site embody the least detailed level of the three, followed by the circulation cores which contain the main vertical circulation spaces, and six predefined construction types, such as wood construction, concrete construction, etc. The latter have the highest level of detail because they contain information about the materials and how those are assembled. As one example for possible evaluation criteria of buildings the Life Cycle Performance (LCP) was picked for this case study. The performance goal of the case study is the generation of design solutions with the maximum LCP.

2.1 Parametric Model Generation

The design process is reduced to an optimization process. Optimization requires the creation of variety which can be achieved by generating dissimilar design variants. Therefore, a parametrically defined generative model is necessary. Developed from the design problem, this model incorporates multiple design components.[1]

---

[1] For this case study, the model has been visually programmed using the software Grasshopper for Rhinoceros3D.

The design problem outline of this case study is as follows: On a rectangular site which is shaded at three sides, a configuration of two to four residential buildings with an optimal Life Cycle Performance (LCP) is to be designed. For study purposes the floor area ratio (FAR) is kept very low at 0.6, ensuring a broad solution space (high FAR leads to geometrically similar solutions). Every configuration of buildings provides a gross floor area of 2500 m^2 which is divided into subareas for the individual buildings on the site. Minimum and maximum dimensions are set to ensure reasonable sizing of the building volumes. The buildings can have two to four floors and the glazing area is constantly 30% of the exterior wall area. Natural lighting within the building is provided by ribbon windows. Due to the parametric positioning of the buildings on the site it is likely that these initially overlap. Therefore, an algorithm, which resolves the overlaps plus maintains a pre-set minimum distance between the buildings, has been developed. Circulation cores, preferably located in the shaded areas to keep the solar gains to the usable floor spaces, are included. To enable natural lighting and ventilation, they solely can be positioned at exterior walls of the buildings. The circulation cores contain the main vertical circulation spaces within the buildings. If a building exceeds a defined building size, further circulation cores are added. Figure 2 shows the parametric building model generation process which includes all the features mentioned in the design problem outline. Every combination of parameter values generates different design variants. The building analysis starts automatically after the creation of a design variant.

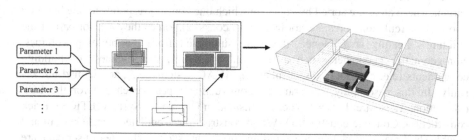

Fig. 2. Parametric building model generation with an inbuilt algorithm for resolving building footprint overlaps (left)

This design problem involves making optimal use of available daylight by taking into account the shading conditions on site, plus the overshadowing that buildings create by themselves. Furthermore, the shape, volume, and position of the buildings need to be considered in order to achieve best LCP results. A set of six potential construction types is provided.

2.2   Building Model Analysis

Life Cycle Assessment (LCA) is increasingly gaining importance in regards to building sustainability evaluation [7]. It takes into consideration both the operational and the embodied energy over the building's whole life cycle. LCA can be defined as a "compilation and evaluation of the inputs, outputs and the potential environmental impacts of a product system throughout its life cycle" [8]. Considering LCA at the very early stages of design process can have a significantly positive impact on the LCP of the building. However, the evaluation of the design through LCA is not sufficient on its own, if it does not improve the design [9]. Moreover, the calculation results should be used as feedback about the design variant in order to support decision-making during the design process. A measure of the resulting environmental performance of variants during their whole life cycle is the Life Cycle Performance (LCP). By means of the LCP, different design variants can be compared, which is used within the case study of this paper.

A previously developed parametric LCA method is used for the calculation of the LCP [7]. This method is fully integrated into a programming software allowing the calculation of operational energy demand and embodied environmental impact of design variants. Since both, the LCA method and the parametric model, are programmed in the same software, exporting and re-importing of data is not necessary thus enables the application of optimization processes. Furthermore, the parametric LCA tool is able to provide results in real-time (<0.1 s). That facilitates finding optimal design solutions in a reasonable amount of time. The LCA method divides all necessary input into three categories, namely geometric information, non-geometric information and surrounding conditions. All of those are defined parametrically to permit quick adaptation to changing parameters.

As geometric information, surface areas are automatically extracted from a design variant. These areas are sorted by zones, in which one zone corresponds to one building floor. The circulation cores are not taken into consideration as they are not part of the building's heating area. Hence, these are subtracted from the building volumes. Non-geometric parameters such as material properties, the thickness of building components (e.g. exterior walls, insulation), HVAC systems, etc., are defined numerically. In this case study, six common construction types are chosen for the LCP calculation. These are: External Thermal Insulation Composite System (ETICS), Brick construction, Concrete construction, Wood construction, Ventilated façade system and Double shell masonry system. Surrounding conditions, such as climate or user data, are taken from standards. The shading value that indicates to which extent the windows are shaded by surrounding buildings is derived from the solar radiation analysis.

Since one building configuration in the case study contains two to four buildings, an LCP value is calculated for each of the buildings. However, the buildings need to be assessed as one complete configuration for optimization. Hence, a weighted average is calculated from the individual LCPs. The weighting is determined by the gross area of each building.

2.3 Optimization Process

Every design stage can contain either an enormously large number of possible variants or an identifiable number of variants. In the latter case, an exhaustive search can be applied. An example for an exhaustive search within the case study is the six selected construction types. However, the number of potential variants very large, a heuristic search becomes necessary in order to find solutions for the design problem within a reasonable time frame. In the case study, Evolutionary Algorithms (EA), also referred to as optimization strategies, are used for that matter. EA mimic biological evolution, namely, the process of natural selection and the 'survival of the fittest' principle [10]. The application of EA cannot guarantee to find an optimal solution, yet it might find one or multiple solutions which can be regarded as good enough from the planner's point of view.

EA require genomes and a fitness with an assigned goal in order to start operating.[2] Genomes are all parameters which can be varied during the optimization to generate design variants. The fitness is a numeric mathematical function which can include one or multiple performance criteria, such as average solar radiation and Surface Area to Volume Ratio (S/V). These criteria are combined by means of addition. Depending on the optimization goal, a positive or negative prefix is assigned to each criterion. The optimization goal can either aim to maximize or minimize the performance results calculated by the fitness function. Consequently, if the optimization goal of the complete function is set to maximization, each criterion which is to be maximized has a positive prefix. In contrast, each criterion that should be minimized gets a negative prefix. The opposite is the case if the optimization goal aims for minimization. Often negative and positive prefix are included in one fitness function. That means one criterion cannot be improved without having a negative impact on at least one other criterion. Furthermore, all criteria need to be scaled to the same numeric range to avoid overly dominant behavior of some criteria towards the other criteria. In the case study, a range from 0 to 1 is applied. Additionally, these criteria can be weighted according to their significance to the performance. However, the difficulty of the weighting processes is to identify how these criteria influence the performance. For example, it is known that the S/V impacts the LCP, but it is not clear how it should be weighed against other criteria like solar radiation in the fitness function in order to represent its significance to the LCP. The fitness function delivers a performance value for each generated design variant which is crucial for optimization processes.

Usually, an optimization stops when a termination condition is reached. In the case study, the optimization process was stopped after the 40th generation. Every generation contained 50 design variants.

2.4   Multi-stage Decision-Making Trees

Rittel's [4] theory of the MD process implies the need of visualizing produced design solutions according to the design stages used for the process. MD trees serve this need as they provide a clear overview of the generated data by arranging it in a tree-like structure. This makes comparing results easy for the planner. The design phases are represented by stages and the alternative design solutions in these stages are organized by branches. As MD trees are controlled parametrically, a vast amount of data can be

---

[2] Galapagos which is a component included in Grasshopper, was used for conducting all optimizations within the case study.

visualized with least effort. Saving the data of the design solutions according to a defined file name structure, and including the resulting file paths in the algorithm, enables automated data input. Moreover, the MD trees are updated in real time as soon as new results are saved or changes are applied to the already existing ones. The average, minimum and maximum values, etc. can be computed automatically, providing fast numeric evaluation methods for the planner. Figure 3 displays the optimization process plus the saving of graphical and numeric data of the optimized design solution for the automated creation of MD Trees.

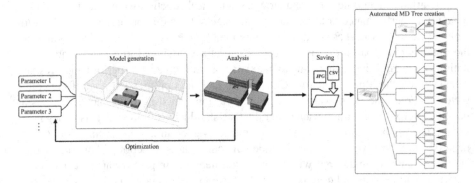

Fig. 3. Optimization process and automated MD Tree creation

2.5   Design Sequences

Part (1) of the study addresses the fragmentation of a design problem into design stages for the application of MD processes. It focuses on the influence of defining separate stages for design components in comparison to combining certain components in one stage in regards to resulting design solutions. Therefore, two MD processes with two different sequences are compared by considering the geometries and the performance values of their design solutions. In sequence 1 (MD process 1), all three design components (building volumes, circulation cores, construction types) are separated into three stages (see Fig. 5 left). Starting with the building volumes and their locations on the site in stage 1, continuing with the positioning of the circulation cores in stage 2, and concluding with assigning the construction types in stage 3, is the stage order of sequence 1. This order corresponds to the level of detail of the components as described above. However, this stage order is not solely determined by the level of detail. Logical constraints need to be considered in this example since the cores can only be placed within the building volumes. That makes it impossible to optimize core positioning without the building volumes. Because of the connection of the cores to the building volumes, the latter must be defined first in this sequence.

In sequence 2 (MD process 2), the building volumes and the cores are combined in stage 1 (see Fig. 5 middle). The six construction types are subject of stage 2. This sequence is based on a hypothesis of the authors and represents typical assumptions that planners may make of design solutions. The hypothesis refers to the solar radiation accessibility on the building façades. Generally, it can be assumed that in order to achieve acceptable solar radiation on all façades, the buildings may tend to maintain high distances to all shadow casting objects such as other buildings of the configuration and the surrounding buildings (see Fig. 4 left). This would be the case for sequence 1 where the volumes and their positions are defined in the first stage. After the volumes are placed on the site, the cores would be positioned in the areas where least solar radiation is identified in order to leave the spaces with good daylight accessibility to the apartment areas. In contrast, the hypothesis states that purposely created shaded areas on the building façades for the core placement can improve the solar radiation. A higher solar radiation may lead to better LCP values. The idea behind this assumption is to decrease the distance of some buildings on the site to achieve highly shaded, yet small areas. In these areas, the cores can be positioned (see Fig. 4 right). By decreasing the distances between the buildings on the site, the distances to the surrounding buildings increase. This can reduce the shading on the building façades caused by surrounding buildings which simultaneously improves their average solar radiation values. This hypothesis can only be considered if the building volumes, their positions, and the cores are optimized in the same stage. If they are divided into separate stages, the influence of the cores cannot be taken into account during the formation and positioning of the building volumes.

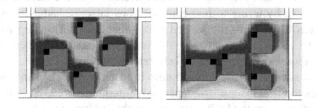

Fig. 4. Author's hypothesis: large building distances (left); small building distances (right)

Resulting from this hypothesis, a fitness function is developed. Sequence 2 requires only one fitness function since both criteria which are to be optimized are included in a single stage. The six construction types in stage 2 are already predefined and do not need to be optimized in this case study. Generating design solutions with high LCPs is the aim of the optimization. However, it is not possible to take the LCP as the fitness function and its maximization as the fitness goal in stage 1 of sequence 2. The reason for that is the missing information about the construction type which is content of the subsequent stage. Therefore, the planner needs to assign a fitness function for stage 1 of sequence 2 which does not contain the LCP but aims for optimization oriented towards the LCP.

The first step for creating such a fitness function is to define important performance criteria which influence the LCP. Moreover, it has to be possible to analyze the design variants of the regarded stage according to those performance criteria. One major performance criterion is the Surface Area to Volume Ratio (S/V) which is an indicator for the compactness of a building volume. It is calculated by dividing the area of the building envelope by the volume of the building. The S/V is an important criterion for determining a building's heat gain and heat loss. That means, a bigger surface area induces more heat gain in warm weather conditions and increased heat loss in cold conditions. Consequently, a minimized S/V is of great benefit to the LCP as it reduces the energy demand of the building. To provide one S/V value for the fitness function, an average of all S/V in a building configuration is calculated.

Another LCP influencing criterion is the solar radiation. It shows to which extent the building façades are exposed to sunlight and indicates the potential amount of daylight in the interior. Daylight accessibility of the building interior is of significance as it impacts the solar heat gains in cold weather conditions, and energy consumption in regards to artificial lighting. Thus, a reasonable amount of daylight in the buildings improves the LCP. As a solar radiation value is calculated for each analysis point on the façades, an average solar radiation value needs to be identified for the complete configuration of the buildings in order to create one value which can be included in the fitness function. However, the areas where the cores attach to the building façades are excluded from the average solar radiation value since they are not part of the heated apartment areas. That implies, that by placing the cores in shaded areas the average solar radiation of the remaining façade areas increases.

In regards to the earlier explained hypothesis of the authors, a shading factor for the cores is added. This factor is included to facilitate the creation of shaded areas where the cores should be positioned for improving the average solar radiation of the buildings. In order to achieve that, it aims to decrease some distances between the buildings on the site by trying to find core positions in semi-shaded areas. Choosing semi-shaded areas instead of fully shaded ones should aid positioning the cores not necessarily at the most shaded areas of the façades (primarily located at the north façades), but at those which are created between the buildings.

Weighting is always included in a fitness function, even when the planner only scales the values to the same numeric range. All criteria involved in a fitness function have a certain influence on the LCP depending on their values, i.e. a higher value has a higher impact on the performance. Additional weighting can be applied if the planner assumes that some criteria are more important than others. In this case study, all three criteria included in the fitness function are not additionally weighted. The weighting resulting from the scaling process seems appropriate enough from the author's point of view. Adding all criteria delivers the fitness function for sequence 2.

Next, the fitness goal needs to be assigned which determines the prefixes of the criteria in the fitness function. In this case, it is set to minimization. The adjusted fitness function for sequence 2 is the following:

$$\text{Fitness}_{\text{Seq.2}} = \text{S/V} - \text{average solar radiation} + \text{shading factor} \qquad (1)$$

This function expresses, that the S/V and the shading factor aim for minimization, whereas the average solar radiation should be increased.

To enable comparison of the design solutions resulting from sequence 1 and sequence 2, the fitness functions involve partially the same performance criteria. Since sequence 1 includes two optimization stages, accordingly two fitness functions are required. The first stage of sequence 1 where the building volumes and their positions on the site are optimized, aims for minimization and has the fitness function of:

$$\text{Fitness}_{Seq.1.1} = \text{S/V} - \text{average solar radiation of building volumes} \qquad (2)$$

The average solar radiation in this function is calculated from all solar radiation values on the façade because the cores are not included in this stage. For the second optimization in sequence 1 which aims for maximization, the following fitness function is used:

$$\text{Fitness}_{Seq.1.2} = \text{average solar radiation} \qquad (3)$$

At this point, the volumes and their positions are already optimized and therefore, the S/V is not included in the fitness $_{Seq.\ 1.2}$. The average solar radiation of the façade can be improved by positioning the cores in shaded areas. The shading factor is not relevant at this stage of the sequence because the building volumes and their positions are already determined and their distances cannot be changed. Therefore, the shading factor is not included in both fitness functions of sequence 1.

The (2) part of the case study serves the investigation of the impact of stage order on design solutions in an MD process. The initial sequence for this approach is sequence 2 from part (1) of the case study. Choosing this sequence facilitates the change of stage order as this MD process has only two stages. In stage 1 the building volumes, their positions on the site, and the cores are optimized. Stage 2 contains six different construction types which do not require optimization. By swapping these two stages, sequence 3 (MD process 3) is created (see Fig. 5 right). Its first stage holds the six construction types, whereas the optimization of the building volumes, their positions on the site, and the cores is conducted in the second stage. As the optimization in this sequence is content of the last stage, it is possible to take the LCP as the sole performance criterion in the fitness function and its maximization as the fitness goal.

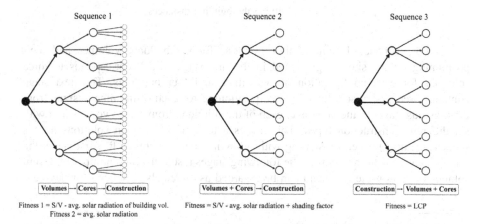

Fig. 5. MD Tree 1 for sequence 1 (left), MD Tree 2 for sequence 2 (middle), MD Tree 3 for sequence 3 (right)

Consequently, the main difference of the solution generation in these two sequences lies in their fitness functions. The fitness function of sequence 2 is determined by the author's assumptions about the design solutions. In contrast, the fitness function of sequence 3 is fully determined by the LCP calculation which simultaneously is the final assessment method of the generated design solutions.

3 Results

In order to ensure systematic comparison between the sequences, several evaluation factors are established.[3] They sum up the design solution data of each individual MD process by creating average values. The first evaluation factor in this case study is the average LCP of a complete sequence. A higher LCP indicates better environmental performance of a design solution. The average of the S/V and the solar radiation on the façades are further evaluation factors for design solutions. By means of the average building distance the geometries of the design solutions can be differentiated. It is calculated by measuring the distance from each building to all the other buildings of a design solution. In the next step, the shortest distance for each building is identified (see Fig. 6). Based on the shortest distance values, the average building distance is calculated for each design solution. The average of these values again, is the average building distance for a complete sequence.

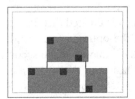

Fig. 6. Identifying the building distances

(1) For sequence 1, nine design solutions for the building volumes and their positioning on the site are generated in the first stage, which corresponds to three solutions for each configuration of two, three and four buildings. The next stage contains three design solutions for core positioning for each of the nine designs from the previous stage. In the last stage, each of the solutions from stage two is paired with six different construction types. This makes a total of 162 design solutions in this sequence (Fig. 7). Even by starting with a low number of items in the first stage, the multiplications with the items of the following stages result in a high number of design solutions. This on the one hand can be regarded as extremely beneficial for having a

---

[3] Another important information to keep in mind when evaluating design solutions is that slight deviations in the results are common for optimization processes which operate based on EA. These deviations are to be considered before making conclusions about the different sequences.

variety of design options to choose from for the planner. On the other hand, this process can easily become very time-consuming if a high number of optimizations has to be conducted within an MD process. That should be kept in mind when determining the number of desired design solutions.

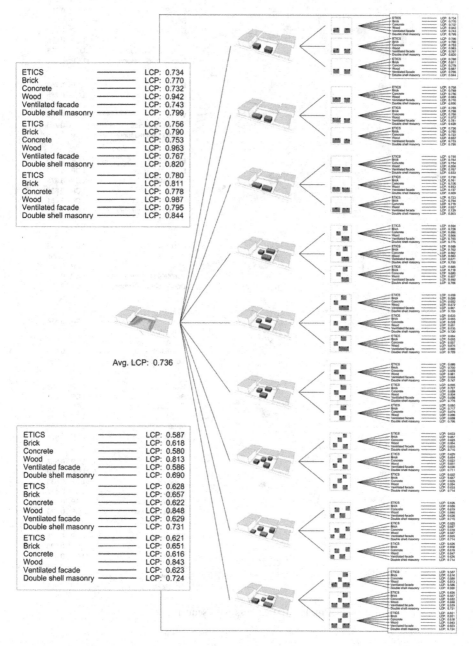

Fig. 7. MD process with sequence 1 with zoom-in parts for better readability

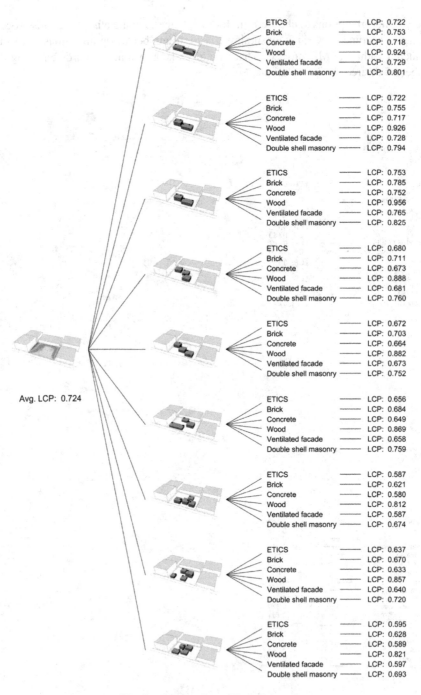

Fig. 8. MD process with sequence 2

The number of design solutions in sequence 2 is significantly lower than in sequence 1 due to the combination of two optimization stages in one. In the first stage of sequence 2, nine design solutions are produced, three for each configuration. They involve the building volumes, their positioning on the site and the core positioning. In combination with the six construction types in the subsequent stage, a total of 54 design solutions is produced in MD process 2 (Fig. 8).

Table 1. Evaluation values of sequence 1 and sequence 2

Average	Sequence 1	Sequence 2	Difference
LCP [WBP]	0.736	0.724	−1.7%
Distance [m]	8.50	4.52	−53.2%
S/V [m^{-1}]	0.352	0.352	±0%
Solar radiation [kWh/m^2]	403.027	370.477	−8.8%

The evaluation values of both sequences are summarized in Table 1. It can be observed that the average LCP of 0.736 resulting from sequence 1 is slightly higher than the average LCP of 0.724 from sequence 2. An enormous difference can be noted in the average building distances where the value of sequence 1 is almost twice that of sequence 2. In contrast, the average S/V values of both sequences are the same.

The MD trees of both sequences (Figs. 7 and 8) show a pattern in the individual LCP values which is caused by the different construction types. If for each individual design solution all LCPs resulting from the six construction types are sorted from the best to the worst, a specific order can be observed: wood construction, double shell masonry, brick construction, ventilated façade, ETICS and concrete. This order is constantly the same for both sequences. This indicates, that it is not dependent on the sequences. Instead, each construction type has a specific influence on the LCP.

The results from part (2) of the case study can be regarded in Figs. 8 and 9. As described above, in the first stage of sequence 2, nine design solutions are generated which makes three for each configuration of two, three and four building. The second stage of this sequence holds six construction types, which makes a total of 54 design solutions (Fig. 8).

Changing the stage order leads to a different number of design solutions. In sequence 3, the six construction types are content of the first design stage. The second stage of this sequence provides three design solutions for each of the construction types

Table 2. Evaluation values of sequence 2 and sequence 3

Average	Sequence 2	Sequence 3	Difference
LCP [WBP]	0.724	0.750	+3.6%
Distance [m]	4.52	10.27	+127.2%
S/V [m^{-1}]	0.352	0.352	±0%
Solar radiation [kWh/m^2]	370.477	399.170	+7.7%

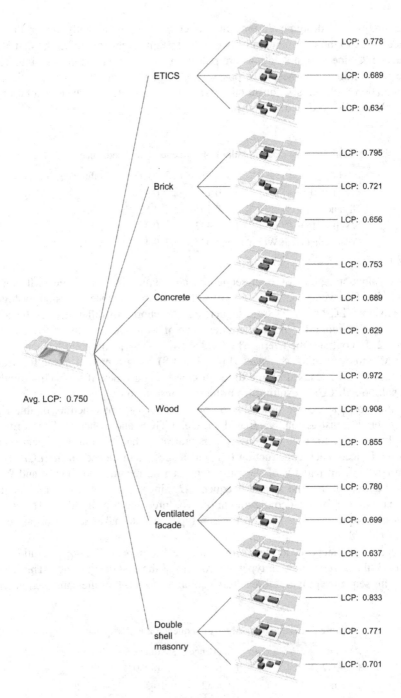

Fig. 9. MD process with sequence 3

from the previous stage. This corresponds to one design solution per building configuration. In total, 18 design solutions are generated for sequence 3. The outcomes of sequence 3 can be regarded in MD tree 3 (Fig. 9).

Both sequences differ significantly in the computation time they required to generate all design solutions. This can be explained by the number of optimizations they include. Sequence 3 has double the number of optimizations in comparison to sequence 2.

Table 2 displays the evaluation values of sequence 2 and sequence 3. Comparing the average LCP values of both sequences, it can be noted that sequence 3 delivers a higher value than sequence 2. Furthermore, the average building distance in sequence 3 is more than a double in comparison to sequence 2. This can be regarded in relation to the average solar radiation on the façades which accordingly, is higher in sequence 3 than in sequence 2. The building volumes in both sequences are of the same compactness.

4 Discussion

The comparison of sequence 1 and sequence 2 shows that both deliver different performances and geometries. As the LCP is the main focus of the comparison, it is crucial to explore the reasons for the difference in the results. Sequence 1 provides a better average LCP than sequence 2 which does not match with the expectations of the authors to create better performing design solutions by combining two design stages in one. In order to investigate the reasons for this discrepancy, it is necessary to take a closer look at the geometry evaluation values. As the average S/V of both sequences is nearly identical, it can be assumed that the solar radiation on the façades is the reason for the difference. The average solar radiation of sequence 1 is higher than that of sequence 2. Regarding these values in conjunction with the building distances, a direct numeric relationship becomes apparent, i.e. the higher the building distance, the higher the solar radiation. By maintaining a high distance, the shading on the façades gets reduced, hence leading to higher solar radiation values. The reason for such a difference in the building distances are the fitness functions used in both sequences for optimization. In sequence 1, the building volumes and their positions on the site are optimized in the first stage by applying a fitness function which contains the S/V and the solar radiation. Both performance criteria are directly related to the aspects which are to be optimized. The S/V influences the formation of building shapes and volumes, whereas the solar radiation aims for a placement of buildings in high distances to minimize shading. This fitness function is based on fundamental knowledge of building forms. Same applies to the second optimization stage of sequence 1 where the average solar radiation is to be maximized by placing building cores in shaded areas. These two fitness functions of sequence 1 are established without further assumptions from the author's side. In contrast, the fitness function of sequence 2 additionally incorporates a hypothesis stated by the authors. According to the hypothesis, a shading factor is added to the fitness function which already involves the S/V and the solar radiation. Since the shading factor is the only difference between the first fitness in sequence 1 and the fitness in sequence 2, it is obvious that this must be the reason for the different average building distances. The EA aims to find core positions with the desired shading condition. It, therefore, places buildings in smaller distances to each other to increase shading in some areas and then position the cores in these shaded zones. However, the idea of the hypothesis does not match with the outcome because the created shaded areas are too big in relation to the area which can be covered by the cores. This causes even more shading than in sequence 1 and consequently lowers the LCP values. By adding the performance criteria in one fitness function after scaling them to the same numeric range, all of them have a similar value since no further weighting is involved. This means, the author's assumption is of similar significance as the S/V and the solar radiation to the LCP. After conducting the case study, it can be concluded that this weighting is not appropriate in regards to the overall goal to generate design solutions with maximal LCP. This outcome represents the difficulty that comes with fragmenting a design problem into design stages.

If the assessment method which is used for the final evaluation of the complete design (LCA) cannot be taken for optimization purposes in all stages of the MD process, other fitness functions need to be established. The design solutions are highly dependent on these as the case study has shown. Consequently, it is the planner's task to define appropriate fitness functions. An ideal fitness function should include all performance criteria relevant to the LCP which can be applied to the design variants in the selected design stage. Additionally, appropriate weighting that matches with the weighting in the final design assessment method should be assigned to the performance criteria. In regards to the example of the case study, that implies that the weighting of the three performance criteria in the fitness function of sequence 2 should be adjusted according to the impact each criterion has on the LCP. Since the shading factor was introduced by the authors but is not included in the LCP, it should be removed from this fitness function.

Another example for a problem that can occur when establishing fitness functions is the following: Performance criteria which are relevant to the LCP and can be applied to design variants at the selected stage are not included simply because the planner is either completely unaware of them, or he does not know how these might influence the LCP. Such a case is exemplified in the second fitness function of sequence 1 where the solar radiation is taken as the sole performance criterion for the core positioning optimization. A second criterion which is relevant but not included at this stage is the S/V. Since the building volumes are already formed in the first stage of sequence 1, it may seem that the S/V does not change anymore by positioning the building cores. However, in regards to the LCP calculation, it is of relevance. As previously explained, in the energy demand calculation, the volumes of the cores are excluded from the building volumes as they are not part of the heated building volume. Consequently, their position is relevant for the S/V. Two positions can be identified, the sides and the corners (see Fig. 10). Positioning a core at a corner creates a different surface area than positioning it at a side. The latter causes a bigger envelope area in comparison to the core located at the corner. This difference influences the energy demand, especially

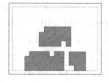

Fig. 10. Different positions of the circulation cores subtracted from the footprints

when a higher number of cores is involved. If the planner is not highly familiar with the way the LCP is calculated, he might miss out certain criteria in the fitness function as this example demonstrates.

Regarding the difficulties of establishing fitness functions described above, three main problems are shown in this first topic of the case study:

(1) The shading factor which is based on the author's hypothesis represents ideas planners may have in regards to design solutions, but do not exactly know how these might affect the LCP. By trying to incorporate such ideas, it is likely that the created fitness function is much more oriented towards the hypothesis than towards the LCP. That can lead to design solutions with worse LCP values as the case study shows.

(2) Even when the planner relies on fundamental knowledge to determine performance criteria, the problem of the weighting occurs. In order to assign weighting values, specific knowledge about the influence of different performance criteria on the LCP is required. This knowledge is highly dependent on the design problem and on the set of performance criteria involved. Therefore, high effort is necessary to determine weighting tailored to the LCP. The more components are involved in one design stage, the more complicated it becomes to define performance criteria and especially, their weighting in the fitness function.

(3) Furthermore, the planner should have high knowledge of the LCA method in order to incorporate relevant performance criteria and identify appropriate weighting factors. Therefore, the task of formulating fitness functions according to the LCP is difficult to incorporate for planners in practice, mostly due to very limited time for design exploration.

In regards to the research questions of the (1) part of the case study, it can be concluded that the fragmentation of a design problem into design stages affects the design solutions in multiple ways. Assigning design stages can lead to sequences which require fitness functions formulated by the planner. The problems he is most likely to experience with this task are described above. These problems can lead to worse LCP values as the case study shows. Furthermore, it can be noted that it is important to consider possible relationships between the design components before separating them into different stages. However, combining multiple design components in one stage where the LCP cannot be taken as the fitness function, can make establishing a fitness function very complicated. Therefore, the approach of separate design stages can be beneficial in terms of formulating fitness functions oriented towards the LCP.

In part (2) of the case study, both sequences differ in their LCP values. The reason for that lies in their fitness functions as these determine the optimization processes. Due to the stage order of sequence 2, the optimization processes are conducted in stage one. In stage two, their outcomes are combined with different construction types. The LCP can only be calculated after the last design stage of this MD process. Consequently, in order to calculate the LCP of a design variant from stage one, it needs to be paired with a construction type. Therefore, the planner needs to assign a fitness function which does not contain the LCP, but is highly oriented towards the LCP. Formulating such a fitness function is a task of high complexity if multiple performance criteria have to be involved in the function. The two main difficulties in this process are identifying performance criteria which are relevant to the LCP plus can be applied at the selected design stage, and assigning their weighting according to the impact they have on the LCP. Establishing appropriate fitness functions requires specific knowledge of the design assessment method (LCA), the design components and the performance criteria. As the results of sequence 2 show, formulating fitness functions, especially if assumptions of the planner are involved, does not necessarily lead to satisfying design solutions in regards to the performance goal.

By changing design stages, the problem of formulating additional fitness functions can be avoided as demonstrated in sequence 3. Stage one of sequence 3 contains the six construction types. For each of them, three designs are optimized. In contrast to sequence 2, here the LCP can directly be used as the fitness function. That is possible because the optimizations are conducted in the last stage of the sequence where the construction types are already determined. This provides the necessary information for calculating the LCP. The most efficient way of finding design solutions according to a performance goal is to use the same design assessment method for optimization and for the final evaluation of the design solution. That is the reason why sequence 3 delivers better performing design solutions.

It can be concluded, that stage order in MD processes can significantly affect design solutions as the case study shows. As fitness functions determine the direction of the optimization process, their formulation is of major importance for the outcome. The establishment of fitness functions is highly dependent on the position of the stages where optimization is conducted in MD processes. If not all information for the LCP calculation is available at a stage, a fitness function which does not contain the LCP has to be established. Since that is a very complex task, especially if several performance criteria have to be involved, it is possible that this fitness function does not lead to satisfying design solutions in regards to the overall performance goal of the design. Using the assessment criterion for the final solutions as the fitness function for optimization is the most effective way of generating design solutions according to the performance goal, because no further fitness function has to be formulated by the planner. That ensures, that the optimization is directly oriented towards the performance goal and is not manipulated by other fitness functions. Furthermore, the case study shows that the strategy of following the level of detail from the least to the most detailed for assigning design stages to the design components is not necessarily the best way to generate design solutions with high performances.

5 Conclusion and Outlook

To investigate the impact of stage order on design solutions in MD processes, a case study was conducted by the authors. In this case study, multiple different sequences were applied for solution generation. The results were displayed in corresponding MD trees to enable a visual comparison of the design outcomes. Additional evaluation values were used to provide a numeric comparison of the design solutions in each individual sequence. By means of this workflow, theoretical knowledge of the MD process was gained. It is worth mentioning, that all statements concerning the research questions are made solely based on this case study and do not claim general validity for all design scenarios. It is possible, that other examples of architectural design problems deliver different results in regards to the posed research questions. In regards to all findings of the case study, it can be concluded that defining an appropriate sequence for the MD process is highly dependent on the individual design problem. The sequence needs to be tailored towards the performance goal while considering all components and their relationships. It is important to consider possible relationships between the design components before separating them into different stages to avoid neglection of possibly better performing compromise solutions.

Consequently, in an ideal scenario, all components would be optimized in one stage. That may be an effective sequence for small design problems which involve a very small number of parameters. However, that does not apply to design problems with a higher number of parameters. The reason for that is the variant space which expands with each added parameter which decreases the chance of finding satisfying design solutions in a reasonable timeframe. Therefore, it can be stated that compromises have to be made between the number of stages in a sequence and the size of the variant space of each stage. Conducting optimization in the last stage of the sequence is beneficial because at this point, the performance goal can be selected as the fitness function. In this way, the optimization is directly oriented towards the performance goal which is most efficient for finding design solutions according to this goal. Additionally, the stage order may induce the need of formulating fitness functions which do not contain the performance goal as a performance criterion, but aim for optimization oriented towards it. If the design problem is very complex, case studies may be needed in order to investigate how design components affect each other and what impact they have on the performance goal. The lack of such knowledge can lead to worse design solutions. However, in practice, deadlines are short and designers cannot afford to undertake research for each design problem. This makes the investigation of fundamental aspects of MD processes such as the sequence an important task to provide basic guidelines which ideally, are applicable to many design problems.

Another approach for further studies can be a higher level of detail in the design that comes with a higher number of components. Furthermore, studies of exploring how the LCP can be influenced by certain building components may be helpful for developing a better understanding of the weighting factor. Further research on MD processes is highly recommended by the authors in order to provide the necessary knowledge for a computational application of the MD process. For the implementation in practice especially, further recommendations for assigning design stages and formulating fitness functions would be beneficial to planners who use the MD process for solution space exploration.

Acknowledgements. This study was carried out as part of the research project 'Integrated Life Cycle Optimization' funded by the German Federal Ministry for the Environment, Nature Conservation, Building and Nuclear Safety through the research initiative ZukunftBau.

References

1. Gero, J.S.: Design prototypes: a knowledge representation schema for design. AI Mag. **11**(4), 26–36 (1990)
2. Markus, T.A.: Design Methods in Architecture. Lund Humphries, London (1969)
3. Maver, T.W.: Emerging Methods in Environmental Design and Planning. MIT Press, Cambridge (1970)
4. Rittel, H.W.J.: Planen Entwerfen Design Ausgewählte. Schriften zu Theorie und Methodik. W. Kohlhammer GmbH, Stuttgart (1992)
5. Lawson, B.: How Designers Think. The Design Process Demystified, 4th edn., p. 33. Architectural Press, Oxford (2006)
6. Mitchell, W.J.: Computer-Aided Architectural Design. Van Nostrand R, New York (1977)
7. Hollberg, A.: A parametric method for building design optimization based on life cycle assessment. Dissertation, Bauhaus University Weimar, Weimar (2016)
8. ISO 14040: DIN EN ISO 14040:2009 Umweltmanagement - Ökobilanz - Grundsätze und Rahmenbedingungen, p. 11. DIN Deutsches Institut für Normung E.V., Berlin (2009)
9. Wittstock, B., Albrecht, S., Colodel, C., Lindner, J.: Gebäude aus Lebenszyklusperspektive - Ökobilanzen im Bauwesen. Bauphysik **31**, 9–17 (2009)
10. Rechenberg, I.: Evolutionsstrategie '94. Stuttgart, Frommann Holzboog (1994)

Why Do We Need Building Information Modeling (BIM) in Conceptual Design Phase?

Ömer Halil Çavuşoğlu[✉] and Gülen Çağdaş

Istanbul Technical University, Istanbul, Turkey
contact@omercavusoglu.com, cagdas@itu.edu.tr

Abstract. Many researchers point out that, in conceptual design, many significant decisions are taken to directly affect functional qualities, the performance of the building, aesthetics, and the relationship of the building with the natural environment and climate, even if there is no certain and valid information to create and obtain satisfactory design solution. The focus of the study is to observe and explore how BIM can be used in conceptual design phase and also to investigate how and how effectively BIM can help architects during the process. To develop an understanding to these aims, a case study implementation within sketching and BIM environments which consists of three stages was carried out in an educational setting by three participants who are undergraduate degree students of Faculty of Architecture. Qualitative research methods were used as research methodology and the findings of the implementation were discussed with prominent related literature in the same context.

Keywords: BIM · Building information modeling · Conceptual design phase · Conceptual design analysis · Energy modeling

1 Introduction

There are always adversative opinions whenever conceptual design and building information modeling are mentioned in the same context. So, first of all, it is significant and meaningful to discuss about the answers of these two sequential questions:

- Why do we need Building Information Modeling (BIM) in conceptual design phase?
- How and in what way can BIM help us to address unprecedented contemporary challenges in AEC industry which are evolved to be crucial that cannot be ignored anymore?

Before discussing the answers of these questions, it is important to unveil the current state of AEC industry under the influence of ongoing drastic changes and paradigm shifts. Starting with the Industrial Revolution and following World Wars; mechanical and electrical systems were invented and developed at a great pace, and this situation changed the fundamentals, opportunities, and requirements of the period. Due to this rapid progress, an expeditious increase in building sector has started which eventually causes some crucial global issues such as high energy consumption, global warming, depletion of natural resources, and so on.

G. Çağdaş et al. (Eds.): CAAD Futures 2017, CCIS 724, pp. 121–135, 2017.
DOI: 10.1007/978-981-10-5197-5_7

Researches show that AEC industry is directly responsible from this situation. For instance, while all consumed energy of the United States used up by the buildings is 48,7% [1], it is 40% in European Union countries [2]. Furthermore, during next twenty years, it is expected to be needed more than doubling the built environment [3]. This situation leads us to a much more critical position which cannot be ignored anymore.

Numerous researches show that one of the most important reasons of this consumption is that many essential decisions (building orientation, building shape, structural system, building envelope and so on) which are taken at the early stages of architectural design are taken without any valid and certain information [4–7]. These decisions which are taken with often inadequate information on the site, climate, geography, also provide a basis for the final performance and the aesthetics of the final outcome.

Within this context, Foqué [8] expresses that 'intuitive thinking and rational thinking are not opponents; they are the twin poles between which the artist structures reality'. Apart from this, he also asserts that with the emergence of modernity, architecture practitioners hover between science and art [9]. In accordance with Foqué's explanations and in order to find a solution to recent challenges, new BIM processes and capabilities have been started to be developed which are acknowledged as inadequate for the conceptual design process, but can have a huge potential to support conceptual design with their existing and potential capabilities.

From this point of view, the focus of the study is to observe and explore how BIM can be used in conceptual design phase and also to investigate how and how effectively BIM can help architects during the process. To develop an understanding these aims, a case study implementation within sketching and BIM environments, which consist of three stages was carried out in an educational setting by three participants who are undergraduate degree students of Faculty of Architecture.

This study consists of five main chapters. Firstly, we review the literature on conceptual design, its characteristics, aspects, requirements and its significance within the scope of design cognition field. And also, we examine into BIM processes, what opportunities BIM can offer in conceptual design phase and how it can help us to address with recent challenges that we have to face. In the following section, we describe and discuss why we have preferred to use qualitative research methods and how we have used them. Also, we describe the precautions in terms of reliability and validity. The next section describes the design task, the scope of the implementation and what was done during the implementation stages. At the end of the section, we also present the findings of analysis and evaluation of the implementation. In Conclusion and Future Works section, we discuss about the findings of the study and prominent topics from the related literature in the same context to reveal an answer for research topic of the study. Finally, we reconsider about our other findings which are not presented in the findings chapter as they are not exactly related to this study's aim and shared them as worthy research topics which can be studied in future works to investigate deeply about the conceptual BIM approach and also take it a step further.

2   Conceptual BIM Approach

2.1   Conceptual Design and Its Significance

Many researchers identify design as a process of generating new, valuable and desirable solutions [10–14]. Design is also accepted as one of the most complicated cognitive process of human beings [15–18] which is mostly accepted as a problem solving activity. Design problems usually have open-ended, wide-ranging, complicated and ambiguous characteristics [19, 20]. They are interacted with various criterion to generate design ideas and concepts [10, 21]. Goel [22] expresses that design problems are constituted of lots of different parts and elements, and these do not need to be logically connected. This makes design a cyclical process which is fed from feedbacks of the ongoing process. To deal with these complicated and ill-defined problems, Alexander [23] asserts to separate design problems into smaller sub problems. Thus, it will be possible to obtain more defined problems which can be solved successfully with rationality [24].

Besides these information, studies from design cognition field showed that sketching and drawing with paper and pencil still has a significant role for exploring possible design alternatives, evaluating ideas and also communication with self [21, 25–29] in architectural concept design. In concept design phase, designers are supposed to decide on some significant factors such as building orientation, building shape, structural system, building envelope and interior finishes with inadequate and indefinite information as mentioned before. These decisions directly provide a basis for the final performance of the ultimate design outcome.

This situation makes conceptual design important not only for aesthetic and functional aspects but also for sustainability. To find a solution to this problematic situation and enhance conceptual design processes, some researchers and practitioners have focused on developing new design tools and information management databases for meeting the new requirements of the current practices. In this context, BIM comes to the forefront with its current and potential capabilities.

2.2   Conceptual BIM

National Institute of Building Sciences [30] defined BIM as a model and process: "A building information model is a digital representation of physical and functional characteristics of a facility. As such, it serves as a shared knowledge resource for information about a facility forming a reliable basis for decisions during its life cycle from inception onward. A basic premise of Building Information Modeling is collaboration by different stakeholders at different phases of the life-cycle of a facility to insert, extract, update or modify information in the model to support and reflect the roles of that stakeholder". Building Information Model is a data-rich, object-based, intelligent and parametric digital representation of the facility, from which views appropriate to various users' needs can be extracted and analyzed to generate feedback and improvement of the facility design [31].

BIM allows the generation and management of all numeric and non-numeric data in coordinately, collaboratively, coherently, synchronously, and computable way from the conceptual design to the end of the building's life [3, 32–34]. This integrated and parametric model which is also an intelligent and object-based virtual model provides to obtain directly abstract forms of representations, inferences, work and time schedules, analyzes, simulations, and so on. The characteristics and capabilities of BIM are discussed with many reports and publications in both industry and academic settings [35–38].

Although BIM offers unique capabilities during the drafting and construction processes, it was regarded as being unsuccessful as a conceptual design tool for a short time before. Especially in the last 10 years, BIM tools were able to meet the skills of other CAD tools commonly used in the industry and reached a level of competitiveness with them for conceptual design. Today, BIM stands out with its 'intelligent and parametric modeling capabilities and 'simulation, analysis and inference capabilities' when comparing with conventional CAD tools in terms of conceptual design process.

As mentioned in the previous sections, the intent of developing BIM as a conceptual design tool is directly related with the recent global challenges which AEC industry are obligated to face. Studies show that the difficulty of evaluating the performance of the building in the early stages of design has caused the products generated to be inadequate in achieving the desired performance [39]. Regarding studies which are investigating how to achieve more sustainable design approaches, the necessity of evaluating sustainability criteria from the initial stages of design has been determined [40]. With BIM approach, even in the first stages of conceptual design, designers can begin to work on models to analyze and redesign their designs according to performance and efficiency criteria using specific pre-defined presumptive data without requiring any advanced engineering knowledge.

Since many important building-related decisions have not yet been taken at the conceptual design process, the capability to analyze and simulate the geometric design models (mass models) of the BIM tools is a distinguishing feature, which is one step ahead of conventional design tools. In this context, the passive and active strategies identified by Krygiel and Nies [3] for the sustainable BIM approach are reduced and sorted according to the possibilities BIM can provide in the conceptual design phase: Building Orientation, Building Massing, Solar and Shadow Analysis, Daylighting Analysis, Conceptual Energy Modeling, Potential Renewable Energy Analysis.

As a brief, it is emphasized that taking advantage of essential information about design task in conceptual design process is useful and crucial. BIM environment with its information capability operates as an improved design (support) tool with powerful 2D and 3D drafting features, performance simulations, and visual analysis feedbacks. These feedbacks are helpful as visual and numeric outcomes of the design which enable the evaluation of the designed mass. Then, the design relies on the functional, aesthetics, sustainable realities and the subjective judgements of designers. In this section, we studied the current realities of conceptual design and building information modeling by literature review, and then, we explained why and how we need BIM in conceptual design phases.

3   Methodology

To clarify and reveal the current state of conceptual BIM approach in conceptual design phase, series of implementations were carried out by three participants in three sessions. Due to the aims of the study, qualitative research methods were used as research methodology. In this section, the reasons why qualitative research methods are preferred for this study will be explained and their roles within the research will be defined.

Qualitative research methods have been developed by social scientists who want to develop a detailed understanding of human behavior [41]. With qualitative research, complicated text based definitions can be obtained about how individuals experience the research topic. With this feature, qualitative research methods have differentiated from other research methods and strengthened their place in scientific field. Another important feature that distinguishes qualitative research from other methods is that it is a research approach that allows starting the study with a minimum of preliminary acceptance and bias about the topic. This situation provides that the research context is updatable and adaptable throughout the process. Because the method limitations are more flexible, unpredictable and unexpected findings can be come out and many important details cannot be passed over which are not realized while planning the research [42]. This allows the researchers to start with less foresight and acceptance about the research by taking only basic decisions about what they are looking for [43], and to be able to update the scope of the research in the process and move toward to the unforeseen issues and results [44]. Another important feature of qualitative research in relation to this situation is that it proves itself as an effective research method for exploratory researches. Also, qualitative studies are also being actively used to obtain rich and in-depth information from small groups of participants [45].

As the purpose of the study desires to explore new things about an existing situation, and is necessary to be carried out with fewer participants in a limited time, qualitative research methods are considered appropriate and useful for this study.

3.1   Observation as Data Collection Method

Observation method is a qualitative research method that is based on traditional etnographic research, aspiring to learn the opinions of inspected populations. The observation method is carried out in the natural environment of the targeted communities which are determined in the direction of the research questions. All observed data are recorded by the researchers for being ready to be evaluated. By this way, it is possible to understand and interpret the behaviors and actions of individuals, and interaction of them with other individuals, contexts, ideas, rules and events [44].

In this study, the method of observation was applied during the case study implementation while participants were working on the design problem. Researchers also carried out observation process in interviews and focus group discussions. All these processes were recorded coordinately and thus made it possible for the researchers to experience and observe relevant processes over and over again.

Apart from observation, semi-structured interview method was used as the second data collection method in order to obtain data from a different perspective on the subjective understanding and interpretation of the researchers and to verify the collected data and findings.

3.2   Semi-structured Interview as Data Collection Method

The interview method is a research technique that is developed to reveal the participants' detailed views about the research topic. In this method, the researcher listens the participant's answers carefully and provides the details with consecutive questions. Throughout the interview, the participants are expected to naturally convey all their thoughts about the research topic. The interview technique allows individuals to express their feelings, thoughts and experiences with their own sentences. This also enables the participants understanding how they interpret and perceive the research topic [44].

In this study, semi-structured interview technique was used. Accordingly, the previously prepared interview protocol enabled the interview to proceed in a certain systematic flow. But also, it provided an opportunity for the researchers to ask for additional questions in order to deepen the data collection process and to elaborate the answers given by this way [46].

3.3   Focus Group as Validity Check Method

Focus group is a qualitative research method in which data collection is carried out through the discussion group of a few participants about a research topic in the same environment. With this method, the researchers are able to ask open ended questions to the participants and can direct the discussion of the focus group to reveal common and contrary ideas of the participant group about the research topic [44].

In this study, after completion of the implementation, a focus group discussion was held with three participants and the participants' opinions on the research topic, implementation, design process, and conceptual BIM approach were discussed. The focus group method was used in this study to present the validity and reliability of the data obtained through observation and interview, and the findings of the data set.

3.4   Reliability and Validity

Data collection and analysis processes in qualitative research are largely under the control of the researcher and the objectivity of qualitative research is being discussed. Despite this, the qualitative research methods are more likely to yield more efficient results in certain fields of study than other research methods, and therefore are preferred by many researchers.

Verification of the validity and reliability of the research in studies conducted with qualitative methods can be more challenging than other research methods and therefore it is important to consider this situation. In order to verify the collected data and the objectivity of the findings of the study, the following ways will be followed:

- The researchers will deliberately try to suppress their subjective thoughts and to bring objective findings to the forehand.
- Different data collection and analysis methods and findings will be compared with each other and the appropriateness of data and evaluation outcomes will be checked by triangulation method.
- In order to clarify the data collection and the correct interpretation of the findings, participants' feedback will be provided by the focus group method after the implementation and the data and findings will be examined in this context.

4   Case Study Implementations

The implementation process was structured in such a way that it consisted of three successive stages which constituted a single design process. During the first implementation stage, the participants were asked to start the study in sketching environment. In the second implementation stage, the design study carried out in the previous sketch environment was transferred to the Revit environment and the design ideas continued to be developed with Revit's mass modeling capabilities. In the last stage, developed design ideas were evaluated using Revit's performance-based simulation and analysis capabilities and developed to have more energy efficient performance, also taking into account the aesthetics concerns of the participants.

The case study was carried out by three undergraduate degree students of Faculty of Architecture who attend Computer Applications in Architecture course as a student and accepted to be volunteer in this study. Two of them are at their fourth year in architectural education while the other one is at second. All participants indicated that they were familiar with at least one well-known CAD tools to use it as drafting, modeling, and designing tool. On the other hand, they had no experience about using BIM, Conceptual BIM, and energy modeling tools. In the process from beginning of the course to the beginning of the practice, a series of operations were carried out in order to make the participants ready to practice.

First of all, since participants had no experience about BIM related concepts which would be used in this study; a series of theoretic and practical lessons had been given for six weeks. By this way, we tried to provide an adequate basis for students to achieve a successful research process within a limited time. A preliminary interview was held with the participants the week before from the implementation start date and brief information about research topic was summarized and the demographic information of the participants were obtained. After this interview, the design location and the design task were announced in general terms to the participants and provided an opportunity for preliminary investigation. Finally, just before the implementation, all information about the design location and the task was shared with the participants, and participants' questions about the study were responded. Immediately after responding the participants' questions, the Stage I process was initiated.

4.1 Design Task and Scope of the Implementation

In this study, the design task of the case study is determined as 'designing a multi-purpose student center as a comfortable environment where students can experience as a gathering and meeting center, and conduct educational and social-based activities'.

To ensure that design study can be completed within the specified time and to design the study in such a way as not to hinder the purpose; the overall design expectation is supported with three main criteria as functional, contextual, and sustainable objectives. The description of these objectives is as follows:

- Functional Objective: To develop design ideas by taking into account the functional characteristics of the spaces given in the Architectural Programme Requirements table. And also, to design direct or indirect connections of spaces which have different functions, privacy levels, and working hours.
- Contextual Objective: To design the multi-purpose student center within the consideration of integrating it successfully with its neighboring buildings, nearby environment and also the entire campus.
- Sustainable Objective: To continue design study in the context of energy efficiency and to develop design alternatives to achieve more efficient energy performance.

In addition to these expected design objectives to be reached, the architectural programme requirements of the design problem are determined as academic study areas, administrative offices, recreational areas, exhibition areas, multi-purpose hall and foodcourts which constitute a total of 12000 m^2 construction area.

4.2 Implementation Stage I: Sketching

At Stage I, participants were asked to develop their first design ideas in the sketch environment in the direction of the design problem. At this stage, participants were not expected to directly assess sustainability and energy efficiency principles, but were asked to evaluate aesthetic, functional, and contextual objectives. The main reason for incorporating the sketch environment into this study is to provide an environment for the participants to create their initial design ideas in a familiar environment. Thus, it is aimed to increase the productivity of the participants and to provide a productive environment for the implementation process. Since the data collection at this stage are not directly related to the purpose of the study, the actions performed in Stage I will be briefly summarized.

The participants performed similar actions in order to solve the design problem despite of being with different levels of priority and importance. Though they had little differences with each other, they all generally started their processes by performing an analysis of the design site, the task, and the nearby environment. Initially, the size and the contextual location of the area, the strong axis in the vicinity, the pedestrian circulation, the built environment, the green areas and all the possible points of interest were determined. In the next step, the results obtained from these analyzes were associated with architectural program requirements and design expectations. In accordance with this associate, as being the first design decisions, the building's settlement area and setbacks were identified and ideas were developed by using functional zones to locate the spaces. Based on the draft settlement plan that was created in the continuation of the process, 2D plan analysis and the first decisions about the building form were taken. Towards the last parts of this stage, the participants drew their study as elevation, section, and perspective representations and continued to improve their designs by evaluating it in this way.

This phase was limited to 120-minute for each participant and each participant's working environment was recorded with an allocated camera. Participants told that they could develop and finish their study as they wished. In this context, the duration of the 120-minute implementation period for Stage I was adequate and satisfactory for the participants.

4.3 Implementation Stage II: Mass Modeling in BIM Environment

In Stage II, the participants were asked to transfer their design studies they had developed during the previous implementation to the Revit environment and they were supposed to develop new design alternatives. At this stage, the participants didn't use performance-based analysis and simulation tools directly, but they continued their study to make the necessary decisions to move on to that stage.

The participants started their study by examining the 3D site model given to them as a mass model. Immediately afterwards, they continued their studies by creating masses in Revit for the representation of the previous design studies they had performed in sketching environment. Since they thought of their designs as both 2D and 3D in the previous stage, they tried to do the modeling process quickly by knowing what they wanted to do from the beginning of the stage. At this stage, participants preferred to use the query feature of BIM schedules to make sure that they met design requirements by controlling the related criterion given in architectural program requirements.

When the mass modeling process for the first design alternative was over, the participants customized the overall energy analysis settings of the model by updating the specific data for each mass as they desired. At this stage, each participant tried to represent their designs visually and behaviorally as closely as possible in the direction of their own design ideas by adjusting the specific settings of masses and surfaces that they created. After the initial design alternatives were finalized in terms of creating mass modeling and defining conceptual energy settings, each participant used the remaining time to develop different design alternatives. At this point, all of the participants preferred to make small transformations and interferences at which they wanted to differentiate with their first design alternative for developing new design alternatives.

Although the participants at the end of the Stage II had completed their study as requested it was observed throughout the process that participants' command of the tools was not at the desired level and the troubles experienced in this direction that directly affected the process. Looking at the results after the implementations, the participants completed the implementation stage successfully, even though they experienced certain difficulties throughout the process.

The 120-min implementation in Stage II was found appropriate and adequate by the participants. The participants reported that they were able to complete the study and had no more action to do for this stage. During the implementation, each participant's computer screen was recorded via software.

4.4   Implementation Stage III: Design Improvement Toward Energy Efficiency

In Stage III, the participants were expected to evaluate the mass models they had developed in the previous stage in the context of Revit's conceptual energy modeling capabilities to obtain a more efficient energy performance. By the beginning of the process, the participants checked and arranged the energy analysis settings of the masses they had developed in the previous implementation and started to study by opening the energy analysis mode. At this stage, all of the participants took a conceptual energy analysis of the different mass alternatives they had realized and preferred to see the performance of each alternative and then compare them with each other. They thought about how to make their designs more energy efficient by looking at the analysis reports that had been provided to them by the tool's energy analysis capabilities. At this point, because the participants had limited knowledge and command of sustainability principles, they compared the available alternatives and determined the most effective solution. Thus, they tried to figure out which output in the analysis report matches with what input in the design model and how they could use this information to improve their designs.

After initial comparisons, the participants started to develop their design alternatives in line accordance with the inferences they made from the analysis report. From this stage onwards, each participant continued to develop their designs in terms of the aesthetic, functional and sustainability objectives. In this period, the participants were more interested in making small touches on the topics such as designing the solid/void ratio of the mass surfaces forming the facade, making partial transformations about the orientation and form of the mass designs, and selecting different conceptual materials according to the needs of each facade.

After the initial comparisons at the beginning of the Stage III, it was determined that the remaining design process developed cyclically as follows: (1) taking design decisions, (2) finalizing the modeling process, (3) updating of the required data entries, (4) performing the analysis process, and (5) evaluating the results and comparing with the other results. This process continued cyclically in this way until the implementation process was over and the participants indicated that they had achieved a satisfactory result.

At this stage, it was observed that the participants could use the interface provided by the tool more effectively and had less difficulty in command. However, because of having limited knowledge and command of sustainability principles, it was found that participants were not be able to provide enough theoretical and practical knowledge in an efficient manner and were not be able to benefit competently from the analysis and simulation outputs provided by the tool. Throughout the process, the participants were more engaged in the design development as they did through trial and error, and were not able to take full advantage of the features offered by the tool.

As the participants did more of the necessary actions at this stage by trial and error, it was not possible for the researchers to test the suitability of the 120-min implementation time in this context. On the other hand, implementation time for Stage III was found to be sufficient and appropriate by the participants. Participants reported that they were able to complete the study within the period. During the implementation stage, each participant's computer screen was recorded via a software.

4.5   Findings and Evaluations

In this study, the researchers examined the conceptual design practice, which was realized with the conceptual BIM approach by three participants, by using observation, interview and focus group methods. At the end of this process, we made some determinations about the conceptual BIM approach, process and it's tools. These findings and evaluations will be shared in this section.

The implementation process was started with sketching. Thus, it was provided that participants took their first design decisions in an environment where they were more familiar with, and also it was planned to protect the nature of the design process as much as possible. During Stage I, although they were not specifically requested of them, the participants took decisions on plan analysis, such as building layout and building circulation, while developing their designs. It was also seen that the participants frequently took notes on sketch paper and writing enhanced their cognitive activities. In interviews conducted after the implementations, the participants indicated that taking first design ideas with sketching and then improving them in conceptual BIM environment was a very effective way of working. They also emphasized that these two environments had different characteristics and capabilities for conceptual design phase which were supporting each other to make the process more efficient. In this context, participants indicated that it was more effective and easier to make the first design decisions in sketching environment where they could draw any complex form they wanted, but it was more difficult in BIM environment. On the other hand, no participant preferred to design very complex and organic forms, even in the sketch environment. Therefore, the question of whether these determinations are related to preferring the tool to which they are familiar with or whether it is based on a real restriction is still to be investigated.

In the mass modeling implementation during the Stage II, the participants interactively used 2D and 3D representation interfaces of the tool. All participants performed basic modeling operations in the 3D environment and preferred to use elevation and section representations for design review and detail modeling. Even in the stage of mass modeling, the formation of all the geometric and non-geometric elements which are parametrically connected with each other has been seen and used by the participants very usefully. At this point, after each revision on the design model the participants checked the rules of architectural program requirements to ensure that they went on the right direction. That situation showed that BIM's calculation and schedule capabilities are also useful at this stage. In addition to controlling the numerical data, some adjustments that take more time to be performing over the mass model have been assigned over schedules, gained time for the participants.

In this context; within the triangle of design problem, design thinking and modeling interface, the whole model can work parametrically, and the strength of the interaction between the geometric and numerical data provided seems to be an important factor. By this way, even this study does not aim for a parametric design implementation, participants benefited of using a parametrically associated working environment for modeling the masses, assigning presumptive attributes to the mass elements and checking whether the alternatives have met the requirements. With this feature, conceptual BIM tools offer different capabilities for mass modeling compared to other CAD tools and are able to differentiate the process.

In Stage III, the participants took an analysis of the design alternatives they developed and compared them to each other. From this moment on, it has been seen that the design process evolved from an intuitive to a systematic design approach. At this stage, participants were asked to evaluate their aesthetic and functional concerns coordinately in consideration with performative realities while developing design alternatives. Another important situation identified in Stage III is the conceptual energy analysis capabilities of the BIM environment need sustainability and performance-based design knowledge at a certain level. As participants did not have enough sustainable design experience, they did more of the design development study by trial and error and tried to figure out how to achieve a more efficient performance by comparing the different performance outputs of different alternatives.

In this context, the participants have reviewed mostly the Energy Use Intensity, Life Cycle Energy Cost, Renewable Energy Potential and Annual Carbon Emissions tables, which are presenting the result outcomes only. In addition, they have benefited from Monthly Heating Load and Monthly Cooling Load which they have found easier to read. The other outcomes of the analysis could not be understood easily by participants. This situation seems to be directly affecting and directing the design process, but the main problem in that case is based on participants' lack of experience about sustainability issues. So they focus more on the subject that they can evaluate to develop a solution. Despite this restrictive situation, all participants expressed that the decision support environment offered by the tool was an innovative and stimulating feature.

5   Conclusion and Future Works

The main objective of the study is to observe and explore how BIM can be used in conceptual design phase and also to investigate how and how effectively BIM can help architects during the process. To develop an understanding to these aims, a case study has been implemented. In previous section, we have described the implementation and discussed the findings of the study.

Kymmell [47] describes the basic concepts of human action and interaction as being interwoven with each other as visualization, understanding, communication and collaboration, and explains how the direct and indirect features of BIM have fed these four concepts. BIM offers a more effective and interactive work environment than traditional design approaches, with its powerful visualization and collaboration tools, and allows design practice to be maintained over many different participants, inputs and targets. Thus, it is now possible to incorporate many different factors, which are often overlooked or difficult to assess nowadays, into the design process. This situation is also directly related to conceptual BIM approach's contribution to conceptual design process. Kymmell explains this situation through the phrase "a picture is worth a thousand words" as follows: "then how much will a 3D model be worth, or a movie of a timed sequence of events?"

In a similar vein, Miller [48] has shown that short-term memory of individuals is limited to 7 ± 2 elements during data processing. Because of the assumption that design moves made during a problem-solving action are the representations of the minds at that moment are considered to be connected to each other in the range of 7 ± 2 moves [24]. Thus, as Kymmell points out, the building information model and all the inferences derived from it helps designers to search for a more effective design by playing a reminder and decision support role for many design criteria that are prone to ignoring in the conceptual design process and disappearing from the working memory.

BIM's ability to store, inference, and analyze the data related to the building serves as a decision support system for architects in conceptual design and serves as a reminder and a guide for the factors that architects value in decision making processes.

BIM offers a competitive drawing and modeling environment with a series of decision support capabilities which use the parametric relationship logic of BIM approach. By this way, designers can continue to design while they are considering both aesthetic, functional and also sustainable factors within a cyclical design process [49]. Moreover, there are more potential capabilities which BIM can offer in conceptual design phase such as estimation, analysis, and simulation which lead it to be more improved decision support system.

Beyond the focus of this study and the findings of the implementation, we noticed and determined some situations and topics that can be investigated in future to develop an deeper understanding about conceptual BIM approach, to find a way to improve it and also to reveal what tool capabilities we need to have in conceptual design phase which make BIM a better design and decision support tool.

First of all, we think that using protocol analysis as a supplementary method to our research methodology will be better to obtain more detailed data collection and also more innovative data analysis outcomes about how participants experience the process and how BIM interacts with its users' cognitive abilities. Furthermore, it will be useful to study with more crowded participant groups who are graduated from Faculty of Architecture with reasonable professional experience, have a good command with related BIM tools and have a basic knowledge about sustainability principles. With this setup, we believe that the implementation will be much more efficient which directly affects to the data collection and the outcomes. From another perspective, conceptual BIM approach can be investigated within a professional context which architects are dealing with a real design problem in order to complete a real design task. Such a study has its own benefits and provides to test conceptual BIM in a real setting with naturally composed conditions such as design task, time limitation, satisfaction level, assessment criterion, and so on.

In conclusion, BIM offers many benefits to its users not only for drafting and construction processes but also for conceptual design. It may have a way to become a better design tool and a decision support system. But, as we have mentioned before, it already has much more capabilities than conventional CAD tools in conceptual design phase.

References

1. Architecture 2030. http://goo.gl/o4FC5X. Last accessed 03 May 2017
2. The European Union: Directive 2012/27/EU of the European Parliament and of the Council of 25 October 2012. Official Journal of the European Union no. 55 (2012). doi:10.3000/19770677.L_2012.315.eng
3. Krygiel, E., Nies, B.: Green BIM: Successful Sustainable Design with Building Information Modeling. Wiley, Indianapolis (2008)
4. Gervásio, H., Santos, P., Martins, R., Simões da Silva, L.: A macrocomponent approach for the assessment of building sustainability in early stages of design. Build. Environ. 73, 256–270 (2014)
5. Granadeiro, V., Correia, J.R., Leal, V., Duarte, J.P.: Envelope-related energy demand: a design indicator of energy performance for residential buildings in early design stages. Energy Build. 61, 215–223 (2013)
6. Hong, T., Chou, S.K., Bong, T.Y.: Building simulation: an overview of developments and information sources. Build. Environ. 35(4), 347–361 (2000)
7. Gratia, E., De Herde, A.: Design of low energy office buildings. Energy Build. 35(5), 473–491 (2003)
8. Foqué, R.: Building knowledge in architecture. In: ASP/VUBPRESS/UPA (2010)
9. Foqué, R.: Building knowledge by design. In: Texto Apresentado na IV Jornadas Internacionales Sobre Investigación en Arquitectura y Urbanismo (2011)
10. Casakin, H.: Factors of design problem-solving and their contribution to creativity. Open House Int. 33(1), 46–60 (2008)
11. Woo, H.R.: Creative abilities in design. Int. J. Creat. Probl. Solving 15(1), 101–113 (2005)
12. Buchanan, R.: Design research and the new learning. Des. Issues 17(4), 3–23 (2001)
13. Galle, P., Kroes, P.: Science and design: identical twins? Des. Stud. 35(3), 201–231 (2014)
14. Galle, P.: Foundational and instrumental design theory. Des. Issues 27(4), 81–94 (2011)
15. Liu, Y.T.: Is designing one search or two? A model of design thinking involving symbolism and connectionism. Des. Stud. 17(4), 435–449 (1996)
16. Akin, O.: Exploration of the design process. Des. Methods Theor. 13(3/4), 115–119 (1979)
17. Oxman, R.: Cognition and design. Des. Stud. 17(4), 337–340 (1996)
18. Gero, J.S., Mc Neill, T.: An approach to the analysis of design protocols. Des. Stud. 19(1), 21–61 (1998)
19. Pinch, S., Sunley, P., Macmillen, J.: Cognitive mapping of creative practice: a case study of three English design agencies. Geoforum 41(3), 377–387 (2010)
20. Carmel-Gilfilen, C.: Creating mature thinkers in interior design: pathways of intellectual develpment. J. Int. Des. 35(3), 1–20 (2010)
21. Goldschmidt, G.: Problem representation versus domain of solution in architectural design teaching. J. Archit. Plan. Res. 6(3), 204–215 (1989)
22. Goel, V.: Sketches of Thought. The MIT Press, Cambridge (1995)
23. Alexander, C.: Notes on the Synthesis of Form. Harvard University Press, Cambridge (1964)
24. Goldschmidt, G.: Linkography: Unfolding the Design Process. MIT Press, Cambridge (2014)

25. Do, E.Y.L.: Drawing marks, acts, and reacts: toward a computational sketching interface for architectural design. AI EDAM **16**(03), 149–171 (2002)
26. Lawson, B.: Design in Mind. Architectural Press, London (1994)
27. Herbert, D.M.: Architectural Study Drawings. Van Nostrand Reinhold, New York (1993)
28. Graves, M.: Necessity for drawing-tangible speculation. Archit. Des. **47**(6), 384–394 (1977)
29. Schön, D.: The Design Studio. RIBA, London (1985)
30. NBIS, Building Information Modeling (BIM). http://www.wbdg.org/building-information-modeling-bim. Last accessed 03 May 2017
31. GSA, GSA BIM Guide. https://goo.gl/3Vamrd. Last accessed 03 May 2017
32. Garber, R.: Optimisation stories: the impact of building information modeling on contemporary design practice. Archit. Des. **79**(2), 6–13 (2009)
33. Eastman, C., Teicholz, P., Sacks, R.: BIM Handbook: A Guide to Building Information Modeling for Owners, Managers, Designers. Engineers and Contractors. Wiley, Hoboken (2011)
34. Deutsch, R.: BIM and Integrated Design: Strategies for Architectural Practice. Wiley, Hoboken (2011)
35. Eastman, C., Tiecholz, P., Sacks, R., Liston, K.: Building Information Modeling Handbook: A Guide to Building Information Modeling for Owners, Managers, Designers, Engineers and Contractors. Wiley, Hoboken (2008)
36. Azhar, S.: Building information modeling (BIM): trends, benefits, risks, and challenges for the AEC industry. Leadersh. Manag. Eng. **2011**(11), 241–252 (2011)
37. buildingSmart. www.buildingsmart.com
38. AGC, The Contractors' Guide to BIM. http://www.agc.org
39. Schlueter, A., Thesseling, F.: Building information model based energy/exergy performance assessment in early design stages. Autom. Constr. **18**(2), 153–163 (2009)
40. Attia, S., De Herde, A.: Early design simulation tools for net zero energy buildings: a comparison of ten tools, In: Proceedings of Building Simulation 2011: 12th Conference of International Building Performance Simulation Association, Sydney, Australia, pp. 94–101 (2011)
41. Denzin, N.K., Lincoln, Y.S.: The Sage Handbook of Qualitative Research. Sage, Thousand Oaks (2005)
42. Knight, A., Ruddock, L.: Advanced Research Methods in the Built Environment. Wiley-Blackwell, Oxford (2008)
43. Miles, M.B., Huberman, A.M.: Qualitative Data Analysis: An Expanded Sourcebook. Sage, Thousand Oaks (1994)
44. Mack, N., Woodsong, C., MacQueen, K.M., Guest, G., Namey, E.: Qualitative Research Methods: A Data Collector's Field Guide. Family Health International, North Carolina (2005)
45. Patton, M.Q.: Qualitative Evaluation and Research Methods. SAGE, Newbury Park (1990)
46. Berg, B.: Qualitative Research Methods for the Social Sciences, 4th edn. Allyn and Bacon, Boston (2000)
47. Kymmell, W.: Building Information Modeling: Planning and Managing Construction Projects with 4D CAD and Simulations. McGraw Hill Professional, New York (2008)
48. Miller, G.A.: The magical number seven, plus or minus two: some limits on our capacity for processing information. Psychol. Rev. **63**(2), 81–97 (1956)
49. Azhar, S., Brown, J., Farooqui, R.: BIM-based sustainability analysis: an evaluation of building performance analysis software. In: Proceedings of 45th ASC Annual Conference, Florida, USA (2009)

Challenges in Raising Digital Awareness in Architectural Curriculum

Guzden Varinlioglu[⊠], Lale Basarir, Ozgur Genca,
and Zeynep Vaizoglu

Izmir University of Economics, Sakarya Caddesi no:156, 35330 Izmir, Turkey
guzdenv@gmail.com

Abstract. The issue of bringing digital technology into architectural education necessitates a paradigmatic change. Achieving this change within a conventional framework presents a number of challenges. However, challenges are presented by the rapid change of technological tools and the frustration of updating the architectural scholarship, especially for schools with a traditional curriculum. This paper focuses on a case study of an update in the architectural curriculum for a CAD course. An approach to understanding the impact of digital tools and methods on digital awareness and a sustainable development of the students and pedagogy are presented, discussed, and demonstrated. Based on questionnaires, the students' learning outcomes are evaluated.

Keywords: Digital awareness · Architectural curricula · Learning outcome

1 Introduction

The integration of digital awareness in the architectural curriculum is a common challenge for design educators. Parametric and algorithmic design tools alongside advanced representation tools necessitate an update in traditional pedagogical methods and tools. Since 2001, when Mark et al. initiated a discussion in eCAADe conference on the digital architectural curriculum, the theoreticians, practitioners, and educators have offered a range of studies and recommendations. To date, there are several studies [1–6] focusing on the implementation of computational design tools in the design education. In most of these cases, the availability of tools and methods and the available resources in digital design setups are flexible, open to change and update. However, even for these advanced setups, there are few studies on the students' learning outcomes through digital fabrication, representation, and thinking courses, and/or which skills are most needed. Especially in traditional design schools with fewer available tools, the learning/teaching strategies are important, in particular in the junior years of architectural design education. In order to guide the current state of change in architectural education curriculum, it is important to ask certain questions. How can the new generations of students develop an awareness of digital architecture within the constraints of a traditional curriculum? Within limited allocated classes on computation and computerization, how can educators concentrate on building awareness using deep learning/teaching strategy? How can we teach/mentor/guide the students to learn without reprogramming them? How can we increase their digital awareness? With

G. Çağdaş et al. (Eds.): CAAD Futures 2017, CCIS 724, pp. 136–150, 2017.
DOI: 10.1007/978-981-10-5197-5_8

these in mind, referring to the teaching method of "learning by doing", this paper focuses on pedagogical strategies based on the learning outcomes of the students of FFD201 Computer Aided Architectural Graphics.

In this paper, within the above-mentioned constraints, it is important to note that the studio setup is discrete, that is, the studio is not fully integrated to the other lecture classes. Within a very limited weight on computational courses, there are only two required courses on CAD: FFD104 Computer Aided Technical Drawing, and FFD201 Computer Aided Architectural Graphics. The course outline presented in this paper is a digital architectural graphics course (FFD201), a 4-hour class for 14 weeks. At this stage, we might say that the first course (FFD104) followed Oxman's statement that "theories and methods of digital design can no longer be conceptualized as the merging of computational tools with conventional formulations of design". The main focus of this paper explores the implications of this statement within a traditional course setup [7]. The course and the student outcomes presented in this paper reflect the integration of digital tools of representation within a conventional formulation. The study needed two major challenges: the skills to be covered within the course and the effort needed to incorporate the design strategies. The constraints will be discussed later in the paper, such as students' lack of design background and adaptive problem solving capabilities from their previous education, or the integrated studio model of their first-year architectural education.

With the widespread use of low-budget virtual reality (VR) devices, the high demand on Building Information Modeling (BIM) skills, and the affordable computer aided manufacturing (CAM), the architectural curricula and discourse have undergone change. Several studies have been conducted to determine the extent to which methods by which the digital paradigm shift in architectural discourse is currently integrated to the architectural curriculum. Mandhar and Mandhar [8] propose a design teaching approach of BIM to bridge the gap between the graduate skill sets and the changing needs of the profession. Horne and Thompson [9] present a research on the integration of VR within the built environment curriculum, and aim to investigate the role of VR and 3D modeling on the architectural curriculum. Celani [1] discusses the role of the new digital fabrication laboratories in architectural education. However, few studies display the student learning outcomes via digital design and fabrication courses, with a specific focus on the junior years of architectural design education. Interaction with BIM, VR, and CAM in the early stages of architectural curricula can help shape later education. However, there is limited time allocated to computational courses in the current curriculum. Replacing the conventional digital tools with more advanced digital tools and methods may risk failing to cover the basic skills needed for architectural practice. To evaluate our approach for integrating digital thinking, application, and experience in architectural education, this paper aims to analyze the process and the outcome of second-year coursework at our university.

2 Definition of Terms

Due to the widespread use of technology, it is necessary for architectural education to produce well-qualified and well-prepared professionals. Employers demand that graduates not only have the required knowledge, but also the appropriate skills to be effective and productive in the workspace. To adapt to these challenges, universities need to redesign their academic models. Besides the highly demanding professional expectations, academia in design faculties demands highly sophisticated outcomes. The professional requirements might bring an education system which resembles a version of vocational high school education, focusing on non-academic skills such as preparing students for only supportive roles in the profession. Technical courses which focus on skill building are (e.g. drawing courses of an architectural curriculum) in particular risk of losing its ability to evolve in parallel to the ever-changing technology, which lead to changes in designerly way of thinking. Due to the rapid changes, especially compared to past centuries of the profession, it gets more difficult to keep pace with the demands of the professional world. While maintaining an academic approach for further development, it is also necessary to provide students the ability to improve and adapt themselves in this rapidly changing world. To discuss further we present the constraints in the process of building digital awareness in the architectural curriculum by describing the academic context including the educational background of students, the overall curriculum of the faculty, and the background of the instructors.

Besides some efforts of extending the duration of the program one more year, architecture education in Turkey, i.e. the undergraduate B. ARCH degree, is a 4-year university degree. Parallel to European and American models, undergraduate architecture departments in Turkey have various education systems and methods [10]. Following Duarte's discrete studio model, in some universities, drawing and representation courses are separate courses; while in others these courses are integrated to design studio [11]. Based on the declarations of EU and International Union of Architects (UIA), there was an effort to extend the architectural education to 5 years [12]. Moreover, any attempts by individual departments to create solutions for insufficient time allocated to design education are restricted and controlled by the regulations of YÖK, the Council of Higher Education in Turkey [13]. In the last decades, creativity classes are included in primary and secondary education curricula to create a designerly way of thinking, as stated in the "design strategy document and action plan" of 2014–2016 [14]. As stated in the same document, the insufficient design culture in Turkey is rooted in insufficient basic design education in the pre-university curriculum. Some minor efforts aimed at stimulating a design culture were made in the form of workshops organized by the Ankara Chamber of Architects [15]. However, such limited efforts are still far from creating a substantial change in the background formation of the high school students prior to the architectural design education.

Within these constraints in updating digital courses, the students' lack of autonomous capabilities is one of the main challenges. This results in digital courses becoming technical courses, in which various software is taught mot-a-mot, leading to difficulties in the implementation of digital tools into design education. Students' lack of design thinking leads to a search for specific answers, rather than defining the problem, and following the design process towards generative results.

At Izmir University of Economics (IUE), design education is relatively new, and the first two years of the architecture department curriculum is partly integrated to other design departments. The first year of design education at IUE comprises several interdisciplinary courses aiming to teach students the designerly way of thinking rather than skills specific to professions. Students from five departments (architecture, interior

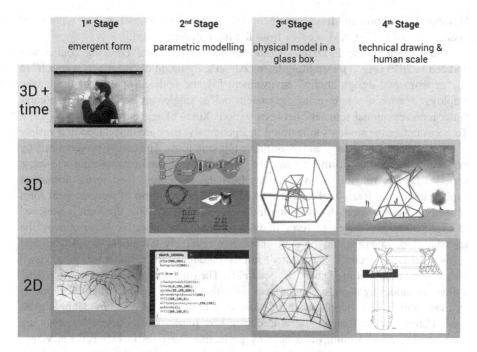

Fig. 1. Stages of the inter-representational transfer in FFD104

architecture, industrial design, visual communication design, and fashion design) are introduced to the materials and the tools for the first time, since there are no basic design classes at K12 level education in Turkey. In terms of course schedule and credits, the emphasis is on this two-semester interdisciplinary design studio FFD 101/102 that are based on the Bauhaus pedagogical approach. The students work with color, shape, and material, independent from function, space, and context [16]. Running parallel to this studio class, another approach is Introduction to Architecture (ARCH 101/102), where students learn to express form using analog techniques and understand the correlation between 2D and 3D representations of architectural forms, as well as being exposed architectural vocabulary. In addition, in the first semester of first year during an interdisciplinary drawing course, FFD 111, students learn various freehand and technical drawing techniques, including orthographic and perspective projection. The aim of the course is to develop basic drawing skills that are not specific to any profession. The second semester of first year includes another drawing course, which is also interdisciplinary, but one that is limited to architecture, interior architecture, and industrial design departments. This course, called "FFD 104 - Computer Aided Technical Drawing" will be described in more detail here, since it is the first course to introduce CAD/CAM to students [17]. Similar to the first year core basic design studio, the computational course (FFD 104) reflects the pedagogy of teaching architectural elements, human scale, and abstract forms without functional requirements. This interdisciplinary approach as described above introduces a discrete studio model, while requiring independent professional courses for each discipline [3].

However, an important disadvantage of this pedagogical model is the separation/ dissociation of CAD/CAM courses from the main design studio.

The content of the FFD104 - Computer Aided Technical Drawing course was updated in 2015 (Fig. 1). Departing from Oxman's argument of "design as research" in an "experimental design studio" environment [5], the updated content of the course employs a reverse engineering approach on a single project that incorporates "inter-representational transfer" between various kinds of representational tools [17]. To accustomize the students to learning independently, they are introduced to a variety of representation, modeling, and algorithmic thinking tools. The course project starts by exploring an emergent form (in this case, foam bubbles), and representing it using a variety of tools ranging from video to freehand sketching. The initial formative exploration of the foam bubbles is followed by video recording of the emergent form generation process. Then, by sampling the emergent shapes in 3D, the form is sketched to explore various stages of form finding process. The objective is to convey the knowledge of layering and timeline through a relatively complicated video editing software. In the second phase, the form is parametrically remodeled in a visual scripting environment in 3D and recoded in 2D. The digital model is later transferred to a physical model by using a Grasshopper definition for finding the structural elements by triangulation. The second phase is followed by building a physical model in a 'glass box'. Using this physical model placed in a box frame, 2D technical drawings are produced by using a plump and later by projecting the lines in between the views. Before converting to CAD format, the human scale is introduced together with basic functional requirements. Finally, the drawings are explored in representation software and placed into a web-based digital portfolio. In other words, the course allowed students to explore the generation and representation of complex forms (e.g. by projection, triangulation), and facilitate the transition between different media and representation techniques.

The second year of architectural education has two classes using CAD/CAM skills. Being the first studio on architectural design, the second year studio focuses on spatial explorations, architectural forms, and elements in relation to our bodies and senses. Visual, environmental, structural, and functional aspects are considered throughout the design process. The students focus on two consecutive phases of design: creation and delivery of information. They first come up with a design idea and then deliver representation of that set of ideas. The inter-representational transfer in several design ideas and tools are favored to display their skills in representation, architectural conventions, as well as a designerly way of thinking. To raise this awareness, we simplify the design problem and limit the length of the design stage focusing on process of their design.

Based on the student evaluation of second-year CAD classes and personal observations of faculty in their second-year architectural design studio, we explore ways of integrating CAD/CAM tools into the curriculum. To avoid the disadvantages of the discrete studio model, computational design tools and methods were applied in a separate course, entitled "FFD201 - Computer Aided Architectural Graphics," combining the traditional course with CAD/CAM skill building.

3   Computer-Aided Design Classes

3.1   Student Setup

The student body in 2016–2017 fall semester was affected by exceptional circumstances, both in IUE and in Turkey. Several universities were closed at short notice by YÖK (Council of Higher Education in Turkey) and their students were allocated to other universities. This change occurred without time for universities to adjust their syllabi or hire new staff. Therefore, in 2016–2017 fall semester, out of the 170 students taking FFD 201 Computer Aided Architectural Graphics course, 18% had originally started their undergraduate studies at different universities' Architecture or Interior Architecture departments. In addition, 35% of the students were from IUE Department of Interior Architecture and Environmental Design (IAED), and had not taken FFD 104 Computer Aided Technical Drawing course in its updated format as described above, but in its old format, with a traditional syllabus teaching orthographic, axonometric, and perspective drawing by hand and computer [17]. Finally, only 47% were from IUE Department of Architecture, and had taken the updated FFD 104 Computer Aided Technical Drawing course the previous year. Thanks to the updated syllabus of FFD 104, these students are more likely to be accustomed to independent researching and learning, and have more experience with inter-representational transfer and parametric tools. In brief, the class consisted of three groups of students with different backgrounds in CAD studies.

The instructors of the course also had varying backgrounds and preferences. Of the 7 instructors of the course, approximately 30% were proficient in teaching architectural conventions; another 40% preferred to work with computerized representation; and the final 30% were experts in computational design. Hence, the group had the opportunity to assign instructors to subjects/steps of the project according to their expertise.

3.2   FFD201 Computer Aided Architectural Graphics

This second-year course is conducted as a single unit for both interior design and architectural design students. The challenge was to offer a syllabus covering the basics of 3D modeling, architectural graphics, and professional conventions in a single one-semester course. As this is the second and the last of the required CAD courses, it was necessary to incorporate several topics into it. The course introduces the essential techniques of architectural graphics in two and three dimensions, and it stresses their incorporation and application within the virtual technology. The learning outcomes are:

This study develops a critical outlook to current approaches in design computing:

- To be able to realize architectural and interior architectural drawings by using the conventions of technical drawing through CAD
- To be able to realize three-dimensional drawing by using different software through CAD
- To be able to present three-dimensional models through rendering.

Information constituting the initial design created in the form of primitive forms (e.g. sugar cubes) exists at the core stream of the course. Students are not expected to develop their designs any further than the minimum initial requirements. Instead, they are repeatedly encouraged to re-elaborate the initial design within a variety of media. Therefore, the same information is remodeled with different tools for representation (Table 1).

Table 1. Syllabus for the CAD course for 2nd year 1st semester 2016. Software brands are listed for information purposes only and are subject to change as the course is updated.

Content			Software		Period
			Cloud based	Desktop based	(weeks)
3D	3D design of a house	Design of architectural elements and space organization with 3D diagrams	Autodesk 123D Catch App	Autodesk Autocad/3Ds Max, Rhinoceros, SketchUp Pro	1
	3D modelling of a house	Detailed 3D model with revisions			2
Digital fabrication		Quiz 1		Autodesk Meshmixer	1
Render		Creating scenes		Vray plug-in	1
	Render of the designed house	Material and environment	HDRI maps	CrazyBump	1
	Post-processing for rendered scenes			Adobe Photoshop	1
VR			SketchFab		
2D	Drawing set with architectural conventions	2D orthographic drawings the house from 3D model together with architectural conventions		Autodesk Autocad	3
	Presentation	Refining render and technical drawing outputs		Adobe Photoshop	2
				Adobe Illustrator	
BIM		Quiz 2			1
Graphics	Conventions and plotting			Adobe Photoshop	2
	Web portfolio design	Language/presentation		Adobe Illustrator	

3.3   Methodology

Starting with modular integrity of sugar cubes of orthogonal geometries, students organized a small-scale living unit with minimum requirements of a living room, wet areas, and a bedroom, all placed in an imaginary landscape (Fig. 2). The modular nature of sugar cubes allowed students to play with the architectonics of various volumes of equal size, and to decide on the proportions of subspaces. If needed, they melted, sanded, and trimmed the sugar cubes to achieve organic forms. Then, using photo-modeling software, they documented the process of form generation with their mobile phones. This short exercise is followed by "Hello World" week, referring to the introduction of the latest technology in computational design. Recent and future capabilities of visualization, computation, and fabrication in architectural practice are presented in relation to the assignments in the syllabus. At this stage, course instructors held two opposing ideas. On the one hand, there was the potential benefits from innovations made possible by BIM software, such as manageability of huge amounts of information and data, and collaboration; on the other hand, there were concerns that without knowledge of solid modeling, architectural elements, and materials, students would be limited by BIM software, specifically their components of various building elements. To avoid unnecessary risks, we decided to continue with conventional CAD models, while letting the students select the 3D modeling software. Instead of teaching them specific software, we introduced common commands and their alternatives on different software, and taught analytical thinking for modelling purposes. When the expected skill building of CAD modeling software is achieved, we introduced the students to BIM software at two stages. First, the main properties of a BIM software was introduced as the central model (the database holding all the information of the virtual building), the object base rather than a geometry base of information, and the way drafting standards are represented in such an environment. Second, the massing/morphing tools of BIM software enabled conventional

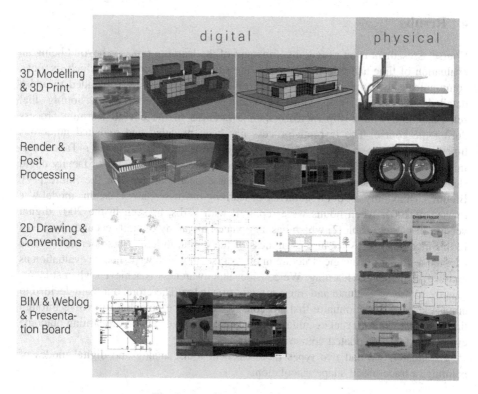

Fig. 2. Sample projects in FFD201

sketching practice to continue within this software environment. The latter was necessary for resolving the conflict stated among instructors that the BIM environment limits creativity at the early stages of design.

Within the limits of this course, the use of solid modeling has the potential to lead to three consecutive topics: Building Information Modeling (BIM), parametric modeling (form finding), and digital fabrication (CAM). We chose to finalize the 3D modeling by digital fabrication, as it introduces a rather new type of production, accessible by using conventional solid modeling programs. The 3D model obtained during the initial weeks of the course, subsequently became a playground in which students experienced different digital rendering and post-processing techniques. As required by the 3D to 2D flow of the course, the aim is to encourage students to think and design three-dimensionally. Orthographic drawings and drawing conventions are introduced after the completion of intensive 3D work. Producing conventional orthographic drawings from the house model creates a fluent transition, since students are in control of the three dimensionality of their design. This process is followed by 2D rendering techniques for the digital presentation of the orthographic drawings. During the final weeks of the course, in addition to the digital presentations via web portfolios, the physicality of the drawings are emphasized by introducing plotting techniques and physical portfolios.

4   Results

Course assessment is an essential component of the learning process, beyond being an evaluation of time and effort. It provides the students a platform with which they can communicate their views about their learning [18]. Therefore, we intended to add a detailed student self and course evaluation into the process envisioning that self-evaluation would help increase their awareness of the overall learning process during the course. The learning process has been modeled and revisited numerous times by educators, and among the most influential models is Bloom's Taxonomy. Initially it was intended to provide a database where various groups of faculty could share their assessment tools for use in similar educational items in the future [19]. Bloom's Taxonomy set out a hierarchy of learning processes; however, this model was revised in 2001, when nouns were replaced with verbs, as seen in the 2007 digital version of model (Table 2) which has an updated hierarchy of skill sets and objectives [20]. Since our goal is to raise awareness of the digital thinking in students, we have adopted a similar pedagogic structure in our course, in which we conceive evaluation as an integral element of learning. We consider that awareness is achieved when students gain the ability to evaluate and transfer their knowledge. Therefore, our team decided to employ a basic questionnaire that we considered had the potential to evolve through time and that would reveal eventually reveal an alternative version of learning outcome evaluation for our updated course FFD 201.

Eventually, we had two types of assessment tools: analog and digital modes of painting, a trace-based shape calculation.

Table 2. Andrew Churches's suggestion for "Bloom's Digital Taxonomy".

		Knowledge dimension			
		Factual	Conceptual	Procedural	Metacognitive
Cognitive process dimension	Remember	List	Recognize	Recall	Identify
	Understand	Summarize	Classify	Clarify	Predict
	Apply	Respond	Provide	Carryout	Use
	Analyze	Select	Differentiate	Integrate	Deconstruct
	Evaluate	Check	Determine	Judge	Reflect
	Create	Generate	Assemble	Design	Create

- An instructor team to assess and give feedback on students' learning process, through assignments and quizzes during and at the end of the semester,
- Students' self-assessment of their own learning outcomes and evaluations of the delivery of the course, through a questionnaire.

To evaluate the learning outcomes, students complete a questionnaire evaluating the challenges faced, the methods used in the class, and the effort needed in this learning process. The questions and the students' further her comments can be classified as four approaches:

- Level of Expertise-Based: Students were mentored by instructors with different levels of expertise at different domains, and their expectation for the learning outcomes were monitored.
- Content-Based: The importance of the order of delivery of the content was highlighted in the following comment: *"Also, some things had to be taught at the beginning of the semester. For example..."*
- Self-Assessment-Based: Students were encouraged to evaluate themselves in terms of course outcomes and how they perceived their own learning processes.
- Physical Conditions-Based: Among basic concerns of students were the studio population, and physical aspects of learning environments in general, for example, heating. One comment was: *"There are too many students in one studio to learn these subjects efficiently"*.

Initially, there were only two approaches, i.e. content and self-assessment based. The above classification evolved after receiving student responses and comments, and two further items were added: Level of expertise-based and physical conditions-based evaluations.

The questionnaire encourages comments and suggestions for both positive and negative evaluation. Content-base was surveyed with the following questionnaire items:

- I gained experience on quick mass sketching (Through "Sugar Cubes", "123D Catch App" Exercises). On a linear scale of one to four from "Not Really" to "Definitely", with 68.4% positive response.

- I have experienced how to easily make 3D sketches of structures in various software options. "Not Really" to "Yesss!", with 70.4% positive response.
- Gained experience in 3D modeling of a building in various software environments. "Disagree" to "Definitely", with 80.3% positive response.
- Improved my rendering skills. "Disagree" to "Definitely", 67.8% positive
- I gained experience in preparing 3D models for 3D printing". "Not Sure" to "Yesss!", with 78.3% positive response.
- I can present a building design to anyone by getting them to navigate it virtually (SketchFab Exercises). "Not Really" to "Definitely", with 78.3% positive response.
- I have learned the process required to get a 3D printout for my projects. "Not Really" to "Definitely", with 78.3% positive response.
- I can submit a project to the Municipality tomorrow and guarantee my project to pass (Conventions) "Not Really" to "Definitely", 56.5% positive.
- I now have experience in presentation techniques within various environments "Not Really" to "Definitely", with 66.4% positive response.
- I have learned the techniques for getting plots for my projects. "Not Really" to "Definitely", with 83.5% positive response.

Another content-based evaluation e.g. multiple choice grid was presented for subjective evaluation on the difficulty of the content of each course. The respondents had to choose one of four levels of difficulty: "Extremely Hard", "Average", "Easy", and "Very Easy". The results provided the following ranking in terms of difficulty, descending from the hardest to easiest; 3D rendering, rendering for VR, building information modeling (BIM), portfolio, architectural drafting conventions, 3D modeling, 3D printing and massing with sugar cubes (Fig. 3).

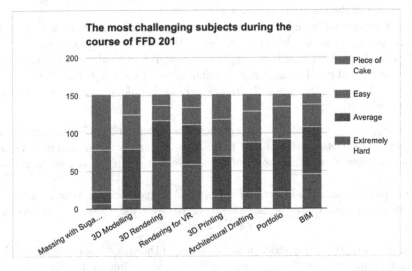

Fig. 3. Bar chart of "The most challenging subjects during the course of FFD201"

Apart from a possible objective measurement of difficulty level for each subject, it is important for our team to understand students' perceptions of the underlying factors that affect the difficulty of each subject. Therefore, we prepared another self-assessment question concerning the learning abilities and circumstances of students. Self-assessment based evaluation on a multiple-choice grid revealed ratings on four evaluation comments. Responses to the statement "It is impossible to learn by myself", from highest to the lowest rate were: Rendering for VR, 3D Rendering, 3D printing, Building Information Modeling (BIM), 3D Modeling, Architectural Drafting Conventions, Portfolio, Massing with Sugar Cubes.

To gauge the success of the self-learning process for each exercise, students were asked to complete the statement: "The subject that I could self-learn by devoting extra out-of-class hours is ……". In this, students were given multiple choice answers: It is impossible to learn by myself/Couldn't find enough resources/Repeating in-class tasks is enough for doing the assignments and applications/I didn't have extra time for learning (Fig. 4).

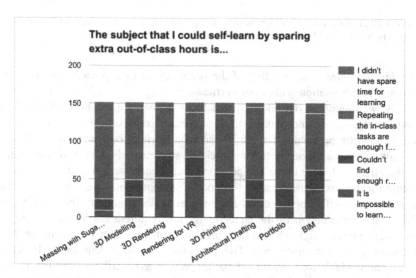

Fig. 4. Bar chart of "The subject that I could self-learn by sparing extra out-of-class hours is…"

Level of expertise-based evaluation, i.e. multiple-choice grid, was surveyed with the questionnaire items: "I believe working on the following subjects will contribute to my future study and work." The students rated each item on the provided list of exercises by selecting from the following ratings: (1) "It was unnecessary, should be removed from the course; (2) Not sure whether it will serve me or not; (3) Happy to have learned it; (4) Would be better if delivered in a different way, with different methods (Fig. 5). The evaluation revealed a consensus that all course content would definitely contribute to students' expected level of expertise. However, approximately 30% had some reservations in terms of course content delivery methods. It can therefore be inferred that teaching methods could be enhanced by collecting more data,

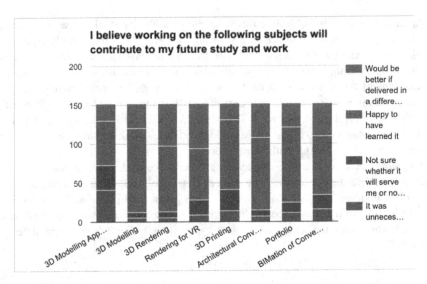

Fig. 5. Bar chart of the answer of "I believe working on the following subjects will contribute to my future study and work"

and gaining a greater understanding of the pedagogy of raising awareness of digital architectural representation within our curriculum.

Finally, we monitored our findings in matrices, allowing our team to evaluate each exercise in terms of its contribution to the aimed learning outcomes. This is a preliminary data collection phase for our research on learning outcome assessment, and will constitute a basis for our further research. 80 students volunteered to contribute to further inquiries and were invited to provide contact addresses. A planned follow-up evaluation for the next semester aims to improve students' self-assessment of learning highlighting their skills improvement, and broader understanding of their profession.

During the introduction of the challenging skill requirements for the course, the students were encouraged to choose their preferred software since no specific software was recommended by the instructors. The instructors advised students on the limits and constraints of available software on the market, as well as describing their own level of software expertise. As students had basic knowledge of a variety of digital tools and software from the prerequisite/preceding course, e.g. FFD104, they had gained an understanding of the main concepts common to modeling software, instead of simply learning step-by-step about a single software/product. This approach gave students sufficient flexibility to operate across various platforms and interfaces, based on a core understanding of the operation of computer graphics software in the 3D environment. This was possible because the commands, menus, and methods of 3D modeling software are widely standardized.

5 Conclusion

This study explores the pedagogical strategies that are aimed to encourage students to explore digital architecture and increase their digital awareness within the limits of a traditional curriculum. The implementation of digital tools in design education is discussed with particular reference to the analysis and outcome of second-year coursework. By means of a simple design problem, the students are encouraged to experiment with different software and media, exploring various computational and representational techniques. A generally positive response from the students is evident in the evaluation of the learning outcomes at four levels.

The 3D models presented in this paper may be classified as CAD and formation models according to Oxman's definition [7]; furthermore, the coursework utilizes computers only for representation and parametric levels during the course [6], and does not cover all the paradigmatic classes of digital design levels and computerized methods. However, our main aim is to introduce and explore computer aided information modelling (CAIM) in this course; therefore, we are aware of the need for the integration of further levels of 3D modelling and computerized models into the design courses in an updated curriculum.

Most architecture schools in Turkey approach digital representation tools in education via discrete pedagogical models, due to the insufficiency of the technical infrastructure and/or lack of experience of the design studio tutors. In this study we observed that integrated pedagogical modeling had the potential to provide novice architecture students with the adaptability necessary for the digital comprehension of digital fabrication, virtual reality and information-modeling processes. Until further research produces wider ranging results allowing a fundamental shift, our attempt of integrating computational tools into conventional methods can serve as a guide to helping students develop an awareness of digital design, especially when allocated courses are limited. Especially, method of "introducing tools", without specifically teaching them may enable the required flexibility for future applications. Therefore, this study may be considered as an initial attempt to develop integrated pedagogical models as the basis for the development of architecture curricula in the future.

Acknowledgements. We would like to thank, Sema Alacam, Gunes Atakan Peksen, Metin Sahin, Selin Anal and Zeynep Edes for their valuable support in conducting these experimental courses and Murat Kumbaracı and Seyit Koyuncu for sharing their course materials.

References

1. Celani, G.: Digital fabrication laboratories: pedagogy and impacts on architectural education. Nexus Netw. J. **14**(3), 469–482 (2012)
2. Cross, N.: Styles of learning, designing and computing. Des. Stud. **6**(3), 157–162 (1985)
3. Duarte, J., Celani, G., Pupo, R.: Inserting computational technologies in architectural curricula. In: Gu, N., Wang, X. (eds.) Computational Design Methods and Technologies: Applications in CAD, CAM and CAE Education, pp. 390–411. IGI Global, Hershey (2011)

4. Mark, E., Martens, B., Oxman, R.: Preliminary stages of CAAD education. Autom. Constr. **12**(6), 661–670 (2003)
5. Oxman, R.: Digital architecture as a challenge for design pedagogy: theory, knowledge, models and medium. Des. Stud. **29**(2), 99–120 (2008)
6. Kotnik, T.: Digital architectural design as exploration of computable functions. Int. J. Archit. Comput. **8**(1), 1–16 (2010)
7. Oxman, R.: Digital design thinking: in the new design is the new pedagogy. In: CAADRIA 2006 Proceedings of 11th International Conference on Computer Aided Architectural Design Research in Asia, Kumamoto, Japan, pp. 37–46 (2006)
8. Mandhar, M., Mandhar, M.: BIMing the architectural curricula: integrating Building Information Modelling (BIM) in architectural education. International Association for Engineering and Management Education (2016)
9. Horne, M., Thompson, E.M.: The role of virtual reality in built environment education. J. Educ. Built Environ. **3**(1), 5–24 (2008)
10. Nalçakan, H., Polatoğlu, Ç.: Türkiye'deki ve dünyadaki mimarlık eğitiminin karşılaştırmalı analizi ile küreselleşmenin mimarlık eğitiminin etkisinin irdelenmesi. Megaron **3**(1), 79–103 (2008)
11. Gökmen, H., Sayar, Y., Süer, D.: Yeniden yapılandırma sürecinde mimarlık eğitimine eleştirel bir bakış. Mimarlık **337**, 63–67 (2007)
12. MOBBİG XXIV Toplantı Sonuç Bildirgesi (2007)
13. Özelgül, E.: Universality of architectural education and particularity of educational institutions of architecture: a critical and comparative look at four educational institutions of architecture in Turkey. Master thesis, Middle East Technical University, Ankara, Turkey (2009, unpublished)
14. Tasarım strateji belgesi ve eylem planı (2014–2016), Resmi Gazete, 29163, Başbakanlık Basımevi, Ankara, Turkey (2014)
15. Gülay Taşçı, B.: Çocuk-mimarlık çalışmalarının değerlendirilmesi ve ilköğretim için yapılı çevre eğitim programı önerisi. Doctoral dissertation, Dokuz Eylül University, Izmir, Turkey (2014, unpublished)
16. Varinlioglu, G., Halici, S.M., Alacam, S.: Computational thinking and the architectural curriculum: simple to complex or complex to simple? In: Österlund, T., Markkanen, P. (eds.), Complexity & Simplicity—Proceedings of the 34th eCAADe Conference, 1, Oulu, Finland, pp. 253–259 (2016a)
17. Varinlioğlu, G., Alaçam, S., Başarır, L., Genca, Ö., Üçok, I.: Bilgisayar destekli teknik çizimde yeni yaklaşımlar: temsil araçları arası dönüsüm. Yapı **419**, 137–141 (2016)
18. Lindström, L.: Creativity: what is it? can you assess it? can it be taught? J. Art Des. Educ. **25**, 53–66 (2006)
19. Savic, M., Kashef, M.: Learning outcomes in affective domain within contemporary architectural curricula. Int. J. Technol. Des. Educ. **23**(4), 987–1004 (2013)
20. Doyle, S., Senske, N.: Exploring learning objectives for digital design in architectural education. In: Architecture Conference Proceedings and Presentations, p. 86 (2016)

SILVEREYE – The Implementation of Particle Swarm Optimization Algorithm in a Design Optimization Tool

Judyta M. Cichocka[1]([✉]) [iD], Agata Migalska[2], Will N. Browne[3], and Edgar Rodriguez[4]

[1] Faculty of Architecture, Wroclaw University of Technology, Wrocław, Poland
judyta.cichocka@gmail.com
[2] Faculty of Electronics, Wroclaw University of Technology, Wrocław, Poland
agata.migalska@pwr.edu.pl
[3] School Engineering and Computer Science, Victoria University of Wellington, Wellington, New Zealand
will.browne@ecs.vuw.ac.nz
[4] School of Architecture and Design, Victoria University of Wellington, Wellington, New Zealand
edgar.rodriguez@vuw.ac.nz

Abstract. Engineers and architects are now turning to use computational aids in order to analyze and solve complex design problems. Most of these problems can be handled by techniques that exploit Evolutionary Computation (EC). However existing EC techniques are slow [8] and hard to understand, thus disengaging the user. Swarm Intelligence (SI) relies on social interaction, of which humans have a natural understanding, as opposed to the more abstract concept of evolutionary change. The main aim of this research is to introduce a new solver Silvereye, which implements Particle Swarm Optimization (PSO) in the Grasshopper framework, as the algorithm is hypothesized to be fast and intuitive. The second objective is to test if SI is able to solve complex design problems faster than EC-based solvers. Experimental results on a complex, single-objective high-dimensional benchmark problem of roof geometry optimization provide statistically significant evidence of computational inexpensiveness of the introduced tool.

Keywords: Architectural Design Optimization (ADO) · Particle Swarm Optimization (PSO) · Swarm Intelligence (SI) · Evolutionary Computation (EC) · Structural optimization

1 Introduction

Design processes based on parametrically variable elements allow designers to explore thousands of potential solutions and can be enriched by computational optimization [1–4]. Thus, the subfield of engineering that uses optimization methods to aid designers in studying and solving design problems plays a vital role in modern practice. Architectural engineering and design problems are usually classified as difficult

© Springer Nature Singapore Pte Ltd. 2017
G. Çağdaş et al. (Eds.): CAAD Futures 2017, CCIS 724, pp. 151–169, 2017.
DOI: 10.1007/978-981-10-5197-5_9

problems, since they correspond to five reasons why problems might be difficult according to Michalewicz and Fogel [2]:

1. An exhaustive search for the best answer is forbidden due to the large number of possible solutions in the search space.
2. The optimization problem is complex and any simplification of it would lead to discovering useless solutions.
3. In many cases a series of solutions rather than a single one is required due to the fitness function's noisiness or variety in time.
4. Due to numerous constraints on the search space the construction of even one feasible solution is difficult and discovering an optimal result even more so.
5. The person solving the problem is not satisfactorily prepared or faces some mental barriers that prevents him/her from discovering a solution.

The complexity of design problems often results in non-convex fitness landscapes. Due to this non-convexity conventional approaches (e.g. gradient-based optimization) are commonly regarded as inappropriate for design problems [3]. Moreover, in complex problems, often instead of a single solution, a number of different solutions could be optimal. Therefore, although deterministic approaches can address this problem, they cannot provide the set of different feasible solutions as they would yield always the same result. In general, gradient methods are ill-defined for non-differentiable functions and may not be suited to non-linear, multi-modal or discontinuous objective functions that often define engineering optimization problems [4]. Therefore the algorithms from the fields of Computational Intelligence, Biologically Inspired Computing, and Metaheuristics have been applied to address such functions [5]. Moreover, often the high complexity of optimization problems might be simply due to errors in the optimization problem's statement that is common in the design space. An optimization procedure (problem formulation/fitness function) constructed by architects and designers need be considered as black-box as it is in metaheuristic methods [5]. Metaheuristics such as techniques rooted in Evolutionary Algorithms or Swarm Intelligence, can be applied to 'almost any kind of the optimization problem, regardless of the type (e.g. continuous/discrete, linear/nonlinear, convex/nonconvex) and number of variables' [3, 5], as opposed to more conventional approaches that require specific objective functions.

Thanks the universal use of metaheuristics, there has been noteworthy growth in the field of nature-inspired optimization for the last few decades. Natural processes like Darwinian evolution, foraging strategies or social group behavior are widely applied in difficult real world problems ranging from industry to commerce [6]. There are two main families of the algorithms that constitute this field today: Swarm Intelligence (SI) algorithms and Evolutionary Computation (EC) Algorithms. In this work we will refer to the following system of classification presented by Brownlee [5]:

"Swarm Algorithms (SI Techniques): Particle Swarm Optimization, Ant System, Ant Colony Optimization, Bees Algorithm and the Bacterial Foraging Optimization Algorithm. Evolutionary Algorithms (EC Techniques): Genetic Algorithm, Genetic Programming, Evolution Strategies, Differential Evolution, Evolutionary Programming, Grammatical Evolution, Gene Expression Programming, Learning Classifier System, NSGA and SPEA".

Currently, mostly the EC-based algorithms are exploited in the optimization tools for designers and architects. Therefore, it is unknown how the SI techniques can perform in solving design problems. Although, evolutionary solvers can address most of the design problems [3, 7], they are very slow [3, 8]. Thermal, solar, structural or acoustic analysis may take a minute/several minutes per iteration [9], thus 'a single process may run for days or even weeks' [8] and 'even with a powerful hardware set-up, the repetition of hundreds or even thousands of analyses might transform the optimization process into an extremely long task' [10]. In many cases the high computational cost of each optimizer run prevents designers from using optimization techniques [3], thus many revolutionary design solutions are not discovered. In this study, the recently developed technique PSO is hypothesized to be able to solve complex design optimization problems faster than existing EA-based tools. The PSO-optimizer prototype was developed on multiple 'toy' problems [11] and this paper develops a fully-working tool - SILVEREYE and tests its use for a real-world application.

The main aim is to introduce a new optimization solver called Silvereye that implements a bespoke PSO algorithm in the Grasshopper framework. PSO is selected as demonstrator of SI optimization processes in design tools, as it constitutes the foundation for the other SI algorithms [5]. The second objective is to evaluate its computational speed and accuracy in solving design problems based on a comparative complex benchmark real-world problem. These initial benchmark tests were conducted on minimizing displacement of shell roof structure inspired by the Crematorium of Kakamigahara – Meiso no mori – Toyo Ito. Experiments have confirmed that Silvereye is faster in single-objective high-dimensional optimization problem as it outperforms existing EA-based alternatives (Galapagos, Octopus) in the search time criteria. Therefore, SI techniques are considered to be competitive to existing EA-based optimizers in solving complex design problems.

At the time when 'the importance of effective problem solving has never been greater' [2] facilitation of an extremely compact algorithm is anticipated to speed up the optimization process and improve the human-machine interaction. This could develop widespread adoption of solvers, popularize them among practitioners and thus enable discoveries of high performing solutions in design space.

2   Background

2.1   Solvers In Design Software – State Of Art

Nature-inspired intelligent computation has become recently an essential part of the interdisciplinary design process. Solvers based on EA obtainable in design systems reflect the principles of the evolution found in nature as they have an implicit parallel interactive search for solutions. The most commonly used of the current design platforms that enable visual programming with the embedded optimization solvers (if applicable) are presented in Table 1. The implemented optimization algorithms confirm that the design optimization field is dominated by EC techniques. Currently, in the most popular application enabling visual programming, Grasshopper for Rhino3D modeling environment [1, 12, 20] there are 4 optimization solvers available: Galapagos, Goat, Opossum and Octopus. The second most popular visual programming design application is Dynamo for Autodesk's Revit Architecture. Optimo – a plug-in for Dynamo [12] is based on the Non-dominated Sorting Genetic Algorithm II (NSGA – II). The other parametric platforms do not have generic solvers developed.

Table 1. Selection of design application with facilitated visual programming techniques.

Producer – Software	Visual programming/ parametric plug-in	% users [12]	Optimization plug-in / optimizer	Optimization algorithms	Category	Author and date of implementation
Gehry technologies: digital project	n/a	3%	n/a	n/a	n/a	n/a
Bentley systems: microstation	Generative Components	0%	Prototype design evolution	GA	EC	Bentley Applied Research, 2011
Autodesk: revit architecture	Dynamo (2011)	7%	Optimo (2014)	MOEAD	EC	Mohammad Rahmani Asl and Dr. Wei Yan, 2014
McNeel & associates : Rhinoceros3D	Grasshopper (2008)	90%	Galapagos	GA	EC	David Rutten, 2008
				SA	other[a]	David Rutten, 2011
			Goat	COBYLA, BOBYQA, Sbplx, DIRECT, CRS2	other[b]	Simon Flory, 2010–2015
			Opossum	Surrogate models	model-based	Thomas Wortmann, 2016
			Octopus	SPEA- 2 and HypE	EC	Robert Vierlinger, 2013
Nemetschek North America: vectorworks	Marionette (2015)	<1%	n/a	n/a	n/a	n/a

[a]Simulated Annealing belongs to the class of Physical Algorithms
[b]Goat interfaces NLopt, a collection of mathematical optimization libraries

2.2   The PSO algorithm

PSO is a sub-field of Computational Intelligence. It belongs to the field of Swarm Intelligence and Collective Intelligence [5]. PSO has both ties with Artificial Life and Evolutionary Computation and conceptually 'seems to lie somewhere between genetic algorithms and evolutionary programming' [13]. In terms of computational expensiveness the PSO algorithm lies 'between evolutionary search, which requires eons, and neutral processing, which occurs on the order of milliseconds' [13]. PSO is a type of biological system, where the collective behaviors of individuals interacting with each other and their environment form the optimization process. PSO was inspired by bird flocking and fish schooling [13] and its simulation was motivated by the need to model 'human social behavior' [13]. The interaction of agents within the PSO method is familiar to humans, since humans share with them some behavioral patterns (e.g. avoiding physical collision) [13].

3 Method

3.1 Method Selection

As shown in the study conducted by Zhang, Wang and Ji [14] 'the number of publications per year related to PSO is the highest among all seven SI-based algorithms. This suggests PSO is the most prevalent SI-based optimization algorithms'. None of SI algorithms has been implemented in any design software application so far, thus PSO is recommended as it is a baseline algorithm for many variations of SI algorithms [5]. Particle Swarm Optimization is the apt representation of the SI family of algorithms as it corresponds to the basic five principles of swarm intelligence [13–15]:

1. Proximity principle – the group should be able to carry out *'elementary space and time computations'* [15].
2. Quality principle - besides the time and space considerations, the population should be able to act in response to the quality factors.
3. Principle of diverse response – the population should seek to distribute its activities along many modes.
4. Principle of stability - the group should not change its behavioral mode upon every environmental fluctuation, unless it is worth the computational price.
5. Principle of adaptability - the population should alternate its behavior, when it is worth the computational price.

It is worth noticing that above rules resemble numerous *'economic decision making principles or folk maxims'* [15] like time is money, only buy the best, don't put all your eggs in one basket, better safe than sorry, a bird in the hand is worth two in the bush, invest for the future, etc. [16] that may indicate the search rules are similar to human common sense. PSO is extremely simple and it has already demonstrated its computational inexpensiveness in feature selection [17] and robustness in the areas of the biological, chemical, medicine, mechanical and civil engineering, fuel and energy, automatic control, and others [14]. Moreover, the PSO algorithm has been already shown to be a promising method for solving complex design problems [11]. Therefore the initial version of PSO presented by Kennedy and Eberhart in 1995 with introduced internal weight factor [18] is selected for the first implementation of SI- based algorithm in a design optimizer.

3.2   Method Description

The unique concept of PSO in comparison to EC techniques is that potential solutions 'fly' through the hyperspace, when in evolutionary computation potential solutions are represent as locations in it [13]. In PSO every single solution is a particle ('bird') in the multi-dimensional hyper-volume of the solution search space. A velocity component enables the system to progress quickly in the direction of good solutions. In practice velocity defines how much each parameter (dimension) can be adjusted in the forthcoming step. The goal of the PSO algorithm is to direct all the particles to the optima in the hyperspace of parameters [5]. The process is initialized with a random population of particles, each representing a solution. In every time step the fitness value is sampled and the velocity of each particle is updated. The velocity is constructed based on the current velocity, the best known global position (the best result sampled by the whole population - gbest) and the best position discovered by the particle (pbest) [5]:

$$pbest(i,t) = \underset{k=1,\dots,t}{argmin}[f(P_i(k))], i \in \{1,2,\dots,N_p\},$$

$$gbest = \underset{\substack{i=1,\dots,N_p \\ k=1,\dots,t}}{argmin}[f(P_i(k))] \tag{1}$$

When these two values are known, the position (P) and velocity (V) of each particle is updated using the following equations:

$$V_i(t+1) = \omega V_i(t) + c_1 r_1(pbest(i,t) - P_i(t)) + c_2 r_2(gbest(t) - P_i(t)) \tag{2}$$

$$P_i(t+1) = P_i(t) + V_i(t+1) \tag{3}$$

Where, V denotes the velocity for particle i, ω is the momentum coefficient for the whole swarm, $r1$, $r2$ are uniformly distributed random variables within range [0, 1], $c1,2$ are the positive constant parameters called '*acceleration coefficients*' or '*learning factors*'. Table 2 presents the commonly set internal tuning parameters of the PSO algorithm. These values have been determinate based on much empirical testing to ensure robustness across a wide range of problem domains [5, 13, 19] (Fig. 1).

The pseudo code of the implemented procedure is as follows:

The implemented algorithm includes inertia weight (ω) introduced by Shi and Eberhart in 1998. ω is also called the momentum coefficient and is used to 'balance the global exploration and local exploitation' [14]. It was demonstrated by the authors, that introduction of ω improves the PSO performance [19]. In the implemented PSO algorithm stochastic factors $c1$, $c2$ are equal to two, as was suggested by Kennedy and Eberhart [13]. Computational expensiveness depends on the size of the population, compliance of the communication rules between different agents [17] and directness of behavioral response to environmental stimuli [15]. The default swarm size is set to 20, as this number is the least expensive recommended swarm size [5]. It is common to set an upper bound for the velocity component. The maximum value of the velocity

Table 2. PSO – commonly set internal parameters of the PSO algorithm.

Internal parameters of the PSO algorithm:	
1. Number of particles	Low, around 20–40
2. The maximum speed a particle can move (max. change in its position per iteration) (*Vmax.*)	Should be bounded as to the percentage of the size of the domain
3. Learning factors (biases towards global and personal best positions) *(c1)*, *(c2)*	Between 0 and 4, typically 2; 2 in the PSO from 1995
Additional factors that can be introduced:	
4. A local bias factor (local neighbourhood)	Only when neighbours are determined based on the Euclidean distance between particles
5. An inertia or momentum coefficient (ω)	0.3 [19]

Step 1. Initialization

    For each particle i $= 1, \ldots, N_p$, do

    (a) Initialize the particle's position with a uniformly distribution as $P_i(0) \sim U(LB, UP)$, where LB and UB represent the lower and upper bounds of the search space

    (b) Initialize *pbest* to its initial position $pbest(i, 0) = P_i(0)$.

    (c) Initialize *gbest* to the minimal value of the swarm: $gbest(0) = \arg\min f[P_i(0)]$.

    (d) Initialize velocity: $V_i \sim U(-|UB - LB|, |UB - LB|)$.

Step 2. Repeat until a termination criterion is met

    For each particle i $= 1, \ldots, N_p$, do

    (a) Pick random numbers: $r_1 r_2 \sim U(0,1)$.

    (b) Update particle's velocity. See formula (2).

    (c) Update particle's position. See formula (3).

    (d) If $f[P_i(t)] < f[pbest(i, t)]$, do

        (i)   Update the best known position of particle i: $pbest(i, t) = P_i(t)$.

        (ii)   If $f[P_i(t)] < f[gbest(t)]$, update the swarm's best known position: $gbest(t) = P_i(t)$.

    (e) $t \leftarrow (t + 1)$;

Step 3. Output $gbest(t)$ that holds the best found solution

Fig. 1. Pseudocode of a standard PSO. Source: [14].

(Vmax) should be calculated based on the size of the domain, so it is individual to each design problem.

A comprehensive survey of studies deliberating on the adjusting the internal tuning parameters was done by Carlisle and Dozier [20]. Discussion of setting optimized values for the design problem domains in the Grasshopper framework is an issue of further research. Currently, the identified values are robust and proper across a wide range of problems, which simplifies the adaptation of the PSO technique into design practice such that it is straightforward.

4 Silvereye

The implementation of PSO in the framework of the most popular parametric modeling platform – Grasshopper [1, 12, 21] will enable direct comparison of the new tool based - Silvereye with existing EC –based solvers (Galapagos, Octopus). We implement our Particle Swarm Optimization solver in C#, which is one of the languages available for custom component scripting in Grasshopper as a Silvereye add-on component (Fig. 2). The central part of the component is a ParticleSwarmOptimization.dll file, a shared library containing an implementation of the core version of the Particle Swarm Optimization algorithm. A Graphical User Interface (GUI) is implemented separately and shipped in a form of a Grasshopper Assembly file, Silvereye.gh. In our current implementation the input parameters, the fitness input and the sliders correspond to the input arguments of the objective function and internal tuning parameters. The output is a list comprising of the best solutions found at each iteration of the algorithm. In order to solve an optimization problem, the Silvereye component has to be placed on the Grasshopper canvas and connected to a number of input parameters, either to number sliders or to gene pool components. These N input parameters constitute an N-dimensional search space S, $S \subseteq R^N$, of the optimization problem in question. The component is also connected to a number component from which the value of a fitness function is retrieved. As in the standard form of an optimization problem definition the optimization objective is to minimize a fitness function, however a user can change the objective to maximization. In a default scenario, once an optimal solution search is initiated a swarm of 20 particles is created with each particle located at a uniform random position in S. The swarm searches for a solution to a minimization problem in 60 iterations. The maximal velocity of each particle is the same in all N directions and is chosen as 0.2 of the maximal range of the input parameters (See: 8.1 Conclusions).

The Silvereye GUI presents a user with a form where the default values of the optimization settings are displayed. The optimization settings comprise of an optimization objective, a swarm size, the number of iterations and a maximal velocity. An execution of the solver is then terminated either after the time has elapsed or after the number of iterations is reached, whichever occurs first. Finally, a user can choose to use an initial position. If this option is selected, one of the particles takes on the current values of the input parameters.

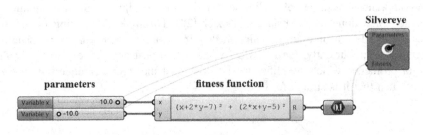

Fig. 2. Silvereye component on the GH canvas.

5   Initial Tests/Benchmarks - Results

5.1   Problem Formulation

In this section, the functionality of Silvereye is presented based on a structural optimization of a free-form roof structure benchmark problem inspired by a real architectural project (Fig. 3). As a case study we selected the Meiso no Mori Crematorium (from the Japanese words meaning Forest of Meditation), designed by Toyo Ito and Mutsuro Sasaki consultants at Kakamigahara City, in Gifu Japan. This building is located in the park-like cemetery between wooded hills and a small pond and it replaced the previous demolished crematorium [22]. Toyo Ito says, that his design is *'not as a conventional massive crematorium but as architecture of a spacious roof floating above the site like slowly drifting clouds, creating a soft field'* [23]. The 20 cm-thick roof of white reinforced concrete is made up of concave and convex forms and rises up to 11.5 m in parts. The roof is supported by twelve freely scattered cone columns dropping from the ceiling [24] and four structural cores [22]. Although the roof seems to be free in its form, it was designed through rigorous structural analysis. In the original project the optimal solution was discovered by modifying the initial shape defined by the architect through the optimization process on minimizing the total strain energy and deformation based on the Sensitivity Analysis method [25, 26].

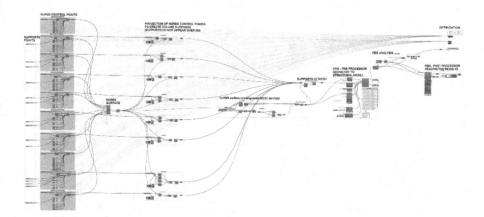

Fig. 3. Grasshopper definition of the optimization problem (adopted from the initial Alberto Pugnale's GH definition [28].

Contrary to the form improvement in the original procedure, in the problem studied by Pugnale and Sassone the optimization process was turned into a form exploration [10]. This case study was elaborated by Pugnale and Sassone in 2007 [27] and reanalysed in 2013 by Pugnale [28]. In 2007 the geometrical information and the optimization process with *'a specially developed Genetic Algorithm'* [27] were written in the programming environment embedded in Rhinoceros – RhinoScript [28]. In 2013 Pugnale reinterpreted the problem to the Grasshopper environment and used Karamba

[29] for FEM (Finite Element Method) analysis and Galapagos' Genetic Solver for the optimization procedure. In his exercise the roof geometry of the original Toyo Ito's project was exemplified in rather a free manner [28], '*acting as design tool of investigation/exploration*' [27]. In the study we adopted the problem presented by Pugnale [28] in order to evaluate the performance of the Silvereye solver in comparison to the existing tools (Galapagos, Octopus). The crucial parameters for the structural efficiency evaluation are maximum nodal displacement (m), the mass (maximum total force of gravity) and strain energy. Minimizing all of them leads to more efficient structures [30]. Displacements are a vector field and in contrary to the strain energy it can reveal both local and global weaknesses [10]. In the presented problem, we chose to minimize total maximum nodal displacement because it is a factor minimizing effectively the strain energy in the whole model [30], and a parameter that can indicate the weakest points of the structure, as maximum displacement returns the values of the local peaks of the analyzed mesh. The aim of the optimization search is to find the shape of the roof within the boundary conditions (Fig. 4) (Table 3) that will have the smallest possible maximal displacement. In the experiment we are preserving the dimensions of the real free-curved surface: length - 80 m, width - 60 m and thickness - 200 mm [26]. The roof structure is described by the means of the third degree NURBS surface (i.e. a rational polynomial continuous function, defined by a set of control points) with a grid of 10×10 control points in a plan projection restricted to the boundary presented in Fig. 4.

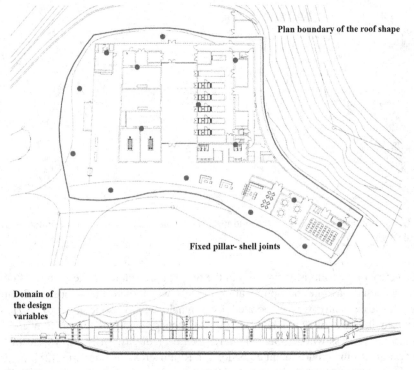

Fig. 4. Boundary conditions in plan and elevation. Source: [31].

The z-coordinates of the control points of the NURBS surface defining the roof geometry have been set as the parameters of the problem to be optimized. Their vertical domain is limited to the range -10.000 and 10.000 m with 20 000 degrees of freedom (as the number slider component's accuracy was set to 3 decimal places). For the FEM analysis the continuous geometry is translated to the triangular discrete finite element mesh – quadratic grid of size 35×20 with complementary diagonals. The dead-load and mesh load 6 kN/m^2 were applied to the 20cm thick concrete shell (C25/30 defined by Eurocode[1]) as it is considered as sufficient approximation of real load situation for the initial design stage. The height and position of 15 pillars, the planar projection of the roof boundary and thickness of the shell are the boundary conditions for the elaborated problem. The formulations of the design problem in our tests and in the previous studies are described in detail in Table 3.

The problem is interesting both from an architectural and a scientific point of view. The size of a set of solutions can be calculated as: X^N, where X is number of possible states, and N is a number of design variables (parameters), therefore in this case it is equal to 20 000^85 possible solutions. The calculation of the entire set of solutions, under the assumption that the calculation of one solution takes one microsecond, would take about $1.23 * 10^{352}$ years! Simplification of the problem would lead to discovery of useless solutions. Thus this problem is constrained with both hard-constraints, such as x,y coordinates of the position of the columns or the roof outline, and with a penalty method included in the fitness function that prevents the tapered pillars becoming too high. Moreover, a number of solutions could be optimal and discovering even one feasible solution might be difficult. Therefore, this problem is considered a difficult optimization problem.

5.2   Hardware and Software

Tests were conducted with the use of a personal computer, which is typically available for modern architectural and design practices: Dell XPS 12 (Processor: Inter® Core (TM) i5-4200U CPU @, 2.30GHz, installed memory: 4.0 GB, Graphics: Intel (R) HD Graphics 4000).

6   Results

The introduced tool, Silvereye, and the existing EC-based alternatives (Galapagos and Octopus) were tested on the presented complex design problem (See Sect.: 5.1 Problem formulation) in two runtime categories. Firstly, tests with a 15-min runtime limit to investigate the software applications' abilities to discover different high quality solutions when a user only has short runtime available. The 8-h tests were conducted only with the best performing in short runs set of settings for each solver in order to examine solvers' capability of finding the best possible solution if the longer time was available

---

[1] E = 3100 [kN/cm^2],   G = 1291.67 [kN/cm^2],   gamma = 25 [kN/m^3],   alphaT = 1.0E−5[1/C°], fy = 1.67 [kN/cm^2].

Table 3. Problem formulation and design tools used in the previous and current analysis.

	Original Project 2004–2006 [26]	Study 2007 [27]	Study 2013 [28]	Study 2017
Design tools				
Geometry modeler	CAD/CAM	Rhinoscript in Rhinoceros	Grasshopper	Grasshopper build 0.9.0076
FE solver	NASTRAN	Ansys	Karamba	Karamba ver. 1.1.0
Optimization tool/ algorithm	Iterative gradient-based optimization technique -shape design method used sensitivity analysis	GA scripted in RhinoScript	Galapagos (GA)	Silvereye (PSO) build 0.0.1
Problem formulation				
Shell Geometry	"Triangulated shell-elements following the one-meter grid compose', 3600 elements 20 cm–thick	Mesh – triangular grid 50 × 50 2500 elements 15 cm-thick	Mesh – triangular grid 35 × 20700 elements 25 cm–thick	Mesh – triangular grid 35×20 700 elements 20 cm–thick
Solution domain	Small, local search from predefined by architect shape	"1/5 of the edge length of the roof plane projection" [31]	Sliders in range: −10 m and 10 m	Sliders in range: −10 m and 10 m
Loads	Gravity load Dominant load – 6.0 kN/m² [26]	Load 1 kN/m² [10]	Self-weight and live load (6 kN/m²)	Self-weight and mesh load (6 kN/m²)
Constraints	Columns as roller supports withstand only vertical load Walls and other columns withstand horizontal load	*'Horizontal coordinates of NURBS control points'* and *'vertical coordinates of control points that represent the pillar-slab joint'* [31]	x,y coordinates of the pillars are fixed; projection of the roof outline is fixed; penalty function as the restriction of the max. height of columns	x,y coordinates of the pillars are fixed; projection of the roof outline is fixed; penalty function as the restriction of the max. height of columns
Variables	z-coordinates of the NURBS surface	z-coordinates of the NURBS surface	z-coordinates of the NURBS surface: 85 parameters	z-coordinates of the NURBS surface: 85 parameters
Fitness function	Strain energy	Vertical displacement	Total displacement	Total Displacement

for testing. Silvereye was tested for sensitivity to the velocity parameter, with different maximum velocities ranging from 0.5 to 20, as it needs to be robust for ease of use. Twenty particles were initialized in each test. Galapagos was tested on two sets of settings: Set 1-settings used by Pugnale in his original definition of the problem [28]: population = 50, initial boost = x5, maintain = 3%, inbreeding = +60% and with default settings: Set 2:population = 50, initial boost = x2, maintain = 5%, inbreeding = +75%. For test purposes, Octopus was tuned with default internal parameters: Elitism = 0.500, Mut. Probability = 0.100, Mutation Rate = 0.500, Crossover Rate = 0.800, Population size = 100. All results for 30 runs of each tested solver are presented in Table 4. In the 15-min tests Silvereye with implemented PSO on average discovered solutions that are about 2.5 times better than those found by Galapagos and about two times better in comparison to the results achieved by Octopus.

The maximum deflection (d) of any structure should be such that people using feel safe and comfortable. As a rough rule of thumb it should be limited to d <= L/300 [30], where d is the maximum deflection and L is a span between the supports. The minimum span between columns in the benchmark problem is 8.82 m, consequently for initial design stage the acceptable value for the maximum deflection, understood as the degree to which a roof structure is displaced under the loads, is about 3 cm. In almost all tested runs Silvereye discovered solution under 3 cm, when neither Galapagos nor Octopus managed to find a feasible solution in thirty runs of the 15-min tests (results underlined in Table 4). The local nodal displacements exceeding 3 cm are marked in the Fig. 5.

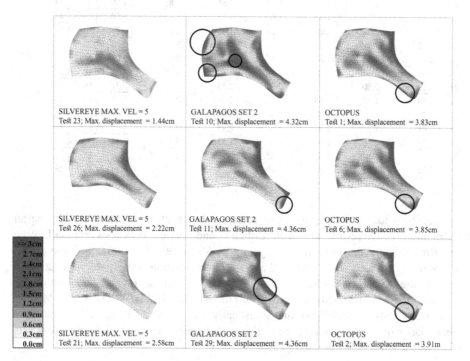

Fig. 5. Different solutions discovered during the optimization process during 15-minute tests.

Table 4. Results achieved by Silvereye, Galapagos and Octopus: 15-minute tests on the benchmark problem.

Runtime limit = 15 Min								
Silvereye						Galapagos		Octo-pus
Result [cm]						Result [cm]		Result [cm]
Test	Vmax = 0.5	Vmax = 1	Vmax = 2	Vmax = 5	Vmax = 10	Vmax = 20	Set 1	Set 2	Set
1	2.93	1.73	1.47	1.92	2.83	2.74	4.73	5.53	3.83
2	2.59	1.64	1.72	2.13	2.52	1.72	6.27	4.03	3.91
3	2.94	1.98	1.50	1.90	1.97	2.77	5.38	4.40	3.85
4	1.77	1.48	1.53	1.47	1.85	2.33	5.66	4.59	3.85
5	2.08	1.89	1.62	1.86	2.73	2.67	5.93	4.65	3.83
6	2.51	1.93	2.57	1.79	1.78	1.86	4.04	5.06	3.85
7	2.48	1.44	2.30	1.66	2.00	1.90	5.25	4.75	3.83
8	1.68	1.99	1.91	2.36	2.15	2.29	4.79	4.91	4.43
9	2.31	2.13	1.80	1.15	1.82	2.36	5.48	4.43	4.43
10	2.13	1.27	1.96	2.07	1.63	1.48	5.51	4.32	4.43
11	2.48	2.09	1.51	1.63	2.40	2.31	5.85	4.36	4.33
12	2.43	1.97	2.06	1.85	1.73	2.32	5.85	4.91	4.33
13	2.99	2.52	1.25	1.51	2.23	2.82	5.49	5.23	4.33
14	2.74	1.72	1.59	1.51	1.73	1.69	5.43	4.87	4.33
15	3.48	2.69	1.58	1.52	2.22	2.02	6.07	4.80	4.33
16	2.55	1.74	2.60	1.53	2.02	2.83	5.91	3.55	4.33
17	2.76	1.54	1.24	1.76	3.24	2.68	6.68	5.42	4.33
18	1.73	1.63	1.71	1.98	2.29	2.73	3.22	5.18	4.33
19	5.01	1.47	1.48	1.33	1.86	1.88	4.78	4.31	4.33
20	2.33	2.20	1.98	1.69	1.72	2.45	6.50	4.90	4.43
21	3.40	2.34	2.66	2.58	1.49	2.04	6.29	4.73	4.33
22	2.42	1.84	1.62	1.82	2.95	2.87	5.16	3.76	4.33
23	2.43	1.63	1.52	1.44	1.98	1.61	5.05	4.56	4.33
24	2.66	2.01	1.78	1.78	1.74	1.98	4.50	6.47	4.33
25	3.19	2.80	1.76	2.02	2.53	1.92	6.21	4.56	4.33
26	3.58	1.86	1.65	2.22	2.38	2.78	5.35	4.10	4.33
27	3.26	2.92	1.99	1.54	1.89	2.31	4.85	5.04	4.26
28	2.95	1.27	2.28	1.64	2.15	2.39	4.74	5.23	4.33
29	3.38	2.16	1.81	1.57	1.61	3.76	4.15	4.36	4.33
30	2.42	4.52	1.82	2.35	2.11	2.21	5.73	5.18	4.81
Av.	**2.72**	**2.01**	**1.81**	**1.79**	**2.12**	**2.32**	**5.36**	**4.74**	**4.25**

Statistical test selection procedure included the check of the normality of the all distributions of the results with K-S., Lilliefors and Shapiro-Wilk tests and the Levene and Brown-Forysythe tests of Homogenity of Variances. The normality assumption ($p < 0.05$) is not satisfied in all tested cases. The tests of homogeneity of variances also decline the hypothesis zero. Therefore, for the comparison of the results the non-parametric corresponding tests are used.: Kruskal-Wallis ANOVA and Median Test. Both tests indicated on the statistically important differences. The multiple comparisons of p value indicate the statistical differences between the independent sets of results when p is below 0,05 (Table 5).

Table 5. Multiple comparisons p values between all sets of the results of 15-minute tests on benchmark problem.

Depend.:	Multiple comparisons p values (2-tailed); Independent (grouping) variable: SetName Kruskal-Wallis test: H (8, N = 270) = 205,4970 p = 0,000								
Set	Silvereye 05	Silvereye 1	Silvereye 2	Silvereye 5	Silvereye 10	Silvereye 20	Galapagos 1	Galapagos 2	Octopus
	R:141,97	R:79,000	R59,000	R58,267	R:94,700	R:113,83	R:244,93	R:226,07	R:201,73
Silvereye Vmax = 0.5		0,064433	0,001394	0,00119	0,686148	1	0,000012	0,001091	0,109198
Silvereye Vmax = 1	0,064433		1	1	1	1	0	0	0
Silvereye Vmax = 2	0,001394			1	1	0,235258	0	0	0
Silvereye Vmax = 5	0,00119	1	1		1	0,210627	0	0	0
Silvereye Vmax = 10	0,686148	1	1	1		1	0	0	0,000004
Silvereye Vmax = 20	1	1	0,235258	0,210627	1		0	0,000001	0,000469
Galapagos Set 1	0,000012	0	0	0	0	0		1	1
Galapagos Set 2	0,001091	0	0	0	0	0,000001	1		1
Octopus	0,109198	0	0	0	0,000004	0,000469	1	1	

Non-parametric tests indicated that Silvereye with the Vmax between 1 and 20 performed statistically better than Galapagos with Set 1 and Set 2 and Octopus with default settings. They have also proven than PSO can perform statistically better or worse depending on tuning the Vmax internal parameter (Silvereye with Vmax = 0.5 performed statistically worse than Silvereye with Vmax = 2 and Vmax = 5) (Figs. 6 and 7).

Results of the 15-min tests revealed that Silvereye with the maximum velocity restricted to be between 1 and 10 discovers the best results. The maximum velocity may be understood as the '*maximum jump*' between values on the number sliders

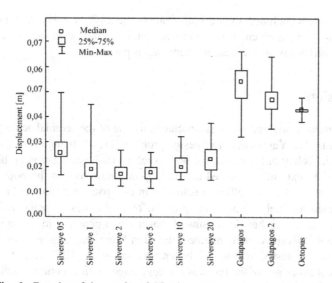

Fig. 6. Boxplot of the results of 15-minute tests on benchmark problem.

Table 6. Results achieved by Silvereye, Galapagos and Octopus - 8-hour tests on the benchmark problem.

Runtime limit = 8 h								
Silvereye						Galapagos		Octopus
Result [cm]						result [cm]		Result [cm]
Test	Vmax = 0.5	Vmax = 1	Vmax = 2	Vmax = 5	Vmax = 10	Vmax = 20	Set 1	Set 2	Set
1	–	0.6	0.7	0.9	1.1	0.9	–	2.8	1.6

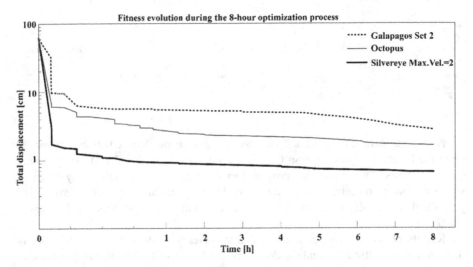

Fig. 7. Graph of the structural performance improvement during 8-hour tests. Source: [32].

(design parameters included in the optimization process) in every iteration. It was observed that the most efficient maximum velocities should be in the range 1/20 and 10/20 of the variability of the design optimization parameters.

7 Discussion

Enhanced computational modeling is concluded as one of the seminal achievements of the 20th Century [1]. Vast majority of design problems are of an engineering nature and modeling social behavior is an effective way to solve these optimization problems [13]. Facilitation of an extremely focused and fast optimization tool in the popular design platform may allow the most efficient solutions in the space of design and architecture to be discovered routinely, thus enabling a new quality in design practice. The introduced PSO-based solver has demonstrated that it has a potential to become this revolutionary tool. Silvereye demonstrated the significant prevalence over EA-based alternatives in the tested real-world benchmark problem. However, it has to be underlined, that every run of the test was not conducted in the identical conditions. The solvers' performance was also influenced by the current computer's performance, which was affected by other processes running in the background and current temperature of the processor that was rising during the series of tests. During each run the optimization process was also slowing down due to the file storage.

However, throughout all experimentations, in a single 15-min test Galapagos managed to produce 20–27 generations, whereas Octopus only between 8 and 11. It has to be remarked upon that Octopus implements the SPEA-2 algorithm that belongs to the family of Multi-Objective Evolutionary Algorithms and is mostly dedicated to solve multi-criteria problems. Silvereye within the same time frame searched through 60–76 iterations. Despite differences in number of iterations or generations, each application within this time sampled the fitness landscape about the same amount of times ranging from 1200 to 1600, which allows us to compare the results.

Although the introduced PSO-based solver outperformed the tested alternatives, there is no silver bullet for solving all design optimization problems and it should be acknowledged that "A prerequisite to handling the real world as a multiplayer game is the ability to manipulate an arsenal of problem – solving techniques, namely, algorithms that have been developed for variety of conditions" [2].

8 Conclusion and Future Work

8.1 Conclusions

We introduced a new tool Silvereye that is a first implementation of Particle Swarm Optimization – an algorithm from the field of Swarm Intelligence in the most commonly used parametric design system. Unlike EA-based solvers Silvereye is intuitive as it is based on social behaviour rather than the concept of evolution. The PSO-based solver is shown to be applicable to complex, real-world design problems. The presented results are the evidence for its computational inexpensiveness and robustness in solving a high-dimensional design problem of roof-shape optimization. Silvereye discovered high-quality solutions faster than the tested alternatives based on Genetic Algorithm (Galapagos) and Strength Pareto Evolutionary Algorithm 2 (Octopus).

The quality of the solutions discovered by Silvereye depends on the maximum velocity parameter. The results indicate that the best performance of solver is achieved with the maximum velocity limited to the value in range between the 1/20 and 10/20 of the variability of the optimization parameters. The wide range of effective maximum velocities makes the tool easier to tune for practical implementations.

In almost every 15-min test Silvereye discovered a high-quality solution that met the structural criterion in contrast to the tested alternatives. Therefore, it shown to be not only an efficient optimization solver, but also its potential to become a solution-exploration tool, as it can produce more feasible solutions in short run times than alternative approaches. This feature is especially appreciated in design space, where the incomputable aspects like aesthetics has a significant influence on the final solution chosen. Thus by providing an extremely fast tool the decision-making process can be enriched by the possibility to compare different high-quality solutions (Table 6).

8.2 Future Work

PSO has fewer tuning parameters than existing evolutionary solvers and the underlying fundamental rules exemplifying Swarm Intelligence may be regarded as more familiar to humans than principles of neo-Darwinian theory of evolution. However, the Silvereye optimizer, as with the other EA-based solvers embedded in Grasshopper requires an 'aware' user as the formulation of the fitness function and solution space can significantly influence the time of search and quality of solutions discovered. Although there are numerical benchmark tests available in literature, to the best of our knowledge, very few publications can be found that address the issue of intuitive control over optimization processes as a factor significantly influencing the achieved results. Like numerous problem studies, in the presented study it is avoided to "immerse deeper into the issues of problem formulation and convergence behaviour" [1], so this is an issue of further research.

Future work should explore more the intuitiveness of the tool, as this is a significant factor influencing its overall performance and user-friendliness. Further research should improve the machine-tool interaction and increase the control over the optimization process. This could be achieved by definition of the rules for the solver tuning in the different design problem domains in the Grasshopper framework and by the extension of the basic set of the tuning parameters.

Acknowledgements. This work is partially supported by the "THELXINOE: Erasmus Euro-Oceanian Smart City Network". This is an Erasmus Mundus Action-2 Strand-2 (EMA2/S2) project funded by the European Union.

References

1. Vierlinger, R.: Multi Objective Design Interface. Technischen Universitat, Wien (2013)
2. Michalewicz, Z., Fogel, B.D.: How to Solve It: Modern Heuristics, 2nd edn. Springer, Berlin (2004)
3. Wortmann, T., Costa, A., Nannicini, G., Schroepfer, T.: Advantages of surrogate models for architectural design optimization. Artif. Intell. Eng. Des. Anal. Manuf. **29**, 471–481 (2015). doi:10.1017/S0890060415000451
4. Wetter, M., Polak, E.A.: Convergent optimization method using pattern search algorithms with adaptive precision simulation. Build. Serv. Eng. Res. Technol. **25**, 327 (2004)
5. Brownlee, J.: Clever Algorithms. Nature-Inspired Programming Recipes, First, LuLu (2011)
6. Marques, A.I., Garcia, V., Sanchez, J.S.: A literature review on the application of evolutionary computing to credit scoring. J. Oper. Res. Soc. **64**, 1384–1399 (2013). doi:10.1057/jors.2012.145
7. Rutten, D.: Navigating multi-dimensional landscapes in foggy weather as an analogy for generic problem solving. In: 16th International Conference on Geometry Graph (2014)
8. Rutten, D.: Evolutionary principles applied to problem solving. Adv. Archit. Geom. (2010)
9. Nguyen, A.T., Reiter, S.: Passive designs and strategies for low-cost housing using simulation-based optimization and different thermal comfort criteria. J. Build. Perform. Simul. **7**, 68–81 (2013). doi:10.1080/19401493.2013.770067

10. Pugnale, A., Echengucia, T., Sassone, M.: Computational morphogenesis, design of freeform surfaces. In: Adriaenssens, S., Block, P., Veenendaal, D., Williams, C. (eds.), Shell Structures Architecture Form-finding Optimization, pp. 250–61. Routledge (2014)
11. Cichocka, J.M., Browne, W.N., Rodriguez, E.: Evolutionary optimization processes as design tools. In: Proceedings of 31th International PLEA Conference Architecture in (R) evolution, Bologna, 9–11 September (2015)
12. Cichocka, J.M., Browne, W.N., Rodriguez, E.: Optimization in the architectural practice—an international survey. In: Janssen, P., Loh, P., Raonic A., Schnabel M. (eds.), Flows Glitches, Proceedings of 22nd International Conference Association Computer Architecture Design. Res. Asia 2017, Paper, p. 155. The Association for Computer-Aided Architectural Design Research in Asia (CAADRIA), Hong Kong (2017)
13. Kennedy, J., Eberhart, R.: Particle swarm optimization. In: IEEE International Conference on Neural Networks, Proceedings, vol. 4, pp. 1942–1948 (1995). doi:10.1109/ICNN.1995.488968
14. Zhang, Y., Wang, S., Ji, G.: A comprehensive survey on particle swarm optimization algorithm and its applications. Math. Probl. Eng. (2015). doi:10.1155/2015/931256
15. Millonas, M.M.: Swarms, phase transitions, and collective intelligence. In: St Fe Inst Stud Sci Complexity-Proceedings, vol. 30 (1994). doi:citeulike-article-id:5290209
16. Geanakoplos, J.D., Gray, L.: When Seeing Further Is Not Seeing Better n.d. (1991)
17. Xue, B., Zhang, M., Browne, W.N.: Particle swarm optimization for feature selection in classification: a multi-objective approach. IEEE Trans. Cybern. 43, 1656–1671 (2013)
18. Shi, Y., Eberhart, R.C.: A modified particle swarm optimizer. In: Congratulation Evolution Computer, pp. 69–73 (1998)
19. Eberhart, R.C., Shi, Y.: Comparison between genetic algorithms and particle swarm optimization. In: Ep' 1998, pp. 611–616 (1998). doi:10.1007/BFb0040812
20. Carlisle, A., Dozier, G.: An off-the-shelf PSO. Proc. Part. Swarm Optim. Work 1, 1–6 (2001)
21. Martyn, D.: Rhino grasshopper. AEC Mag. 42 (2009)
22. Webb, M.: Organic embrace. Archit. Rev. 222, 74–77 (2007)
23. Toyo Ito & Associates.: Meiso no Mori Crematorium Gifu, Japan Toyo Ito & Associates Meiso no Mori Crematorium Gifu, Japan Toyo Ito & Associates n.d
24. Municipal Funeral Hall in Kakamigahara, Detail, 48,786–90 (2008)
25. Sasaki, M.: Flux Structure. Toto Publishers, Tokyo (2005)
26. Sakamoto, T.: Ferre A. From control to design: parametric/algorithmic architecture. In: ACTAR (2008)
27. Pugnale, A., Sassone, M.: Morphogenesis and structural optimization of shell structures with the aid of a genetic algorithm. J. Int. Assoc. Shell Spat. Struct. 48, 161–166 (2007)
28. Pugnale, A.: Computational Morphogenesis-with Karamba, Galapagos—Test on the Crematorium of Kakamigahara—Meiso no mori—Toyo Ito (2013) https://albertopugnale.wordpress.com/2013/03/25/computational-morphogenesis-with-karambagalapagos-test-on-the-crematorium-of-kakamigahara-meiso-no-mori-toyo-ito/. Accessed 30 Nov 2015
29. Preisinger, C.: Linking structure and parametric geometry. Archit. Des. 83, 110–113 (2013). doi:10.1002/ad.1564
30. Preisinger, C.: Karamba User Manual (version 1.1.0) (2015)
31. Pugnale, A.: Engineering Architecture. Advances of a technological practice, Ph.D. Thesis. Politecnico di Torino (2009). doi:10.1017/CBO9781107415324.004
32. Cichocka, J.M.: Particle Swarm Optimization for Architectural Design. Silvereye 1.0, Code of Space, Vienna (2016)

Solar Collection Multi-isosurface Method

Computational Design Advanced Method for the Prediction of Direct Solar Access in Urban Environments

Francesco De Luca[(✉)] and Hendrik Voll

Tallinn University of Technology, Tallinn, Estonia
{francesco.deluca,hendrik.voll}@ttu.ee

Abstract. Direct solar access and daylight requirements contribute significantly when it comes to shaping the layout and appearance of contemporary cities. Urban planning regulations in Estonia set the minimum amount of direct solar access that existing housing has the right to receive and new premises are required to get when new developments are built. The solar envelope and solar collection methods are used to define the volume and shape of new buildings that allow the due solar rights to the surrounding buildings, in the case of the former, and the portion of the own façades that receive the required direct solar access, in the case of the latter. These methods have been developed over a period of several decades, and present-day CAAD and environmental analysis software permits the generation of solar envelopes and solar collection isosurfaces, although they suffer from limitations. This paper describes an advanced method for generating solar collection isosurfaces and presents evidence that it is significantly more efficient than the existing method for regulation in Estonia's urban environments.

Keywords: Urban planning · Direct solar access · Solar envelope · Solar collection · Computational design · Environmental design

1 Introduction

Architecture has been connected with and dependent on the exploitation of daylighting throughout the evolution of the built environment. Daylighting is the efficient use of the quantity and quality of natural light available every day all around the world for the illumination of external urban environments and the interiors of buildings.

The use of daylighting as the main source of illumination for interiors lasted until the first half of the twentieth century, when fluorescent lamps became affordable and energy cheap [1]. This way, the interiors of buildings and façade layouts became independent from natural light and ventilation, in some extreme cases even becoming completely unnecessary. A renewed interest in daylighting started again during the 1970s as a result of the oil crises and consequent shortage of energy [2].

If the amount of interior and exterior illuminance is precisely measurable with many different metrics, the quality of daylight is subjective, as it involves health aspects [3]. Daylight is the most appreciated source of light by people for the illumination of

© Springer Nature Singapore Pte Ltd. 2017
G. Çağdaş et al. (Eds.): CAAD Futures 2017, CCIS 724, pp. 170–187, 2017.
DOI: 10.1007/978-981-10-5197-5_10

interiors of buildings of any kind, including residential, office, production and commercial buildings.

The appreciation of daylight is due to its full range and balanced spectrum of
colors, from the violet to the red, with a peak in the blue-green area that increases the
comfort of vision. At the same time, the alternation of day and night and the characteristic of variability of natural light in daytime from sunrise to sunset improves the
circadian rhythm and health of humans [4]. Therefore, daylight is a critical aspect for
the physiological and psychological wellbeing of occupants of buildings [5].

Daylighting is generated by direct and diffuse sunlight. Although natural light
diffused by the sky and by the reflection from the surrounding environment is a
valuable source of daylighting, direct solar radiation is the most appreciated. Albeit the
need to control it through the appropriate design of building features, it is crucial in
order to avoid or minimize downsides such as higher energy use due to internal heat
gains during cooling dominated periods and discomfort of vision by glare, direct
sunlight is the most efficient source of natural light for its quantity, quality and
distribution.

Quantity refers to the illuminance intensity required to perform specific tasks in the
interiors of different kinds of buildings and to perceive the surrounding ambient with
ease. Quality is relative to the already mentioned ability of natural light to render colors
without variations, thereby increasing the level of comfort of vision and making
interiors more pleasant to the occupants [6]. Distribution is the potentiality of natural
light to be uniformly spread and scattered in interiors through a proper floor plan and
facade glazing layout, to maximize the usable floor area and minimize the difference
between the quantity of light in different parts of a building's interior [7].

Planning and building regulations set the required quantity of daylight to be
guaranteed in living and working environments in different ways from country to
country. The differences are in the metrics used for the measurements and in the actual
quantity of daylight required.

In Estonia the access to natural light, during the season in which it is available in a
significant way, is an important requirement and is regulated by the standard "Daylight
in dwellings and offices" [8]. The standard sets two main targets. One requires that in
an urban environment a new building cannot decrease the amount of hours of direct
solar access received by the surrounding buildings' premises by more than 50% for
every day of the period between the 22nd of April and the 22nd of August. The other
states that in a new residential building at least one room of the premises, among living
room and bedrooms, is required to receive at least 2.5 h of direct sunlight every day
during the same period. This requirement is particularly challenging in dense urban
environments because in an ideal open field a building, regardless of its orientation,
will receive more than 2.5 h of direct sunlight in the specified period at the Estonian
latitudes between 57.5°N and 59.7°N.

The massing and plan layout studies of new developments, which have to fulfill the
two requirements described above, can be done using the solar envelope and solar
collection methods.

The solar envelope is an efficient method developed by Knowles [9, 10] to calculate
on a given plot the maximum buildable volume that the new buildings cannot exceed in
order to guarantee the quantity of direct sunlight hours required on the surrounding

façades during a specific period and time frame. The solar envelope method is more efficient than that of the setbacks because it takes into account a building's characteristics, such as latitude, orientation and distances, and the required period of the year and time of the day during which the direct sunlight has to be guaranteed in the premises of the surrounding buildings. It is also the most conservative planning tool for natural light requirements in the interior of buildings, comparing zoning ordinances or daylight tools that take into account skylight and reflected light as well [11].

The solar collection method is a development of the solar envelope method. It predicts on a given plot the minimum heights at which a new building's windows and glazed areas should be located to receive the minimum required amount of direct sunlight hours per day in the specified period of the year and time of day [12, 13].

As with the solar envelope, the solar collection method also considers the layout, latitude, orientation and distance of the plot from the surrounding environment. Nevertheless, its main characteristic is to take into account the heights of the neighboring buildings. This way the solar collection isosurface generated on the plot is the lowest location of the points not shaded by the neighboring buildings in the required period of the year and time frame. The two methods can be used simultaneously to determine the maximum mass and layout of buildings and the usable portion of façades.

The present work discusses an advanced method to generate solar collection isosurfaces that is more efficient than the existing in relation to the complex Estonian daylight standard in urban environments. The existing method and the environmental analysis software available are not sufficiently adequate to allow for an efficient prediction of the lowest heights at which windows and glazed areas of new buildings should be located to fulfill the requirement of 2.5 h of direct sunlight per day during the period between the 22nd of April and the 22nd of August (Fig. 1).

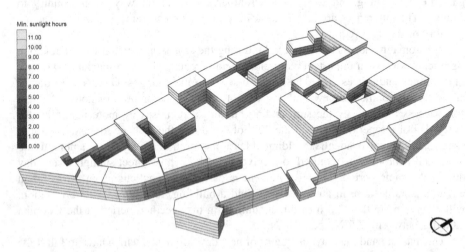

Fig. 1. Analysis of direct sunlight hours on building façades in the city of Tallinn and calculation of the minimum amount received per day from the 22nd of April to the 22nd of August.

2 Existing Methods

The current section discusses the generation of both the solar envelope and the solar collection isosurface using existing methods. Being that the two procedures are equivalent, even though they produce opposite results, their joint discussion strengthens the scope and introduces the background of the present research.

Both the solar envelope and solar collection are intuitive methods that permit one to easily calculate the relative shapes, even on paper. The necessary data for the calculation is the plot's layout, the solar azimuth and altitude at every specific hour of the period of the year, and the distances and heights of surrounding buildings. Nonetheless the procedure of calculation on paper can be used only for very simple plots and surroundings layouts, and is anyway a long, tedious and error prone process even for expert designers.

A useful chart for the selection of the size and shape of solar envelopes has been developed by Brown and DeKay [14] using calculation on paper. Depending on the orientation of the plot the chart indicates the slopes angle and the ridges horizontal angle for different latitudes from 0° to 72°, for different time frames during the two equinoxes and the two solstice days.

Pioneering computer-based tools to create solar envelopes have been studied and developed for many decades. Tools like SolVelope, developed by Yeh [15], permit one to generate solar envelopes by selecting the latitude and orientation of the site, the time and days in which neighboring buildings should not be overshadowed, and the shadow limits, but can only be used for rectangular and horizontal plots. These shortcomings were solved by the computer tool SolCAD, developed by Juyal et al. [16]. It used DXF files to import the plot boundaries and outlines of neighboring buildings and it took into account complex plot layouts with convex and concave boundaries and sloping sites. The solar envelope was generated as Mesh from the grid of point of the plot's sub-division and it took into account different shadow limit heights on the surrounding buildings.

An automated system, called SustArc, was developed by Capeluto and Shaviv [17, 18] to automatically calculate the Solar Rights Envelope, the Solar Collection Envelope and the Solar Volume in between the two for the generation and evaluation of different urban fabrics. It utilizes a series of poles located at the intersections of a grid that divides the plot into small samples.

Using the angles of the solar azimuth and altitude at the specific hours of the given period it is possible to calculate the maximum height for every pole so that its shadow does not extend beyond the desired limit, i.e. the footprint of the surrounding buildings or the edge of the sidewalk not to be shaded. The three dimensional matrix of points at the top of all the poles constitutes the upper surface of the Solar Rights Envelope.

The same poles on the plot's grid are used for the generation of the Solar Collection Envelope. In this case the shadows cast on the poles by the surrounding buildings at every hour of the given period indicate the lowest heights at which to locate the windows of future buildings at the same location as the pole. This way, the premises will receive direct sunlight for all of the hours and days of the period of the year taken into account.

Environmental analysis software and plug-ins for CAAD and parametric programs based on the existing methods currently permit one to generate solar envelopes and solar collection isosurfaces and to realize custom scripts for special tasks [19–22]. The necessary inputs are the latitude, the contour line of the plot, the size of the subdivision of the plot, baselines or rooflines of the surrounding buildings, depending respectively on whether a solar envelope or a solar collection isosurface has to be generated, and the sun vectors of every hour, or portion thereof, of the period to be considered. The final result, in both cases, is a surface defined by the points of the grid on the plot translated along the Z axis (Fig. 2).

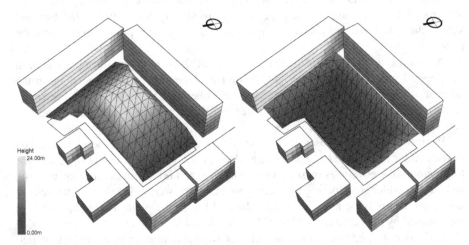

Fig. 2. Solar envelope surface (left) and solar collection isosurface (right) generated with the existing method for a plot located in Tallinn for the 21st of June from 07.00 to 17.00.

The points that generate the solar envelope are the highest among those that allow the neighboring façades to receive direct sunlight at the specified hours of the period. The shape of the solar envelope is then defined by the volume between the surface and the ground. The points that generate the solar collection isosurface are the lowest among those that receive direct sunlight at the specified hours of the period.

Both the existing methods, and the available computer tools based on environmental software to generate solar envelopes and solar collection isosurfaces are inadequate when used in relation to the Estonian standard in urban environments.

The existing solar envelope method is not efficient because, during a specific period of the year, it takes into consideration specific hours of the day during which direct sunlight has to be guaranteed on the surrounding façades with a fixed start and end time. Since different façades with different orientations receive different quantities of direct sunlight hours, especially in an urban environment, due to the particular overshadowing of the surrounding buildings, it is not possible to efficiently use the same start and end time for different façades in case the target is the 50% of the actual quantity of sunlight hours as required by the Estonian regulation.

This shortcoming has been tackled by De Luca [23], who developed an advanced method for the generation of solar envelopes. This advanced method uses multi-objective optimization to generate a solar envelope, calculating by simulation the actual amount of direct sunlight hours received by each sample of the façades surrounding the plot. The main objectives of the optimization process are the minimization of the deviations between the direct sunlight hours that each sample receives at each iteration (solar envelope variation), and the required 50%, and the maximization of the solar envelope size. This strategy permits to generate solar envelopes the size of which is more accurate, usually larger that of the solar envelopes generated with the existing method, and to guarantee that the façades surrounding the plot receive the required direct sunlight every day in the specified period, and at the time in which the intensity of direct solar radiation is higher [24].

The existing method to generate solar collection isosurfaces, applied in the most advanced environmental analysis software, has two critical aspects. It subdivides the plot with a horizontal grid of points used to calculate the solar access in the different locations on the plot, and, similarly to the solar envelope method and available software tools, it uses a fixed start and end time for every day of the analysis period.

The first aspect is a shortcoming because a point on a horizontal plane, the plot, receives a number of direct sunlight hours during a day larger than a point on a vertical plane, like the façade of a building which has a specific orientation.

A free point on a plot could receive a number of direct sunlight hours equal to the duration of an entire day from sunrise to sunset if not overshadowed by surrounding buildings. Whereas the amount of direct sunlight hours per day on an unshaded façade facing South, that has the longest sun exposure, e.g., in Tallinn, Estonia (Lat. 59°26′N Lon. 24°45′E) is a maximum of 11 (Fig. 3). This way, the solar collection isosurface generated with the existing method accounts for a larger quantity of direct sunlight hours and the height of its points above the ground is not correctly predicted.

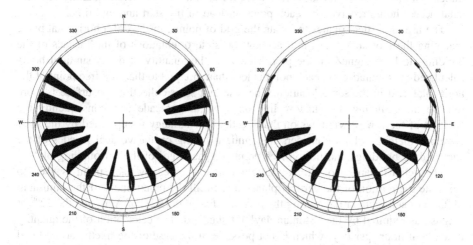

Fig. 3. Sun paths for the city of Tallinn indicating the sun positions for the period from the 22nd of April to the 22nd of August and the sun's rays falling on an horizontal unshaded plane (left) and on a vertical unshaded façade facing south (right).

The second critical aspect makes the existing method suitable only for cases in which solar collection is required for specific hours (e.g., from 10.00 to 14.00, for the entire day, at noon) every day of the selected period or for one single day, due to the setting of the fixed start and end time. In the case of the Estonian daylight standard, in which the requirement is 2.5 h of direct solar access, the existing method is hardly applicable. It does not permit one to know a priori if and at which hours a specific point on the plot in an urban context receives the required direct sunlight; hours that should be used to set the start and end time for the calculation.

Furthermore, different points on different façades would require different start and end time settings. In the case of the Estonian regulation the existing method is applicable only if the plot is not surrounded by any buildings. In this case, every façade's orientation, and the entire façade receives the minimum of 2.5 h of direct sunlight every day during the required period. The resulting solar collection isosurface would be a horizontal plane corresponding with the plot itself.

The present work proposes a method for the generation of solar collection isosurfaces that is more efficient than the existing method for the requirements of Estonian daylight standards in an urban context. The following sections discuss the advancements of the proposed method and present the results and the comparison with the existing method.

3 Proposed Solar Collection Method

The proposed method to generate solar collection isosurfaces tackles the two shortcomings of the existing method, so that it can be efficiently used in the case of the Estonian regulation in urban contexts through two main improvements: it uses vertical planes, instead of horizontal, on which the points used to determine the quantity of direct sunlight hours the façades receive are located; it uses the actual quantity of direct solar access hours received by each point, instead of the start and end time.

The use of vertical planes to locate the grid of points, instead of a horizontal plane matching the plot area, takes into account possible orientations of the façades of the buildings to be designed on the plot. This way, the quantity of direct sunlight hours calculated by simulation on each point is less than or equal to that of a free point of the horizontal grid in the same location. The resultant solar collection isosurface is more reliable in predicting the shadow line on a building façade and consequently the location of the lowest windows on that façade. This strategy is supported by the solar envelope method, which considers the sunlight falling on the vertical façades of the surrounding buildings and not on free points on the edges of the surrounding plots.

The actual quantity of direct sunlight hours received by each point is used to calculate the portion of the vertical planes that fulfill the requirement of the minimum of 2.5 h of sunlight per day during the period between the 22nd of April and the 22nd of August, as required by the Estonian daylight standard. The calculation of the quantity of sunlight hours per day, which is not possible in the case of the fixed start and end time used by the existing method, is necessary because different façades with different orientations receive light at different hours during the day and in different quantities in a complex urban environment. This strategy is based on the findings of De Luca [23] on an advanced method for the generation of solar envelopes.

By using environmental analysis tools integrated into parametric design software, both of the above mentioned strategies are possible. The programs used for the present study are Rhinoceros [25], as the 3D modeling environment; Grasshopper [26], for the parametric and algorithmic design; and Ladybug Tools [27], for environmental analysis and simulation.

3.1 Multi-isosurface

The key aspect of the proposed method is to split the generation of the single solar collection isosurface of the existing method into multiple isosurfaces. Four isosurfaces have been used for the present study, in order to keep the investigation as simple as possible, one aligned with the main plot edge and the others forming a rectangle with the first (Fig. 4). The reason multiple isosurfaces are being used is due to the fact that the proposed method is based on the use of vertical planes for the location of the analysis points. The vertical planes simulate possible orientations of building façades and it has been assumed that at least one orientation is parallel to the main plot's edge. The same method could use as many isosurfaces as needed to take into account plots with complex layouts or buildings with orientations different than the plot edges.

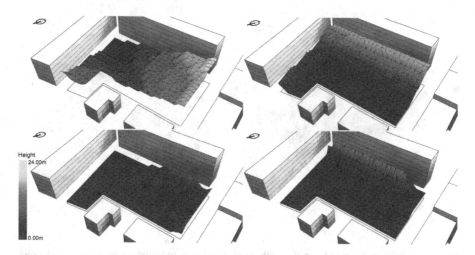

Fig. 4. The four solar collection isosurfaces generated with the proposed method for the relative plot orientations, using the southwest edge of the plot as the main alignment.

Therefore, each solar collection isosurface generated through multiple vertical planes with the same orientation is associated with the possible orientation of one building's façade. This way, each generated solar collection isosurface can predict more exactly the portion of the relative façade that does not fulfill the requirement for minimum direct solar access. Although generated separately the isosurfaces are used simultaneously for the solar collection prediction, hence the name of multi-isosurface.

3.2   Algorithm Design

For the investigation and development of the proposed method and for comparison with the existing method a multi-stage algorithm has been developed through the integration of environmental analysis tools and parametric design.

In the first stage a solar collection isosurface, using the existing method, is generated for a performance comparison with the proposed method. The plot's horizontal plane is subdivided into a regular grid of square samples 3-meter sized. Located at the center of each sample are the points used to calculate the minimum quantity of direct sunlight hours that fall on the plot per day during the period from the 22nd of April to the 22nd of August.

An array of surfaces with the same plot layout is generated along the Z axis in the positive direction at a distance of 3 m, each corresponding to the standard floor to floor height of residential buildings. The number of surfaces corresponds to the maximum buildable height on the plot. Each surface is subdivided into a grid of samples in the same way as the first surface on the plot and the calculation of minimum direct solar access per day is performed for each horizontal surface (Fig. 5).

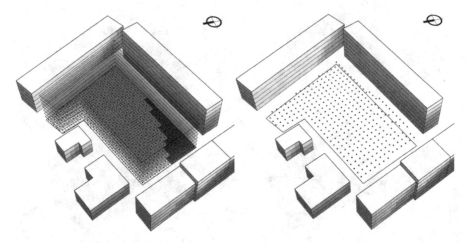

Fig. 5. The horizontal grid of samples with those that do not meet the requirement in dark color and the surface array (left), the selection of the lowest points that meet the requirement (right).

This process corresponds to the use of vertical poles at each grid point on the plot to determine which portion of the pole receives direct sunlight during the day in the specified period of the year, although it takes into account the actual quantity of direct sunlight received by each sample instead of whether the sample receives direct sunlight during a fixed time of the day. Actual environmental analysis software needs discreet surfaces (the grid samples) to perform calculations of sunlight hours on their centroids.

Once the three dimensional grid of points that fulfills the minimum of 2.5 h of direct sunlight per day has been obtained, a selection algorithm identifies those with the smallest Z coordinate among those sharing the same X and Y coordinates (Fig. 5). Consequently the points are used to generate the solar collection isosurface.

In the following step, a procedure similar to the previous one is applied to vertical planes, the innovative aspect of the proposed method.

A rectangular polyline bounding the plot is generated, with one or more sides parallel to the plot's edges. An array of vertical planes is generated, at a distance of 3 m, for each of the four orientations of the rectangle bounding the plot. The height of the planes corresponds to the maximum buildable height on the plot and they are subdivided into a 3-meter sized grid of square samples to ensure the same level of accuracy as the procedure used in the existing method (Fig. 6).

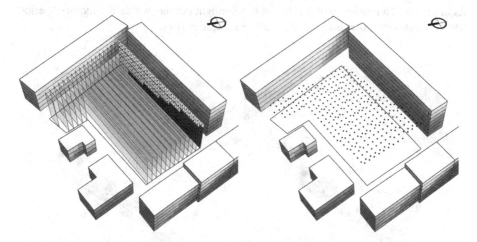

Fig. 6. The vertical grid of samples, for one of the orientations used, with those that do not meet the requirement in dark color (left), the lowest points that meet the requirement (right).

Through the use of an iterative algorithm the calculation of direct sunlight hours is performed on each vertical plane and the process is repeated for each of the four orientations. The same algorithm used for the horizontal planes of the existing method calculates the minimum amount of hours of direct solar access per day on each sample in the specific period. The result is four different three-dimensional grids of points, one for each orientation. The algorithm then selects the points for each orientation with the smallest Z coordinate among those that share the same X and Y coordinates (Fig. 6). The four resulting groups of points are used to generate four solar collection isosurfaces that are used at the same time to constitute one multi-isosurface.

In the following stages performances evaluation and comparison of the proposed and existing methods is performed through computation by simulation of the actual portion of the façades that do not meet the requirement of a number of buildings and analysis of the predictions of both methods.

The buildings used for the test of the two methods are simple "shoe-box" models. A specific portion of the algorithm generates all the possible variations of footprints of the buildings, based on a 3-meter sized square module, different for size, ratio of the two dimensions and location within the plot. One of the four orientations of the footprints of the buildings is parallel to the main plot edge and to the rectangle used for the generation of the multiple isosurfaces of the proposed method.

The footprints are extruded to generate the shapes of the buildings with an incremental step of 3 m up to the maximum allowed height for the buildings. The algorithm selects among each series the highest that is completely contained inside the solar envelope previously generated with the advanced method described [23].

The calculation of direct solar access hours, using environmental analysis software, is performed on the façades of each building variation, subdivided using 3-meter sized grids of square samples. The algorithm computes samples which do not meet the requirement of a minimum of 2.5 h of direct sunlight per day within the required period and calculates the total area (m^2) for all four façades (Fig. 7).

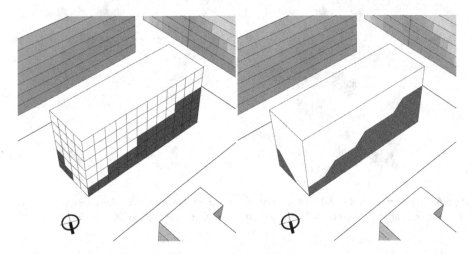

Fig. 7. Areas of a building's variation façades that do not meet the requirement in dark color, computed by simulation (left), predicted through proposed method solar isosurface (right).

The task of the solar collection isosurface method is to predict the portion of a building that does not meet the requirement for direct solar access through the intersection of the isosurface with the façades. The portion of the building's façade below the isosurface does not meet the requirement; the part above meets the requirement.

The isosurface generated with the existing method is intersected with all four façades of each building's variation and the area (m^2) of the portion of the façades below the isosurface computed. Each isosurface of the multi-isosurface generated with the proposed method using one orientation is intersected with the façade with the corresponding orientation for every building's variation and the areas (m^2) of the portion of the four façades below the isosurfaces are computed and summed (Fig. 7).

The last step of the algorithm computes, for all of the building's variations, the ratios between the areas of the façades that do not fulfill the requirement predicted by the solar collection isosurfaces generated with both methods and the areas of the same façades that do not fulfill the requirement computed by simulation. The computed ratios are used to evaluate and compare the efficacy of each method.

The isosurface method is a quick procedure to assess the solar collection potentialities on a building whereas the direct calculation of sunlight hours on many building's variations is a time-consuming trial-and-error process.

3.3 Urban Areas

The proposed method has been tested and compared with the existing method in four different cases, each one related to plot located in a different urban area in the city of Tallinn, Estonia. The four areas have been chosen for their different layout and the pattern of neighboring buildings, one low density suburban area and three high density urban areas with different characteristics (Fig. 8).

Fig. 8. The four plots of the study cases: 1 top left, 2 top right, 3 bottom left and 4 bottom right. Source of images: Estonian Geoportal 2016–2017

Case 1. The Padriku Street plot is located in the low density suburb called Pirita, in the North-East sector of the city, developed mostly during the beginning of the 2000s. A few small residential buildings of four floors are located beyond the East and North edges of the plot. As a result, the plot is mostly free in all orientations.

Case 2. Kaupmehe Street, located in the City Center, is characterized by different types and sizes of buildings, mostly residential, dating from the second half of the 20th century. The buildings surrounding the plot are located at different distances, with a minimum of 8 m as required by fire regulations, and have different heights, varying from 3 to 8 stories. This makes the area a dense and varied environment.

Case 3. Pärnu Street, located in the City Center, is characterized by buildings with different heights, ranging from 5 to 8 stories and built during the 20th century. The peculiarity of this plot is that two of the surrounding buildings lay on two edges of the plot due to the fact that they constitute a street continuous façade. The other buildings are at different distances, from a minimum of 8 m to 20 m across the nearby street.

Case 4. This case plot is located in the Sääse high density neighborhood, in the Soviet era quarter of Mustamäe. The plot is surrounded on all sides by panel housing blocks of five stories to the East and West, and nine stories to South and North. The distance to all the buildings is the minimum of 8 m. This case is the most uniform in terms of the heights and the distances of surrounding buildings.

4   Results

The performance of the solar collection isosurface method is measured by the capacity to predict the portions of building façades that do not fulfill the requirement.

To analyze the performances of the two methods a large number of building mass variations have been generated for each of the four cases, varying in terms of footprint size and ratio, and location within the plot. Each building's façade has been divided into samples and the number of samples that do not meet the requirement of the minimum of 2.5 h of direct sunlight per day has been computed through simulation. A large number of building variations are necessary in order to obtain a broad data set that guarantees the reliability of the results.

Consequently, the existing solar collection method isosurface and the proposed method multi-isosurface have been generated for each plot and have been intersected with the variation of each building's mass to compute the areas of the façades portions not fulfilling the regulation. Finally the areas predicted through isosurfaces have been compared with the areas obtained by simulation and the deviations computed with Formula 1. The best performance is a deviation percent of the predicted area (Ap) against the simulated area (As) of 0.

$$(Abs\ (As - Ap))/As \qquad (1)$$

The results of Case 1 show that the deviations between the multi-isosurface method with simulated sunlight hours are in the range 0–29.2% for all 151 building variations. The deviations of the existing method are in the range of 0 to 95.9%, with most of the results above 50% and the rest below 10%. Evidence shows that in low-density areas the existing method has differentiated performance, depending on the distances from the few surrounding buildings, whereas the multi-isosurface method consistently performs better with 77.6% of the variations below 10% of deviation (Fig. 9).

The area of Case 2 is characterized by buildings with varying heights and distances. Comparing sunlight hours calculated by simulations of 134 building variations the deviations of the proposed method, which are in the range of 0–28.3%, with 68.6% of

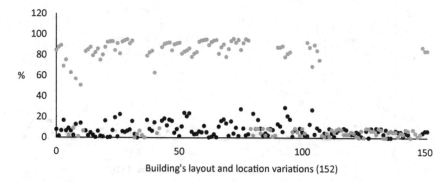

Fig. 9. Results of the deviations in Case 1, using the proposed and the existing method.

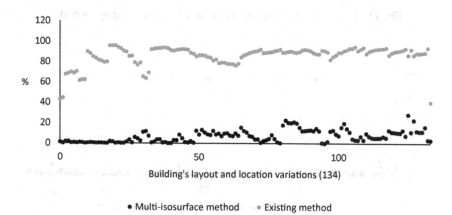

• Multi-isosurface method   • Existing method

Fig. 10. Results of Case 2 using the proposed and the existing method.

the variations below 10% of deviation, present consistently good performances. The consistent deviations of the existing method, which are in the range of 40.3–96.0%, show that in dense urban environments the existing method underestimates the area of façades that fail to meet requirements (Fig. 10).

The plot of Case 3 is surrounded by buildings of different heights and distances, with two of them located adjacent to the plot. The difference in performances between the proposed and the existing method is more evident for all 143 building variations. The deviations of the first are in the range of 0.1–23.6%, with 85.3% of the variations below 10%, whereas those of the latter are in the range of 55.7–96.3% (Fig. 11).

The buildings surrounding the plot of Case 4 are very close and tall. It is the most occluded of the four plots analyzed. Consequently the difference in performances is the most significant. The multi-isosurface method predictions have a deviation range comparing the simulation results of 0.1–15%, with 98.4% of the 192 variations below 10%, whereas the deviations range of the existing method is 93.5–98.4% (Fig. 12).

The results show that in dense urban environments the multi-isosurface method performs consistently better than the existing method. The proposed method shows

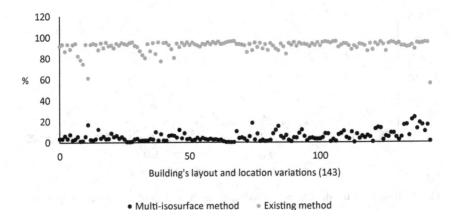

Fig. 11. Results of Case 3, using the proposed and the existing method.

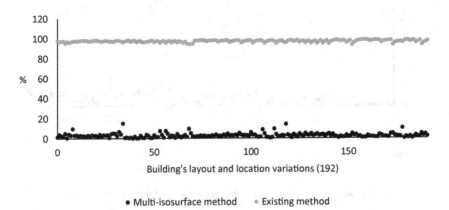

Fig. 12. Results of Case 4, using the proposed and the existing method.

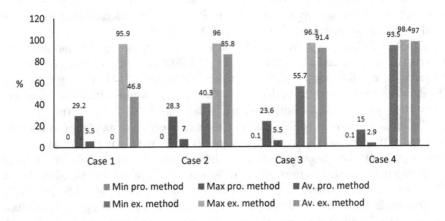

Fig. 13. Min, Max and Average (Av.) deviations for the proposed and the existing methods.

excellent performance in all cases, with small average deviations of 5.5%, 7%, 5.5% and 2.9%, respectively. The average prediction deviations of the existing method are considerable and increase with the increase in density of the area. They are 46.8%, 85.8%, 91.4% and 97%, respectively. This makes the existing method failing for the Estonian daylight standard, whereas the proposed method is adapt (Fig. 13).

5 Conclusions

This paper has discussed an advanced method for generating solar collection isosurfaces through the use of computational design and environmental analysis tools. The study is part of a broader research agenda arising from the need to develop efficient prediction tools for the requirements of the Estonian daylight standard. The regulation states that new residential buildings have to be designed in such a way that the premises' interiors receive a minimum of 2.5 h of direct sunlight every day during the period from the 22nd of April to the 22nd of August.

In an urban context, the actual solar collection method and the software tools based on it are very inefficient when it comes to predicting the portion of a building's façade that does not fulfill the requirements. There are two main shortcomings: first, it calculates the solar collection potentials on horizontal planes; and second, it uses a fixed start and end time to determine the daily period in which the direct sunlight has to be guaranteed.

The proposed method tackles the above-mentioned shortcomings with two innovative procedures. The first is the utilization of vertical planes to compute which parts fail to fulfill the requirement. This way the results are more reliable, since vertical planes simulate the orientation and location of the building's façades. The sets of vertical planes generate different solar collection isosurfaces to be used in association with specific building façades. The result is a solar collection multi-isosurface.

The second is the computation by simulation of the actual quantity of direct solar access hours on the vertical planes. Since, in an urban context, different façades receive different quantities of sunlight at different times of the day, this strategy permits one to predict more efficiently which portion of the vertical planes, i.e. the façades of buildings, fulfills the requirements.

The proposed method has proved to be superior in each of the four analyzed cases. Results show that in the urban context with increasing density the difference of prediction performance of the existing method and the proposed method increases. In the case of low density areas the existing method has a variety of performances whereas in the cases of high density areas the results are very poor. On the contrary, the proposed method shows excellent results for all types of urban areas.

The solar collection isosurface method has proven to be a reliable tool for the prediction of solar access on building façades, if the proposed advancements are taken into account. Nonetheless, the method can only be used for simple "shoe-box" shaped buildings. It is not possible to use the solar collection isosurface method for buildings with articulated shapes because it does not take into account the self-shading of opposite or concave façades.

Future work with the research agenda will include investigating methods for buildings' massing generation from solar envelopes and layout optimization for solar collection based on the analysis of the performances of different architectural typologies.

Acknowledgements. The research has been supported by the Estonian Research Council, with Personal research funding grant PUT-652.

References

1. Turnbull, P., Loisos, G.: Baselines and barriers: current design practices in daylight. In: Proceedings of the 2000 ACEEE Summer Study on Energy Efficiency in Buildings, vol. 3, pp. 329–336. ACEEE, Washington, D.C. (2000)
2. Reinhart, C., Selkowitz, S.: Daylighting – light, form and people. Energy Build. **38**, 715–717 (2006). doi:10.1016/j.enbuild.2006.03.005
3. Veitch, J.A., Newsham, G.R.: Quantifying lighting quality based on experimental investigations of end user performance and preference. In: Proceedings of the Right Light Three: 3rd European Conference on Energy-Efficient Lighting, vol. 1, pp. 119–127. National Research Council of Canada, Ottawa (1995)
4. Samuels, R.: Solar efficient architecture and quality of life: the role of sunlight in ecological and psychological well-being. In: Saygh, A.A.M. (ed.) Proceedings of the Energy and the Environment into the 1990's: 1st World Renewable Energy Congress, pp. 2653–2659. Pergamon Press, Oxford (1990)
5. Altomonte, S.: Daylight for energy savings and psycho-physiological well-being in sustainable built environments. J. Sustain. Dev. **1**(3), 3–16 (2008). doi:10.5539/jsd.v1n3p3
6. Reinhart, C.: Daylighting Handbook I. Fundamentals. Designing with the Sun. The MIT Press, Cambridge (2014)
7. Johnsen, K., Watkins, R. (eds.): Daylighting in Buildings. Energy Conservation in Buildings & Community Systems & Solar Heating and Cooling Programmes, ECBCS Annex 29/ SHC Task 21. AECOM, Birmingham (2010)
8. Estonian Centre for Standardization: EVS 894:2008/A2:2015 Daylight in Dwellings and Offices. Tallinn (2015)
9. Knowles, R.L.: Sun Rhythm Form. MIT Press, Cambridge (1981)
10. Knowles, R.L.: The solar envelope: its meaning for energy and buildings. Energy Build. **35**(1), 15–25 (2003). doi:10.1016/S0378-7788(02)00076-2
11. DeKay, M.: A comparative review of daylight planning tools and a rule-of-thumb for street width to building height ratio. In: Burley, S., Arden, M.E. (eds.) Proceedings of the 17th National Passive Solar Conference, pp. 120–125. American Solar Energy Society, Boulder (1992)
12. Capeluto, I.G., Shaviv, E.: Modeling the design of urban fabric with solar rights considerations. In: Proceedings of the IBPSA 1999 Conference, pp. 1341–1347. International Building Performance Simulation Association, Toronto (1999)
13. Capeluto, I.G., Yezioro, A., Bleiberg, T., Shaviv, E.: From computer models to simple design tools: solar rights in the design of urban streets. In: Proceedings of the IBPSA 2005 Conference, pp. 131–138. International Building Performance Simulation Association, Toronto (2005)

14. Brown, G.Z., DeKay, M.: Sun, Wind and Light. Architectural Design Strategies, 2nd edn. Wiley, New York (2001)
15. Yeh, U.P.: Computer Aided Solar Envelope Design. ProQuest, Ann Arbor, MI (1992)
16. Juyal, M., Kensek, K., Knowles, R.L.: SolCAD: 3D spatial design tool to generate solar envelope. In: Klinger, K. (ed.) Proceedings of the Connecting >> Crossroads of Digital Discourse ACADIA 2003 Annual Conference of the Association for Computer Aided Design in Architecture, pp. 411–419. ACADIA, Indianapolis, IN (2003)
17. Capeluto, I.G., Shaviv, E.: On the use of 'solar volume' for determining the urban fabric. Sol. Energy **70**(3), 275–280 (2001). doi:10.1016/S0038-092X(00)00088-8
18. Shaviv, E.: A direct generative CAD tool for the site layout of communities with solar access to each building. In: Agger, K. et al. (eds.) Proceedings of the CAAD: Education-Research and Practice eCAADe Conference 1989, pp. 9.17.1–9.17.9. Education and research in Computer Aided Architectural Design in Europe, Brussels (1989)
19. Marsh, A.: Computer-optimized shading design. In: Proceedings of the IBPSA 2003 Conference, pp. 831–837. International Building Performance Simulation Association, Toronto (2003)
20. DIVA for Rhino Homepage. http://diva4rhino.com/. Last accessed 14 Apr 2017
21. Sadeghipour, M., Pak, M.: Ladybug: a parametric environmental plugin for GRASSHOPPER to help designers create an environmentally-conscious design. In: Wurtz, E. (ed.) Proceedings of the IBPSA 2013 Conference, pp. 3128–3135. International Building Performance Simulation Association, Toronto (2013)
22. Niemasz, J., Sargent, J., Reinhart, C.: Solar zoning and energy in detached residential dwellings. Environ. Plan. B Plan. Des. **40**, 801–813 (2013). doi:10.1068/b38055
23. De Luca, F.: Solar envelope optimization method for complex urban environments. In: Szoboszlai, M. (ed.) Proceedings of the Back to Command 2016 CAADence in Architecture Conference, pp. 223–229. Faculty of Architecture, Budapest University of Technology and Economics, Budapest (2016). doi:10.3311/CAADence.1657
24. Ratti, C., Morello, E.: SunScapes: extending the 'solar envelopes' concept through 'iso-solar' surfaces. In: Raydan, D.K., Melki, H.H. (eds.) Proceedings of the PLEA 2005 22nd Conference on Passive and Low Energy Architecture, pp. 815–820. NDU Publishing, Washington (2005)
25. Rhinoceros Homepage. http://www.rhino3d.com/. Last accessed 14 Apr 2017
26. Grasshopper Homepage. http://www.grasshopper3d.com/. Last accessed 14 Apr 2017
27. Ladybug Tools Homepage. http://www.ladybug.tools/. Last accessed 14 Apr 2017

Studying Design Behavior in Digital Environments

Making Sense of Design Space

What Designers Do with Large Numbers of Alternatives?

Naghmi Shireen[⊠], Halil Erhan, Robert Woodbury, and Ivy Wang

School of Interactive Arts and Technology,
Simon Fraser University, Burnaby, Canada
{nshireen, herhan, rw}@sfu.ca, ivy.ye.wang@gmail.com

Abstract. Today's generative design tools and large screen displays present opportunities for designers to explore large number of design alternatives. Besides numerous studies in design, the act of exploring design space is yet to be integrated in the design of new digital media. To understand how designer's search patterns will uncover when provided with a gallery of large numbers of design solutions, we conducted a lab experiment with nine designers. Particularly the study explored how designers used spatial structuring of their work environment to make informed design decisions. The results of the study present intuitions for development of next generation front-end gallery interfaces for managing a large set of design variations while enabling simultaneous editing of design parameters.

Keywords: Parametric design · Alternatives · Design space exploration · New interfaces · New media · Protocol analysis · User study

1 Introduction

Designers explore design variations at each design stage throughout the process. As they explore, they reflect on their design decisions [16], and interact with the already explored design space [23] for sense-making [19] and revisiting decisions [1]. We know this behavior from repeated studies in the design literature [1, 4, 6, 7]. An important and considerably under-researched question is *how* designers can interact and reflect on the design space when the solution space grows faster and larger than they can handle using the conventional design media. In particular, when we consider availability of the increased computational power and new interaction devices—such as large screen displays—we should seek for new design media addressing how to support generating *a large* numbers of design variations. It may take a "good" system to generate thousands of design variations from a parametric model almost instantly. Therefore, the challenge for designers is the interaction with such large numbers of solutions. The legacy tool features and conventional approach to design pose a bottleneck. For example, most of these tools still only allow working on a single-model at a time [21], are not equipped to help store and navigate through the generated design space, and are not even able to display alternative solutions side-by-side, a basic strategy for quick comparison promoting reflection and sense-making.

© Springer Nature Singapore Pte Ltd. 2017
G. Çağdaş et al. (Eds.): CAAD Futures 2017, CCIS 724, pp. 191–211, 2017.
DOI: 10.1007/978-981-10-5197-5_11

Particularly, interaction on single-model, i.e. one-at-a-time interface strategy is because most of these tools are designed for a limited display space, e.g. for desktop computing. This is contrary to the findings from the field studies on observing expert designers that show evidences of them working through multiple design variations on large office walls [22]. The mismatch between the tool and task of design exploration is one of the major impediments for working with large number of alternatives. Hence, our research goal is to reduce—if not eliminate—this mismatch between the technology for design and the design exploration behaviors. As a first step, we aim to develop interfaces that can support working on a large design space for sense-making and an informed design decision.

The literature shows that working with multiple designs in parallel results into a more efficient design process and creative design solutions [5, 15, 18, 24]. However, we also contend that there is a cognitive cost associated with working on large number of design variations simultaneously. Experiments in marketing [11] suggest that when decision makers are confronted with extensive options, the result is a *choice-overload problem*, producing frustration and dissatisfaction. In addition, relevant cognitive science studies suggest that when experts are to work with multiple objects, they resort to workspace management to reduce the cognitive overload, e.g. by intelligently laying out cues for themselves within the environment they are working in [10, 13, 14].

Although the previous studies look at the decision makers' behavior when they were asked to make choices among given alternatives, we have yet to see how the lessons learned could translate to design where the alternatives are created and chosen by the same agents. In addition, we need to explore how designers' strategies for managing alternatives may differ when they were given computational tools that can enable working with large numbers of possible alternatives and the associated choice overload problem.

We believe that developing interface solutions for working with a large numbers of design alternatives is highly coupled with understanding how designers make sense of design space. In this paper, we present an experiment conducted in a simulated design task environment where designers are asked to choose plausible design solutions among given 1000 alternative. In the environment, designers work with alternative solutions generated from a parametric model printed on index cards using vertical and horizontal working surfaces. The goal of the experiment is to study how designers may use their task environment as a cognitive ally, while (re)structuring their design workflow. Hence the collected data is analyzed and presented with emphasis on two inter-related concerns: what are the manifested design moves and in response how the spatial structuring corresponds to the observed design moves.

1.1 Design Process

One dominant view to design accepts it as a creative but complex problem solving process [19], in which designer's actions, domain expertise, individual preferences along with the external conditions and design media together defines the outcome [10]. The studies on the invariants in problem-solving process confirms that a designer starts with ill-defined problem structures usually with a solution-focused strategy [1, 16].

The designers are highly opportunistic in their behavior with frequent 'switching of types of cognitive activities' [4, 6]. When needed, they exercise their creative freedom, by changing design goals and constraints [4, 16], as their understanding of problem develops and definition of solutions proceeds [1, 4, 16]. Most of these findings are derived by observing designers during laboratory based protocol or ethnographic studies in various design domains where the design medium has primarily been sketching or computer-aided design (CAD) tools where the delegation of controls lies with the human designer during the process of exploration.

With increasing use of generative design methods for design exploration, *sketching-a-solution* is now complemented by *filtering-a-bunch* of plausible solutions out of a large set. The set can be created using computer-assisted or computer-generated techniques [12, 22]. Our focus for this experiment is to explore how this technological shift has impacted the design process and the embedded design tasks. To our knowledge, there is limited research that studies designer's search patterns when the design alternatives are computationally generated; selectively filtered and are presented back to the designer for further exploration and reflection. In our experiment, we observed designers working with a large set of computer-generated design solutions in a minimally structured exploratory setting. The results from the study, as expected, show design exploration patterns and a set of exploratory (goal-oriented) design tasks. In the follow up studies, we aim to abstract these to a set of system functions for (design) gallery style interfaces to explore a computationally generated design-space.

1.2 Spatial Structure

As noted earlier, experts in different domains tend to use their own work environment as a cognitive ally when confronted with cognition-intensive task [10]. They structure their surrounding space to simplify choice, perception and internal computation [13]. However, to the best our knowledge, no research has been carried out studying 'designer' to confirm these behaviors, especially when they are cognitively challenged to find solutions from a large set of alternatives. Such a research study would hold value and novelty in exploring the interaction patterns of designers within the design space. In our research, we report spatial patterns of design media use and correlate them with the design process observed. We aim to apply the lessons learned to design front-end interfaces, considering the physical surfaces and digital screens (e.g. table-top displays) both have equally limited real estate to work with.

According to the literature [13], spatial structuring happens at three levels: *high, medium and low*. *High level structuring* is a long-term setting of a workspace to restore the environment to a state that agents can deal with for a longer period; "thereby diminishing uncertainty, reducing number of contingencies that have to be built into a program and allowing streamlining of plans" [13]. *Medium* and *low-level structuring* on the other hand, involves setting up a workspace for a task that spans across a limited period (usually known beforehand). This structuring is cognitively intense and experts have been observed to improve efficiency by strategically setting stations and allocating spaces for different tasks. They also keep on re-arranging and re-assigning stations and their contents.

For an in-depth analysis of spatial structuring, the participants in our study were pre-emptively exposed to a high-level structuring of the space by providing them with an arranged room space; hence prompting them to explore the design solutions at a finer granularity through medium- and low-level structuring of the space.

2 Research Design

"Bridging the gulf of execution requires mapping the psychological goals to the physical actions, permitted by the mechanism of that system. Bridging the gulf of evaluation, in turn is a mapping between physical state of the system to the psychological goals and intentions." - p. 43
Norman [17]

Generally, there are two ways to improve a system design: (1) by bringing the system closer to its user, or (2) by moving the users closer to system. This research design focuses on the former approach by first studying user's actions in an approximation of a natural setting then, based on the observed action patterns, suggesting "an interface that matches user's needs, in a form that can readily be interpreted and manipulated" [17].

We also know that there can hardly be an action without its effects on the medium in which it is performed. For our purposes, tabletop workspace with secondary cognitive artifacts (e.g. pencil and paper) is the basic work environment representing an interface. In our analysis, we ignored the effects of this work environment and have devised conclusions beyond it, to infer system requirements; more specifically front-end interface solutions. In our lab setting, we adapted the lessons from previous ethnographic studies for identifying some of the cognitive phenomena involved in using a task environment in developing a meaningful design exploration structure while working with computer-generated design solutions.

We chose to run a lab experiment over an ethnographic study because we wanted to overload designers with a large number (~ 1000) of computer generated design solutions, which may not have been guaranteed in a field setting. In a real setting, designers may move back and forth between design phases, (conceptualizing may overlap with prototyping for instance). Due to time and resource constraints, we limited our observations to the conceptual design development stage only, because this stage is amenable to exploring huge amounts of alternatives early in design. In addition, we wanted to observe designers' interaction with work surfaces to fully understand and infer lessons for interface design. Our possible interruption might alter designers' workflow in real setting that may not be desirable for both the designers and our goals. In addition, in a lab setting we could pre-plan the experiment in a way to capture the entire task environment and control it to avoid possible threats to our findings.

2.1 Generative Design Model

"If you want to get the most out of a sketch, you need to leave big enough holes." - p. 115
Buxton [2]

Before designing the experiment, the first step was to devise a hypothetical yet real world inspired design scenario that could align with the research objectives. The two most important objectives while developing a 3D model to be used in the experiment were: (1) it should be parametric, i.e., capable of generating a large set of variations, and (2) it should be appropriately abstract, i.e., the base design and its successors should have sketch-like characteristics[1] [2]. To capture the design intentions and processes, an abstract 3D model with sketch-like characteristics was conceived that facilitated exploration rather than evaluation of a detailed design. The model was meant to be a catalyst to an appropriate conversation between the designer and the design. It exhibited generative capabilities to seed millions of variations. It also had enough ambiguity to suggest and not tell, and be interpreted in millions of different ways, with new relationships observed every time a designer looked at the solutions.

It is a hypothetical apartment building, modelled using a parametric CAD[2] software with three basic design components, namely residential units, vertical circulation spaces, and open spaces such as terraces colored gray, red, and green respectively (Fig. 1). All three design components are parametrically defined boxes. The distance (space) between the same type of components in the model is defined by a non-linear parametric function[3] such that changing the point position and direction, will vary the spatial distribution of the related components. For example, the second gray box can be one unit away from the first one, while it can be 1.5 units away from the third depending on the output from the function. For the complete list of parameters used in the model and their value ranges see Fig. 2.

2.2 Alternative Generation

To make certain that selected design for the experiment looked visually different, we followed several steps (Fig. 3). First, a random number generator was used to generate combinations of values shown in Fig. 2. This resulted into $\sim 7^{25}$ possible input combinations that were next filtered based on a dissimilarity matrix, which was programmed to produce a set of 1000 design variations [8]. These combinations (based on model inputs) were used to generate parametric models along with their rendered outputs with a fixed camera position, background, material and light parameters using a parametric CAD system – *GenerativeComponents*®.

2.3 The Design Scenario

Keeping with Buxton's [2] suggestive ambiguity, we developed an open-ended design scenario to promote exploration using incomplete requirements rather than well-defined

---

[1] Buxton (2007) defines a sketch-like characteristic as, quick, inexpensive, disposable, clear, distinct and minimal; which is appropriately ambiguous to suggest and explore designs rather than confirming one early on.

[2] CAD: Computer-Aided Design.

[3] Order 4 Bezier curve.

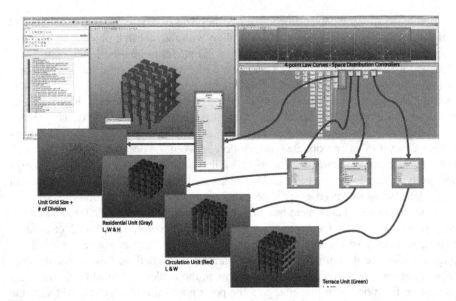

Fig. 1. The structure and sequence the model in which the components (residential units in gray, vertical circulation in red, and open spaces in green) were created and updated in relation to their respective parameters. (Color figure online)

No.	Parameter	Range (Min to Max)	Step Size
1	Building Length (Max)	2 to 14	2
2	Building Width (Max)	2 to 14	2
3	Building Height (Max)	2 to 14	2
4	Unit Grid Division (X, Y, Z)	2 to 1 (X,Y,Z each)	1
5	Resident Units (Gray) (H, W, L)	0.2 to 5 (H,W,L each)	0.2
6	Circulation Units (Red) (H, W, L)	0.2 to 5 (H,W,L each)	0.2
7	Terraces (Green) (H, W, L)	0.2 to 5 (H,W,L each)	0.2
8	Space Controller Point01(x,y) on X-plane	0 to 1 for both x and y positions	0.1
9	Space Controller Point02(x,y) on X-plane	0 to 1 for both x and y positions	0.1
10	Space Controller Point03(x,y) on Y-plane	0 to 1 for both x and y positions	0.1
11	Space Controller Point04(x,y) on Y-plane	0 to 1 for both x and y positions	0.1

Fig. 2. (Left) Sample of independent parameters that controlled the model; (Right) Model's design constraints

goals to avoid promoting a mere selection. We asked the participants to consider themselves as chief architect in a team which had come up with a large set of computer-generated conceptual models for a multi-storey residential building. Participants were unaware of the exact number of variations in the set. They were told that their job was to go through the designs and set goals for the next design phase (Fig. 4).

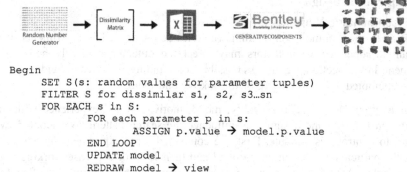

```
Begin
        SET S(s: random values for parameter tuples)
        FILTER S for dissimilar s1, s2, s3...sn
        FOR EACH s in S:
                FOR each parameter p in s:
                        ASSIGN p.value → model.p.value
                END LOOP
                UPDATE model
                REDRAW model → view
                SAVE  view
        END LOOP
```

Fig. 3. The pseudo code for generating each alternative as a dissimilar solution to others.

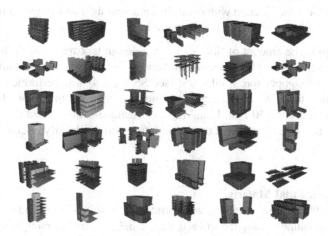

Fig. 4. A small sample of the dissimilar design variations

2.4 Participants

We used a mixed method sampling technique–*purposive random sampling*[4] to select participants for our study, who were randomly selected and approached through email correspondence. Respondents were further pre-screened with respect to their experience in parametric modelling and design expertise to avoid outliers in the data.

Ten participants (including the pilot participant) completed the given tasks. The pilot was performed in a different lab setting; hence the data from that study is excluded to maintain the validity of between-subject data analysis. The remaining nine participants had expertise working with computer-aided design tools in different capacities, and most, if not all, had some experience in working with parametric modelling.

---

[4] Random sampling: every individual has equal chance of being selected. Purposeful sampling: individuals are selected because they have experienced the central phenomenon.

2.5   Experiment Design

2.5.1   Confounding Variables

In addition to the common confounding variables across most lab experiments, it is important to identified what factors may affect the outcome explicitly before the experiment. In this section, we discuss possible confounding variables individually and how we attempted either to control or to look beyond them.

Human Factor: Designers' personality, mood, motivation and experience with the given design task and the design may influence the search pattern. We adopted two strategies to control this variable. First, we conducted a pre-experiment survey, confirming the participant's design background and their level of expertise working with programmable CAD tools (see Sect. 2.5.4). And second, an honorarium was offered to all participants to keep their motivation level consistent.

Lab Controlled Environment: To reduce the effect of tools and design environment, all participants were provided access to the same lab material and each session was conducted in the same location with controlled ambient light and temperature. The time of day was set to be convenient for the participants.

Limited Time: The amount of time spent on a design task may vary with the design strategy adapted, hence the experiment results. In the interest of fairness for a between-subject comparison, a pilot test (see Sect. 2.5.4) was performed to estimate task completion time. We found that the estimated time used to explore 1000 design alternatives was around 50 min. Using this as benchmark, we advised the participants that the task may take 60 min, but they were left free to finish early or take longer time if needed.

2.5.2   Experimental Material

Post-filtered 1000 design variations were printed on a plain $4'' \times 6''$ index cards along with a random number assigned to each variation. This random number was initially considered important to keep a track of mostly-viewed (between-subjects) or double-viewed (within-subject) variations. However, we ignored these numbers in this analysis, but a follow up study with different questions may use them (Fig. 5 Left). The set of 1000 index cards became the basic material for the experiment along with a table ($6' \times 4'$), two whiteboards ($8' \times 5'$), board markers, sticky notes, pen, pencils, extra whitepapers, erasers, board magnets, and masking tapes.

2.5.3   Experimental Setup

Each experimental session was video recorded using four different cameras (Fig. 5 Right). One GoPro® camera (GoPro#2) was head-strapped to the participant's fore-head, with an intention to roughly capture participant's focus of attention. Another (GoPro#1) was used to capture the aerial view of the table specifically, and most of the room's view generally. The other two cameras were set up to capture the two whiteboards and participant's hand movements or any other action outside the coverage area of two GoPro® cameras. Figure 6 shows the views from each of the camera to illustrate

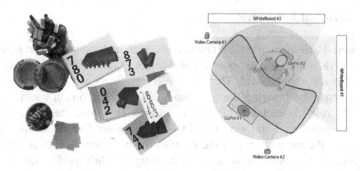

Fig. 5. (Left) Experimental material; (Right) Experimental setup

Fig. 6. Views from the video recorders used, which later consolidated into one stream of video

the effectiveness of experimental setting and the amount of coverage details. We consolidated the four views into one video stream for data analysis.

2.5.4 Pilot Study

The pilot study served two purposes: First, it was used to confirm the overall logistics of the study, such as the experimental set up (e.g., room arrangement, camera locations, video/audio settings), the experiment flow, and the effectiveness of pre- and post-experiment questionnaires and sequence of questions. Secondly, and most importantly the video and audio data from the pilot study was used to develop a set of preliminary design actions and activities, which were later refined based on the actual experimental data. We used the preliminary findings from the pilot for developing the initial coding scheme and the patterns that we needed to look for in the analysis of the final data. The pilot study also played an important role in determining the time required for successfully carrying out an experiment session.

2.5.5   Experiment Procedure

Introduction: Each participant completed the task individually. There were two researchers in the room: one to observe and take note, and the other provided assistant to the participants when needed. They were less interfering as much as possible. The experiment began by bringing the participant into the experiment room, presenting them to the high-level structuring of the design space. They were then briefed about the study, its (potential) risks and were asked to sign a consent form to release video and audio rights to the researchers and the confidentiality of their identities. Participants were specifically requested to vocalize their thoughts while performing the task to emulate and capture the design through processes.

Pre-experiment Questionnaire: After the briefing, the participants were asked to fill out a pre-experiment questionnaire, which was intended to collect data on demographic and experience. They were asked whether they had any design experience, if so, how long and in what field. In addition, they were asked to rate their experience in various CAD tools on a 5-level Likert scale, where 1 represented 'Novice' and 5 represented 'Expert'. We used this information largely to interpret the spread of expertise and to reason out any anomaly in the data.

Design Task: The participants were then introduced with the design scenario. They were asked to voice any clarifications they might need to further understand the given task. After the participants confirm their understanding of the task and design requirements, we gave them a single stack of randomly ordered 1000 index cards. We, then, asked them to start the design selection task. During the study, one of the two researchers in the room answered the participants' questions and reminded them to keep voicing their thoughts. Once the participant verbally notified the completion of the task, the researchers asked the participant's final decision on the design solutions and performed a formal follow up post-experimental interview.

Post-experiment Questionnaire: The post-experiment interview began with a structured questionnaire followed by documentation of case-specific clarifications and observations made by the researchers during the experiment. The questionnaire consisted of sixteen questions and was aimed to analyze if the participants were overloaded with the amount of information they had to process during the task and if they knowingly used their environment in effective ways to help make a design decision.

3   Results

The audio/video data collected from this experiment was coded at three levels determined after the pilot study and literature review: action, activity and task.

We adopted a bottom-up approach to develop these codes; the process was cyclic and ran multiple times until an exhaustive list of design actions, activities and tasks was identified. Due to the space limitation, we leave the presentation of the complete list of codes, their definitions and the data analysis process to another paper. In this paper our focus is to outline some potential features for a future CAD system supporting large numbers of alternatives. Each of these features is motivated by findings from the above experiment. We support these features with exemplary interactions and episodes observed directly from the experimental data.

For simplicity and clarity, we first briefly discuss the high-level design patterns observed repeatedly across participants which are then correlated to the spatial patterns observed during various embedded design tasks. A detailed analysis of the process and its embedded design tasks with respect to managing large number of alternative solutions will also be discussed in another paper.

3.1 Design Process

Consistent with the design literature, we observed that the participants followed a cycle of design process, which at the outset began by clarifying and defining the initial design criteria based on their preliminary immediate study of a randomly selected set of alternatives (Table 1). The initial criteria could be based on experience, understanding, knowledge or designer's insight; it could be subjective or objective, internal or external; but as the understanding of the overall design task developed, the criteria became richer.

Working with large number of design solutions, designers moved back and forth between interacting-with-criteria and interacting-with-designs. Once the preliminary criteria were identified, participants tested the criteria over a few designs before they continued using them over a larger set of solutions in the next cycles. In each cycle, the search became faster and participants very often reflected on their design decisions. They orally confirmed their decisions, spent time looking at a collection, asked questions for clarity, looked for inspiration, and did housekeeping (clearing up the table for the next filtering cycle for instance). These observations resulted with four main tasks: criteria building, criteria testing, criteria applying and reflection (Fig. 7).

3.2 Spatial Structure

This is the key section from an interface design perspective. Each observation in this section is reported with an empirical view describing what participants did. The future work involves complementing each of these empirical observations with a design view suggesting how a future system design may accommodate the structure.

3.2.1 Zoning

Participants devised various spatial structures by partitioning the work surfaces into zones. More prominently they developed three types of spatial zones: active, analysis and storage zones. Each of these zones initially had tentative locations and loosely defined boundaries, later participants relocated and resized them as needed (Fig. 8).

Active Zone: The active zone was the immediate workspace with respect to the designer for accessing to perform tasks like comparing, filtering, or focusing. The content of this zone continuously and very often rapidly changed as design decisions

Table 1. Design moves observed and corresponding spatial organization

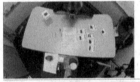	*P01 [00:15:00–00:17:25] "started off with having 8 cards displayed in front of him while speaking out loud the design task from the requirement sheet and what he is expected to do"*
	*P02 – [00:03:54–00:04:45] "...I am just looking over them trying to get a bigger picture..."*
	*P04 – [00:00:00–00:04:17] "okay let's see what we have here...how big is the site?" "At this time, using these sample designs, I am just trying to understand what the problem is? And how the firm has already approached it?"*
	*P05 – [00:58:01–01:01:00] "First off to begin with - I will just take as many as to cover this whole table. I am spreading them in a grid and leaving some space in between each two designs"*
	*P06 – [00:00:00–00:01:52] "Let me just take few of them and have a look at them. Looking at these, just 5 or 6 of them, some of them are really un-realistic and unfeasible"*
	*P08 – [00:00:00–00:04:46] "Right now I am trying to get a sense of what is happening here and what the requirements are and how is the design space. Obviously, there are lots of alternatives, so I am just going to spread them to see what is happening"*

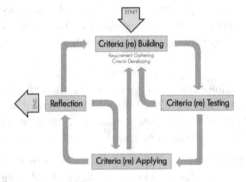

Fig. 7. The cycle of design tasks

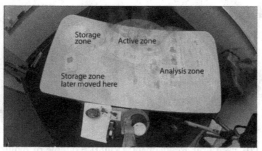

Type of Zone	Core purpose	Design Task performed	Focus time per design	Focus time overall	Focus shift while working in a zone
Active zone	Quick decision making	Criteria Testing & Applying	Seconds	~30 - 50% (no evidence)	Frequent shifts to Analysis zone
Analysis zone	comparative analysis	Criteria Building & Reflection	Minutes	~45 - 70% (no evidence)	Long focus with no immediate shift
Storage zone	Storing less-used items	None	No-attention zone	~5%	No immediate shift

Fig. 8. The spatial zones and details of their use

were made. Its boundary expanded and contracted per the need of the activity. Sometimes an active zone occupied a small part of the table surface (e.g. for comparing two solutions side by side); and other times the complete table became an active work-zone, e.g. when multiple alternatives were arranged onto the table to understand the spread of the design space. The viewing direction and the spatial orientation of the zone also changed with respect to the participant's position—analogous to a person holding a torch looking his way on a map, as the person moves closer, the cone of light gets smaller and details clearer. The active zone changed more frequently during criteria testing and applying cycles when the decisions were made quick and alternatives were replaced rapidly.

The active zone mostly contained few (~ 3) to many (~ 40) design alternative at a time. The latter is mostly observed when the active and analysis zones overlapped, mostly during criteria building. The more the objects were in a zone, the more actions for comparing solutions were observed.

Analysis Zone: The analysis zone was the *primary and opportunistic workspace* where the designers analyzed the selections and reflected on the decisions made, such as actions performed to develop, refine and revisit criteria. The content of the analysis zone is always more than four design cards at a time.

This zone occupied the largest spatial area compared to the other two zones. Some participants worked with more than one analysis zone or partitioned the zone to multiple sub-zones (Fig. 9 Right). The structure and size of the zone was largely dependent on the activity and its content, but mainly it remained consistent compared to the active zone, except during criteria building task. The analysis zone was used for three purposes: (1) to build criteria based on close observations and comparisons (this

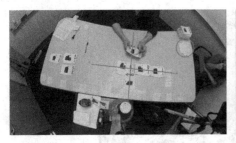

Fig. 9. (Left) P01 used grid arrangement; (Right) Example of multiple Analysis zones

is when active and analysis zones overlapped), (2) to group and cluster alternatives after analysis–the core purpose of the zone, and (3) to reflect on the design decisions made. As it occupied the largest area of the workspace; the analysis zone was naturally kept at a certain distance (an arm's length in most cases) by the participants.

Storage Zone: The storage zone was the *secondary workspace* where items were stored and left to be used in the later stages. It was the no- or less-attention zone. Location and size wise, it was the farthest and least-space-occupying workspace. There were one or multiple storage zones depending on the stage in the process. Most of its content included the unseen, discarded, or to-be-revisited design piles, the task sheet, and other aiding devices (such as pencils, erasers).

In the beginning of the experiment, almost all participants kept the storage zones closer to their position, but as the process developed the zone moved away. In fact, sometimes participants moved it to the side table to open space for other zones.

The items in this zone were only retrieved when needed, and returned to the zone afterwards. The common example was during the filtering rounds (e.g. in criteria applying), when the unseen designs became part of the active zone. They remained in an active zone until the cycle finished, that is when the 'seen and selected' were moved to the analysis zone, and the remaining unseen were moved back to the storage zone.

3.2.2 Meaningful Local Orientation and Global Arrangement

Experts construct arrangements for three reasons [13]: to simplify choice, to simplify perception, and to simplify internal memory or computation. In this study, participants made local and global arrangements when performing the design tasks.

Participants plotted informational cues highlighting the opportunities to help make an informed choice. Aside making global arrangements (zones), participants coded local spaces inside zones, particularly within analysis zone to simplify design decisions. They used aiding devices such as markers and colored sticky notes to mark alternatives with added information and to code a workspace based on its internal functional property. For instance, P01 (Fig. 9 Left) used low-level (detailed) grid arrangement (within the medium-level arrangement of zones) by making stations onto the workspace to filter design solutions. Not only these vertical column-like stations marked a criterion under which each design solution was considered, they also marked the order (left to right in case of P01) each design was evaluated in. This way participant used the workspace as an extension to his mind by off-loading his memory to remember his choices.

For instance, looking at a design in the sixth column on the table surface, it is understood that it has been considered for all the previous criteria on left.

Like informational cues, participants also plotted *physical constraints* [13] to block designs from viewing. For instance, some participants placed design cards upside down (Fig. 9 Left) to visually mark them as 'seen and rejected', again eliminating the need to remember and to minimize the visual clutter on the work surface.

One thing we found very interesting and unexpected was the meaningful use of design-card's orientation. We know that the physicality of design-cards with designs printed in landscape allowed only few possible arrangements within the constraints of media, mostly involving grid-like structure. Even then we observed participants placing the cards in portrait orientation to indicate designs with certain property or interest, while placing the others horizontally (Fig. 9 Left). This may be used to make an immediately recognizable orientation contrast. For example, in the middle of an experiment, P01 placed a card vertically just because, although the design on it didn't fit any of his already-built design criteria, P01 still wished to keep the design. P01 visually marked the solution using the cards physical property. Similarly, when P03 (Fig. 10) grouped design variations based on their architectural language, he made two clusters within each group to mark the boundaries of next generation cycle with do's and "don't". Interestingly, he placed the do's designs horizontally and don'ts vertically. This way both participants (P01 & P03) used the physical property of a design-card to highlight the obvious choice in their design process.

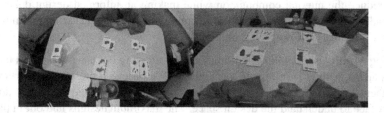

Fig. 10. P03 grouping designs marked using the physical property of design cards

Another interesting arrangement simplifying the visual perception was observed when a participant clustered design based on their visual weights and content (Fig. 11 Left). P06's spatial arrangement (within the analysis zone) was a perfect example of clustering using colors to sharpen perceptual activity. She made visual groups of designs, such as, minimum to no-red group, too much red, too little green, too much gray etc. The designs in these groups were also organized in a way, for instance in this case P06 used partial overlapping to highlight their visual content without having a need to remember their location. Consequent to her visual process of rejection, her final selection was designs with balanced distribution of red, green and gray areas. Out of these designs came final candidates for the next design stage.

Fig. 11. (Left) P06 clustering designs using visual properties of designs; (Right) A participant allocating groups using written marks

Other participants used written markings (Fig. 11 Right) or visual tags (Fig. 9 Left) to cluster designs with common attributes.

Aside these local arrangements, participants kept the objects needing immediate or frequent attention closer to themselves, which may imply that the frequency of use demands proximity of access. This pattern surpassed any arrangement.

3.2.3 Scanning Mechanisms

When it comes to viewing and managing thousands of design alternatives, the crucial scanning and arrangement techniques are highly coupled. In our study, we paid close attention to these activities. Each viewing style that we discussed has an inherent layout associated with it. However, they present a common cognitive implication: participants aim to reduce the internal computation while making an informed design decision.

Broadly we observed three styles of scanning mechanisms: (1) scanning multiples, (2) serial viewing, (3) Comparing multiples.

Scanning Multiples: Scanning multiples involved laying out usually not less than six designs and scanning them together as a group. We observed most of our participants began their design process with this activity. They laid out average 23 cards onto their work surface to understand the design space. The maximum designs laid out in parallel at a single time were 40 cards. Three of our participants (P02, P05 and P08) used this maximum limit while scanning multiples. We believe this number could have been the limitation of our study, since this was the maximum the table surface we provided can accommodate. We need a further study to understand the effect of work surface or the size of design cards on the number of solutions scanned at once.

Out of the four design sub-tasks of managing multiple designs, criteria building seemed to require layouts of multiples the most. To build a criterion, the relationship among a set of designs should be evident, many times quick comparisons within a set was needed, resulting into a juxtaposed arrangement of design variations. In this study, we observed that scanning multiples was mostly used when participants actively built and tested criteria over a pool of designs spread across their workspace. Their scanning multiples episode may be something like this: *the participant scanned multiple designs looking for similarities, made criteria based on the observations; applied criteria over laid out designs by dividing them into groups, rejected the remaining designs by moving them out of sight into the rejection pile* (Fig. 12).

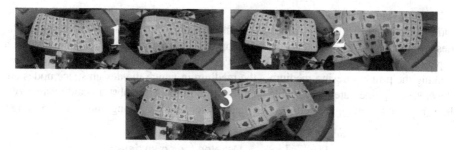

Fig. 12. A simultaneous criteria-building and testing episode while scanning multiple

Serial Viewing: This involved studying designs one by one. Slow-serial viewing is when a participant focused on one design at a time to make a design decision, whereas rapid-serial viewing, such as flickering through design-cards, was used for high-speed off-loading of internal computation, relying heavily on visual memory and contrast (Fig. 13 Right). Both viewing styles are effective when criteria are *known* and have been tested that is when the person holds a mental model (or has recorded notes) as to what constitutes a criterion. In these styles, designs are judged serially against that model for inclusion or exclusion from the set representing the criterion. Hence serial viewing can be a preferred mode of interaction during criteria applying stage.

Fig. 13. Comparing two (Left), Comparing multiples (Middle), Rapid serial viewing (Right)

Comparing Multiples: In this study, we made a distinction between comparing multiples and scanning multiples. Comparing multiples involved a criterion based synthesis of two or more designs whereas scanning multiples involved skimming through designs to create a criterion. Participants were observed comparing two or more designs at a time. When they compared two designs, for example, they hold each on one hand. When they compared more than two designs, they sometimes placed them in their both hands, by making a fan of designs. This could be due to the cards' physical affordances. While comparing, they used techniques like juxta-positioning, i.e., comparing designs by placing them side by side, and super-positioning, i.e., comparing designs by placing them overlapped (complete or partial).

Interestingly, when participants compared a design against a set, they hold a card besides a spread of designs and compared it with various designs in parallel. While keeping the card in hands and they scanned through the complete set at the same time.

3.2.4 Develop Design Space

During the experiment, most (if not all) of the participants, expressed a wish to edit the design parameters, to be able to draw on top of them or to sketch independently on a separate sheet of paper (Fig. 14). We believe that from interface design point of view, making the primary design medium—the medium in which the design space nodes are developed—immediately accessible is highly important. More abstract and faster tools, like free hand drawing should also be enabled for quick marking and brainstorming.

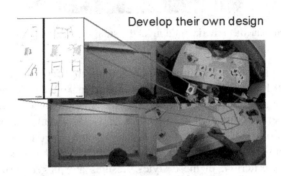

Fig. 14. A participant sketching his own designs inspired by the computer-generated design space

3.2.5 Wall Mounted Exploration

We observed that wall-mounted exploration happened at the later stages of the process most of the time, i.e. during reflection and final decision making.

Possible explanations could include: (1) The wall display provides more free space for thought, i.e., more space to arrange and re-arrange a candidate set and more space between sets (e.g., between candidates and contenders in Fig. 15); (2) People move to think—though we don't have a good explanation for this. It would involve a claim that moving closer and further ways from (parts of) a collection might afford different focus and point of view; (3) Although it is not part of this study, walls displays are better for collaboration as we must stand back from them, hence personal spaces don't overlap so much with a wall. If this is true, then sending a set to a larger display (and retrieving it from a larger display) needs to be an integral operation in a future system.

Fig. 15. A participant reflecting on his decisions on wall-mounted work surface

4 Discussion and Future Work

The results of the experiment provide insight to the design of interactive gallery for design alternatives. Zoning suggests the future digital media provides graphical indication of zones, of which focus zones are but one example. These zones should be interactive, that is being moveable, sent-to-back or brought-forward as needed, semantically zoomed in or out, and flexible, that is their boundary be shrinkable and expandable. Within zones, user-editable layout templates should be provided for meaningful arrangement of design alternatives. The arrangements should be complemented with tools to enable grouping, tagging and marking. While grouping physical, visual and semantic properties of alternatives should be made visible and available to use. Actions on single and groups of alternatives should be supported. Revisions should become cheap (with least cognitive load) and quick with minimum effort and locus of attention shift. Interactions at various levels—such as at alternative, group, and zone levels—should be supported. Scanning mechanisms such as scanning multiples, serial viewing (rapid and slow), and comparing designs using juxtaposed and superimposed techniques should be made available. Sharing or transferring a set of designs between multiple digital surfaces should be supported with editable parameters.

The suggested system features above are motivated by the results of the study and we contend that they will be important to the success of a system supporting working with large numbers of alternatives. However, their effectiveness should be verified on prototype of system interfaces and by conducting separate evaluations.

We believe that the study presented here has two main limitations. The first is the size of the layout spaces provided. Several participants used all of the horizontal surface, thus their work strategies were limited by the media involved. We do not know what they would have done with significantly larger surfaces. The second is that the cards enforce a rule that an alternative can only be present in a display in one location. Thus, it cannot belong to two spatially-displayed categories simultaneously. This may have constrained layout strategies. Both limitations should be kept in mind while designing future systems for working with large numbers of alternatives.

5 Summary

To investigate the designer's behavior when presented with large numbers of design alternatives, we conducted a lab experiment in a simulated design environment. Participants were presented with a hypothetical yet realistic design scenario where they were asked to explore 1000 computer-generated design alternatives of a parametric design model. The designs were printed on index cards. Participants, who did not know about the number of design alternatives, were asked to complete a design selection task by thinking-aloud throughout the experiment. They performed four primary tasks in cycles: criteria-building, -testing, -applying and reflection. They managed and explored the large numbers of design alternatives using their work environment as a cognitive ally. They formed active, analysis, and storage zones to perform high-level tasks. Mostly, *active zones* were used during criteria applying task, where participants used *serial viewing* (slow and rapid) mechanisms to make design decisions. *Analysis zones* were used during criteria building task, where *scanning multiples* was a crucial technique when building criteria. Analysis zones were essential for recording design groups using layouts with embedded informational cues and physical constraints. *Informational cues* helped highlight opportunistic designs, whereas *physical constraints* blocked unwanted designs from viewing. Storage zones were the no-attention zone holding least used items such as unseen design cards and aiding devices pencils and erasers. The structure of the design space kept on changing and maturing throughout the design process. Some participants also used wall displays to reflect on their final designs.

In the future, we will work on developing a *gallery system* that will apply the lessons learned from this study to enable designers to view and manage design alternatives with least effort, and that will seamless integrate with primary design media such as parametric modelers. This combination of modeler and gallery will be able to both generate and interact with thousands of design solutions.

References

1. Akin, O.: Variants in design cognition. In: Eastman, C., Newstetter, W., McCracken, M. (eds.) Design Knowing and Learning: Cognition in Design Education, pp. 1–17. Elsevier, New York (2001)
2. Buxton, B., Buxton, W.: Sketching User Experiences: Getting the Design Right and the Right Design, p. 115. Diane Cerra (2007)
3. Clark, A., Chalmers, D.: The extended mind. Analysis **58**(1), 7–19 (1998)
4. Cross, N.: Design cognition: results from protocol and other empirical studies of design activity. In: Eastman, C., McCracken, M., Newstetter, M. (eds.) Design Knowing and Learning: Cognition in Design Education, pp. 79–103. Elsevier Science, Amsterdam (2001)
5. Dow, S., Glassco, A., Kass, J., Schwarz, M., Schwartz, D., Klemmer, S.: Parallel prototyping leads to better design results, more divergence, and increased self-efficacy. ACM Trans. Comput. Hum. Interact. **17**(4) (2010). Article 18
6. Eastman, C.M.: On the analysis of intuitive design processes. Master thesis, Department of Computer Science, Carnegie-Mellon University, pp. 21–37 (1968, submitted)
7. Eisentraut, R.: Styles of problem solving and their influence on the design process. Des. Stud. **20**(5), 431–443 (1999)
8. Erhan, H., Wang, I., Shireen, N.: Harnessing design space: a similarity-based exploration method for generative design. Int. J. Archit. Comput. **13**(2), 217–236 (2015)
9. Foz, A.: Some observations on designer behavior in the parti. Master thesis, Department of Urban Studies and Planning, Massachusetts Institute of Technology, p. 151 (1972, submitted)
10. Hollan, J., Hutchins, E., Kirsh, D.: Distributed cognition: toward a new foundation for human-computer interaction research. ACM Trans. Comput. Hum. Interact. **7**(2), 174–196 (2000)
11. Iyengar, S.S., Lepper, M.R.: When choice is demotivating: can one desire too much of a good thing? J. Pers. Soc. Psychol. **79**(6), 995 (2000)

12. Marks, J., Andalman, B., Beardsley, P.A., Freeman, W., Gibson, S., Hodgins, J., Kang, T., Mirtich, B., Pfister, H., Ruml, W., Ryall, K., Seims, J., Shieber, S.: Design galleries: a general approach to setting parameters for computer graphics and animation. In: Proceedings of the 24th Annual Conference on Computer Graphics and Interactive Techniques (SIGGRAPH 1997), pp. 389–400. ACM Press/Addison-Wesley Publishing Co., New York (1997)
13. Kirsh, D.: The intelligent use of space. Artif. Intell. **73**(1–2), 31–68 (1995)
14. Lave, J.: Cognition in Practice: Mind, Mathematics, and Culture in Everyday Life. Cambridge University Press, New York (1988)
15. Lunzer, A., Hornbæk, K.: Subjunctive interfaces: extending applications to support parallel setup, viewing and control of alternative scenarios. ACM Trans. Comput. Hum. Interact. **14** (4), 1–44 (2008)
16. Newell, A., Simon, H.A.: Human Problem Solving. Prentice-Hall, Englewood Cliffs (1972)
17. Norman, D.A., Draper, S.W.: User Centered System Design: New Perspectives on Human-Computer Interaction, vol. 3, p. 43. Erlbaum Associates Inc., Hillsdale (1986)
18. Schön, D.A.: The Reflective Practitioner. Temple-Smith, London (1983)
19. Simon, H.A.: The Sciences of the Artificial, 1st edn. MIT Press, Cambridge (1969)
20. Smith, B., Xu, A., Bailey, B.: Improving interaction models for generating and managing alternative ideas during early design work. In: Proceedings of Graphics Interface 2010 (GI 2010), pp. 121–128. Canadian Information Processing Society, Toronto (2010)
21. Terry, M., Mynatt, E.D., Nakakoji, K., Yamamoto, Y.: Variation in element and action: supporting simultaneous development of alternative solutions. In: Proceedings of the SIGCHI Conference on Human Factors in Computing Systems (CHI 2004), pp. 711–718. ACM, New York (2004)
22. Woodbury, R.: Elements of Parametric Design. Rutledge, London (2010)
23. Woodbury, R.F., Burrow, A.L.: Whither design space? AI EDAM **20**(02), 63–82 (2006)
24. Yasuhiro, Y., Kumiyo, N.: Interaction design of tools for fostering creativity in the early stages of information design. Int. J. Hum. Comput. Stud. **63**(4–5), 513–535 (2005)

Studying Co-design

How Place and Representation Would Change the Co-design Behavior?

Leman Figen Gül[(⊠)], Can Uzun, and Süheyla Müge Halıcı

Istanbul Technical University, Beyoğlu/Istanbul, Turkey
fgul@itu.edu.tr

Abstract. This paper reports the results of a protocol study which explores behavior of designers while they design in pairs using sketching (analogue and remote) and 3D modeling tools (co-located and remote) in co-located and remote locations. The design protocol videos were collected, transcribed, segmented and coded with the customized coding scheme. The coded protocol data was examined to understand the changes of designers' co-design process and their activities of making representation in four different settings. This paper discusses the impact of location and types of representation on collaborative design. The paper concludes that designers were able to adapt their collaboration and design strategies in accordance with the affordability of the used digital environments.

Keywords: Collaborative design · Remote sketching · Augmented reality · Virtual worlds · Protocol analysis

1 Introduction

With the advances in information and communication technologies, developing digital design environments to facilitate collaborative working has become a major research area. Today the construction industry deals with complex design problems that require more knowledge than any single person because the knowledge relevant to a problem is usually distributed among stakeholders [1]. Generating a shared understanding among these stakeholders can facilitate having new insights, new ideas and new artifacts. The shared understanding among collaborators requires working in shared platforms where ideas would be generated, discussed and developed together. Many researchers have studied the developments of shared-virtual design platforms in order to support collaborative activity. For example, the early version of the Augmented Reality (AR) technology in architecture and urban design [2, 3], in design collaboration and management [4], in a mixed reality visualization [5] and sketching in 3D [6, 7] have contributed to the field. In most of those early studies, the technology implementation was usually considered as the tool of representation/documentation for the evaluation of the design idea.

The recent mobile Augmented Reality (AR) and Virtual Reality (VR) technologies have the potential to offer new opportunities to designers as the new co-design

© Springer Nature Singapore Pte Ltd. 2017
G. Çağdaş et al. (Eds.): CAAD Futures 2017, CCIS 724, pp. 212–230, 2017.
DOI: 10.1007/978-981-10-5197-5_12

platforms. With those technologies, digital 3D models are generated with the immediacy and accuracy that would be superimposed to physical environment for the visual analysis of the design proposal. Thus, the AR and VR can provide experiences, embodiment and immediate feedback to its users that would not be possible within CAD or traditional design media. Designers can therefore work three-dimensionally since every object within the virtual environment is experienced through movement and interaction. This possibility offers a different 'conversation' with their design idea that is otherwise not obvious or possible [8].

The aim of the study is to understand this new conversation with the design idea. We conducted a protocol study with the participation of designers that collaborated across different design medium. Particular focus of the study is on the impact of 'place' and 'types of the representation' on collaborative design behavior. Having knowledge of similarities and differences of co-design behavior across different digital design medium is thought to be informative for developing innovative collaborative design environments.

2 Studying Design Collaboration

Collaborative designing that resembles the thought processes of individuals is a collective problem solving activity. Researchers argue that the essential elements of design problem solving activity do not change when the expert designers work in groups [9, 10]. Designers' creative practice can enable collaborative projects to build upon and transcend participants' expertise and expectations through 'creative exchange' [11]. Thus based on the individuals' expertise on the given design problem, the designer would work intensely in the close-coupled process, or they would work separately in the loose-coupled process. According to Kvan et al. [9], in the close-coupled process, participants work intensely with one another, observing and understanding each other's moves, the reasoning behind them and the intentions. Furthermore, in the loose-coupled process, the participants work separately on the agreed-upon parts and then they put them together. The participants work together because each has a particular expertise that can contribute to the solution process. Kvan et al. [9] characterized the cognitive model of design collaboration that consists of cyclic joint expert actions (meta-planning, negotiation and evaluation) and separated parallel expert action (individual work), each of short durations.

With the recent developments on the information and communication technologies, collaborative design activity has taken place in computer mediated design environments (CMDEs). The CMDEs will possibly become a common working platform allowing the co-located and remote participations. Researchers argue the possible benefits of the CMDEs' employment on the workplace, enhancing the perceptual activity [12] and increasing the activities on the information exchanging [13].

In the context of design, the information and design ideas are communicated between co-designers through external design representations such as sketches and models. The act of sketching itself is regarded as important in team design activities in conjunction with having the function of communicating and discussing ideas through sketches [14]. Researchers argue that in synchronous CMDEs, when designers have shared representations and viewpoints, sketching plays an important role providing an efficient platform for exchanging ideas and collaboration during design process [15]. In the asynchronous context, however, sketching could have adverse effects when incomplete, inaccurate and inconsistent representations do not reflect the original creators' intentions.

Models, however, represent the concretization of design ideas, by getting as close as possible to the actual design intention. Investigating the exterior and interior form, structure, color and lighting would become easy. Models can help within the creative process of visualizing 3D space directly as well as by functioning to help with complex visual relationships, thus models outperform drawings [16]. With the introduction of the digital environments into the design processes, the digital models are considered as new design representations. These have a consistency and a long life span, and do not require continuous reconstruction. This is, in contrast to sketches and physical models, which involve considerable redrawing, tracing and scale-model making [17].

Early research points out that although most digital design systems try to simulate or imitate traditional tools and offer their digital counterparts, the interface of these tools usually affects the 'network' [18]: The 'network' is defined as being between people's mental images, visual perception, hands and representation. The early research also argues that the structured actions with palettes, menus, default values and system messages could break the balance in the 'network', interfering the 'creative flow' [19] and "leading the designers to make decisions prematurely" [20].

In recent years, there are improved systems for conceptual designing with potential to not affect the 'network' and permit the 'creative flow'. This can be only achieved through understanding the design behavior better. Emerging design technologies are encouraging designers to consider new media for effective and efficient collaborative design; the cognitive impact of the emerging technology on designers must therefore be addressed.

3 Proposed Study

Our primary motivation was to design effective digital design environments that would facilitate effective design collaboration. Although the study presented in this chapter focuses on the behavioral change and cognitive impact of digital tools on collaborative design, it is a part of a larger research effort dealing with the development of advanced digital design tools to support co-design activity. Only the result of two pairs of designers' protocol analysis is presented here. The research is funded by The Scientific and Technological Research Council of Turkey (TÜBİTAK) under project number 115K515.

Our initial study consisted of two pairs of designers as they collaborated across four different design environments. Consequently, we setup an empirical study for the purpose of gaining deeper understanding of the changes on the designers' collaboration and their interaction within the given environments. The assumption of the study was that a comparison of the same designers in four different environments would provide better indication of the impact of the environments than using different designers and the same design task (similar to the earlier studies [21]). With these ideas in mind, a study with four different settings was developed, as indicated in the Table 1: (1) face-to-face analogue sketching (F2F), (2) remote sketching (RS), (3) co-located 3D modeling with marker-based mobile AR application (MAR), and (4) remote 3D modeling in a Virtual

Table 1. Research matrix, location and representation.

Research matrix		Locations	
		Co-located	Remote
Representations	Sketching	Face to face sketching (F2F)	Remote sketching (RS)
	3D modeling	Co-located modeling with marker-based mobile Augmented Reality tool (MAR)	Remote 3D modeling in Virtual World (VW)

World (VW). The below section explains the experiment apparatus and the environments.

3.1 Experiment Apparatus and Set-Up

Two pairs of architects participated in the study. They were given the consent of participation and some training information about the digital platforms prior to the experiments. Then, they were provided with four different design briefs with similar difficulty and were asked to come up with schematic design solutions in 30 min in each of the design settings. In the design briefs, the participants were asked to consider the

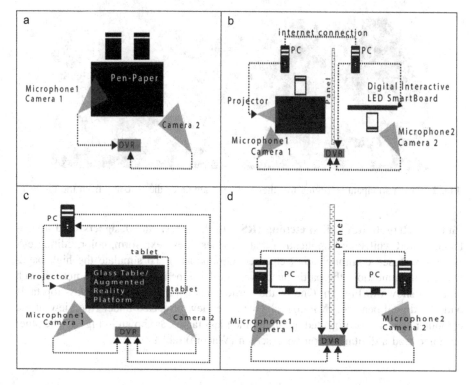

Fig. 1. Experiment apparatus and set-up for the phases

climate of the region, the context of the surrounding and the relation with its neighbors. In terms of the context of design, they were expected to consider open, semi-open and closed spaces for different public functions. Figure 1 shows the overall set-up of the experiments: (a) the first setting shown in Fig. 1a was the face-to-face sketching (F2F), (b) the second phase was the remote sketching (RS) as shown in Fig. 1b, (c) the third phase that was the co-located 3D modeling with mobile augmented reality tool (MAR) is shown in Fig. 1c, and (d) the final phase, shown in Fig. 1d, was the remote 3D modeling in a virtual world (VW). To simulate high bandwidth Internet connection, the participants were in the same room separated with a panel between them, as shown in Fig. 1. Camera views, screen views and a microphone were connected to a Digital Video Recoding (DVR) system that was used to capture the collaborating participants' actions and communications in all sessions.

Phase 1: Face-to-face analogue sketching (F2F). The first design environment is the co-located face-to-face analogue sketching. Two designers were given analogue tools (pen and paper, rules etc.) during the design process. Figure 1a shows the experimental set-up of the F2F phase, in which two architects were working together around a table. Figure 2 shows that two participants were working together around a table (on the left), and the view of some of their sketches (on the right).

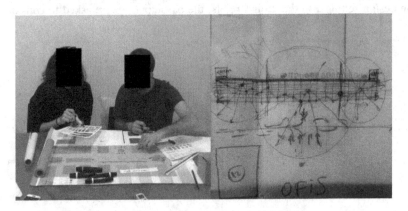

Fig. 2. Two participants working together and an example of the outcome from the Phase 1.

Phase 2: Remote (digital) sketching (RS). In this phase, the designers used a web-based shared whiteboard application that provides lines, text, form, color, editing etc. and a text-based communication channel (Groupboard). To simulate the high band-width communication, the participants were in the same room, but could not see each other, as shown in Fig. 1b. One of the participants used a customized glass-top table with the digital pen tool (MimioTech) with the view projected under (the view of the computer screen was projected out under the glass table), as shown in Fig. 3. The other designer used a digital pen on wide-screen (Wacom) tablet.

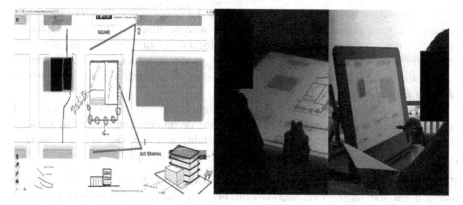

Fig. 3. The screen shot of the shared whiteboard application and views from the Phase 2.

Phase 3: Co-located 3D modeling with a Marker-based Augmented Reality Tool (MAR). In the third phase, the co-located 3D modeling, designers were given two 9′ tablets with the MAR, several markers and an enhanced design environment that consists of the physical model of the site in 1:500 scale, and the shared view of one of the tablets is projected under the glass-top table, as shown in Fig. 4.

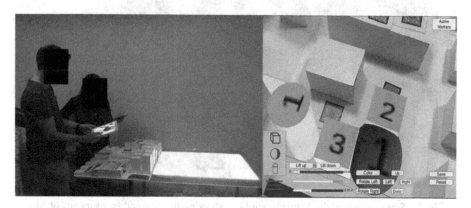

Fig. 4. The interface of the developed MAR tool and a view from the phase 3.

MAR: The Marker-Based Mobile Augmented Reality Tool. An AR application was developed using the Unity 3D game engine with the Vuforia AR plug-in that offers the set of target objects' library, object recognition and extended tracking (see [22], for the details of the system).First, a set of marker images was defined in the Vuforia AR library, and then the data set of the image targets was uploaded in the Unity 3D platform. The image targets were the unique predefined 2D shapes, similar to the QR codes, which were recognized by the device's camera. In the Unity 3D platform, the data set of the image markers was set to correspond with the primitive geometric objects (cube, sphere and cylinder) that would be the design elements for the phase 3.

The interaction with the tablet screen achieved a direct manipulation of the design elements. Several scripts were written to allow manipulations as follows: scaling the objects on the x, y, z directions, changing the location of the object on the x-y plane and z direction, rotating the object on the x, y, z polar coordinates, and changing the color of the objects. In addition, the reset, save and activate options were implemented on the interface, as shown in Fig. 4.

One of the tablet screens was shared through a mirroring application, thus both participants were able to create and modify the objects on the scene. In addition, a large shared display was provided on the glass-top table and a model of the context to provide an enhanced design environment, as illustrated in Fig. 4.

Phase 4: Remote 3D modeling in a Virtual World (VW). In the last phase, designers used a collaborative 3D VW, Second Life. For this phase, designers were given 24′-wide screen desktops. Second Life (SL) is a multi-user collaborative WV with the object-based 3D modeling capabilities that consists of a library of the basic geometries (cube, sphere and cylinder etc.) and wide range of editing tools. In SL, an island – VirtualStudioITU-, with some buildings are already on it, provided as a context for the designers to work on, as shown in Fig. 5. Similar to the other remote design phase, we put a panel between the participants to simulate the high-bandwidth communication.

Fig. 5. Screen shots of the VirtualStudioITU, showing the edit and build menus of SL

Following the collection of the designers' actions and verbal expressions, a thorough investigation has taken place using the protocol analysis method.

4 Methodology

Since the early studies of Watson where the verbalization is at the core of thinking [23], 'researchers have primarily relied on verbal behavior as a significant trace of the cognitive activities mediating between stimulus and response' (as indicated in [24]) This understanding has been applied to study cognitive activities on several design-related fields. For example, in the engineering domain, protocol analysis is a well-documented approach to understand what a participant is thinking while solving a problem [25]. Later, studies acknowledge the importance of external representations and drawings that are associated with the design thinking which can be interpreted through verbal expressions [26, 27].

In collaborative design studies, unlike the think-aloud and retrospective protocols, the design dialogues are the context of the analysis. We are adopting a Vygotskian [28] view on the relationship between thought and speech, as discussed in detail in [29]. Thus, in the area of design collaboration, studies contemplate that communicating with others has been seen as similar reflections of cognitive processes [29, 30]. We reflect on the teams' design protocols that resemble the 'think aloud' method, since the design dialogues during a joint task have potentials to offer data that is indicative of the cognitive abilities of the team members. The analysis of the design protocol is a complex process that includes collecting, indexing, structuring large video data and investigating the relationships and the patterns of designers' behavior, explained as follows.

4.1   Segmentation

The transcription of the data is the first step, and then there is the segmentation phase that means dividing the design protocols into smaller units. In collaborative design studies, the data contains a large continues stream of dialogues and video recordings. Since we aim to understand the role of the place and representations on collaborative design, a thorough investigation of designers' communication and the activities on the external design representation has to be done. A hybrid method was used for the segmentation of the protocols based on two sources: (1) Gero and McNeill [31] 's definition: 'flag the changes in actions and intentions', (2) Maher et al.'s [21] definition: 'flag when there is a change in the 'who' and 'what' items. The next step was to assign a code for each of the segments in order to measure the changes of the designers' cognitive activities.

4.2   Coding Scheme

Following the segmentation of the design protocols, we examined the activities using a coding scheme, as shown in Table 2. The basis for the development of the coding scheme was the expected results of the study that 'types of presentation and location would have an impact on co-designers behavior'. Thus measuring the changes in activities of (1) the co-designing and (2) the representation-making were essential. Table 2 shows the classes, the related codes for each class and the descriptions of the codes.

Table 2. Coding scheme.

Classes	Codes	Descriptions
Co-design model* [9]	Meta-planning	Planning the design process
	Negotiation	Talking about an issue or an aspect of design
	Evaluate	Determination of the values of design proposals.
	Individual work	Team members are working alone
Realization action [10]	Write	Typing about aspects of design
	Create	Generating a visual proposal for the first time
	Continue	Continue modeling with created proposal
	Delete	Erasing a part of generated proposal
Realization process* [10]	Decision	Agreement on a proposal
	Describe	Explaining an issue or an aspect of design
	Modeling	Discussing on making a representation (model – sketch)
Design process*	Analyze	Examining an issue of a design proposal
	Propose	Stating a new idea about the design
	Setup goals	Planning for achieving a goal
	Synthesize	Reaching a result by combining analyzes
	Evaluate	Determination of the values of design proposals.
Design space*	3D	Modeling action in three dimensional space
	2D	Modeling action in two dimensional space
Collaboration mode	Individual	Team members are working alone
	Team	Working collaboratively
Shared content	On given model	Working with given information about design task
	On proposal	Working on design proposal
Design exchange* [32]	High level	Dealing with general concepts of design task
	Low level	Dealing with details of design task

*Classes are determined by the investigation of the verbal expressions only.

4.3   Coding Process and Data Analysis

Two researchers coded the segments separately (see [25], for more on the coding process) which includes validating the segments in arithmetic order by listening-viewing the audio-video recorded data as well as reading the transcripts of the segments. Based on the researcher's understanding of the segments and the coding scheme, each segment was assigned with a code from the above scheme. After both researchers finished the individual coding, they combined their results in a joint arbitration process, as described in [33].

The occurrence frequency of each classes and codes (see Table 2) was investigated with the behavior analysis software, INTERACT 15. The software gave us information about the specific time interval indicating the changes in the co-design activity, see [34] for the details of the supporting software.

5 Results

This section presents the empirical evidence for the changes of the designers' co-design activities when they use digital tools. To measure the similarities and differences of designers' activities in each of the design sessions, the duration percentages of each class and codes were calculated within each environment. To examine the changes caused by the design environments, the pattern of behavior was also explored visually through the timeline graphs, as follows.

The shift of attention was examined by an analysis of the segment durations in each session, as shown in Table 3. Since a continuous stream of video data was segmented based on the hybrid method, the segment numbers and durations provide us with the information about how frequently the changes/shifts occurred. The biggest segment number is observed in the F2F phase for both pairs (199–166), the smallest segment number is observed in the VW phase for both pairs (151–131), as shown in Table 3. The most frequently occurring segment durations are smaller in both sketching environments: F2F (4.52–2.76) and RS (4.77–3.91) and are higher in both 3D modeling environments: MAR (5.41–6.05) and VW (6.04–7.04), as shown in the mode durations below. The mode values and maximum segment durations increase when the virtuality is introduced to the design activity, comparing F2F-RS and MAR-VW. The similar increase on the standard deviation values is also shown this tendency. The segment durations for all sessions are positively skewed. The high kurtosis values show that the distribution of the durations of segments is not flat. The distribution of the segment durations along the segment numbers in the design phases is shown in Fig. 6. The timeline also shows that the segment durations are longer in both 3D modeling environments (MAR and VW).

Table 3. Statistics on the duration of segments.

	Co-locate		Remote		Co-locate		Remote	
	Sketching				3D modeling			
Segments	F2F		RS		MAR		VW	
(second)	Pair 1	Pair 2	Pair 1	Pair 2	Pair 1	Pair 2	Pair 1	Pair 2
Median	7.37	6.56	7.16	7.36	7.6	8.56	7.73	7.66
Mode	4.52	2.76	4.77	3.91	5.41	6.05	6.04	7.04
Max	47.82	81.01	57.24	82.98	70.95	83.54	75.91	92.23
Min	1.33	0.98	0.86	1.21	1.14	1.25	1.03	1.04
Skewness	2.40	3.90	2.70	3.18	3.15	2.49	2.35	2.74
Kurtosis	8.16	13.07	11.26	12.77	14.86	8.07	6.57	7.97
Stan.Dev.	7.18	11.96	7.43	12.36	10.21	12.47	12.80	16.97
Segm.Num	199	166	197	162	172	144	151	131

Overview of the Classes. The duration percentages of the classes are shown, in Fig. 7. The duration of each class is divided by the total elapsed time for each design session (within each phase - 30 min), and then the average duration percentage is determined.

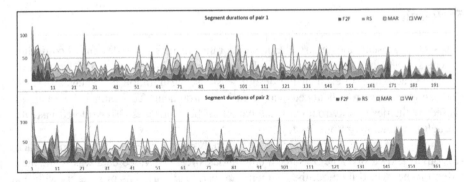

Fig. 6. The distribution of the segment durations

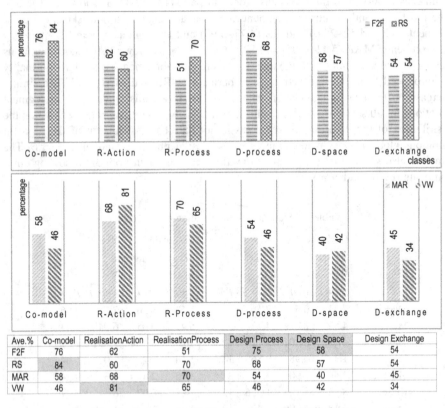

Ave.%	Co-model	RealisationAction	RealisationProcess	Design Process	Design Space	Design Exchange
F2F	76	62	51	75	58	54
RS	84	60	70	68	57	54
MAR	58	68	70	54	40	45
VW	46	81	65	46	42	34

Fig. 7. Average duration percentages of overall classes

First, we examine the overall durations of each class: The duration percentage of the design process class is higher in the F2F (75%) session (that are determined from the verbal expressions), followed by a drop in remote sketching and both 3D modeling environments (MAR and VW). The classes are the co-modeling (76% in F2F – 84% in

RS and 58% in MAR – 46% in VW), the design process (75% in F2F – 68% in RS and 54% in MAR – 46% in VW), the design space (58% in F2F – 57% in RS and 40% in MAR – 42% in VW), and the design exchange (54% in F2F – 54% in RS and 45% in MAR – 34% in VW) classes, as shown in the Fig. 7.

Only the duration percentages of the realization classes are higher in the 3D modeling environments: the realization process (51% in F2F – 70% in RS and 70% in MAR – 65% in VW) and the realization actions (62% in F2F – 60% in RS and 68% in MAR – 81% in VW). The 'realization process' class represents the verbal expressions that are related to the making of the design representation in the given setting, explaining how to make the model, describing what the objects on the scene would mean etc. The discussions about making the model increase in the 3D modeling environments and the highest duration percentage of the realization actions (create-continue-delete-write actions- that are determined from the video data) is seen in the VW session (81%). Those finding were investigated further below.

5.1 Design Process

We report the results of the analysis of the comparison across different place, co-located versus remote (F2F vs RS and MAR vs VW): Only the duration percentages of the design process class (75% in F2F vs 68% in RS and 54% in MAR vs 46% in VW) is higher in the co-located phases, as shown above in Fig. 7. Thus, we investigate the design process class in detail; the duration percentages for each code within each phase is plotted on the same chart for the comparison, as shown in Fig. 8. The highest duration occurs in 'propose' in both sketching phases, followed by the MAR (16%) and the VW (14%) phases. The durations of 'analyze' and 'synthesize' codes are also higher in the F2F, followed by the RS, the MAR and the VW phases, as shown in Fig. 8. The higher duration of 'set-up goal' occurs in the remote locations, 9% in the VW, followed by the RS (6%), as shown in Fig. 8. Most 'evaluation' code occurs in the RS phase, followed by the MAR, the F2F and the VW phases.

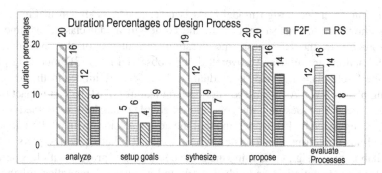

Fig. 8. The average duration percentages of the design process class in all sessions

5.2   Realization Actions

We report the results of the analysis of the realization activities comparing across two media: sketching versus 3D modeling: (F2F - RS vs MAR - VW): the overall duration percentages of the realization action are higher in both 3D modeling environments, as shown above in Fig. 7. Thus, we further investigate this class that is determined through the investigation of the video data, as shown in Fig. 9. The realization action class represents the interaction with the design representation that is related to the making activities including creating and modifying the external design representation (sketches and models) see [15] for more details). The duration percentage of 'continue' action (includes all kinds of modifying/editing activities) is higher in the 3D modeling phases: the VW (74%) phase is the highest, followed by the MAR (52%), the F2F (31%) and the RS (18%). The duration of create action is higher in the RS (32%), followed by the F2F (26%), the MAR (11%) and the VW (5%). The write and delete activities occur for a short period of time, as shown in Fig. 9.

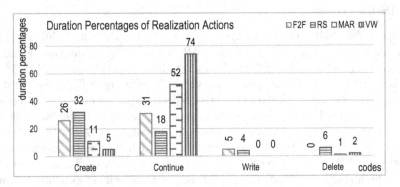

Fig. 9. The average duration percentages of the realization action class

5.3   Co-design Model

The duration of the co-design model class is investigated as shown in Fig. 10. This analysis shows the average durations of the co-design model class over time in all design phases. In the RS phase, the duration percentages of the 'negotiate' and 'evaluate' actions are higher. An overall drop is observed in the 3D modeling phases, except the 'meta-planning' and 'individual-work' is slightly higher in the remote 3D modeling phase (VW). As discussed later, several features of SL had an impact on this. Based on the verbal design protocols, closed-coupled and loosed-coupled working models, as suggested by [9] iterated in all of the design sessions with a different pattern. This result also confirms previous design studies [9, 10] that show designers work on their collaborative design tasks using the same collaborative process with less iterations (meta-planning, negotiation, individual work and evaluation) regardless of the technology change. This finding also confirms that 'designers adapt the nature of their communication to the bandwidth of the channel available without compromising their collaborative strategy or expert contributions' [35].

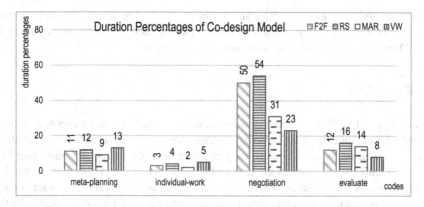

Fig. 10. The average duration percentages of the co-design model class

To investigate this model further, the classes of the 'co-design model' and the 'realization activity' are plotted along the timeline of the phases, as shown in Fig. 11. Each horizontal bar indicates the durations of each operations; the beginning is on the left whereas the end is on the right. Figure 11 shows the co-design model class along the timeline of the phases; the pattern of the model starts with the meta-planning activity in all phases, continued with the 'negotiation' action in longer time segments, followed by the 'individual-work' action and shorter 'evaluation'. There are some long empty time slots as indicated with the dotted lines in the 3D modeling phases, as shown in Fig. 11. This happened when designers are not articulating and expressing their thoughts verbally, instead their attention shifted to the making of the 3D model. Thus, we plotted the class of realization activity onto the same timeline, as shown in Fig. 11.

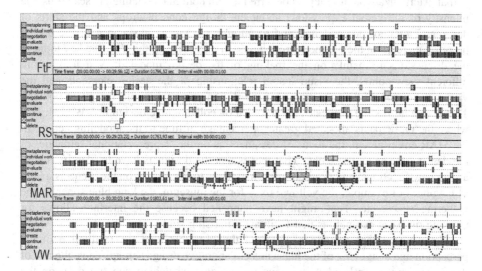

Fig. 11. Timeline of parallel actions – co-design model and realization activities

The 'create' and 'continue' activities are synchronous with the design and collaboration process (having verbal expressions) in both sketching, but they become separated in both 3D modeling environment, as shown in the timeline.

6 Discussions

The findings of the shifts of attention suggest that the designers had more new actions and shifted them quickly in the co-located phases (less time – more segments). But they spent more time on an action before they engaged in a new action demonstrating less and longer shifts of attention in the remote locations; when comparing F2F versus RS and MAR versus VW sessions. This consistent finding suggest that the remoteness and technology inclusion in the collaborative design activity would have an impact on the designers' cognitive load in a certain degree as designers had to pursue each action in more detail in the remote digital design environments.

During the design sessions, we observe that designers were able to adapt their collaboration and design strategies in relation with the affordability of the given digital environment. The appropriation that is 'the process by which people adopt and adapt technologies, fitting them into their working practices' [36] demonstrating similar semantic '(change in meaning or significance of the technology in context) and behavioral (novel usage patterns)' [37] adaptation. We advocate that the affordances of the tools and interface contribute the developing of the 'appropriation' by demonstrating new design behavior. This appropriation generates a transformation of the attention of designers' on the specific design aspect in relation to the features of the employed design tool.

The findings of the realization class suggest that both sketching environments (whether or not technology is involved) encourage designers to communicate about the development of the design concept more than the 3D modeling environments do. The verbal externalizations of thoughts occurred less in both 3D modeling phases. Thus, the intensity of the verbal expressions about the design concept drops and the shifts of designers' attention to modeling and examining the visual appearance of the design proposal increase in the 3D modeling phases. In particular, in the VW, the key topic of the discussions is mainly on the making of the design model, how it looks from different view-points, the visuo-spatial relationship of the design elements and the visual evaluation of the appearance of the design proposal within the given context. This particular finding replicates the research on collaborative design in VW [15]; [38] where the participants allocated greatest percentage of time to the modeling action. In the MAR environment, the focus of designers' is on the 'representational semantic' of the design objects on the scene. That means that the designers have to identify and to assign new functional and programmatic narratives to the objects on the scene as a kind of tagging. For example, the yellow box is for the museum, the long blue sphere is the gathering space, etc. That might have happened because the interface allows for working on basic geometries that facilitate a massing study.

Sketches are representations of visual thoughts that help the facilitation of the perception and conveying of the ideas in a collaborative design setting. Thus, the rise of the design process related discussions on analogue sketching and the drop on the communication about design development in the remote digital environments (the drop of the duration percentages of the 'analyze', 'synthesize' and 'propose' codes) are not surprising. However, the evaluation of the design proposal and the set-up goal activities do not follow this trend. We speculate that since being in remote places requires an additional attention on monitoring and managing collaborative activities, designers thus assigned roles to each other in the remote digital environments. In particular, in the VW phase, the design objects shared in SL that encourages designers to allocate some tasks to each other for modifying the model. For example, one designer stood on top of the design model while the other designer inspected and instructed what to do with the model in SL. Similarly, the shared whiteboard on the remote sketching phase encourages the designers to work together facilitating the closed-coupled process (92% team mode), thus designers tend to confirm every design decision to proceed. Thus, the duration percentages of the evaluation code become higher in the remote sketching phase. Similarly, the MAR phase also includes the shared view of the tablets and provides the shared operations on the design objects. The sharing of the working environment encourages designers to work in the close-coupled process. This finding confirms that the affordability of the interface had an impact on the collaboration process, as indicated by [12]: 'the dense collaborative actions is said to be that the user interface helps the designers to get focus on the different aspects of design which make designers work much more engaged in the process of conceptual design'. Thus, to proceed further for the design development, designers need to evaluate every step of their decisions in the close-coupled mode in the shared environments.

The time spent on the realization of the design representations (including activities related to the making of the model) are longer in the 3D modeling environments. This is due to the nature of the modeling, in the 3D design environments: In SL, one mouse click creates the basic objects on the scene (cube, pyramid, tetrahedron, torus, sphere, cone, tube, cylinder, ring, tree and grass objects etc.) and then, designer needs to manipulate the objects' properties to make other things. During these manipulations, designer would inspect the objects' form in different viewpoints to determine a satis-factory result. Thus, making the 3D model in the SL is a constant modeling activity. This is consistent with a cycle of actions such as move/rotate/transfer/group etc. as pointed out by [39]. In order to have a desired building form, designers need to modify the objects by rotating, moving, scaling and changing color, mapping a texture onto it in the VW. Similarly, in the MAR environment, creating a basic object requires dis-playing a marker to the tablets' camera. Then, the object becomes registered in the system. Then, designer needs to modify the properties of the object to make other things. Thus longer 'continue' action that consists of series of actions requiring a continuing attention on the objects occurs in the 3D modeling environments. During the 'continue' operation, designers also examine the visual appearance of the artifact by zoom in /zoom out and orbiting the view in the SL. In the MAR, the visual examination takes place on the tablets' view through the bodily engagements of the designers by bending their knees, moving up and down the tablet to catch the best scene. Thus, investigating the visuo-spatial properties of the design artifact becomes a major activity in both 3D modeling environments. That is one of the reasons for having 'longer spans of attention' in the 3D modeling environments as well (see Fig. 6).

The plot of the parallel actions on the same timeline suggests that the articulation of design concepts and the developing (making) of design representations are simultaneous collaborative activities in sketching, but they become separated actions in the 3D modeling environments. The externalization of thoughts occurs less in 3D modeling. The loosely-coupled process is mostly observed in the VW, as designers make task allocations to then separate and do their individual modeling tasks. In the MAR environment, on the other hand, they operate the 'continue' action in the close-coupled process, but mostly in a silent mode.

7   Conclusions and Future Remarks

This paper presents the results of a protocol study based on an experiment with pairs of designers working across different design settings. From the protocol analysis, co-designers' activities, their interactions with representations and with the interfaces of the tools have been explored. Results of this study suggest that collaborative designers are able to adopt and adapt technologies in order to achieve satisfactory design solutions. The results indicate that co-designers illustrate behavioral adaptation based on the affordances of the used technology. Each digital design environment provides different experiences of co-design behavior and contextual interaction.

The alchemy of design collaborations across the digital media shows that designers are able to design successfully in all the examined environments generating a design outcome, addressing the briefs. The properties of the environments that are the interfaces and tools, the field of view, sharing of the virtual space have great impact on the collaborative activities and on the behaviors of the designers. The cyclic co-design processes of collaboration with different intensity were occurred across the digital media. In particular, 'what you see is what I see' kind of shared environments support the close-coupled collaboration processes in which designers tend to achieve the consensus of decisions to proceed further. The shared environments where users have their own field of views and options to navigate alone encourage designers to work in the loosely-coupled collaboration process.

Regardless of the involvement of the technology, sketching provides designers a shared platform where they simultaneously generate design ideas and develop the design representations. In the 3D modeling, the model making and the generation of the design ideas become separated activities. In the co-located 3D modeling environment, the broken 'network' between the virtual and physical has been an impact on the process of idea generation, but superimposing the virtual model on the physical model gives them the opportunities to examine and develop the perceptual aspects of the design proposal. The VW with the detailed and complex modeling possibilities and having realistic looking context gives designers the possibilities to articulate the design artifact in more detail.

In conclusion, a design interface which is highly isolated from the interactions in physical reality can generate occlusions in the processes of idea generation. The physical reality context can be a prompting or impeding factor in the design cognition through the processes of idea generation. Thus, the benefits or impacts of superimposing the virtual and the real on the design context which can be provided by the augmented reality environments requires further study.

Acknowledgements. This research is funded by TÜBİTAK under project number 115K515 titled as 'A study of co-design cognition in virtual environments: Do presence and types of representation change design behavior? The authors wish to thank the participants of the study.

References

1. Arias, E., Eden, H., Fischer, G., Gorman, A., Scharff, E.: Transcending the individual human mind—creating shared understanding through collaborative design. ACM Trans. Comput. Hum. Interact. **7**(1), 84–113 (2000). doi:10.1145/344949.345015
2. Kim, M., Maher, M.L.: Comparison of designers using a tangible user interface & graphical user interface and impact on spatial cognition. In: Proceedings of International Workshop on Human Behaviour in Designing, Melbourne, Victoria, pp. 81–94 (2005)
3. Seichter, H., Schnabel, M.A.: Digital and tangible sensation: an augmented reality urban design studio. In: 10th International Conference on Computer Aided Architectural Design Research in Asia, CAADRIA, New Delhi, India (2005). doi:10.1007/978-1-4020-6528-6_1
4. Ko, C.H., Chang, T.C.: Evaluation and student perception of augmented reality-based design collaboration. Management **6**(6), 6 (2011)
5. Anders, P., Lonsing, W.: Ambiviewer: a tool for creating architectural mixed reality. In: ACAADI, pp 104–113 (2005)
6. Sung, W.: Sketching in 3D Towards a Fluid Space for Mind and Body. SMArch Thesis. MIT Architecture, Cambridge (2013)
7. De Vries, B.: Sketching in 3D. In: ECAADE, pp. 277–280 (2013)
8. Schnabel, M.A., Kvan, T.: Design, communication & collaboration in immersive virtual environments. Int. J. Des. Comput. Spec. Issue Des. Virtual Worlds **4** (2002)
9. Kvan, T., Vera, A., West. R.: Expert and situated actions in collaborative design. In: 2nd International Workshop on Computer Support Cooperative Work in Design. International Academic Publisher, Beijing (1997)
10. Gül, L.F.: Understanding Collaborative Design in Different Environments. University of Sydney, Ph.D. Thesis, Australia (2007)
11. Bowen, S., Durrant, A., Nissen, B.: The value of designers' creative practice within complex collaborations. Des. Stud. **46**, 174–198 (2016). doi:10.1016/j.destud.2016.06.001
12. Leon, M., Doolan, D.C., Laing, R., Malins, J., Salman, H.: Application of interactive surfaces to support computer mediated collaborative design environment. In: 18th International Conference on Information Visualisation (2014). doi:10.1109/IV.2014.30
13. Lee, S., Ezer, N., Sanford, J., Do, E.Y.: Designing together while apart: the role of computer-mediated communication and collaborative virtual environments on design collaboration. In: IEEE International Conference on Systems, Man and Cybernetics (2009). doi:10.1109/ICSMC.2009.5346849
14. Remko, V.: Functions of sketching in design idea generation meetings. In: C&C' 02, ACM, Loughborough, Leic (2002)
15. Gül, L.F., Maher, M.L.: Co-creating external design representations: comparing face-to-face sketching to designing in virtual environments. Co-Design **5**(2), 117–138 (2009)
16. Porter, T., Neale, J.: Architectural Supermodels. Architectural Press, Oxford (2000)
17. Achten, H., Joosen, G.: The digital design process-reflections on a single design case. In: Digital Design, 21st ECAADe Conference Proceedings, Graz, Austria, pp. 269–274 (2013)
18. Laseau, P.: Graphic Thinking for Architects and Designers. Van Nostrand Reinhold, New York (1989)

19. Raskin, J.: The Human Interface: New Directions to Design Interactive Systems. Addison Wesley, Boston (2000)
20. Eckert, C., Boujut, J.: The role of objects in design co-operation: communication through physical or virtual objects. Comput. Support. Coop. Work **12**, 145–151 (2003). doi:10.1023/A:1023954726209
21. Maher, M.L., Bilda, Z., Gül, L.F.: Impact of collaboratve virtual environments on design behaviour. In: Gero, J. (ed.) Design Computing and Cognition'06, pp. 305–321. Springer, Netherlands (2006)
22. Gül, L.F., Halıcı, S.M., Uzun, C., Esengün, M.: Understanding the impact of mobile augmented reality on co-design cognition and co-modeling. In: Luo, Y. (ed) Cooperative Design, Visualization, and Engineering, 13th International Conference, CDVE 2016, Sydney, NSW, Australia (2016)
23. Watson, J.: Is thinking merely the action of language mechanism? Br. J. Psychol. **11**, 87–104 (1920). doi:10.1348/000712608X336095
24. Eastman, C.: Explorations of the Cognitive Processes in Design. Department of Computer Science Report, Carnegie Mellon University, Pittsburgh (1968)
25. Ericsson, K., Simon, H.: Protocol Analysis: Verbal Reports as Data. MIT Press, Cambridge (1984)
26. Eppler, M.J., Kernbach, S.: Dynagrams: enhancing design thinking through dynamic diagrams. Des. Stud. **47**, 91–117 (2016). doi:10.1016/j.destud.2016.09.001
27. Suwa, M., Tversky, B.: What do architects and students perceive in their design sketches? A protocol analysis. Des. Stud. **18**, 385–403 (1997). doi:10.1016/S0142-694X(97)00008-2
28. Vygotsky, L.: Thought and Language. MIT Press, Cambridge, MA (1986)
29. Goldschmidt, G.: Designer as a team of one. Des. Stud. **16**, 189–209 (1995)
30. Gabriel, G., Maher, M.L.: Coding and modeling communication in architectural collaborative design. In: Ataman, O., Bermudez, J. (eds) ACADIA'99, pp. 152–166 (1999). doi:10.1016/S0926-5805(00)00098-4
31. Gero, J.S., Neill, T.M.: An approach to the analysis of design protocols. Des. Stud. **19**, 21–61 (1998). doi:10.1016/S0142-694X(97)00015-X
32. Vera, A.H., Kvan, T., West, R.L., Lai, S.: Expertise, collaboration and bandwidth. In: Proceedings of the SIGCHI Conference on Human Factors in Computing Systems, pp. 502–510 (1998). doi:10.1145/274644.274712
33. Cross, N.: Natural intelligence in design. Des. Stud. **20**, 25–39 (1999). doi:10.1016/S0142-694X(98)00026-X
34. Gül, L.F.: Evaluating software support for multimedia data analysis in design studies. In: Computer-Aided Qualitative Research Europe: Lisbon University (workshop) (2010)
35. Alonso, H.V., Kvan, T., West, R.W., Lai, S.: Expertise, collaboration and bandwidth. In: CHI (1998)
36. Dourish, P.: The appropriation of interactive technologies: some lessons from placeless documents. JCSCW **12**(4), 465–490 (2003). doi:10.1023/A:1026149119426
37. Muller, M., Neureiter, K., Verdezoto, N., Krischkowsky, A., Zubaidi-Polli, A.M., Tscheligi, M.: Collaborative appropriation: how couples, teams, groups and communities adapt and adopt technologies. In: CSCW'16 Companion, San Francisco, CA, pp. 473–480 (2016). doi:10.1145/2818052.2855508
38. Cardella, M.E., Atman, C.J., Adams, R.S.: Mapping between design activities and external representations for engineering student designers. Des. Stud. **27**, 5–24 (2006). doi:10.1016/j.destud.2005.05.001
39. Maher, M.L., Bilda, Z., Gu, N., Gül, L.F, Marchant, D.: Collaborative Process: Research Report on Use of Virtual Environment. The University of Sydney (2005)

Association Rule Mining to Assess User-Generated Content in Digital Heritage

Participatory Content Making in 'The Museum of Gamers'

Serdar Aydin$^{(\boxtimes)}$ (ID), Marc Aurel Schnabel (ID), and Iman Sayah (ID)

School of Architecture, Victoria University of Wellington,
Wellington, New Zealand
{serdar.aydin,marcaurel.schnabel}@vuw.ac.nz,
iman.sayah@gmail.com

Abstract. Association rule mining is one of several approaches in game design for discovering correlations among user-generated content items. This paper aims to aid the digital heritage field by analysing user preferences in interactive environments designed for participatory cultural heritage making. Textual and diagrammatic explication of the feedback mechanism introduces the universalization of the knowledge gained in this research that is supported with the outcome of a workshop which offered two gamified interactive environments. Three key pleasures of cyberspace in digital heritage are extended from immersion to meaningful experience and to transformation. User-generated content engenders meaningful correlations that help improve and evaluate digital heritage applications. Qualitative findings explicate the relationship of 'The Museum of Gamers' with the authenticity issue. This paper is among the first to investigate the association rule finding methods in relation to indexical authenticity in digital heritage.

Keywords: Digital heritage · Game analytics · Association rule mining · User-generated content · The Museum of Gamers

1 Introduction

This paper examines the lack of active participation and the authenticity issue in participatory heritage making processes as concomitant challenges. A result of the paradigmatic modalities of sublime authority and aesthetical authenticity - which have consistently put heritage value at odds with the pragmatics of digital – we seek to remedy these two issues with a standard method borrowed from game datamining. Our underlying rationale is to extrapolate how a cybernetic feedback mechanism might benefit digital heritage. Our discussion is based on the results of associative rule mining and frequent pattern finding methods for analysis of user-generated content in The Museum of Gamers.

This paper initially elaborates on the authenticity issue in participatory heritage making (Sect. 2). We then focus on participatory digital heritage making by presenting

© Springer Nature Singapore Pte Ltd. 2017
G. Çağdaş et al. (Eds.): CAAD Futures 2017, CCIS 724, pp. 231–251, 2017.
DOI: 10.1007/978-981-10-5197-5_13

the digital environments designed for The Museum of Gamers (Sect. 3). A cybernetic feedback mechanism is drawn to demonstrate how different aspects of participatory digital heritage making are integrated (Sect. 4). The role of association rule-mining from user-generated content is then detailed (Sect. 5).

Findings are discussed in terms of their meaning, with a discussion based on the notion of *indexical authenticity* that is instrumental to justifying a participatory content-making process in digital heritage. With these theoretical discussions and practical experiments, this paper aims to extend our understanding of authenticity from a digital heritage perspective.

2 Background

Our work sees the challenge of augmenting active participation in the making of heritage as homologous with seemingly incommensurable issue of authenticity. This is an issue that involves conflicting views on meaning and value, defying mediation for their translation.

Projecting authenticity has long been a hallmark practice of Authorised Heritage Institutions (AHI) associated with state and memory institutions such as museums and galleries. The role of these 'authenticators as guardians of knowledge' is challenged by contemporary digital platforms, where individual story making captures more attention [1]. Crucially at stake in authenticity in heritage practices is an understanding of representation as a collective memory, requiring a protocol of shared authorship.

Although a relatively a new scientific domain with fewer than 50 years of history [2], digital heritage is a field that holds immense potential to extend our knowledge of authenticity in the information age [3, 4]. Contemporary understanding of authenticity is no longer based on definitive models (in authenticity [5]; in cultural heritage management [6]; in digital heritage [7]; in museology [8]; in heritage theory [9, 10]). Today, it is less important to come to an ultimate and immediate agreement on the authenticity issue in heritage practice, than it is to reframe it as a process of construction and agreement between conflicting views.

Museums have been seeking innovative means to improve their services for changing visitor demands. As a widespread individual story-telling medium, social media prompts the GLAMs sector (Galleries, Libraries, Achieves and Museums) for more engaging and personalized narration [11]. Long before social media tools such as Facebook and Twitter became an ordinary arena for museums, the New Museology was born in the 1970 s as a movement to promote participation in exhibitions [12, 13]. This movement dispelled initial doubts cast on the use of digital technologies.

Meanwhile the heritage discourse has been dealing with theoretical and philosophical views such as Walter Benjamin's aura [5] and Jean Baudrillard's definition of hyper-reality [14]. These critical views have helped further inform the real value of digital narration as a novel and non-linear format. Digital technologies have been proven to effectively promote knowledge in heritage, yet generate new questions. Do these technologies help content holders or end-users? Is it simply the sum of different media? Does Virtual Reality (VR) refer merely to navigation through digital replicas of the heritage environments?

Parallel to the development of the New Museology movement in the 1990s and early 2000s, the Reality-Virtuality (RV) continuum lingered on in an influential position behind the research and practice of digital applications for museum visitors [15, 16]. It is arguable that, drawn as a conceptual scalar diagram between ultimately real environments and the completely synthetic and virtual, the RV continuum reduces the notion of 'virtuality' (i.e. ability of imagination) to the sole level of the medium.

Moving from object-centered to user-oriented narration, digital heritage discourse entertains the possibility of presenting transcending and conspicuous, however unexplored, aspects concomitantly. In this regard, Murray's identification of '3 key pleasures of cyberspace' provides a foundation for this research [17] – the entanglement of immersiveness (1), agency (2) and transformation (3) defines the anatomy of this research. To imagine a new way of making heritage value more practicable in digital, The Museum of Gamers proposes a ternary standard (Fig. 1).

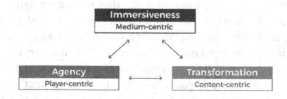

Fig. 1. Murray's '3 key pleasures in cyberspace' are shown in relation to medium-, user- and content-centric perspectives.

3 Designs

3.1 From Immersiveness to Agency

Driven by visual media studies, immersiveness and related technical resolution values have been the common appeal of digital applications [18–20] employed by Authorised Heritage Institutions (AHI) [21]. In this digital heritage project, immersiveness is central to the role of meaningful experience (i.e. agency) as well as to the transformation of both content and users.

A preliminary 2-day workshop was conducted to observe initial encounters between users and content in two digital environments with differing levels of immersiveness. Nine participants (seven onsite and two remote) engaged interactively with the pre-modelled replica of a real heritage environment in a VR system called Hyve-3D [22]. Navigating the narrow alleyways of Kashgar (an ancient Central Asian city in China), participants used tablet devices to superimpose digital sketches on missing parts of textured meshes (Fig. 2, left). Representing the participants' personal presence in an embodying immersive digital environment, the resulting instantaneous and spontaneous lines are ascribable to the notion of 'unmediated heritage' (Fig. 2, right).

Fig. 2. End of the participant engagement with the virtual Kashgar model and their 3D sketches.

Mere immersiveness isolated from a relationship with meaningful experience and content falls short of knowing the essential elements of Kashgar's authenticity. A digital heritage application that dissolves the user into a crudely prioritised level of immersiveness will be subject to questions such as: How does an application extend our understanding of the authenticity in a participatory process in digital? Does putting authority in the hands of participants increase their enjoyment or enhance their learning? How can we measure the depth and quality of their experience in these applications?

The sketching feature of the VR system places the participants in an undefined position of agency. However, the incommensurability of Kashgar's authenticity remains an impediment to immersive digital heritage environments if a systematic inquiry is not undertaken to consider its indexicality for negotiating 'real' heritage value (see the 'atomic real'-'digital real' differentiation in [23, 24]). In a second digital environment called 'The Trace', the same workshop participants inhabited the narrow alleyways of Kashgar individually with a mouse-keyboard control in front of a large HDTV (Fig. 3).

Fig. 3. Player navigating in the photogrammetric model of Kashgar's narrow alleyways.

Here, the participant is tasked with completing a digital model as holes and glitches emerge during the photogrammetry process. Facilitating a dynamic interpretation process, digital errors are utilised in 'The Trace' as part of the game scenario. 'The Trace', in a similar manner to first-person shooter (FPS) games, allows a player to target. Unlike the moving character targets of FPS games, the player here focuses on immobile items, i.e. the mesh model of Kashgar's narrow roads.

The player saves screenshots as 250×250 pixel frames and places them on the incomplete and missing parts of the model (Fig. 4). These areas are highlighted with a fluorescent colour to inform the player.

Fig. 4. The gameplay and collecting of 'objects' in 'The Trace' game.

Shifting the centroid of the digital model by generating new walls and roads, a deliberative agency might demystify the latent value of physical architectural elements, developing correlations between items for analysis. Content generated by one of the workshop participants in 'The Trace' undergoes further analysis in Sect. 5 (Fig. 5).

Fig. 5. Patterns captured by the user.

3.2   From Agency to Transformation

By embarking on a meaningful experience as a subject-in-action, the visitors (players) of The Museum of Gamers are expected to subjugate the rigid structures of pre-designed content by altering the environment with new input. This is the transformative power of games, which results in emergent, innocent and unforeseen outcomes [25]. Transformation itself is too a large topic for a single paper, just as immersiveness and agency are. Our focus, however, is on how their relationship developed in a cybernetic feedback mechanism (elaborated with diagrams in the next section). This section presents a third digital environment featuring the indie-style game 'Missing Duppa' (Fig. 6). Low-poly models that represent Kashgar's architectural components constitute this environment. It is presented here to explain positive and negative feedback loops employed in The Museum of Gamers.

Fig. 6. The main character of 'Missing Duppa' representing the duppa hat worn in Kashgar.

"The Trace" and "Missing Duppa" were designed to be played concurrently. Each player deals with positive and negative feedback cycles that are instrumental in designing a 2nd-order cybernetic system for The Museum of Gamers. The two games differ in style as well as in their making (Fig. 7). Player I experiences Kashgar in an organic manner with perspective view frames; Player II is given a rather abstract and minimalist representation through isometric projection.

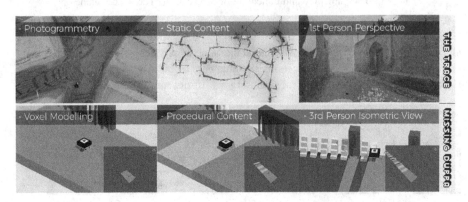

Fig. 7. The making of 'The Trace' (above) and 'Missing Duppa' (below).

To understand the dynamics of the improvisational and interactive nature of an ongoing and two-way conversation between the two players, a feedback mechanism is conceived with an objective of systematically eliciting information generated by users. In 'The Trace' and 'Missing Duppa', players send positive and negative feedback to each other without noticing the presence of a second platform (Fig. 8).

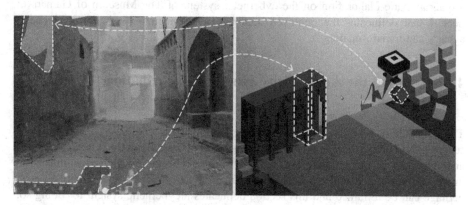

Fig. 8. "The Trace" (left) invites the player to repair the heritage content by collecting and placing new patterns – Conversely, "Missing Duppa" (right) challenges the participant to destroy the given content items by collecting architectural elements to find a secret.

Two players interact without knowing it. The Trace has gameplay based on repairing and completing missing parts of the digital model. The Missing Duppa player is challenged to destroy as many voxelated geons (or components) as possible (Fig. 9). While destroying components, the second player plays with the first's cognitive processes - such as memorisation, causal attribution and decision-making. When a component is destroyed in the second platform, Player I notices missing textures that were previously rebuilt. First player's screenshots are saved as .PNG files and archived in a data folder of the game.

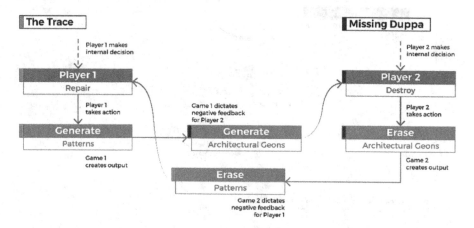

Fig. 9. Negative feedback flow between 'The Trace' and 'Missing Duppa'.

Our inquiry takes place largely within the symbiotic relationship between these two games. We capture the changes in high-level cognitive processes such as memorisation, causal attribution and decision-making. For the purposes of this paper, our presentation covers only the associative rule-mining method applied to user-generated content in 'The Trace', based on the patterns shown above in Fig. 5. Section 5 presents this, after a diagrammatic elaboration on the cybernetic system of The Museum of Gamers in Sect. 4 that delineates the deployed feedback mechanism between immersiveness, agency and transformation.

4   Reframing the Authenticity Issue for Participation in Digital

The authenticity issue in heritage encompasses too many conflicting views for consensus [10]. Today's heritage theories embrace complexity, focus on systems, relations and networks of objects, and are shifting from a form-giving understanding to an understanding of constant conversation [8, 9]. In cyberspace, the authenticity issue in heritage can be reframed and this section delineates a cybernetic system for doing so. The purpose of reframing is not modelling of learning or explanation of communication, but measuring understanding and agreement.

Goal of the Model. This study measures user-generated content as a part of a cybernetic feedback mechanism that considers immersiveness, agency and transformation in a concomitant relationship (Fig. 10). The Museum of Gamers does not presume that authenticity lies solely in a physical, material world or that knowing authenticity is possible and necessary. The system design posits only that it is necessary and possible to be coupled to authenticity by achieving goals, by means of feedback from the components of a system. Relying on game datamining methodologies to describe the transformation of content, The Museum of Gamers attempts to measure the indexicality of Kashgar's heritage value as inherited (or recorded) via digital modelling techniques.

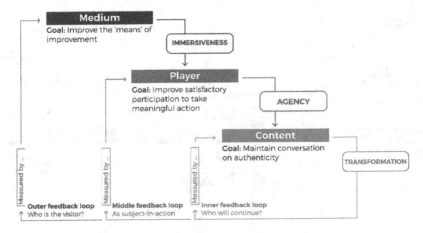

Fig. 10. Diagram of the formal feedback mechanism in The Museum of Gamers.

Description of Components and Processes. Feedback loops are a foundation of cybernetics, assuring conversation between systems [26–31]. The circular, causal system regulates conversations between the variables of medium, player and content in order to maintain participation. The outer feedback loop improves the 'means' of improvement in general. In the middle, local processes are enhanced. The inner loop maintains quality output by regulating conversation around participant-generated dynamic alterations.

Another cybernetic criterion is the clear definition of the system's limitations, so that it is evident when goals are achieved. Here, defining effective resolution, frequency and range values achieves inter-attribute relations between variables of the system (Fig. 11). Connected and unconnected (orthogonal) parameters of variables are laid down to process a feedback loop between input and output. The dimensionality of these values is based not on continuous variables as defined in analog systems, but in discrete forms. A variety is required to comprehend the system's capacity for maintaining conversation at a local level. It is a formal expression defining the nature of internal relations with other parameters in a discrete manifold (see the formal properties of morphological models for wicked problems in [32]).

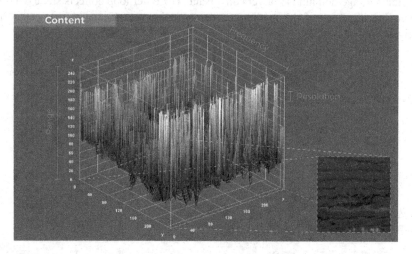

Fig. 11. Defining the resolution, frequency and range of a user-generated content item in 'The Trace' based on the RBG values of the pattern – 3D visualisation is made via 'Interactive 3D Surface Plot' in ImageJ. Together with the results gathered from all items and other players' outcome, figuring out an effective range is instrumental to designing an efficient system.

Similarly, varieties' parameters can be defined for all levels. Inheriting the heritage value of Kashgar, a new map based on the relations designed within the system, is generated to reveal digital value in The Museum of Gamers. This can be counted as an equivalent response to the authenticity issue at a 'global' level. Later we disclose the qualitative statistics based on 'unit' operations in relation to the indexical authenticity (see 'unit operations' in [33]).

The participatory digital heritage environments in The Museum of Gamers produce a dynamic set of relationships between medium, participant and content. Understanding those relationships through the measurable aspects of the system's capabilities, allows us to observe the extent to which the experience is medium dependent, and to what extent the content is meaningful and representative of pure agency — that is how to read and achieve unmediated heritage in digital.

Therefore the effectiveness of the system is defined by how it manages a balance between topological and internal relationships between parameters. We focus here on the inner feedback loop of our diagram (Fig. 12), i.e. the changes in content, measuring these in relation to the role of agency. While following the traces in the narrow lanes of the city, the player journeys through a narrative in 'The Trace'. They first explore a network of Kashgar alleys represented by photogrammetric models, then collect textures from blocks by creating screenshots. Screenshots constitute a user-generated dataset, saved as texture indices that are instrumental to searching associations between items and players. In this way, the inner loop introduces associative rule finding to measure changes in the content. The diagram below (Fig. 12) introduces three terms from the game design field: player profiling, play and player modelling – with which the digital heritage domain is not yet conversant. The outer loop collects static data, for instance specifications of the medium or demographic questionnaires that categorize participants (or players).

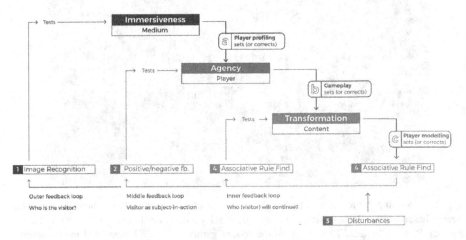

Fig. 12. Examples of measuring tools (image recognition, positive/negative feedback, associative rule finding, respectively) and the positions of game datamining methods (player profiling, gameplay and player modelling, respectively) in the feedback system.

Player profiling is generally about annotating information that does not change during the game. Player profiling methods are used to test how immersiveness can be improved in The Museum of Gamers. The middle cycle is about game mechanics that define the basis for gameplay. The inner loop, which we soon present, benefits from player modelling techniques that are used to understand how participants (usually at the individual level) interact with the content. It focuses on the associative rule finding that is a player modelling method for refining game designs. In this study, however, player modelling is based on extrapolating empirical data from artificial players to make definitive claims and formulations about an 'authentic' digital heritage experience. The reframing of the authenticity issue in this model escapes the constraints of such an either-or approach in the authenticity issue by allowing insight from the user-generated content that is the substance of participation.

5   Findings: Searching for Meaningful Insight

Many methods are employed in game data mining to refine a design. Among the most common are description, characterisation, discrimination, classification, estimation, prediction, clustering and association [34]. One common aspect of all data mining methods is that they become more valid when the analysis is of a large volume of data. The preliminary workshop (see Sect. 3.1) provided us with a set of user-generated content from 'The Trace'. Although the data is small, it is still possible to mine a significant amount of discrete information.

In ImageJ, six patterns captured by a workshop participant were visualised to demonstrate how non-figurative information embedded within images might differ between them (Fig. 13 – top row). Clustering algorithms could analyse and group participant behaviour. For example, understanding what RGB values (first level) receive attention from the participant, could later inform group images based on what their focus areas (second level) are. And this clustering might be strengthened by adding more levels to the dataset in different lookup tables (LUT), providing a new set of parameters with modified values of resolution, frequency and range (Fig. 13 – middle and bottom rows).

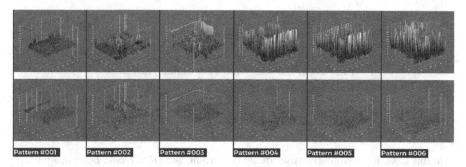

Fig. 13. 3D data visualisation of user-generated content items. The top row shows the distribution of each pixel's RGB value in 3D; the bottom one applies a different range visualised in 'Fire LUT' style.

Among many possible datamining methods, searching associations between clustered groups might offer a better understanding of user interaction, even where the generated data is limited to just six patterns. This part of the paper presents the associate rule mining method used by game designers to, for instance, adapt their game mechanics if players do not inhabit the digital environment as intended. Its use is not limited to 'correcting' player behaviour, but also extends game designers' understanding of player experience and interest; helping to refine their game design.

5.1 Association Rule Finding

Association rule finding performs a correlation (in this paper the terms association and correlation are used interchangeably) analysis to find attributes that are possibly contingent on each other. As a frequent pattern finding technique, association rule mining is an unsupervised method accompanied by a measure of support and confidence [35].

Association rule mining is an increasingly important subject in the game design field. Establishing helpful and unfamiliar data from player interaction, rules are discovered from associations to gain insight for more engaging design outcomes. Attributes of quantitative data are analysed to disclose correlations between individual items generated by the player. For example, players collecting unique sets of items in Minecraft, inadvertently generate associations between their own itemsets and that of other players [36]. These associations remain unknown until analysed. Those individual itemsets can give us a summary of the player experience within the game, drawing attention to items that take their attention in varying orders.

Likewise, every participant exhibits a unique interest in different parts and patterns in a digital heritage environment. A list of collected items can tell a story of a unique virtual journey and include information such as location, angle of view and distance. Calculating the frequent sets of instances is the first method to analyse user-generated content which does not take attributes into account. It is followed by an FP-Growth algorithm in search of association rules between player itemsets. Table 1 shows an example of four player itemsets.

Table 1. Transactional data for 4 players as an example.

ID	List of items
1	*Thick Brick, Darwaza Gate, Pink Curtain, Red Door*
2	*Thick Brick, Mud Wall, Red Door*
3	*Thick Brick, Red Door, Darwaza Gate*
4	*Darwaza Gate, Red Door, Mud Wall, Pink Curtain*

In this case, a possible 2-itemset frequency would be: {*Red Door, Darwaza Gate*}, as three players' transactions contain both *Red Door* and *Darwaza Gate*. In this example, we can show the association rule (with support 3 and confidence 1) as:

$$Darwaza\,Gate \rightarrow Red\,Door[\text{support } = 75\%, \text{ confidence } = 100\%] \qquad (1)$$

However, Darwaza Gate → Red Door and Thick Brick is most likely not a useful association rule because although support condition is met, confidence stays 1/3. A rule A → B is the percentage of the transactions in the whole list that contain both A and B, i.e. $P(A \cup B)$. The confidence of the same rule A → B is the percentage of transactions in the list that contains A provided that it also contain B, i.e. $P(B\backslash A)$.

$$support(A \rightarrow B) = P(A \cup B) \tag{2}$$

$$confidence(A \rightarrow B) = P(B\backslash A) \tag{3}$$

To generate strong association rules, a 'minimum support threshold' and a 'confidence factor' are required. This enables the elimination of trivial rules from results. [37] provides a good summary of the basic concepts involved in association rule mining in large databases.

5.2 Experiment

Participants. Based on the workshop participant's interactive session, an artificial dataset is generated to expand the number of players to a million. One reason for this scenario is that game datamining methods tend to provide more interesting and reliable results when covering a large amount of data. Another is that the purpose of this paper is to arrive at a qualitative outcome while maximising the affordability of the deployed tools and methods.

Experiment Variables. The number of items that can be collected from the virtual environment in 'The Trace' is limited to 10. These items are *Mud-Brick Wall, Timber Wall Structure, Timber Structure, Metal Door, Rec Cobblestone, Hex Cobblestone, Red Door, Blue Door, Mosque Gate* and *Brick Wall*, and the optimal outcome of the workshop participant (ID1) is a 3-itemset sample that includes only *Metal Door, Timber Wall Structure* and *Brick Wall*. This paper discusses the associations found between the 3-itemset ID1 and the rest of the artificial database. By doing so, it binds the argument to the digital experience of the sample workshop participant.

Analysis. The algorithm follows a two-step process to calculate association rules in the database; firstly collecting frequent items and constructing a frequent pattern tree (FP tree) and then mining of the FP tree. This method is called FP-growth. It recursively grows frequent patterns by partitioning the database. In this experiment, the conditional FP-tree of ID1's 3-itemset within the database of all transactions is built from its conditional pattern-base. The implementation of the mining method of the FP tree is as the below pseudocode provided by [37]:

```
if Tree contains a single path P
  then foreach combination (β) of the nodes in the path P
      generate pattern β ∪ α
        with support = minimum support of nodes in β;
else foreach aᵢ in the header of Tree {
    generate pattern β = aᵢ ∪ α
      with support = aᵢ.support;
    construct β,s conditional pattern base
      and then β's conditional FP_tree Treeβ;
    if Treeβ ≠ ∅
      then call F_growth(Treeβ,β);}
```

Findings. Based on the artificial dataset, the transaction of ID1 {*Metal Door, Timber Wall Structure, Brick Wall*} is found to have associations with other 1-itemsets in the following order {*Rec Cobblestone*}, {*Timber Structure*}, {*Mud-Brick Wall*}, {*Hex Cobblestone*}, {*Blue Door*}, {*Mosque Gate*}, {*Red Door*} (Fig. 14). In this scenario, we can presume that the workshop participant is more likely to collect a {*Rec Cobblestone*} pattern than a {*Red Door*} pattern.

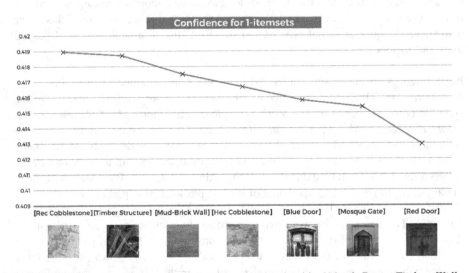

Fig. 14. Confidence graph among 1-itemsets associated with {*Metal Door, Timber Wall Structure, Brick Wall*}.

On the one hand, this information supplies feedback to the middle and outer loops of the system (above Fig. 12). If this is unexpected player behaviour and the narrative is based on an alternative concept — for example, {*Red Door*} is a component designed to be important for the learning process — the designer can adjust the specific area where the problematic component exists.

Conversely, such an unforeseen outcome might tell us a different story, one based on deeper relations between more discrete information embedded within patterns. In that case, the feedback would remain in the inner loop circle to generate new knowledge emerging from the transformation of content as well as user behaviour.

New relations can be sought with n-itemsets. From the infinite number of possibilities offered by association rule mining, we can highlight associations with higher confidence itemsets within the database. Figure 15 shows the confidence for 2- and 3-itemsets in association with the 3-itemset of ID 1, i.e. {*Metal Door, Timber Wall Structure, Brick Wall*}.

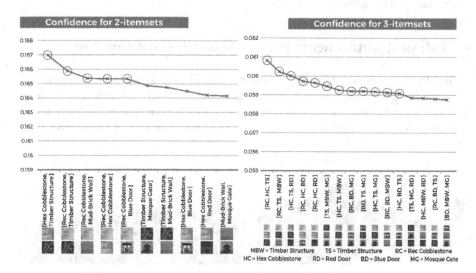

Fig. 15. Confidence graph among 2-itemsets (left) and 3-itemsets (right) associated with the transaction of ID1, i.e. {*Metal Door, Timber Wall Structure, Brick Wall*}. Comparatively higher confidence itemsets are circled.

In this case, we directly observe and interpret a linear relationship between transactions {*Metal Door, Timber Wall Structure, Brick Wall*} and {*Hex Cobblestone, Timber Structure*}. ID1's association rules of 2-itemsets with support = 1% and confidence = 16.6% can be displayed as below (*MD = Metal Door, TWS = Timber Wall Structure, BW = Brick Wall*):

$$\{MD, TWS, BW\} \rightarrow \{Hex\,Cobblestone, Timber\,Structure\} \tag{4}$$

The association rules of 3-itemsets with support = 0.4% and confidence = 6% is denoted as below:

$$\{MD, TWS, BW\} \rightarrow \{Rec\,Cobblestone, Hex\,Cobblestone, Timber\,Structure\} \quad (5)$$

$$\{MD, TWS, BW\} \rightarrow \{Rec\,Cobblestone, Timber\,Structure, Mud-BrickWall\} \quad (6)$$

$$\{MD, TWS, BW\} \rightarrow \{Hex\,Cobblestone, Timber\,Structure, Red\,Door\} \quad (7)$$

Limitations. Yannakakis et al. warns designers using player modelling methods that the player's behaviour in cyberspace is not necessarily reflective of his/her real-life profile [38]. In other words, information gained as a result of player profiling and player modelling methods is subject to a distinction between real-life behaviour and behaviour in cyberspace.

6 Indexical Authenticity: Present Signs of Nonabsent Past

Figure 16 shows how a tall pagoda transmits an overwhelming message about the changing identity of Kashgar with its new silhouette. Yet, only a decade ago, Kashgar was thought to be 'the best-preserved example of a traditional Islamic city to be found anywhere in Central Asia' with minarets stretching out from ground through sky [39].

Fig. 16. North-East silhouette of the Kashgar Old Town. A newly-built pagoda is on the left side, standing higher than anything including a minaret towards the right.

Charles Sanders Peirce's elaboration on the sign is that (1) the final meaning is always the result of a series of successive interpretants, (2) whose never ending combinations give rise to the language of a system of signs, and (3) the interpreter enriches each sign with further signification [40, 41]. In his interpretation, there are three sign types, i.e. icon, index and symbol, whereas a sign can be one of them or all simultaneously. Solving those correlations are the main research gap in heritage studies that seek the dynamics of authenticity. Similarly, the unique architectural heritage of Kashgar [42, 43] is a product of brick layers with different types displaying intermittent changes formulating different manufacturing standards throughout history. All these elements propagate a specific 'Kashgar' language at the material level.

The primary axis for authenticity has always been related to the mode of representation. With the increasing influence of digital tools, this axis has now been broken into discrete and unexplored units [44]. Heritage theories have evolved from material culture to its beyond with social context and even further to our bodily engagements with heritage objects [9, 45]. Analysing indices of a heritage artefact no longer stip-ulates a physical interaction with the original. Although digitising the complexity of an authentic experience is virtually impossible, basic units of visual language are capable of carrying a degree of indexicality to re-examine the question of "what is authentic heritage?" in digital.

The association rules that are discovered in user-generated data might present an intricate relationship between the units of different visual representation types. Figure 11 displayed above how a 2D pattern can escape the boundaries of its technical representation by an interpretation that is circumstantial to unrevealed but non-trivial information. Cross-referencing the values of resolution, frequency and range, one can discover more objective rules within these datasets in order to provide better feedback to the rest of the system (Fig. 17).

Fig. 17. Defining resolution, frequency and range values for the components of immersiveness, agency and transformation allows communication between different aspects of a digital heritage application.

The findings presented here are single-dimensional associations that disclose intra-attribute relationships between user-generated content items. The constituent components of the visual content also involve figurative information such as destina-tion, dimension, brightness, saturation and so on. Improvement on the indexicality involves adding such figurative information to find out multi-dimensional associations in order to seek deeper insight. These inter-attribute relations vertically link player output to, for example, the idiosyncrasies of the digital environment.

For example, frequent itemsets in association can be extended by adding an extra level(s) of 'support'. Finding such cross-object relationships requires a modification in the representation of the itemsets. Classical definition of itemset $\{i_1, i_2, ..., i_k\}$ contains a secondary data to represent itemset in cross-object association rules $\{i_1(\Delta_1), i_2(\Delta_2), ..., i_k(\Delta_k)\}$ [46]. In our case, to discover cross-object associations from user-generated content in The Museum of Gamers itemsets can include, for example, location-based information $\{Brick\ Wall\ (Rd\ 1),\ Mud\text{-}brick\ Wall\ (Rd\ 5),\ Greed\ Door\ (Rd\ 3),\ Brick\ Wall\ (Rd\ 8)\}$. These cross-object associations can increase the translatability of indices from the real heritage environment.

These experiments dealing with basic units of the visual content merit an under-standing of the indexicality that the heritage object holds. The role of these indices found in digital that exist in relationship with each other, can be related to the indices of the real environment. Understanding these relationships better via collective data generation as aimed by The Museum of Gamers, offers an array of options for better heritage management and value. The findings of the association rule mining method demonstrate those patterns more likely to receive attention from the participant. This informs us that, for example, the least likely pattern, graphically demonstrated in Fig. 14, may require improvements in the agency or immersiveness parts of the feedback system shown in Fig. 12. Or, it can be a source of new knowledge that one cannot recognize by simply looking at the visual content. So the indexicality becomes ever closer by testing the validity of these findings through constant feedback via the system. If a pattern that was supposed to have high association with certain itemsets is not generating the anticipated outcome iteratively, it may mean that there is actually no association that one can attribute to it.

As Peirce notes, signification is not a result of a simple dual relationship between sign and object. Interpretation itself as an autonomous and authentic element is central to the signification process that generates a special but natural and ordinary language for conversation and dialog between sign users [40]. In an analogy to Peircean understanding of sign, The Museum of Gamers correlates the indexicality of the heritage value in Kashgar's narrow lanes with the basic units of visual language in digital representations in the form of interactive and engaging experiences.

7 Conclusion

This paper is the first to investigate the association rule finding methods in relation to "indexical authenticity" in digital heritage, which is a way to describe the heritage value beyond materiality in reference to Peirce's concept of the sign in semiotics. It presents a novel digital heritage platform named The Museum of Gamers where a user content generation process is explicated through a real case that extends on a theoretical discussion with regards to the conference theme of 'future trajectories of computation in design'.

There is no digital heritage study that is concerned with a network of tightly entangled relationships between immersiveness, agency and transformation which are described as the 3 key pleasures of cyberspace that are achieved by successful games.

In game design, embedded elements assist in evaluation of game data that lead to player modelling studies. This research does not predicate the authenticity issue on a player modelling study predicting possible user behaviours, however this kind of evaluation methods borrowed from game datamining become the tools for observing the dynamic relations occurring between the user, medium and content.

Our work demonstrates how user-generated content can constitute meaningful correlations that help obtain actionable insights to improve and evaluate digital heritage applications. The findings are instrumental in the study of 'transformation', one of three key pleasure to be found in cyberspace.

The scientific contribution of The Museum of Gamers lies in its success for concentrating on 'digital' and 'heritage' aspects separately as well as combined.

References

1. Howell, R., Chilcott, M.: A sense of place: re-purposing and impacting heritage resource evidence through digital heritage and interpretative practice. Int. J. Intang. Herit. **8**, 165–177 (2013)
2. Münster, S., Ioannides, M.: A scientific community of digital heritage in time and space. In: 2015 Digital Heritage Congress, Granada, Spain (2015)
3. Colley, S.: Ethics and digital heritage. In: Ireland, T., Schofield, J. (eds.) The Ethics of Cultural Heritage, pp. 13–32. Springer, New York (2015)
4. Lowenthal, D.: Authenticity: rock of faith or quicksand quagmire? Getty Newsl. **14**(3) (1999)
5. Cameron, F.: Beyond the cult of the replicant: museums and historical digital objects— traditional concerns, new discourses. In: Cameron, F., Kenderdine, S. (eds.) Media in Transition: Theorizing Digital Cultural Heritage: A Critical Discourse. The MIT Press, Cambridge (2010)
6. Fairclough, G.J.: The Heritage Reader. Routledge, New York (2008)
7. Affleck, J., Kvan, T.: Reinterpreting virtual heritage. In: Digital Opportunities, Proceedings of the 10th CAADRIA, New Delhi, India (2005)
8. Adair, B., Filene, B., Koloski, L.: Letting Go? Sharing Historical Authority in a User-Generated World, p. 335. Left Coast Press, Philadelphia (2011)
9. Waterton, E., Watson, S.: Framing theory: towards a critical imagination in heritage studies. Int. J. Herit. Stud. **19**(6), 546–561 (2013)
10. Harrison, R.: Heritage: Critical Approaches, p. 268. Routledge, New York (2013)
11. Borowiecki, K.J., Forbes, N., Fresa, A.: Cultural Heritage in a Changing World, p. 322. Springer, Basel (2016)
12. Bennett, T.: Museums and the people. In: Lumley, R. (ed.) The Museum Time-Machine: Putting Cultures on Display, pp. 63–85. Comedia/Methuen, London (1988)
13. Ross, M.: Interpreting the new museology. Mus. Soc. **2**(2), 84–103 (2004)
14. Tiffin, J., Terashima, N.: HyperReality: Paradigm for the Third Millennium, p. 165. Routledge, London (2001)
15. Milgram, P., Takemura, H., Utsumi, A., Kishino, F.: Augmented reality: a class of displays on the reality-virtuality continuum. In: Das, H. (ed.) Proceedings SPIE 2351, Telemanipulator and Telepresence Technologies, pp. 282–292 (1995)
16. Aydin, S., Schnabel, M.A.: The museum of gamers: unmediated cultural heritage through gaming. In: Borowiecki, K.J., Forbes, N., Fresa, A. (eds.) Cultural Heritage in a Changing World. Springer, Basel (2016)
17. Murray, J.H.: Hamlet on the Holodeck: The Future of Narrative in Cyberspace, p. 324. MIT Press, Cambridge, MA (1998)
18. Kenderdine, S.: Speaking in Rama: panoramic vision in cultural heritage visualization. In: Cameron, F., Kenderdine, S. (eds.) Media in Transition: Theorizing Digital Cultural Heritage: A Critical Discourse. The MIT Press, Cambridge (2010)
19. Pietroni, E., Adami, A.: Interacting with virtual reconstructions in museums: the etruscanning project. J. Comput. Cult. Herit. **7**(2), 1–29 (2014)
20. Datta, S., Beynon, D.: Digital Archetypes: Adaptations of Early Temple Architecture in South and Southeast Asia, p. 224. Ashgate Publishing Company, Farnham (2014)
21. Champion, E., Bishop, I., Dave, B.: The Palenque project: evaluating interaction in an online virtual archaeology site. Virtual Real. **16**(2), 121–139 (2012)

22. Schnabel, M.A., Aydin, S., Moleta, T., Pierini, D., Dorta, T.: Unmediated cultural heritage via Hyve-3D: collecting individual and collective narratives with 3D sketching. In: Living Systems and Micro-Utopias: Towards Continuous Designing, Proceedings of the 21st CAADRIA, Melbourne, Australia (2016)

23. Negroponte, N.: Being Digital, p. 243. Knopf, New York (1996)

24. Aydin, S., Schnabel, M.A.: Fusing conflicts within digital heritage through the ambivalence of gaming: research through design for a digital heritage project. In: Emerging Experiences in the Past, Present and Future of Digital Architecture, Proceedings of the 20th CAADRIA, Daegu, South Korea (2015)

25. Salen-Tekinbaş, K., Zimmerman, E.: Rules of Play: Game Design Fundamentals, p. 672. MIT Press, Cambridge, MA (2004)

26. Glanville, R.: A ship without a rudder. In: Glanville, R., de Zeeuw, G. (eds.) Problems of Excavating Cybernetics and Systems. BKS+, Southsea (1997)

27. Mathews, S.: The fun palace as virtual architecture: cedric price and the practices of indeterminacy. J. Archit. Educ. **59**(3), 39–48 (2006)

28. Veloso, P.: Cybernetic diagrams: design strategies for an open game. Int. J. Archit. Comput. **12**(4), 379–398 (2014)

29. Pickering, A.: Cybernetics, International Encyclopedia of the Social & Behavioral Sciences, 2nd edn, pp. 645–650. Elsevier, Oxford (2015)

30. Seising, R.: Cybernetics, system(s) theory, information theory and fuzzy sets and systems in the 1950s and 1960s. Inf. Sci. **180**(23), 4459–4476 (2010)

31. Kockelman, P.: Information is the enclosure of meaning: cybernetics, semiotics, and alternative theories of information. Lang. Commun. **33**(2), 115–127 (2013)

32. Ritchey, T.: Wicked Problems Social Messes Decision Support Modelling with Morphological Analysis. Risk, Governance and Society, vol. 17, p. 106. Springer, Heidelberg (2011)

33. Bogost, I.: Unit Operations: An Approach to Videogame Criticism, p. 243. MIT Press, Cambridge (2006)

34. Seif El-Nasr, M., Drachen, A., Canossa, A.: Game Analytics Maximizing the Value of Player Data, p. 800. Springer, London (2013)

35. Drachen, A., Thurau, C., Togelius, J., Yannakakis, G.N., Bauckhage, C.: Game data mining. In: Seif El-Nasr, M., Drachen, A., Canossa, A. (eds.) Game Analytics: Maximizing the Value of Player Data, pp. 205–253. Springer, London (2013)

36. Drachen, A: Frequent Itemset and Association Rule Mining (2012). http://www.gameanalytics.com/blog/frequent-itemset-and-association-rule-mining-or-how-to-know-if-shirts-follows-pants-or-the-other-way-around.html. Accessed 15 Feb 2017

37. Han, J., Kamber, M.: Data Mining: Concepts and Techniques, p. 550. Morgan Kaufmann Publishers, San Francisco (2001)

38. Yannakakis, G.N., Maragoudakis, M.: Player modeling impact on player's entertainment in computer games. In: Ardissono, L., Brna, P., Mitrovic, A. (eds.) UM 2005. LNCS, vol. 3538, pp. 74–78. Springer, Heidelberg (2005). doi:10.1007/11527886_11

39. Michell, G.: Kashgar: Oasis City on China's Old Silk Road, vol. 159. Frances Lincoln, London (2008)

40. Peirce, C.S., Moore, E.C.: Charles S. Peirce: The Essential Writings, Great Books in Philosophy, p. 322. Prometheus Books, Amherst, NY (1998)

41. Merrell, F.: Peirce, Signs, and Meaning, Toronto Studies in Semiotics, p. 384. University of Toronto Press, Toronto (1997)

42. Aydin, S., Schnabel, M.A.: Decoding Kashgar. In: Guidi, G., et al. (eds.) Proceedings of 2nd International Congress on Digital Heritage 2015, VSMM, EUROGRAPHICS, CIPA ICOMOS/ISPRS. IEEE Xplore Digital Library, , Granada, Spain (2015)

43. Aydin, S., Schnabel, M.A.: Augmenting Kashgar. In: Image & Archive, Proceedings of 20th VSMM. IEEE Xplore Digital Library, Hong Kong SAR, China (2014)
44. Galloway, A.: Are some things unrepresentable? Theory Cult. Soc. **28**(7–8), 85–102 (2011)
45. Watson, S., Waterton, E.: Reading the visual: representation and narrative in the construction of heritage. Mater. Cult. Rev. **71**, 84–97 (2010)
46. Ling, F., Eric, T.: Finding cross-object relationships from large databases. In: Systems, Man, and Cybernetics, IEEE SMC '99 Conference Proceedings (1999)

Computing with Watercolor Shapes

Developing and Analyzing Visual Styles

Onur Yüce Gün[✉]

New Balance Athletics Inc., Boston, MA, USA
onuryucegun@alum.mit.edu

Abstract. Computers help run visually creative processes, yet they remain visually, sensually and tactually distant [1]. This research introduces a drawing and painting process that infuses digital and analog ways of *visual-making* [2]. It implements a computationally broadened workflow for hand-drawing and painting, and develops a custom drawing apparatus. Primary goal is to develop a computationally generative painting system while retaining embodied actions and tactile material interactions that are intrinsic to the processes of hand-drawing and watercolor painting. A non-symbolic, open-ended and trace-based shape calculation system emerges.

Keywords: Shape · Computing · Painting · Embodied · Watercolor

1 Introduction: Problem Statement

Advancements in digital computing and human-computer-interaction (HCI) devices help computing become a more interwoven part of visual arts and design processes. Current research concentrates on making the digital aspects of design more material while making material aspects of design more digital so that sensibly, tangibly and digitally infused design and fabrication methods and technologies can be implemented [3]. The visual aspects of design, as processes of design keep expanding into broader disciplines, techniques and scales, become even more prominent for design ideation. Briefly, the definition and ways of *visual-making*[1] keep transforming as a consequence of technical and technological advancements. Yet, a relentless boundary between the digital and the material persists [1–3].

The research presented here aims first to inquire, then to outline and finally to tackle the disconnection between the immediacy and materiality of a hand-drawn trace and the digitally generated counterpart of it. A computationally generated trace is not truly tangible or experiential [4] and in turn a bodily materialized trace cannot directly be digitally computed. This study proposes a method and an apparatus to bring these two distant ends closer.

---

[1] *Visual-making* is the practice of producing visible things for exploring visual ideas. Word *visual* does not only refer to the mode of perception, but it also contains the meaning of the noun version of the word: *visual(n)* making. The making process is not merely visual in perceptual sense, but also visual in an embodied manner, involving tactual and broader senses.

© Springer Nature Singapore Pte Ltd. 2017
G. Çağdaş et al. (Eds.): CAAD Futures 2017, CCIS 724, pp. 252–269, 2017.
DOI: 10.1007/978-981-10-5197-5_14

The main goal is to preserve and leverage the influence of humanly visual and tactile decision making processes within disembodied computational and digital visual-making practices that are becoming dangerously habitual [5]. Centralizing and utilizing the essential acts of *humaning*[2] [6] while exploring a more embodied integration of computing is the main endeavor of this study.

2   Technical and Methodological Developments

2.1   Apparatus

The developed visual-exploration apparatus, the *Broadened Drawing-Scape*, consists of both hardware and software components [2]. The apparatus comprises of a transparent drawing surface on which drawing mediums can be placed, a computational camera that is positioned to capture images from this drawing surface, and a digital projector (Fig. 1).

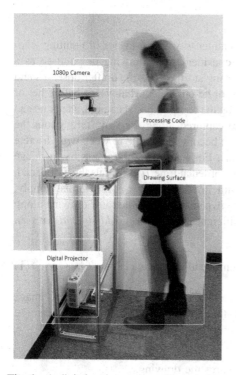
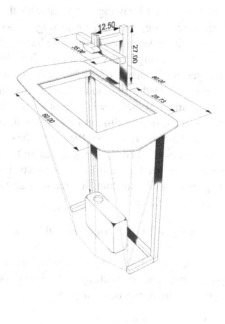

Fig. 1. A digital web-cam is positioned above the drawing area to capture the developmental stages of a water-coloring process. The dimensions of the apparatus are shown in centimeters.

---

[2] *Humaning* is a term coined by Tim Ingold. While the noun *human* objectifies, the verb *humaning* highlights the acts of ever-becoming human.

The software is developed in Processing.[3] The interactive drawing/painting tool helps capture, reconfigure and re-use the embedded bits of a drawing or painting. This enables the painter to pick and choose shapes either from his or her ongoing analog hand-drawing or painting, or from the projected shapes (that fall underneath the ongoing drawing) to continue the painting process.

The apparatus is built upon the idea of fusing the visual richness of rule based drawings with intuitional foundations of hand-drawing and it is meant to become a tool to *visually* think with. This hardware-software setup amplifies the role of the hands and eyes of the painter or the designer, which are intrinsic to processes of visual-making. The argument that computational tools and workflows suppress the dominant role of hands and eyes [1–3], springs from the limitations implied by either the discrete logic of computing or by unhandy human-computer interaction devices. This research proposes a workflow to tackle this limitation and introduce a unique computational drawing process that re-centralizes the role of hands and eyes in visual-making processes.

2.2 Workflow

The Broadened Drawing-Scape enables the painter to work in cycles of painting, capturing, reconfiguring and projecting. If we consider act of drawing or painting as a process that takes place on the timeline T, starting at time $T(0)$, the drafter observes and edits the drawing at any given time $T(n)$. She or he only sees whatever is before her or his eyes in real-time, at $T(n)$. However, by using the computational camera, she or he can compute with the individual frames that are captured along the way, throughout the development of the drawing. In other words, it becomes possible to work with discrete images recorded at different moments in time. For instance, subtraction of an image recorded at time $T(m)$ from the image that is recorded at time $T(n)$ reveals the embedded, excluded or masked bits between these two time frames, along n-m time units. Simply, what is extracted is the difference between the two snapshots of the same drawing along its genesis. Isolating such subtractions and differences reveals embedded—*but not seen* partial images:

$$\text{drawing } [at] \, T(n) - \text{drawing } [at] \, T(m) = \text{empbeddedDrawing } [along] T(n - m) \quad (1)$$

In another instance, a drawing sequence that involves image capturing, image processing and projecting capabilities of the Broadened Drawing-Scape can be described in consecutive steps as:

*step 1_* the user draws,
*step 2_* using the apparatus, the user captures the drawing,
*step 3_* the user draws again, adds a shape or a trace (*x*),

---

[3] As described on the Processing website: "Processing is a flexible software sketchbook and a language for learning how to code within the context of the visual arts." https://processing.org/ [Accessed February 2016].

step *4_* using the apparatus the user digitally isolates the trace *(x)*,

step *5_* the user applies shape rules[4] to digitally multiply the isolated trace *(x)*,

step *6_* *the* user projects the resultant image back onto drawing surface,

step *7_* the user looks, evaluates and picks, traces over projected shapes,

step *8_* the user goes back to *step 1* or one of the other former steps in between.

Proposed sequence can be altered at any moment and the artist may choose to draw or apply shape rules in different ways. Because the workflow is completely flexible, and because the essence of the system lies in the multi-directional interaction of human with materials, computational devices and images, a semi-structured, flowing *un-diagram*[5], describes the interwoven relationship of the human(ing) with the components of the Broadening Drawing-Scape during the act of visual making (Fig. 2).

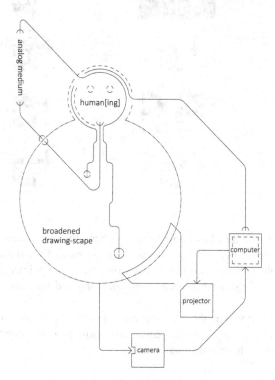

Fig. 2. An 'un-diagram' of the workflow. The human touches, and extends his/her actions and perceptions in an embodied manner while painting. The digital camera, computer and projector are there to take care of the computational end of the painting process.

---

[4] Specifically, in an additive drawing or painting process, the user uses $x \rightarrow x + t(x)$ schema to generate a template that includes multiple instances of the same shape.

[5] This is a *un-diagram*, because diagrams try to represent workflows as completely resolved input-output mechanisms.

The proposed workflow helps develop sophisticated paintings starting with a simple initial shape, and by using this shape (and its unfoldment) as a source of visual inspiration. The apparatus helps digitally capture and extract the embedded bits of drawings from ongoing analog drawing and water-coloring processes. These captured bits are then utilized to generate digital patterns by using shape rules (Table 1). The digital patterns, in turn, are projected underneath the analog drawing surface, and the whole surface yields to an exploratory drawing process.

Table 1. Shapes are drawn by hand, by tracing over the calculated digital patterns, using the apparatus.

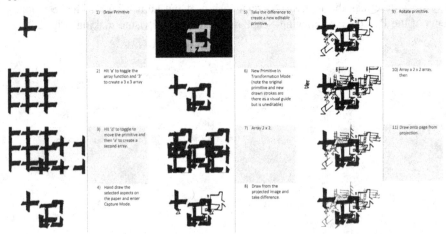

In the first diagrammatical example presented here, the artist begins with a simple marker stroke (an initial shape) and arrives at a visually sophisticated drawing shown at the end of the Table 1. In this abstract visual exploration, the painter aims to create *a visually coherent whole* starting from a simple drawing and through applying certain schemas and rules.

The patterns that appear on the way, especially in reference to the initial shape, look rather expected and arguably homogeneous. This most probably happens due to the limited, a *blind* use of the transformation rule

$$x \rightarrow x + t(x) \tag{2}$$

The initial shape is captured by the digital camera and then multiplied via application of sequential planar transformations. Arguably, every part carries more or less a similar significance or salience in the making of the whole. However, when overlaid, the patterns generate irregularities. Something truly new emerges when the eye and the hands get into work together: at an unexpected moment, the eye captures a new shape, and the hand starts tracing over it. An unforeseen trace appears (Fig. 3). This very shape is not necessarily mandated by a resultant pattern but it is rather seen through drawing, as the eye and the hand work in an unfolding sequence of seeing and doing.

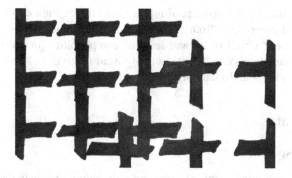

Fig. 3. A new shape is seen and traced over. The new shape is not digitally produced; it is hand-traced over the projection.

The arrival at the final canvas (Fig. 4) involves a series of rule applications, personal choices and embodied actions. The traces on the canvas emerge through analog hand operations and digital captures and projections of shapes.

Fig. 4. The final drawing. Inherently, it doesn't have to be the final as it holds the potential to expand to other drawings.

The method presented here yields to rapidly-developed drawings that come to life as blends of analog medium(s) on paper and digital traces that are drawn by projector's light. The resulting blended (material and projected digital) drawing helps generate ever-changing visual configurations, a dynamic *drawing-scape* [7] to which the drafter or the painter can look into, and draw and paint onto. This suggests new ways of embedding [8], through which an artist or designer can both draw and calculate with the bits that belong to his or her own style. The drawing process introduced here, unlike most of the digital drawing tools, offers a non-symbolic drawing system in which the traces are not created through use of pre-complied mathematical shapes (as it would be in any CAD platform), but rather drawn by hand, using analog mediums. It develops upon the interpretations and insights of artists rather than combinatorically simulated insights of digital computers. Both the method and outcomes of this study yield to understandings about visual styles and level of compatibility (or incompatibility) of current digital computing systems with acts of visual-making. Following experiments lay the groundwork for understanding visual styles.

3 Experiments

3.1 Painting Styles

The experiments presented in this research not only help re-evaluate the limitations of conventional digital (and computerized) drawing environments but also help develop insights about the ways in which visual styles emerge.

Drawings can be thought of as *trace-scapes*, and paintings as *pigment-scapes* [7]. What the drafter or painter does is to embed traces, strokes and pigments to generate *fields* of marks [9] that later accumulate, blend and transform to generate a greater *scape*. One can neither comprehend nor describe a (visual) whole in terms of its parts [10], yet the parts are definitely the means that one intertwines with—and within—the explorative fields of drawings and paintings [11]. Then, the character of a drawing—the style—surfaces as a product of not only the sum of its traces but also the ways in which these traces get embedded into the whole, the bigger picture, over time [8].

3.2 Method: Watercoloring While Calculating

Schemas and shape rules help describe the developmental stages of drawings and watercolor painting as calculations [8]. In the following example, a simple shape, *x* is captured and then multiplied to generate a digital pattern (template) to work with. The painting starts with a *motif* that is painted with a watercolor brush (Fig. 5):

Fig. 5. A simple, gestural watercolor *motif.*

Then, in the digital environment, the shape is transformed several times using the transformation rule

$$x \rightarrow x + t(x) \tag{3}$$

Following three consecutive steps of transformations, the entire calculation becomes

$$x \rightarrow x + t(x) + t'(x) + t''(x)\ldots \tag{4}$$

The resultant digital image is then projected underneath the analog drawing surface, for the painter to trace over the shapes in red [12] ... (Fig. 6)

Fig. 6. A simple motif leads to generation of a sophisticated pattern after consequent application of the rule $x \rightarrow x + t(x)$.

$$<x, 0> \ \rightarrow \ <x, x'> \tag{5}$$

...to generate the watercolor painting. Finally, the artist sees dragons, birds and fish in boundaries of watercolor shapes (Fig. 7):

$$<x, x', 0> \ \rightarrow \ <x, x', b(x) + b(x')> \tag{6}$$

Fig. 7. Final painting and inked edges. Painting by Joie Chang.

3.3   Analysis

The artist evaluates the painting in retrospect to find out the repeating features and she recalls the actions that she has taken over the course of painting (Fig. 8):

Fig. 8. Repeating features that get embedded by tracing over the digital projection. (Color figure online)

#1 shows the initial shape (the very first brush stroke, the *motif* in blue) and the stroke that is created by tracing over the translated shape. The painter uses the schema

$$x \rightarrow x + t(x) \qquad (7)$$

#2 comes to life as an "explosion" of the copy of first stylistic curve, so that the artist uses the part schema

$$x \rightarrow prt(x) \qquad (8)$$

The artist paints a similar shape after shifting the pattern.

#3 is painted after a watercolor wash appears in the projection and gets duplicated after the former shift.

#4 is generated when the artist does a computational operation (image difference) using two latest captured patterns before projecting it underneath the painting.

#5 utilizes the same technique in #4 and finally rotates the final projection to paint an upside-down and traces over a less precise duplicate.

4 Discussion

Developing and analyzing drawings and paintings by using shape calculations help develop insights about how the current computing systems can be altered, modified and reconfigured to better suit open-ended acts of visual-making. *Shapes* prove to be greater than mere *parts* as they (visually) offer more than their *combinations*. In turn, the combinatorial logic of digital computers barely fares against what an eye can see in a sea of shapes.

4.1 Re-thinking Part-Whole Relationship for Visual Computations

If we define a drawing as an ensemble of traces, and a painting as an ensemble of pigments, would this mean that drawings and paintings can be explained through their traces and pigments? What a drafter or a painter does is to embed traces, strokes and pigments to generate fields of marks that later accumulate, blend and transform to generate something greater than the sum of the parts [11].[6] The traces and pigments build the picture towards a whole that cannot be contained in one single description.

What's more is that these bits, marks, shapes, fields are created and interacted with in fundamentally different ways in analog and digital realms. Analog traces are truly immediate and results of direct embodied actions that involve both visual and tactile sensations. Digital traces, on the other hand, are made up of smaller structured bits, and

---

[6] Hill wrote: 'As an individual becomes conscious of the relational laws in drawing, he will begin to take notice of similar relationships in experience. The course of the stream moves both ways: experience in drawing—arranging lines creating form and space, relating parts, exploring various materials—will slowly act upon the vision of a sensitive individual, affecting how he sees, even what he sees.'

can be modified through numerical operations. They can be multiplied almost indefinitely. As a consequence, merging the potentials of embodied painting and computing appears to be an obvious idea to introduce a novel method for creative visual processes. The way in which this should be done; however, remains as one of the core research challenges since the introduction of digital computers [2].

This study reviews the motivations that lead to the development of early computational systems and search for alternative intelligences to root its arguments in the disciple of computer science as much as it does in the discipline of visual arts and design.

4.2   Insight and Intuition: Perceptual Intelligence Versus Machine Intelligence

Computers are acclaimed to play a central role in processes of visual-making for their potential in introducing novel methods of making. Are computers truly intelligent devices or this potential is a result of some other property? The answer to this question heavily depends on how one defines *intelligence*, and there are too many ways to do so. The intelligence of machines has been classified in a different category than that of humans (and animals and plants) with the addition of the adjective *artificial*. The (probable) intelligence of machines is called artificial, because it is being implemented with certain assumptions about the mind's workings [13]. The majority of users might think that computers are intelligent simply because computers can count fast, count numbers at speeds that humans cannot match in any possible way. Yet true intelligence involves many more actions beyond mere computing, such as perceiving, learning, planning, communicating and problem solving. Intelligence extends beyond the physiological boundaries of the human brain and body throughout the surroundings, places [7] and matter. In this respect, research that has been trying to develop disembodied intelligence constantly keeps failing. As Dreyfus states [13]:

> 'In thinking that the body can be dispensed with [...] thinkers again follow the tradition; which from Plato to Descartes has thought of the body as getting in the way of intelligence and reason, rather than being in any way indispensable for it. If the body turns out to be indispensable for intelligent behavior, then we shall have to ask whether the body can be simulated on a heuristically programmed digital computer. If not, then the project of artificial intelligence is doomed from the start.'

Human intelligence for creativity is quite different than the one of machines. Looking into the inner workings of a Turing Machine is definitely helpful in determining the sort of intelligence that a machine can potentially have. In essence, the possibility of developing AI on a Turing machine depends on *'the assumption that human beings produce intelligence using facts and rules'* [13] that so far proved not to be the case. Creating general intelligence on Turing machines is heavily dependent on primary characteristics of the Turing machine, as laid out usefully by Dyson. Dyson highlights the two fundamental assumptions that Turing introduced: *'discreteness of time and discreteness of state of mind'* [14]. In Turing's model, time does not flow in a continuum; the computing duration depends on the speed of the machine, and there is a moment of time when a desired state of mind is reached. The state remains the same until a new set of instructions via a new set of symbols is fed into the machine for new computations. So, whatever is being searched for or is constructed in the machine does not take place until the final state is reached. In a sense, the computing time is totally meaningless. According to Dyson:

> '...the Turing machine [...] embodies the relationship between an array of symbols in space and a sequence of events in time. All traces of intelligence [are] removed. The machine can do nothing more intelligent at any given moment than make a mark, erase a mark, and move the tape one square to the right or to the left.' [14]

All the listed actions undertaken by the Turing machine are done in accordance with the instructions, and as long as there are no physical or logical failures, the machine works in perfect order. In other words, *'the Turing machine follows instructions and it never makes mistakes.'* This also implies that it cannot learn from making mistakes in any way, which in turn is a fundamental characteristic of human intelligence.

Humans seem to overcome the limitations of an inability to make mistakes with intuition. Intuition enables us to make decisions that are neither included nor foreseen in planning or acting processes. Intuition has been the major player in the development of artificial intelligence since the emergence of digital computers, in which intuition has neither been identified nor deciphered nor simulated, and thus remained the major unresolvable limitation of AI. For Turing, *'intuition consists in making spontaneous judgments which are not the result of conscious trains of reasoning, [and] these judgments are often but by no means invariably correct (leaving aside the question what is meant by 'correct'.)'* [13]

Briefly, Turing talks about what we call intuition (or insight) (Fig. 9) that triggers the actions that cannot be planned or explained using reasoning. And visual-making, although it involves various levels of planning, is a purely perceptual act that depends on seeing and making. Insight, intuition, and making mistakes—that cannot be developed or acted out by machine intelligence, constitute the very foundation of perceptual intelligence.

Fig. 9. Human insight is irreplaceable (*intel inside* graphic by Intel and *human insight* graphic made by the author).

4.3   Blind Machines and the Sentient in Seeing

'...in the real world, most of the time, finding an answer is easier than defining the question. It is easier to draw something that looks like a cat than to define what, exactly, makes something look like a cat. A child scribbles indiscriminately, and eventually something appears that resembles a cat. An answer finds a question, not the other way around.' [14]

As understood in Dyson's example, drawing is a sentient approximation more than it is a practice of making definitions. It also involves trials, errors and discoveries such as the one represented in Fig. 4 in the former sections.

If one tries to define the visual properties of a cat, using words and phrases, it would be possible, but it will not be the same as just jotting down a couple of traces that would lead an onlooker to say *'that's a cat!'* (Fig. 10).

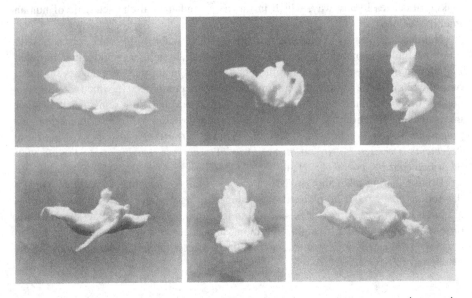

Fig. 10. Ambiguity at work: *equivalents* by Vik Muniz. A dog, a teapot, a cat, a rowing man in a boat, praying hands and a snail. Are they made of cotton or clouds?

The series of acts leading to the appearance of the cat during the course of a child's scribbling involve many errors that help the child learn how to do things the next time, how to utilize her intelligence and how to be creative in making or drawing something that, in the process, ends up looking like a cat. And for a machine to represent true intelligence of humans, it needs to recognize its mistakes and learn from them: *'if a machine is expected to be infallible, it cannot also be intelligent,'* Turing concludes [14].

A design or visual exploration (as explained in the representative example of the cat figure) is more about asking a series of questions without proposing any hurried or definitive answer. The very early adoption of digital computers in creative practices (such as visual arts and design) is due to the power of digital computers in creating, iterating and displaying shapes (and later colors). Such potential applications have long been described as new paradigms [15], and the excess of available colors and shapes (and thereof their combinations) is described as some sort of unprecedented richness. This argument is partly inaccurate, because most computer applications were developed through simulation of colors that have been around humanity from the beginning of times.[7] What was truly novel was the speed and availability of generating and displaying those shapes and colors on computers.

Yet there is still nothing that performs similar to the way in which humans use ambiguity. It is not only about making things but also about seeing things in, on or about whatever visually exists around us. As in the case of drawing something like a cat, one can just see something like a mouse inside waves of string-painted watercolors (Fig. 11).

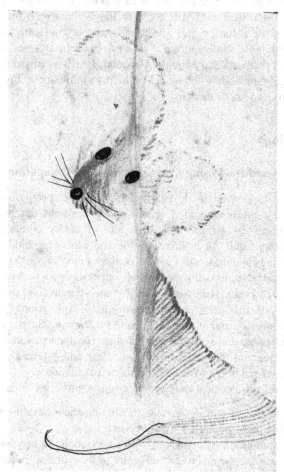

Fig. 11. An answer finds a question: A mouse waiting to be 'found' by the human eye. A string that is dipped into watercolor is then laid onto a paper and pulled from one side. The colored marks of the string become an open invitation for the artist, Nebahat Gün, to *see*. The work parallels Vinci's stains or Cozen's blots as it is a product of visual (re)search in ambiguity.

---

[7] ..and every eye sees those colors ever slightly differently.

4.4 A Non-deterministic Way for Visual-Making

There exists a divide between the embodied actions and perceptions of humans and the purely-discrete and purely-combinatorial nature of binary computing. In other words, humans just do things, and almost none of these things can be explained in terms of combinations of parts [16].[8] Digital computers are programmed to undertake tasks following pre-determined commands within pre-determined domains[9] while a design or a work of art does not come to life following a discrete series of operations. They are rather products of actions undertaken under influence of intentions. A *product*, then, inherently implies a *process*, the process of its making. And as much as this process involves making, what truly makes it come to life is the search for *visual meaning* during its making, the meaning that artists and painters constantly search for. Such understanding highlights the importance of open-ended processes of drawing and painting, processes that are open enough to support the designer and the painter while they think through their bodies—it would be hard to think about any kind of disembodied way to produce art or designs.

5 Contributions

5.1 A Step Forward for Fusing Visual-Making and Computing

This study is a step forward in developing a critical perspective about the divide between human's seamless embodied actions and perceptions that take place during creative visual processes and the discrete nature of binary computing. It aims to introduce a new approach for making visible the otherwise hidden bits that get embedded in paintings and drawings over the course of their becoming. Using this tool, one can do shape calculations using any sort of (intentional, coincidental or accidental) traces. To this end, this study proposes a way to incorporate computational technologies into processes of truly open-ended creative visual explorations [2, 8].

This research develops and introduces Broadened Drawing-Scape, an apparatus that is comprised of hardware and software components. The apparatus makes it possible to bring forth a new method for visual-making, drawing and painting via fusing analog and digital modes of painting, a trace-based shape calculation.

This study develops a critical outlook to current approaches in design computing:

- Analog and digital modes of design and drawing practices have their own potentials and richness but these potentials hardly co-exist.
- Inferential computational systems work with a symbolic understanding of shapes, and thus they cannot use or utilize ambiguity to their utmost potential.
- Current computational design and drawing systems are mostly geared towards production, multiplication and efficiency [17] rather than exploration and discovery.

---

[8] Watts wrote: '...*their technique was to separate things into their component parts and to try to understand them by examination and classification of the pieces; their belief was that the best way of knowing a thing scientifically was to "pull it to bits".*'

[9] Any sort of generative and advanced computing falls into this category.

The conducted experiments and presented drawings help developing ideas and tools towards:

- Centralizing and broadening one's phenomenological and artistic style.
- Merging the visual richness of rule based drawings with intuitional foundations of hand-drawing.
- Developing a drawing environment, in which computational means of drawings (such as coding) meet analogue means (hand & material) of drawing.

To conclude, the outlined study offers a method for expanding one's phenomenological visual design activities and for merging the explorative power of rule based algorithmic drawings with intuitional foundations of hand-drawing.

The variety and distinctiveness of paintings, three of which are showcased here illustrate the flexibility of the system in generating and working with different styles [2].

5.2   Final Thoughts and Reception

If we observe the act of drawing, we draw what is salient[10] to us, or we look at the meaningful parts in what we draw, and because drawing is seeing[11] we keep working with what we see as momentarily salient and what we draw. The significance of *the drawn* does not come from convergence, from a meaning's completion; it rather is a product of meaning's ever-unfolding that points to an ever-expanding emergence. Based on this, what we do during creative visual-making processes is not simply working with discrete parts, but resonating with significance of the whole and its parts. In Watts' words:

> '[...] while [one] cannot see the wood for the trees, the [other] cannot see the trees for the wood. The balanced and integrated mind, however, is that which sees both the wood and the trees in their true relation to one another.' [16]

The method presented here empowers the painter to retain his or her embodied painting process and broadens the process by adding a computational layer for expanding stylistic exploration. This helps develop or further investigate characters (or styles) of paintings and drawings: the watercolor paintings engendered in this study have been acknowledged as a step forward for Shape Grammars [2], for they use schemas and shape rules in making and analyzing watercolor paintings. Knight and Stiny [18] speculate about a making grammar for Sargent's watercolor paintings, but they do not develop one, as they claim *"doing so would be extremely complicated and challenging."*

The presented apparatus was built and iterated many times and used for educational workshops and design studios [19]. The apparatus remains unique in the way it utilizes the hardware and software components that it brings together. Similar setups exist but

---

[10] As unfolded by Edith Ackermann as *'that which currently stands out as capturing our attention or imagination.'* In personal correspondence in 2014.

[11] Hill, Edward. 1966. The Language of Drawing. Prentice-Hall, 25. Hill says: *'Drawing = Seeing.'*

they concentrate either on some sort of conversation between humans and machines, or collaboration between human agents. The software component, developed in processing, became an open source script to be developed and transformed in accordance with the goals of individual users [2].

Last but not the least, this research expands into disciplines that are not frequently involved in computational and generative design studies. It tries to learn from the disciplines of anthropology and philosophy and marry them with disciplines of computing and design to develop a more human inquiry into the role of computing (and in a broader sense—technology) in making and experiencing art and design.

Acknowledgements. This research won the William J. Mitchell ++ Fund in 2015 and the Council for the Arts at MIT Grant in 2016.[12] I am grateful to MIT for funding and supporting my PhD studies. I would like to thank my former assistant Joie Chang for working on the paintings and the Processing code. Late Prof. Edith Ackermann's and Prof. George Stiny's critical approaches to design computing along with Marilyn Levine's multifaceted support played an important role while this research matured. Beyza Şahin's input during revisions, writing and editing was invaluable.

References

1. Petherbridge, D.: The Primacy of Drawing: Histories and Theories of Practice. Yale University Press, New Haven (2010)
2. Gün, O.Y.: A Place for Computing Visual Meaning: The Broadened Drawing-Scape. Ph.D. Dissertation, Massachusetts Institute of Technology, Cambridge (2016)
3. Pinochet, P.D.: Making Gestures: Design and Fabrication Through Real Time Human Computer Interaction. Thesis, Massachusetts Institute of Technology, Cambridge (2015)
4. Noë, A.: Action in Perception. MIT Press, Cambridge (2004)
5. Woods, L.: The Storm and the Fall. Princeton Architectural Press, New York (2004)
6. Ingold, T.: The Life of Lines. Routledge, Milton Park, Abingdon (2015)
7. Casey, E.S.: Getting Back into Place: Toward a Renewed Understanding of the Place-World. Indiana University Press, Bloomington (2009)
8. Stiny, G.: Shape: Talking About Seeing and Doing. MIT Press, Cambridge, MA (2006)
9. Knight, T.W.: Color grammars: designing with lines and colors. Environ Plan B Plan Des **16**, 417–449 (1989). doi:10.1068/b160417
10. Watts, A.: The Book: On the Taboo Against Knowing Who You Are, Reissue edition. Vintage Books, New York (1989)
11. Hill, E.: The Language of Drawing. Prentice-Hall, New York (1966)
12. Stiny, G.: Pictorial and Formal Aspects of Shape and Shape Grammars, 1975th edn. Birkhäuser, Basel (1980)
13. Dreyfus, H.L.: What Computers Still Can't Do: A Critique of Artificial Reason, ix, 235. The MIT Press, Cambridge, MA (1992)
14. Dyson, G.: Turing's Cathedral: The Origins of the Digital Universe, pp. 247–252. Vintage Books, New York (2012)
15. Picon, A.: Digital Culture in Architecture, p. 71. Birkhauser, Basel (2010)

---

[12] http://arts.mit.edu/artists/onurgun/#about-the-artist.

16. Watts, A.: Seeds of genius: the early writings of Alan Watts. In: Watts, M., Snelling, J. (eds.) Seeds of Genius: The Early Writings of Alan Watts, p. 189. Element Books Ltd., Rockport, MA (1998)
17. Solnit, R.: Wanderlust: A History of Walking. Penguin Books, New York (2000)
18. Knight, T., Stiny, G.: Making grammars: from computing with shapes to computing with things. Des. Stud. Spec. Issue Comput. Mak. **41**(Part A), 8–28 (2015). doi:10.1016/j.destud.2015.08.006
19. Gün, O.Y.: Broadened drawing-scape: being, becoming, computing. In: Archi-DOCT E-Journal Issue 2-1 Fields, pp. 62–75 (2014). http://www.enhsa.net/archidoct/

Materials, Fabrication, Computation

Robot-Aided Fabrication of Interwoven Reinforced Concrete Structures

Elif Erdine$^{(\boxtimes)}$, Alexandros Kallegias, Angel Fernando Lara Moreira,
Pradeep Devadass, and Alican Sungur

Architectural Association (AA) School of Architecture, London, UK
{elif.erdine, alexandros.kallegias,
Lara-Moreira}@aaschool.ac.uk, pappurvsa@gmail.com,
sunguralican@gmail.com

Abstract. This paper focuses on the realization of three-dimensionally interwoven concrete structures and their design process. The output is part of an ongoing research in developing an innovative strategy for the use of robotics in construction. The robotic fabrication techniques described in this paper are coupled with the computational methods dealing with geometry rationalization and material constraints among others. By revisiting the traditional bar bending techniques, this research aims to develop a novel approach by the reduction of mechanical parts for retaining control over the desired geometrical output. This is achieved by devising a robotic tool-path, developed in KUKA|prc with Python scripting, where fundamental material properties, including tolerances and spring-back values, are integrated in the bending motion methods via a series of mathematical calculations in accord with physical tests. This research serves to demonstrate that robotic integration while efficient in manufacturing it also retains valid alignment with the architectural design sensibility.

Keywords: Robotic fabrication · Robotic bar bending · Concrete composite · Geometry optimization · Polypropylene formwork

1 Introduction

In previous decades, architecture evolved rapidly through a series of innovations in digital design techniques where geometrical assemblies are generated through computational form-finding methods. At the same time, digital fabrication techniques have witnessed a more compromised level of development, uneven with that of the vast array of computationally sophisticated formations. In recent years, robotic fabrication procedures applied in architecture have begun to incorporate digital and analogue paradigms in an unparalleled way due to the multi-axis freedom of the industrial robot arm, its speed, precision, and low tolerances [1]. The current advancements of robotic fabrication processes in architecture has fueled the emergence of complexity found in mass-customized assemblies, moving away from previous standardized/sheet-material component fabrication [2].

This paper illustrates the outcomes of an ongoing research towards developing an innovative strategy for the construction of three-dimensionally interwoven concrete composite structures. The investigations are conducted as part of the Architectural

© Springer Nature Singapore Pte Ltd. 2017
G. Çağdaş et al. (Eds.): CAAD Futures 2017, CCIS 724, pp. 273–288, 2017.
DOI: 10.1007/978-981-10-5197-5_15

Association (AA) Summer DLAB Visiting School 2016. Research methods include the employment of computational design and robotic fabrication techniques that incorporate geometry rationalization and material constraints. The objectives of the research focus on the evaluation and interpretation of a traditional fabrication process, steel bar bending, towards its development within the domain of advanced computational and robotic methods. Through the review of bar bending technology in traditional manufacturing industries that are well-documented and established, this research serves to examine the evolving complexity of embedding generative form-finding parameters, geometrical rationalization parameters, and material constraints within the computational scene and use of simulation tools. In this manner, the ability to enforce basic mechanical tools and cost-effective fabrication methods for the realization of complex forms becomes a possibility.

Over the last years, research teams have engaged in robotic bar bending methods, developing various workflows. A custom-made, robot-aided CNC bender that is controlled as an additional axis of the generic robotic system has been developed for the "Clouds of Venice" installation at the 2012 Venice Biennale in order to realize mass-customized, robotically bent steel bar elements [3]. Moreover, there is an ongoing research on integrating robotic fabrication constraints within the conceptual architectural design processes via customized algorithms [4]. This research aims to expand on the generic properties of a robotic manipulator, whereby attention is kept on the development of custom-made, versatile programming and simulation workflows without the necessity to develop custom-made hardware elements. Through the careful correlation of data pertaining to material properties, including tolerances and spring-back values of steel bars, with fabrication constraints related to robotic toolpath planning, this research presents a methodology for the integration of generative design tools, geometrical optimization, material opportunities and limitations, and fabrication constraints for the robotic bending of steel bars.

The one-to-one scale prototype and the scaled model presented in this paper are case studies for investigating the design and construction methodologies of a network of 3-dimensionally interwoven concrete composite structures. The design brief for the prototype entails the design and construction of a one-to-one scale pavilion made from reinforced concrete in a forest located in AA's Hooke Park premises in Dorset, United Kingdom, within a limited time frame, three weeks. Three main components of the prototypes' are addressed as the key research objectives: Steel reinforcement bars, Polypropylene formwork, and a fast setting concrete mix. The dimensions of the structure are 3 m in length, 3 m in width, and 2.4 m in height.

2   Computational Methodology

2.1   Computational Form-Finding

In regards to the design approach a computational setup based on formation processes found in examples from nature is devised. Specifically, by extrapolating the basic principles of how waterlogged threads bundle together, a bundling algorithm is developed in McNeel Rhinoceros Grasshopper. The algorithm acts as the initial stage of form-finding explorations for the network generation of interwoven elements. The user is enabled to locally differentiate the amount of connectivity between elements in discrete parts of the overall configuration. These local operations have an impact on the global topology thus allowing for the possibility to enhance the formation's structural stability. The outcomes of this computational process are organized as a series of variations facilitating our understanding of the properties of the different options in terms of structural, environmental, spatial qualities and relations to context (Fig. 1).

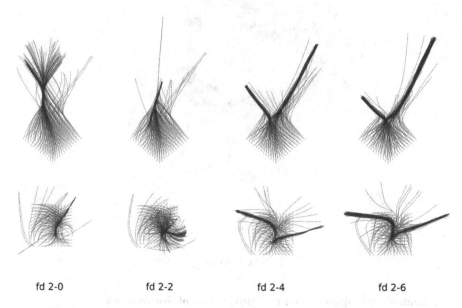

fd 2-0   fd 2-2   fd 2-4   fd 2-6

Fig. 1. Computational form-finding through custom-built bundling algorithms.

2.2   Tool and Jig Development

At the same time, a fabrication strategy is developed for the robotic bending of the custom shaped steel reinforcement bars. The setup is made to accommodate cus-tomization via automation and includes a 6 axis robot (KUKA KR- 150), custom-built bending jig, and pneumatic grippers (Fig. 2). The bending jig system comprises 3 different bending discs, with radii of 50 mm, 100 mm, 150 mm. For the robotic end effector a customized gripper holds the bars in position with a V-shaped metallic channel. This is powered by two pneumatic cylinders placed in distance of 250 mm from each other preventing kinking of the steel bars and allowing for bending longer bars. Apart from the gripper's two pneumatic cylinders, a third gripper is fixed on the bending jig to secure the end of the steel bar when positioned in the jig. This is controlled through the independent IO of the robot.

   With this arrangement, the bar bending process offers a set of constraints that are considered as direct feedback on the computational form-finding process. Opting for 3 specific arc radii has been in order to achieve a gentle transition between 2 consecutive linear members. The smooth transition circumventing extreme angle differentiation between linear members prevents fatigue on the steel bars.

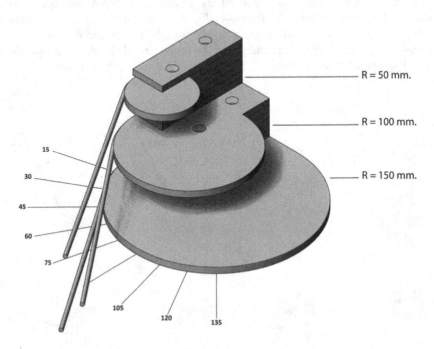

Fig. 2. Robotic bending jig system.

2.3   Geometrical Optimization and Integration of Spring-Back

Prior to the fabrication procedure, and with the aim to establish an efficient transition from the design to the manufacturing stage, two principle schemes are created with the use of Grasshopper, the visual coding plugin within the three-dimensional modelling software McNeel Rhinoceros. In both schemes custom-built Python scripts are developed to incorporate scientific data either from mathematical equations or from physical explorations. At first, the process involves geometrical optimization of the outputs from the initial bundling experiments. The continuous 3-dimensionally curved lines are modified via a custom-built Python script inside Grasshopper. In this setup, each curve is divided into domains at specified intervals. By comparison of the initial path to that of the optimized, each interval's length is defined by considering the continuity of curvature, the steel bar sizes, and the restrictions in the bar connections that may occur during the assembly process. Consequently, each continuous path is split with an interval of 550 mm in length, resulting in a polyline model created according to tangent vector information at each node of the intervals. At this point, every node is assigned one of the three specific jig radii based on the difference among consecutive beams' angles. Specifically, for nodes with an angular difference smaller than 30°, the 50 mm radius is assigned. For nodes with an angular difference between

30° and 60°, the 100 mm radius is assigned. Lastly, for nodes that have an angular difference greater than 60°, the 150 mm radius is assigned. Thus optimization is achieved by rebuilding the path as a series of lines and arcs with variable bending angles. In addition, every member is extended by 100 mm at each end point to provide sufficient overlap between consecutive members during site assembly, thereby creating members of 750 mm in length (Fig. 3). The resulting geometry serves as steel reinforcement bars of the concrete structure that is formulated in later stages of the design. The geometrical end-result of the first scheme is passed as information to the second scheme. In this pre-manufacturing stage all data pertaining to bending location, bending angle, and jig radius is recorded for each individual bar.

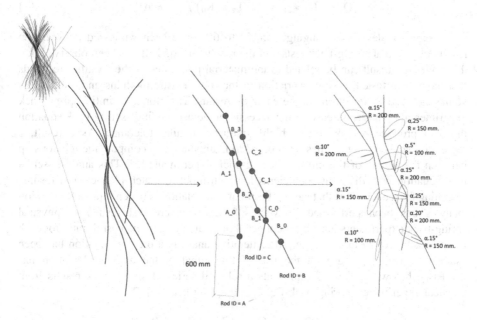

Fig. 3. Geometrical optimization process.

Table 1. Input parameters for mathematical spring-back equations.

T_y *(Yield stress of the material – N/mm²)*	200		
Q_s *(Angle of springback from Q_o)*	VAR		
Q_o *(Target angle)*	VAR		
R_o *(Radius of jig in mm)*	50	100	150
E *(Elastic(Young's) modulus – N/mm²=MPa)*	210000		
d *(bar diameter - mm)*	8		
Coefficient	3.4 (Eq. 1)	−7.86 (Eq. 2)	

The second scheme is developed to counteract the physical phenomenon of the bent bars' spring-back effect. Table 1 presents the input parameters for the mathematical equations that are going to be described in this section. With this set of equations, the spring-back of steel bars is addressed in order to prevent undesired results during robotic bending process. During this stage, physical experiments are carried out to test spring back of steel bars with a fixed diameter, 8 mm, fixed length, 1500 mm, and different jig radii. For each jig radius, physical bending experiments are implemented with 4 different bending angles, increasing from 30° to 120° respectively. The resulting spring-back values from these physical tests have been documented and compared with the results attained from a typical spring-back equation (Eq. 1) [5].

$$Q_s = Q_0 * \left[(3.4 * T_y * R_0) / (E * d) \right] \tag{1}$$

A series of deviations ranging from 5° to 65° have been witnessed between the results of physical spring-back tests and the results of Eq. 1. It has been observed that this undesired result can be related to the material properties of the specific steel rods that have been tested; a slight variation in the rod's elastic modulus and yield stress values can lead to deviations in the equation results. Therefore, the initial spring-back experimentation has resulted with the necessity to devise a refined spring-back equation that can produce results with a highly reduced angular tolerance. As a result, a regression analysis method has been opted to mathematically compute the relationship between the results of the physical spring-back experiments [6]. This analysis sets a new equation with different coefficients for each input to match physical test results, searching for a coefficient that can best estimate the relation between inputs. Regression analysis has been performed in Microsoft Excel where test results of physical spring-back experiments have been collected on a table to find the best fit ratio for each input to achieve the target angle. After iterative analysis a precise equation has been established (Eq. 2), and with the use of this equation the angular deviation has decreased below 5°. Table 2 represents a selected series of spring-back results from physical experiments, spring-back Eq. 1, and spring-back Eq. 2.

$$Q_s = -7.86 + (Q_0 * 0.34) + (R_0 * 0.12) \tag{2}$$

Spring-back Eq. 2 is then implemented in a Python script inside Grasshopper so as to convert target bending angle into actual bending angle that integrates spring-back values. As a result, all bars are bent 15° to 60° more to achieve target bending angles. For example, in order to reach 90° bending with a 150 mm jig, the bar needs to be bent 130.74° to compensate for the 40.74° spring-back value (Table 2 – member B_10). This process is finalized by collecting the data relating to bar location in the global geometry, bending location, bending angle, and grip point of robotic arm for each bar, concluding the preparation of bars for robotic bending process (Fig. 4). Conclusively, this dual-scheme approach enables an analytical relationship between initial form-finding, geometrical optimization, and subsequent manufacturing processes.

Table 2. Comparative analysis of physical experiments, spring-back Eq. 1, and spring-back Eq. 2.

Bar	Target bending angle (°)	Physical bending result (°)	Physical Spring-back test (°)	Spring-back (Eq. 1) (°)	Spring-back (Eq. 2) (°)	Jig Rad. (mm)
B_0	30	15	15	1.21	14.34	100
B_1	30	18,4	11.6	1.21	14.34	100
B_2	30	19.1	10.9	1.21	14.34	100
B_3	30	20.2	9.8	1.21	14.34	100
B_4	30	10.2	19.8	0.61	8.34	50
B_5	30	12.2	17.8	0.61	8.34	50
B_6	60	34.2	25.8	3.64	30.54	150
B_7	66.5	37.8	28.7	4.04	32.75	150
B_8	60	38.1	21.9	2.43	24.54	100
B_9	57	39.6	17.4	2.31	23.52	100
B_10	90	49.7	40.3	5.46	40.74	150
B_11	60	32.6	27.4	1.21	18.54	50
B_12	120	65.1	54.9	7.29	50.94	150
B_13	120	66.2	53.8	7.29	50.94	150
B_14	120	66.8	53.2	7.29	50.94	150
B_15	120	68.4	51.6	7.29	50.94	150
B_16	150	75.8	74.2	9.11	61.14	150
B_17	90	65.7	24.3	3.64	34.74	100
B_18	90	65.7	24.3	1.82	28.74	50
B_19	120	81.3	38.7	4.86	44.94	100
B_20	130	88.8	41.2	5.26	48.34	100
B_21	120	88.8	31.2	2.43	38.94	50

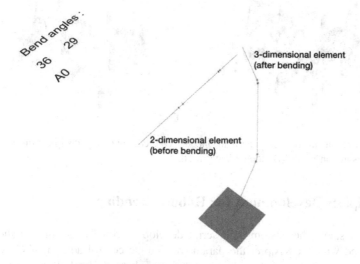

Fig. 4. Data collated for each bar member.

2.4 Formwork Mesh Generation

The outcome of this phase, a series of interwoven 3-dimensional components made of lines and arcs, is given structural thickness via a built-in meshing algorithm inside Grasshopper that generates a high-resolution mesh around the components. This mesh is then modified and triangulated to create developable surfaces that can be unrolled with accuracy in later stages of fabrication (Fig. 5). The diameter of each branch in the structure ranges between 100 mm and 250 mm according to its location in the overall arrangement.

One of the key aims of this research is the integration of structural elements in the initial stages of design in contrast to the conventional approach where the constructional input succeeds the conceptual design development. Here, the geometry of the steel bar reinforcement is considered of equal importance as is the final appearance of the prototypical structure. As described, the geometry rationalization takes place in the initial steps of the design in order to facilitate the later steps of fabrication.

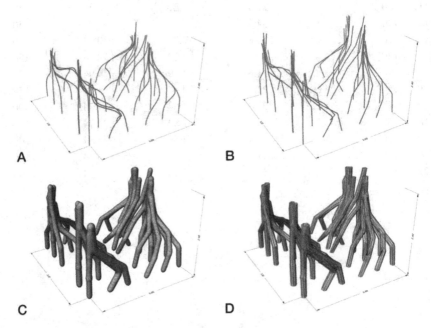

Fig. 5. Development of computational model: (A) continuous paths, (B) lines and arcs, (C) high-resolution mesh, (D) triangulated mesh.

3 Toolpath Development for Robotic Bending

In the next stage, the custom-built script developed with Python in Grasshopper is incorporated with KUKA|prc, the parametric robotic control add-on of Grasshopper [7]. In this way, the information generated for bar-bending, including tolerances and spring-back values, are directly transferred to robotic bending motion. For robotic toolpath planning, steel bar elements of 750 mm length and 8 mm diameter have been coupled in pairs, achieving an overall bar size of 1500 mm. This size has been designated as an optimal length in order to avoid collisions during robotic simulation, as both ends of the steel bars are required to be bent. During robotic toolpath planning process, two sets of data have been key parameters, bending angle and jig radius for each end of the steel bar respectively.

Recent developments in architectural programming interfaces for computational design and fabrication, especially in McNeel Rhinoceros and Grasshopper, have presented users to code and observe real-time results as the robotic simulation is developed. KUKA|prc add-on, developed by Robots in Architecture [8], provides an inverse kinematic (IK) solution within the Rhinoceros-Grasshopper interface, allowing for the prediction and inspection of the problems that can be encountered during robotic simulation. As there is no ready-made robotic toolpath programming solution for the required task of robotic bar-bending, KUKA|prc's built-in command types for Cartesian Coordinate Programming, namely LIN (Linear Movement), PTP (Point to Point Movement), CIR (Circular Movement), are employed. The basic input required for these commands is a plane comprised of XYZABC information, XYZ defining the location and ABC defining the orientation of the end-effector. This information can be easily extracted from planes in Grasshopper, where all geometries and data need to be referenced to the robot base. This process lays the foundation for the development of an in-house robotic toolpath generation method.

During the development of the robotic toolpath, movement from the initial robot position, defined by steel bar before bending, to the final position, defined by steel bar

Fig. 6. Robotic bar bending process.

after bending, has informed the motion of the robot's TCP (Tool Centre Point). This motion is guided by three planes: starting plane, auxiliary plane, and end plane for the bending movement through a CIR (KUKA circular movement command) for smoother bending process. Safe retracts and WAIT commands are included in the algorithm to avoid any collisions and allow sufficient response time of the pneumatic gripper.

The employment of KUKA|prc's IK solver has presented a challenge due to the fact that predicted robotic simulation errors cannot be automatically rectified. Therefore, industrial software packages—like Mastercam/Robotmater—have been taken into consideration. These packages offer highly competent milling strategies and have the capability to tackle the problem stated; however, they lack custom toolpath generation for custom-made end-effectors, and cause limitations in the transfer, handling, development, and manipulation of irregular geometry. Nevertheless, Robotmaster provides a very powerful optimization interface which not only detects the robotic simulation errors, but also provides an intelligent solution to the problem. Hence, the potential of combining the advanced techniques of Robotmaster for optimising robotic simulations and the power of custom-coding in Grasshopper are harvested during robotic toolpath planning. A process is developed in multiple stages: Firstly, on the Grasshopper platform, the custom toolpaths that include handling and manipulation of data are executed. Then, a post processor is written on the same platform to generate XYZIJK of the toolpath in Automatically Programmed Tool (APT) code format. In this format, XYZ defines the Cartesian coordinates of Tool Centre Point (TCP) and IJK defines the vector for tool orientation. Thereafter, the code is imported into Robotmaster using the Robotmaster Import Utility Tool in order to perform robotic toolpath optimization. Although this method provides a two-stage process using two different software platforms, it offers a robust and automated output. In this way, more than 80 steel bars, each bearing a unique bending angle and radius, are robotically bent within a short period of time thanks to the speed, precision, and low tolerances of the custom-made robotic bending protocols (Fig. 6).

4   Fabrication and Assembly

At this stage, in order to ensure an effective conduct of the 1:1 scale construction, initial models of smaller size are designed and fabricated. Three iterations are created to test the key research aspects of the final structure; concrete mix, formwork and strengthening (Fig. 7). Through the making of the three pieces, sized approximately at 600 mm width, 450 mm length and 600 mm height, various assumptions are rendered possible allowing to forestall unexpected situations during the fabrication by taking counter-measures in advance. These conclusions determine certain decisions for the fabrication process of the final structure that are described in this section. From the first smaller size prototypes, regarding the concrete mix, it becomes evident that apart from having defined water-cement-grovel proportions, setting an explicit sequence of pouring is necessary. In this way, consistency in the flow can be guaranteed throughout the various branches of each piece, the absence of which would result in the fast-setting concrete to create various blockage points in undesired parts. In terms of the formwork, the initial sheets that were used to cast the concrete revealed the need to strengthen their connection points against the concrete's hydrostatic pressure. Lastly, it has been realized that strengthening of formwork can be optimized in focusing on strategic parts of the structure rather than the entire geometry of each piece.

Fig. 7. Small scale prototypes.

For the final interwoven concrete structure, the triangulated mesh generated with the geometrical input of steel reinforcement bars acts as the formwork for the structure. At this stage, the fabrication process for the one-to-one scale prototype presents itself with different challenges in regards to the appropriation of complex geometries for digital fabrication methods and the material behavior of concrete during the pouring process. As witnessed by the smaller physical experiments, the formwork necessitates the employment of a material rigid enough to compensate for hydrostatic pressure that acts laterally on the faces of the formwork. Additionally, it is observed that the material needs to provide a smooth surface finish in order to guarantee an effortless de-moulding process. This set of constraints has driven the choice of formwork material to specifically be polypropylene sheets of 2440 mm × 1200 mm × 3 mm.

As the final mesh geometry of the formwork is a developable surface that can be unfolded for a flat sheet fabrication process, the research at this phase focuses on an automated process for unfolding 3-dimensional triangulated mesh geometries. Inspired by traditional mountain and valley paper folding techniques, Pepakura, an origami based software used to translate complex geometries into foldable paper models, is selected as the preferred software tool for mesh unfolding [9]. Initial mesh optimization in Grasshopper is used to re-triangulate and reduce the number of polygons in order to maintain part specific sizes related to the constraints of the Polypropylene sheet material.

Each branching component of the mesh structure is fed to Pepakura, where a strip based approximation method reinterprets the output mesh as regions or stripes by analysing the triangle's topological distance with respect to its new border. The unfolded piece can be further segmented while maintaining its border cutline. A series of outward facing flaps, which aid in the manufacturing process and ensure overall connectivity between the various pieces, are added. The result is a series of foldable stripes that are unrolled flat on sheet material and are thus suited for CNC milling. A nesting algorithm, Rhino Nest, reduces waste of sheet material and optimizes the scoring patterns of mountain and valley folds [10].

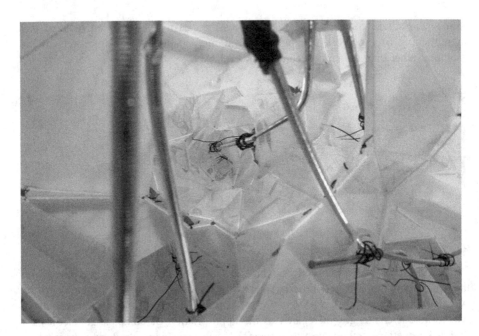

Fig. 8. Steel bar reinforcement bars placed inside Polypropylene formwork.

The fabricated sheets are folded back and tied together with zip ties to generate the 3-dimensional components of the interwoven structure. Each component is further wrapped with cloth-backed adhesive tape in order to enhance the structure's performance against hydrostatic pressure during the pouring process. Naturally occurring gaps between joints, a condition due to polypropylene's material thickness, serve a two-fold purpose: Firstly, gaps provide the flexibility required by the overall structure to find its final resting position once the lateral forces of expanding concrete are in effect. Secondly, they offer much needed ventilation in an otherwise airtight formwork, accelerating concrete curing times. As the formwork mesh has been generated directly from the geometry of the steel bent bars, the self-supporting formwork is guided into position with ease by the robotically bent steel bar reinforcement bars, which have remained at the geometrical center of the formwork (Fig. 8).

During the final stage of assembly, each module is placed on site, guided by the foundation area that bears a depth of 300 mm (Fig. 9). The self-supporting formwork keeps additional scaffolding to a minimum, only requiring temporary supports where needed during concrete pouring process. Furthermore, the elimination of stationary scaffolding grants an accessible work area that allows for a continuous concrete pouring process, lasting 7 h in total. Special attention has been paid to the sequence of pouring. The complexity of the geometry has required each branch to be filled simultaneously from ground upwards, contrary to traditional individual casting methods. Coupled with the triangulation of the formwork geometry, the sequence of the pouring process has helped to balance the hydrostatic pressure throughout the structure, thereby preventing ruptures and minimizing overall displacement.

Fig. 9. Polypropylene formwork with steel reinforcement bars on site.

A special mix of aqueous fast setting concrete mixed with fiberglass additives has been poured in one step to homogenize the setting stage, allowing the concrete mix to

Fig. 10. Global configuration of one-to-one scale prototype.

be cast and cured within several hours. Due to the surface finish of Polypropylene formwork, it has been possible to complete the de-moulding process of the structure in a short period of time (Fig. 10). Additionally, the use of Polypropylene has facilitated a reflective surface quality for the prototype (Fig. 11). The final configuration is characterized by a continuous network of concrete branches that support each other while creating an amorphous spatial enclosure.

5   Discussion

Throughout the design, fabrication, and assembly processes, the strong associations and interfacing between different design, analysis, and simulation protocols have been essential in correlating a multitude of parameters and design drivers. The comparison between the digital simulation of the architectural output and the final output, the prototype itself, provides useful information to be considered and embedded in the future digital simulations. The correlations between the digital simulation and final prototype in the case study have been accurate due to the choice of material for formwork and the precision of robotic processes. It must be noted that the degree of association between digital simulation and physical outcome depends highly on the amount and extent of manual labor during fabrication and assembly processes; it has been observed that an increase in manual labor bears the possibility for a decrease in precision. Future research in the field aims to incorporate real-time structural analysis that can be employed during computational form-finding processes, and real-time calculation of the results of selected robotic fabrication protocols through sensors in order to progressively inform design outputs.

A key challenge during the fabrication process was to have precise control over the sequence of concrete pouring in order to maintain balance of the formwork as well as to resist hydrostatic pressure. This challenge was met by filling each branch simultaneously as to retain a similar height range of fluid concrete in all branches. Nevertheless, future work can incorporate CFD (Computational Fluid Dynamics) simulation of concrete in the digital environment on various selected global configurations in order to test the efficiency of concrete flow. With this method, CFD simulation of concrete flow can serve as a key driver during design development.

In current research processes, the role of robotic fabrication techniques is moving away from a direct design-to-production approach towards the integration of robots within the design process itself. While the employment of complex hard-ware systems and sensors can be a useful method of enabling this integration, this research presents a methodology to develop custom-made, versatile programming and simulation workflows without the necessity to develop custom-made hardware elements. Hence, this research aims to expand on the generic properties of a robotic manipulator by testing the complexity of embedding parameters related to generative form-finding, geometrical rationalization, material constraints, and robotic toolpath planning within the computational environment and simulation tools, hence enabling the capacity to implement simple mechanical tools and cost-effective fabrication methods.

One of the key aims of this research is to illustrate the architectural possibilities of using concrete in a non-conventional way by creating strong associations between computational design methodologies and robotic fabrication processes. Nevertheless, it is argued that a similar methodology addressing the integration of material properties and robotic fabrication constraints in the early stages of design development can be developed for further material systems and robotic fabrication protocols. Through the utilization of material and fabrication parameters as design drivers from the conceptual design phase onwards, the high level of complexity inherent in design processes can be discovered to serve multiple aspects of performance.

Fig. 11. Close-up of one-to-one scale prototype, displaying reflective surface finish.

Acknowledgements. The work presented is part of the research undertaken at Architectural Association (AA) Summer DLAB Visiting School 2016. We would like to thank our tutoring team and students for their great efforts.

AA Visiting School Director: Dr. Christopher Pierce

AA Summer DLAB Programme Heads: Dr. Elif Erdine, Alexandros Kallegias

Tutors: Alexandros Kallegias, Dr. Elif Erdine, Angel Fernando Lara Moreira, Necdet Yagiz Ozkan, Suzan Ucmaklioglu.

Research Collaborator: Alican Sungur.

Robotics Collaborator: Pradeep Devadass.

Students: Artemis Psaltoglou, Anna Rizou, Irini Sapka, Stelios Andreou, Alexandra Marantidou, Melike Culcuoglu, Deniz Ipek Ayasli, Isui Rodriguez, Roger Flores, Reese Lewis, Shang-Fang Yu, Anthony Ip, Mauricio Velarde, Kentaro Fujimoto, Josue Davila, DanielaOrellana, Erik Hoffmann, Zheng Luo, Jeffrey Novak, Veronica Ruiz, Justine Poulin.

References

1. Menges, A.: Morphospaces of robotic fabrication. In: Brell-Çokcan, S., Braumann, J. (eds.) Rob|Arch 2012: Robotic Fabrication in Architecture, Art and Design, pp. 28–47. Springer, Vienna (2013)
2. McGee, W., Feringa, J., Søndergaard, A.: Processes for an architecture of volume: robotic hot-wire cutting. In: Brell-Çokcan, S., Braumann, J. (eds.) Rob|Arch 2012: Robotic Fabrication in Architecture, Art and Design, pp. 62–71. Springer, Vienna (2013)
3. Pigram, D., et al.: Protocols, pathways, and pbaruction. In: Brell-Çokcan, S., Braumann, J. (eds.) Rob|Arch 2012: Robotic Fabrication in Architecture, Art and Design, pp. 143–147. Springer, Vienna (2013)
4. Pigram, D., McGee, W.: Formation embedded design: a methodology for the integration of fabrication constraints into architectural design. In Taron, J.M. (ed.) ACADIA 2011: Integration Through Computation: Proceedings of the 31st Annual Conference of the Association for Computer Aided Design in Architecture (ACADIA), Association for Computer Aided Design in Architecture, pp. 122–131 (2011)
5. Pytel, A., Kiusalaas, J.: Mechanics of Materials, pp. 465–466. Cengage Learning, Stamford (2012)
6. Moore, D.S., McCabe, G., Craig, B.A.: Introduction to the Practice of Statistics, pp. 10–55. W.H. Freeman and Company, New York (2017)
7. http://www.robotsinarchitecture.org/kuka-prc. Accessed 25 April 2016
8. Braumann, J., Brell-Cokcan, S.: Parametric robot control: integrated CAD/CAM for architectural design. In Taron, J.M. (ed.) ACADIA 2011: Integration Through Computation: Proceedings of the 31st Annual Conference of the Association for Computer Aided Design in Architecture (ACADIA), Association for Computer Aided Design in Architecture, pp. 241–252 (2011)
9. Mitani, J. Suzuki, H.: Making Papercraft Toys from Meshes Using Strip-based Approximate Unfolding. University of Tokyo (2004)
10. http://www.tdmsolutions.com/rhinonest/. Accessed 12 May 2016

Computing Stitches and Crocheting Geometry

Özgüç Bertuğ Çapunaman[1(✉)], Cemal Koray Bingöl[2],
and Benay Gürsoy[3]

[1] Istanbul Bilgi University, Istanbul, Turkey
ozgucbertug@gmail.com
[2] Epitome, Istanbul, Turkey
ckoraybingol@gmail.com
[3] Penn State University, State College, USA
benaygursoy@gmail.com

Abstract. This paper presents a study that explores the computability of the craft of crochet. The study involves two consecutive stages: an analytical and systematic approach to crocheting three-dimensional objects to discover the underlying computational aspects, and a formal representation of the deducted computational logic in the form of a computer algorithm. The aim is to explore the computability of hands-on making processes where computation extends beyond the use of computers and digital tools to spatial reasoning in general.

Keywords: Computational making · Parametric design · Digital craft

1 Introduction

Making denotes fully sensory and perceptual activities of manipulating things that have a physical existence. With aspects that reveal throughout the process, making is integral to design reasoning and can be computed [1]. Considering computation in making as a spatial reasoning process extends the understanding of computation to a more improvisational and perceptual kind, one that can involve hands-on making processes, and incorporate *"material things"* [2].

Building on this understanding of computation, this paper presents a study that explores the computability of the craft of crochet. The study involves two consecutive stages: an analytical and systematic approach to crocheting three-dimensional objects to discover the underlying computational aspects, and a formal representation of the deducted computational logic in the form of a computer algorithm. Being able to formally express a process, e.g. as an algorithm, indicates a thorough understanding of the process [3]. Formal descriptions, in return, help to communicate this understanding with others. Thus, the aim of this study is, first, to understand the process of crocheting three-dimensional objects, and second to create a common ground to communicate this deliberate and particular understanding with others.

The analytical approach to crocheting in the first stage involves hands-on explorations. Different materials, tools and techniques are systematically compared to deeply understand their effects on the process of crocheting three-dimensional objects. The comparative analyses enable to delineate the physical constraints of crocheting, and result in the generation of a set of *crocheting rules*.

© Springer Nature Singapore Pte Ltd. 2017
G. Çağdaş et al. (Eds.): CAAD Futures 2017, CCIS 724, pp. 289–305, 2017.
DOI: 10.1007/978-981-10-5197-5_16

In the second stage, the *crocheting rules* are used as guides in the development of a computer algorithm. The computer algorithm generates crochet patterns for three-dimensional objects that are modeled in CAD software. The physical constraints discovered in the first stage through hands-on explorations constitute the variables of the computer algorithm. These include *determinate variables* such as the material properties (yarn weight) and the tool size (crochet hook), but also *indeterminate variables* such as the effect of the *crafter's hand* (grip on the yarn) while producing stitches. The latter, being unique for each individual crafter, is specified through a physical test swatch that the crafter crochets before running the computer algorithm. The output of the computer algorithm is a crochet pattern in conventional text form to *materialize* the digital model. Following the resulting pattern, one is able to *crochet* the digital model by hand. This is yet another formal description to communicate the information necessary for crocheting the digital model. The overall process is thus a transition from the digital to the physical, where physical constraints continuously inform this transition and shape the outcome (Fig. 1).

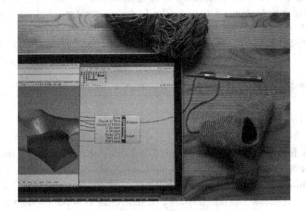

Fig. 1. The computer algorithm developed in Grasshopper for Rhino generates the crochet pattern to crochet the three-dimensional objects modeled in CAD software.

The study is a testimony to the computability of hands-on making processes where computation extends beyond the use of computers and digital tools to spatial reasoning in general. The computation in this study is as much in the delineation of hands-on crocheting rules, as it is in the execution of the computer algorithm. The crocheting rules extracted from the hands-on explorations are not learnt or imposed. They are not absolute certainties either. They are defined through unique and personal inferences of the crafter-researcher and mostly rely on his perceptions. Yet, they establish a temporary framework that enables one to compute, generate novel outcomes, and communicate this process with others.

2 Reasoning for Productivity in Making

Crocheting is a widely recognized craft that involves the repetitive manipulation of a single continuous thread with a hook-like tool. The thread is manipulated to form stitches, which add up to generate not only Euclidean but also non-Euclidean surfaces. The topology of a crocheted surface is relatively complex: the continuous thread undulates, first, to create stitches along rows, and the stitch-loops of one row are pulled through the stitch-loops of the subsequent row to expand the surface. In other words, the crocheted surfaces emerge through the interplay of stitches, where the whole becomes more than the sum of its parts-stitches.

A crochet stitch is a type of knot that is commonly known as *slipknot,* where the loosening of one stitch can lead to unraveling of the entire *system.* The whole process of the generation of crocheted form, thus, demonstrates an *"emergent behavior"* where a number of simple entities operate together in a systematic way to form more complex behaviors [4]. Such *systems* are defined both by bottom-up and top-down relations between parts and wholes. In the case of crocheting, a constant feedback loop of stitches to the whole form is necessary. The size of the stitches, the number of stitches in each row and the relationship between the rows mutually determine the final form. It is, therefore, not an easy task to crochet three-dimensional objects without a crochet pattern at hand that guides the process. Crochet pattern generation requires a deep understanding of the process to determine how, on the overall surface, the stitches should interact to form the desired surface.

Crochet, as it is recognized today, is a relatively new craft dating back to 19th century. Despite vast possibilities that this technique opens up from more conventional craft applications to physical representation of complex mathematical models and theories [5, 6], throughout its short history, crocheting of three-dimensional objects mostly *repeated* and *reproduced* existing crochet patterns. Crochet patterns are specified both with verbal descriptions and a conventional diagramming system that makes use of abstract notations. These two establish a formalism and a common ground to communicate the information necessary for crocheting. In this way, the crochet patterns can be *reproduced* many times and by different people.

In the case of crocheting three-dimensional objects, the information conveyed in crochet pattern diagrams and verbal descriptions commonly involve the generation of revolved surfaces – three-dimensional objects with axial symmetry (e.g. sphere, cylinder, cone, ellipsoid). Crochet patterns of revolved surfaces have regularly distributed changes in stitch counts on each row. The regularity eases the generation of the crochet patterns and the physical execution of the step-by-step crocheting procedure by the maker.

The step-by-step procedure in crocheting is often associated with algorithms [7–10]. There is a set of predefined *rules* that have to be followed while crocheting to achieve a consistent result. These are indicated in the crochet pattern diagrams. Similar to algorithms, the diagrams must be read following a definite order and the *crocheting rules* must be applied respectively. As Bernasconi et al. [10] put forth: *"the bustrophedic reading of the diagram gives the specification, row by row, of the elementary stitches to be performed and essentially represents the algorithm to be executed to realize the piece of work*" in crocheting. Recently, in a study that aligns with the goals and objectives of this paper, knitting is explored within a computational framework [11]. The knit pattern is identified as "*a code*" where "*it is both the physical sequence of stitches and the dynamic properties of each stitch within a digital model*". The exploration similarly involves the generation of a set of knitting rules followed by a reversed process beginning with an informed digital simulation.

The correlation between algorithmic thinking and production techniques such as weaving, knitting and crocheting is not surprising considering that one of the first examples for an elementary computer is the mechanical loom invented by Joseph Jacquard in the early 19th century. The Jacquard loom or the Jacquard machine, was *programmed* by a series of punched cards that were continuously attached together to form a chain. The punched cards controlled the sequence of operations in the machine and were replaceable to allow automated weaving of various complex pattern combinations. The Jacquard loom is considered an important step in the history of computing and in the "*birth of information technology*" [12]. From the Analytical Engine of Charles Babbage to the IBM machines, the logic of punched cards remained in use in computing up until the mid 1980's. After the Jacquard machine, other machines, including the computer-controlled ones, were built for weaving and knitting textiles throughout history both for personal use and industrial production. While these include machines that crochet planar surfaces and laces, there is still no automated machinery for crocheting three-dimensional objects, possibly because of the complexity of the construction of the crochet stitches in three-dimensions. In the course of crocheting, the crocheted piece can spin, twist, and shift in any direction if not held in place by the crocheter. Human eyes coordinate with hand movements and haptic senses to manipulate the crocheted piece so that the crocheter can *see* and decide where to insert the hook.

In the case of crocheting three-dimensional objects, "*good abstraction capabilities are indeed needed to figure the final result out and to map the idea of a pattern into a knitted form*" [10]. As every local change affects the final form of the crocheted object, for crocheting a desired three-dimensional object, one must figure out where exactly to increase and decrease stitches. This requires a deep understanding of the effects of stitches on the crocheted object. Reasoning and unique abstractions are key to develop this understanding and to establish a computational framework for crocheting. The already algorithmic nature of crocheting, and existing abstract notations are helpful in developing this computational framework. When a thorough understanding is developed, crocheting, and any craft technique in general, can be productive, besides solely relying on reproduction.

2.1   Abstraction – Materialization – Abstraction for Creative Reasoning

Reasoning is the ability to deal with situations for which one doesn't have any previous experience. Encountering a new situation, the reasoner does not feel the need to recall previous experiences. Instead, through analysis and abstraction, the reasoner is able to deduct inferences and connect these to tackle with the unknown. "*The art of the reasoner*", according to William James [13] consists of two stages, namely "*sagacity*" and "*learning*". Sagacity is the "*ability to discover parts that lie embedded within the whole"*; and learning is the *"ability to recall a part's consequences, concomitants or implications"* and to apply them accordingly. Referring to William James, Stiny [14], in his theory of shapes, defines visual reasoning in design through sagacity and learning. In visual reasoning processes, sagacity implies seeing, and learning implies the ability to apply rules. Through this visual reasoning process a personal and perceptual act like seeing becomes communicable. According to Stiny, James' definition of reasoning is the *"ability to deal with novelty"*, and this is why *"reasoning makes a difference"*.

Extracting parts out of wholes where and when they are relevant denotes a perceptual, enactive and situated process. Wholes do not always have predetermined parts, as in the case of crocheting. The reasoner, in different occasions, can extract different parts out of the whole. Hence, abstractions can be unique to the reasoner and to the situation. These unique perceptual processes of extracting parts out of the whole are essential for sagacious and creative thinking.

Abstractions create natural stops in the continuous creative process to perceive, think and reason. Transitions between abstract representations and the physical thing in an *"abstraction – materialization – abstraction cycle"* are key to spatial reasoning in making [15]. Abstractions in this cycle are not determinate. They define temporary frameworks and enable the designer to concentrate on a specific aspect of the making activity and to understand it deeply.

This deeper understanding of the underlying principles of a process is possible through reasoning. In return, reasoning allows one to be productive and not solely reproductive. It allows incorporating variations.

2.2 Extracting Rules for Computing Stitches

Hands-on exploration played a crucial role in delineating the computational aspects of crocheting. Through the explorations with materials, tools and techniques, a set of crocheting rules is extracted to address how crocheting can be processed at different levels of complexity. Figure 2 shows abstract representations for three crocheting rules that are used in this study, and their materialization on crocheted surfaces.

First rule, shown in Fig. 2-a, is the rule for *plain stitch (st)* where the number of stitches in two subsequent rows is the same. This results in the crocheting of planar surfaces and even distribution of stitches. Second rule, shown in Fig. 2-b, is the rule for *increase (inc)*. Through this rule two stitches are diverged from one stitch in the subsequent row. This results in an increase in the total number of stitches in the subsequent row, as well as affects the planarity of the crocheted surface. Third rule, shown in Fig. 2-c, is the rule for *decrease (dec)*. As opposed to the second rule, this rule results in a decrease in the total number of stitches in the subsequent row as two stitches are converged into one. Again, this affects the planarity of the crocheted surface.

By combining this elementary set of rules, an infinite number of crochet patterns can be generated with a bottom-up approach. However, to generate the crochet patterns for a specific three-dimensional object, a top-down approach that guides the sequence

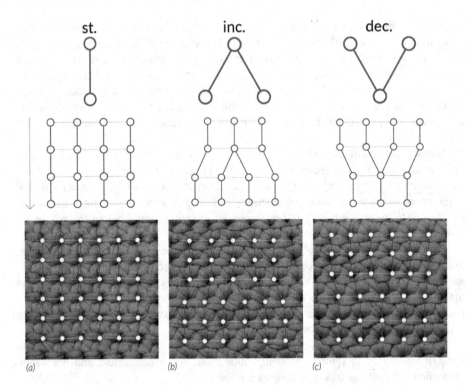

Fig. 2. Abstractions for crocheting rules and their materialization on crocheted surfaces: (a) stitch (st): plain stitch, (b) increase (inc): diverging two stitches from one stitch, and (c) decrease (dec): converging two stitches into one stitch.

of application of these rules must be followed. This requires an additional set of rules that formalize the relations of the stitches to the overall surface.

3   Computing Stitches for Crocheting Non-symmetrical Objects

Commonly available crochet patterns for three-dimensional objects are mostly for the materialization of revolved surfaces – three-dimensional objects with axial symmetry (e.g. sphere, cylinder, cone, ellipsoid). Crochet patterns of revolved surfaces have regularly distributed increase and/or decrease in stitch counts on each row. Regularity eases the generation of the crochet patterns.

Recent studies that explore computer-aided crochet pattern generation for three-dimensional objects, i.e. *Crochet Lathe* [16], and *Knittink's Amigurumi Pattern Generator* [17] enable the users to manipulate two-dimensional, symmetrical shapes that are the inputs of the algorithm and that define the profile curves of revolved surfaces. While both crochet pattern generators facilitate the crochet pattern customization, the outcomes are limited with three-dimensional objects with axial symmetry. This is mainly because of the two-dimensional input geometries and the underlying algorithms that evenly increase or decrease the stitches on every row.

Different than the conventional revolved surfaces, the method presented in this paper is capable of generating crochet patterns for non-symmetrical three-dimensional objects. The input geometry is a three-dimensional object modeled in CAD software. The set of crocheting rules can be unevenly distributed to increase and decrease the number of stitches depending on the input geometry. The input geometries are at present limited with four types of closed and non-closed orientable surface topologies: two-edge non-closed surfaces (Fig. 3-a), one-edge non-closed surfaces (Fig. 3-b), closed surfaces (Fig. 3-c) and branching structures (Fig. 3-d). While the first three topologies challenge the symmetry of revolved surfaces, the fourth topology introduces novelties to crocheting three-dimensional objects.

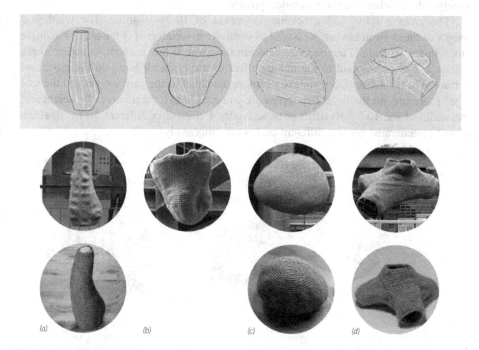

Fig. 3. The four surface topologies used and the crocheted outcomes of each topology: (a) two-edge non-closed surfaces, (b) one-edge non-closed surfaces, (c) closed surfaces, and (d) branching structures

The four topologies selected present increasing levels of crocheting complexity, and individual challenges to crocheting three-dimensional objects. Figure 3 shows the crocheted outcomes of each challenge, with the objects in Fig. 3-a, c and d crocheted in two different scales. The variation in scale is not only the result of changing the yarn weight: the crochet patterns generated by the computer algorithm change as well with respect to the selected yarns and crochet hooks. As a result the resolution of the crocheted surface differs greatly.

3.1   The Computer Algorithm: From Stitches to Digits

Developing a computational framework for the hands-on crafting technique of crocheting requires first, a deep understanding of the process, and second, a thorough abstraction of this process in the form of an algorithm. This algorithm should take into consideration *determinate variables* such as the material properties (yarn weight) and the tool size (crochet hook), but also *indeterminate variables* such as the effect of the *crafter's hand* (grip on the yarn) in producing stitches.

Yarn weight and tool size are quantifiable and can be standardized. However, the effect of the crafter is not known beforehand and can vary from person to person, and even from time to time. While being an *indeterminate variable*, it has a crucial role in crocheting three-dimensional forms. Acknowledging this fact, the crochet pattern generation algorithm developed in this study includes the *crafter's hand* as a primary input in the crochet pattern generation process.

The process starts with crocheting swatches of 10-by-10-stitch. The width and length of these swatches are measured to obtain two variables: (1) the size of a single stitch in a row, and (2) the distance between the rows. While numeric in nature, these values in fact correspond to the unique effect of the *crafter's hand* on the crocheted surface. The swatches also seamlessly capture the effect of the yarn weight and the tool size. Therefore, all the necessary inputs are gathered in two parameters: the height and the width of the 10-by-10-stitch swatch. Figure 4 shows six different 10-by-10-stitch swatches generated by two different crafters for this study.

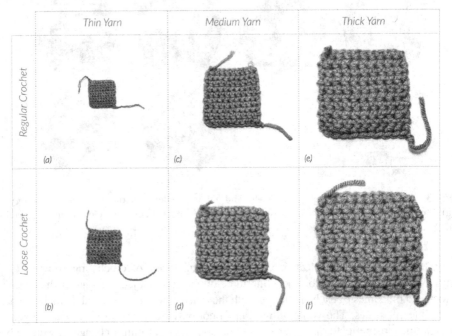

Fig. 4. Six different 10-by-10-stitch swatches to capture the crafter's grip on the yarn.

The swatches in the top row belong to one crafter and the swatches in the bottom row belong to another crafter. Each crafter is asked to crochet 10-by-10-stitch swatches with three different yarn weights using corresponding crochet hooks. While the weights of the yarns have a considerable effect on the outcome, the comparative presentation on Fig. 4 also clearly indicates the differences of each crafter's grip on the yarn.

This calibration is necessary at the beginning of the crochet pattern generation as the algorithm developed makes use of these unique parameters in generating unique crochet patterns. The total number of stitches in a row, as well as the total number of rows in the crochet pattern are both defined with reference to these two parameters obtained from 10-by-10-stitch swatches.

In generating the crochet patterns for three-dimensional objects, the algorithm makes use of the width and length of the 10-by-10-stitch swatches to compute the numbers of rows and stitches. The whole procedure is illustrated in Fig. 5 through the two-edge non-closed surface topology. First, the surface is subdivided into curves in U and V direction as shown in Fig. 5-a. These curves indicate the beginning and the direction of crocheting. Then, the curves in U direction (shown in Fig. 5-a) are divided with respect to the value obtained from the 10-by-10-stitch swatch that indicates the distance between each row. Another set of closed curves in V direction is obtained through this step. These closed curves comply with the row height value of the 10-by-10-stitch swatch. However, since crocheting operates in a continuous process along a single thread, a continuous path should be generated. Therefore, these closed curves in V direction are split from their starting points. The starting point of each curve is shifted gradually towards the end point of the curve in the subsequent row. This connects the starting points of the curves with the end points of the curves in the next row to create a spiral-like continuous path along the surface as shown in Fig. 5-b and magnified in Fig. 5-e. The next step is to generate the *stitches* in each *row*. This time, the width value obtained from the 10-by-10-stitch swatch is used to divide the continuous curve (shown in Fig. 5-b) to stitch points. The division length is equal to the distance between two stitches in the 10-by-10-stitch swatch. The outcome can be seen in Fig. 5-c. Finally, the stitch points are connected to the closest point on the next row. Because of the non-symmetrical geometry, the stitch count in each row is different. The algorithm distributes the increases and decreases evenly along each row. Figure 5-d is the outcome, and Fig. 5-f shows a close-up view of the subdivision.

Currently, the algorithm only works with UV parameterized surfaces and has a limited use with other surfaces (i.e. meshes). There are similarities between the algorithm presented in this paper, the Chebyshev net algorithm [18], and the periodic global parameterization method developed by Ray et al. [19], which are all surface discretization and paneling algorithms. However, the subdivision algorithm presented in this paper is primarily developed for crocheting: the physical constraints of the crocheting activity (i.e. single continuous thread) shape the subdivision method.

The last phase of the algorithm is the translation of the surface subdivision (shown in Fig. 5-d) into a conventional verbal description, so that the crafter can easily crochet the three-dimensional object without having to count the stitches from the CAD software. This last stage liberates the crocheting procedure from the computer environment. By simply taking a print out of the text-based instruction, the crafter can crochet the three-dimensional object without further need of a computer, as in

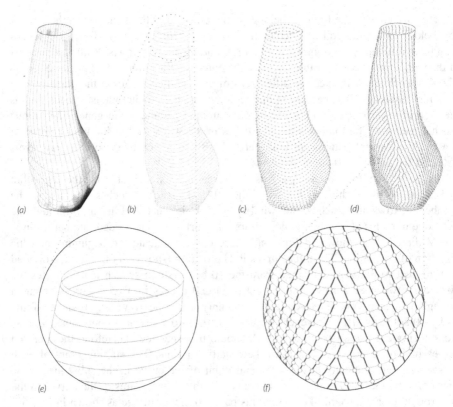

Fig. 5. The steps of the crochet pattern generation algorithm

conventional crocheting processes. The representation of the algorithm in the form of the conventional verbal descriptions for crocheting also plays a vital role in sharing the crocheting procedure with others who are not familiar with the CAD software. The text-based instruction indicates the number of stitches in a row, as well as the specific locations of increases and decreases in between the rows, starting from the first stitch in the first row and ending at the last stitch in the last row. Figure 6 illustrates this conversion from lines and points in CAD software to the text-based representation. Figure 6-a shows the outline of the object with a row extracted from the overall geometry. In Fig. 6-b the row is diagrammatically unrolled and the output verbal description is illustrated.

3.2 Variations on a Theme

Various inputs obtained from 10-by-10-stitch swatches and the outcomes of the algorithm are cross-referenced in Figs. 7 and 8. The first column in Fig. 7 shows six different 10-by-10-stitch swatches crocheted by two different crafters. They are sorted from the smallest swatch that is crocheted using the thinnest yarn with tighter stitches (Fig. 7-a) to the largest one that is crocheted with the thickest yarn with relatively loose

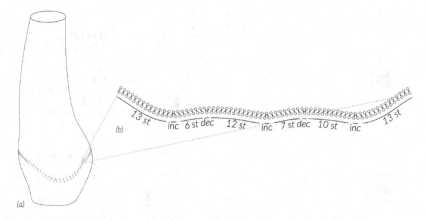

Fig. 6. Translation from lines and points in CAD to conventional verbal description

stitches (Fig. 7-f). Even though the input three-dimensional geometries in CAD software are completely identical, the variables obtained from 10-by-10-stitch swatches affect the process and the output of the algorithm. The second column in Fig. 7 demonstrates the continuous path in between the rows, and the third column shows the distribution of stitches on the surface. As the 10-by-10-stitch swatches enlarge, more sparse crochet patterns are generated. This is a proof that the distance between rows and stitches are generated according to the input swatches. Last column shows the text-based instructions generated. Even though only the first eight rows of each generated pattern is presented, the vast differences in the number of stitches clearly indicate the distinction among the patterns.

The CAD interface enables the user to observe the density of the crochet pattern: the 3D wireframe view gives an idea on how the crocheted product may look like. Although the physical product is different than its wireframe computer representation, the latter still truthfully indicates the dimensions and the number of stitches and rows. In Fig. 8, the crocheted objects resulting from two different swatches are compared. The input geometry is the same in these two explorations: it is the scaled-down version of the input geometry in Fig. 7. However, the 10-by-10-stitch swatches make the difference. The difference is easily perceivable in the columns showing the rows and the pattern. The pattern in Fig. 8-a is much denser than the pattern in Fig. 8-b. The difference is already observable in the *pattern* view, before the physical execution of the crocheting algorithm. The last column finally shows the two crocheted objects that are in the same exact scale but exhibit striking variations in the surface texture. Even though the two crocheted objects are formally the same and in the same exact scale, the text outputs of the crochet patterns for the two objects are totally different. The control over the non-symmetrical forms and the variations in the surface texture transcend the craft of crochet from a solely reproductive technique to a productive one.

The application of the algorithm to other surface topologies is exemplified in Fig. 9. The closed surface topology in Fig. 9-a is particularly challenging, as any discrepancy in the execution of the algorithm would result in problems in closing the surface. However, as previously shown in Fig. 3, all the surface topologies were

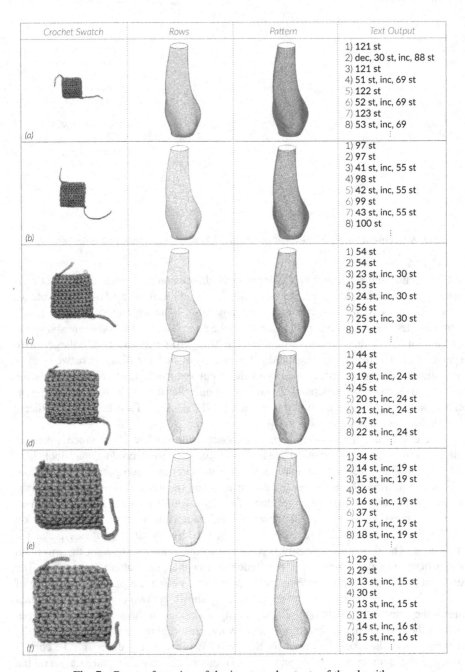

Crochet Swatch	Rows	Pattern	Text Output
(a)			1) 121 st 2) dec, 30 st, inc, 88 st 3) 121 st 4) 51 st, inc, 69 st 5) 122 st 6) 52 st, inc, 69 st 7) 123 st 8) 53 st, inc, 69
(b)			1) 97 st 2) 97 st 3) 41 st, inc, 55 st 4) 98 st 5) 42 st, inc, 55 st 6) 99 st 7) 43 st, inc, 55 st 8) 100 st
(c)			1) 54 st 2) 54 st 3) 23 st, inc, 30 st 4) 55 st 5) 24 st, inc, 30 st 6) 56 st 7) 25 st, inc, 30 st 8) 57 st
(d)			1) 44 st 2) 44 st 3) 19 st, inc, 24 st 4) 45 st 5) 20 st, inc, 24 st 6) 21 st, inc, 24 st 7) 47 st 8) 22 st, inc, 24 st
(e)			1) 34 st 2) 14 st, inc, 19 st 3) 15 st, inc, 19 st 4) 36 st 5) 16 st, inc, 19 st 6) 37 st 7) 17 st, inc, 19 st 8) 18 st, inc, 19 st
(f)			1) 29 st 2) 29 st 3) 13 st, inc, 15 st 4) 30 st 5) 13 st, inc, 15 st 6) 31 st 7) 14 st, inc, 16 st 8) 15 st, inc, 16 st

Fig. 7. Cross-referencing of the inputs and outputs of the algorithm

successfully crocheted-some of them were even crocheted in at least two different scales. The input geometries in Fig. 9 were similar in terms of scale. The crochet patterns in the far right column were all generated with the same 10-by-10-stitch

Topology	Crochet Swatch	Row	Pattern	Objects
(a)				
(b)				

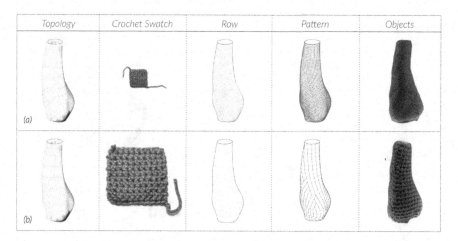

Fig. 8. Cross-referencing of the inputs and final crocheted objects

swatch, hence, for the same crafter, using the same yarns and crochet hooks. The generated patterns with non-recursive increase and decrease rules, show the level of complexity required to crochet non-symmetrical patterns, which without the aid of the computer algorithm would have been nearly impossible to compute.

4   Communicating the Knowledge: From Digits to Stitches

Thorough understanding of the craft of crochet extends beyond previously discussed practices of making and computing. It requires an additional set of knowledge on how computational outcomes can be communicated with others. During the development process, *indeterminate variables* in computation and formal communications with the outcomes were limited primarily with the authors of this paper. These limitations necessitated the expansion of the group of users and testing of the validity of the proposed computer algorithm.

In order to explore the communication of the developed crochet pattern generation method, three workshops have been conducted in three different settings: (1) make@-Bilgi at Istanbul Bilgi University - Faculty of Architecture, (2) at ISMEK (Istanbul Metropolitan Municipality Lifelong Learning Center), and (3) at Atölye Istanbul co-working space. Through these three locations, we were able to reach people with different backgrounds: students, craft enthusiasts, and creative freelance professionals.

Different backgrounds of the participants translated into different levels of knowledge and experience in both computational tools and crocheting. Participants at make@Bilgi were the least experienced group in crocheting, but were fairly competent on the three-dimensional modeling software. The participants at ISMEK represented the other end of the spectrum: great knowledge on crocheting but low to no experience in computational tools. Workshop conducted at Atölye Istanbul, on the other hand, was composed of a fairly balanced group of participants, most of them having moderate insight on both subjects.

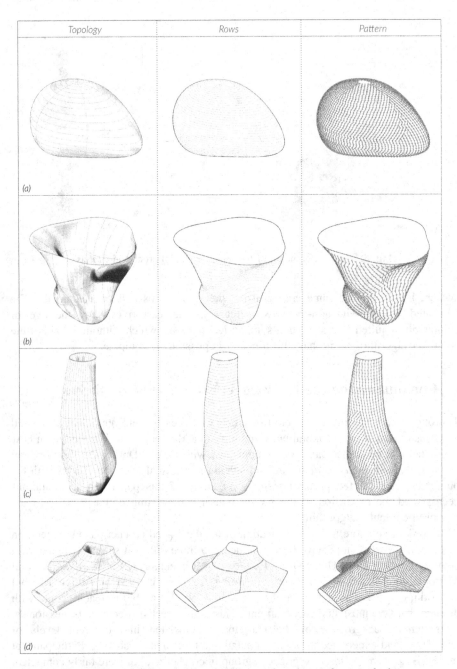

Fig. 9. The application of the algorithm to the other surface topologies

The workshops lasted for approximately 3 h. Participants did not have enough time to complete the crocheting of three-dimensional objects during the time of the workshops. Therefore the physical outcomes of the workshops as crocheted objects are not presented in this paper. The focus during the workshops was rather placed on the process: the use of the computer algorithm by the participants and the communicability of the generated crochet patterns. The workshops provided insights on how to develop the algorithm further and how to communicate and represent the generated crochet patterns.

One of the common discussions held in all three workshops was the legibility of the widely used notation systems; namely the verbal descriptions of crochet patterns and the conventional diagramming system that makes use of abstract notations. Participants compared these two notation systems focusing mainly on their effect on the crocheted geometry and the understandability of the information conveyed by users of any skill level. Compared to the abstract crochet diagrams, text-based notations do not convey much information on the final geometry but ease the communication of the step-by-step procedures. On the other hand, abstract crochet diagrams use symbols that resemble the geometric patterns of the final product.

When both these notation systems are applied on three-dimensional objects, the geometric resemblance that crochet diagrams excels at is undeniably severed. Since crochet diagrams utilize planar projection to illustrate two-dimensional pieces, it struggles to convey geometrical relations in three dimensions, which practically renders this notation system impractical for the aim of this study. At this point, text-based notation system that concatenates repetitive tasks excels at readability of the crochet instructions. In addition to readability, text-based notation system also allows users to execute repetitive tasks without having to go back and forth between crochet instructions since it presents them in chunks rather than step-by-step instructions.

Regardless of the notation system used, the importance of a comprehensive legend for both text-based notations and abstract diagrammatic notations emerged in all discussions. For users with low skill level in crocheting, legend also acts as a reminder of how increase, decrease and plain stiches differ from one another. Since they are new to terminology of crocheting, visual representation of how these crocheting actions manipulate imaginary grid allows users to establish well-founded understanding of them. Similarly, high skill level users struggle in corresponding the terminology with their existing knowledge. Even though they have practical knowledge on each of these crocheting actions, these visual representations allow matching the practical knowledge with the notation system used in the crocheting instructions.

5   Discussions and Future Work

Since this study accounts for a crocheting knowledge that is sharable and communicable to a great extent, further work can be conducted on developing a web repository that will allow the users to convert their CAD objects into crochet patterns, archive these patterns and geometries for future use and develop a community around digital crocheting. Similar web platforms for 3D printing enthusiasts (i.e. Thingiverse, Youmagine) have already emerged. The web platform for *digital crocheting* might allow people with limited CAD knowledge to be able to customize archived geometries by following simple steps and to get actively involved in the computation of crocheting.

This study shares some common grounds with Filament Deposition Modeling (FDM) systems commonly used in commercially available 3D printers. Similar to these systems, the developed algorithm decomposes three-dimensional objects in CAD into layers, which later translate into tool-paths that dictate how objects are materialized. In addition to how geometries are processed, this study also shows similarities on how objects are synthesized additively. Keeping these similarities in mind, the developed algorithm, in a way, proposes a new medium for additive manufacturing systems, and positions computed crocheting in the context of additive manufacturing.

From this perspective, one future study can explore how this proposed manufacturing system can become automated in order to better suit more precise manufacturing needs. Since this study relies on users to crochet the final object, the manufacturing can easily become a meticulous and lengthy process that may take many hours of consecutive crocheting. For these reasons, automating this manufacturing can allow non-crocheters to be able to use this fabrication, minimize human error to very negligible levels and increase the efficiency during the fabrication process by allocating repetitive crocheting tasks to an electronic system that can directly communicate with the algorithm.

In addition to the challenge of crocheting non-symmetrical topologies that this study focuses on, there are other geometrical challenges that can be further explored. One of them is crocheting geometries that have three or more openings on one piece. Such objects would need an alternative approach on depicting the crocheting rows. Currently the developed algorithm treats crocheting rows as one continuous line, which would be disrupted when it attempts to decompose an object with 3 or more openings.

As much as this study is successful in its attempt to develop a computer algorithm for crochet pattern generation, the developed algorithm is restricted by various constraints. The computational platform that has been chosen, namely Grasshopper for Rhinoceros 3D, constitutes one of the constraints. Lack of native iterative tools in Grasshopper limits how repetitive tasks are processed within the algorithm. Additionally, since Grasshopper is operational only through Rhinoceros 3D, it is better in evaluating NURBS surfaces. As a consequence, the algorithm relies on NURBS UV divisions and has a limited use with other surfaces (i.e. meshes).

Although the computer algorithm takes into consideration the *indeterminate variables* that change from person to person, the approach is mainly top-down: the resulting form is predetermined on the computer before running the algorithm. The process is not open to mistakes and emergent discoveries. The crafter needs to follow the sequence of rules generated by the algorithm. Any mistake would lead the whole process to fall down. The crafter would need to unravel the wrong stitches and start over in order to crochet the form generated on the computer. A future study can explore a reverse process where the *emergent* three-dimensional crocheted forms can be translated to digital models in CAD software.

Finally, the computational framework for making can extend beyond the specific case of crocheting exemplified in this paper. The implications of this approach can be especially seen in crafts. Introducing computational thinking in their making can enhance the long-existing craft knowledge to make variations possible. Craft grown knowledge can thus become part of contemporary design practices and lead to innovations rather than sole reproductions. As exemplified in this study, incorporating digital design and parametric tools at this point can expand the possibilities even further.

Acknowledgements. The authors would like to thank Can Altay, Ayşenaz Toker and Gizem Öz, instructors of the ID 402 studio, for their early feedback on the development of this study by Özgüç Bertuğ Çapunaman as his graduation project at Istanbul Bilgi University - Faculty of Architecture in 2016, and Serpil Çapunaman who provided insight and expertise that greatly assisted Özgüç Bertuğ Çapunaman in learning and discovering basics of crocheting. All images are retrospective (except Fig. 1) and are created by Özgüç Bertuğ Çapunaman for this paper.

References

1. Gürsoy, B., Özkar, M.: Visualizing making in design: shapes, materials and actions. Des. Stud. **41**, 29–50 (2015)
2. Knight, T., Stiny, G.: Making grammars: from computing with shapes to computing with things. Des. Stud. **41**, 8–28 (2015)
3. Knuth, D.E.: Computer science and its relation to mathematics. Am. Math. Mon. **81**(4), 323–343 (1974)
4. Küçükoğlu, G., Çolakoğlu, B.: Algorithmic generation for crochet technique. In: Computation and Performance 31st eCAADe Conference, Delft, Netherlands (2013)
5. David, W.H., Taimina, D.: Crocheting hyperbolic plane. Math. Intelligencer **23**(2), 17–28 (2001)
6. Osinka, H.M., Krauskopf, B.: Crocheting the Lorenz manifold. Math. Intelligencer **26**(4), 25–37 (2004)
7. Baurmann, G., Taimina, D.: Crocheting algorithms. Cornell J. Archit. **9**, 105–112 (2013). Mathematics
8. Worden, A.G.: Emergent explorations: analog and digital scripting. Unpublished Master's thesis, Virginia Polytechnic Institute and State University (2011)
9. Kenning, G.: Crochet Lace as expression of digital culture. In: Textile Society in America Symposium Proceedings (2008)
10. Bernasconi, A., Bodei, C., Pagli, L.: Knitting for fun: a recursive sweater. In: Crescenzi, P., Prencipe, G., Pucci, G. (eds.) FUN 2007. LNCS, vol. 4475, pp. 53–65. Springer, Heidelberg (2007). doi:10.1007/978-3-540-72914-3_7
11. McKnelly, C.: Knitting behavior: a material-centric design process. Unpublished Master's thesis, Architectural Studies in Computation and Design, Massachusetts Institute of Technology, Cambridge, MA (2015)
12. Essinger, J.: Jacquard's Web. Oxford University Press, Oxford (2007)
13. James, W.: Principles of Psychology, vol. 2. Dover Publications, New York (1980). (Original work published in 1890)
14. Stiny, G.: Shape: Talking about Seeing and Doing. The MIT Press, Cambridge (2006)
15. Gürsoy, B: Formalizing making in design. Unpublished Ph.D. dissertation, Istanbul Technical University (2016)
16. Avtanski, A.: Crochet Lathe, September 2016. http://avtanski.net/projects/crochet/lathe/
17. Monroe, A.: Knittink's Amigurumi pattern maker falls short, September 2016. https://audreymonroe.wordpress.com/2010/10/05/knittinks-amigurumi-pattern-maker-falls-short/
18. Popov, E.V.: Geometric approach to Chebyshev net generation along an arbitrary surface represented by NURBS. In: International Conference Graphicon (2002)
19. Ray, N., Li, W.C., Lévy, B., Sheffer, A., Allies, P.: Parametric global parameterization. ACM Trans. Graph. **25**(4), 1460–1485 (2006)

Discrete Heuristics

Digital Design and Fabrication Through Shapes and Material Computation

Diego Pinochet[(✉)] [iD]

School of Design, Adolfo Ibañez University, Santiago, Chile
diego.pinochet@uai.cl

Abstract. In the case of designers, architects and arts, tools are part of a repertoire of cognitive, symbolic, and semiotic artifacts with which each explores and learn about design problems. Nonetheless, when using digital fabrication tools, a dichotomy between what is ideated and what is made appears as an evident problem since many of the perceptual aspects of sensing and thinking about new things in the making are neglected. It is argued that this establishes a dichotomy between what is ideated and what is executed as an outcome from that idea. How designers can think, learn and augment their creativity by using digital tools in a more relational, exploratory, interactive and creative way? Furthermore, how can we teach design using contemporary fabrication tools beyond its representational capabilities? This paper explores the richness of using digital fabrication tools through the lens of shapes grammars as a design paradigm in order to extend computational making including digital fabrication tools, gestures and material behavior as crucial actors of the design process. Through the use of discrete heuristics - that is, the elaboration of deictic rules for computation with physical objects, materials and fabrication tools in a precise yet perceptual way- this paper shows experiments inside a third year design studio to overcome the hylomorphism present in the digital design and make dichotomy.

Keywords: Digital fabrication · Computational making · Human computer interaction · Shape grammars

1 Digital Fabrication: From Representing to Making

To Flusser [1], our society lives a crisis in terms of creativity. To him, automation of the industrial manufacturing has provoked not only the physical separation between manufacturers and the manufactured but also has omitted observation – as a collective endeavor of the eye and the hand- as a crucial factor in the creative development of our society (p. 43). One can argue that the design practice through technology is constrained by the imposition of an hylomorphic –form over matter- model by a constant imposition of predetermined ideas over matter by *'a violent assault on a material prepared 'ad-hoc' to be informed with Stereotypes'* [1]. Because of this, the designer is forced to pause the creation –that is, the development of an idea, form, concept and so

© Springer Nature Singapore Pte Ltd. 2017
G. Çağdaş et al. (Eds.): CAAD Futures 2017, CCIS 724, pp. 306–326, 2017.
DOI: 10.1007/978-981-10-5197-5_17

on- focusing on the representation and plans for execution of an idea, neglecting the interaction between perceiving and acting which is present in analog processes that involve making something.

In the case of digital fabrication, the assumption that the digital is somehow a sufficient representation of the real has ignored the phenomenological dimension of meaning [2], which involves aspects of materiality or human intervention as an active decision making actor. In the process of making through digital, the process follows a linearity of events from the generation of an idea to the physical prototype [3]. The current methodology for making something through digital fabrication tools comprises a pause or *'creative gap'* [4] in the reasoning process of the development of an idea in order to develop a plan for the physical manifestation of the design. In addition, Gürsoy and Özkar [5] make a clear distinction between *making of* processes and *making for* processes (p. 31) stating that the former do not take into account materialization as a mechanism of reasoning about the design itself, whereas in the latter materialization and design are indistinguishable from one another.

This cause-effect relationship between idea and prototype relies on the evaluation of results in order to modify the structure that originated that output. The translation from idea to, digital models to, G-code to, material to, prototype and so on, involves a series of translations and black-boxed operations that happen without human intervention. Furthermore, these operations are dependent on formal or codified knowledge about *'ways of representing'* that do not take into account the perceptual and phenomeno-logical contingency and interaction of the agents involved (eyes, hands and its gestures, mind, materials, tools and so on). This black boxed world or as Perez-Gómez [2] defined as 'the between dimensions' -from idea to prototype- is an issue that is not present in analogue making processes since they do not rely on predefined structures of codified knowledge. Conversely, these processes are based on 'ways of making', which consider a constant unfolding-evolving processes of applying tacit knowledge as sit-uated action to make something. Moreover, considering Goodman's distinction of arts [6] it is possible to classify digital fabrication as an allographic one, in which the generic outputs derived from a prescriptive set of rules can generate multiple repro-ductions -without human intervention during the process- of a design. One question that this paper tries to address is the one related to how design and make through the use of digital fabrication tools can transcend its allographic nature, into an autographic one where originality and uniqueness are tightly related to the actions that gave origin to a design?

Plotting a drawing, 3D printing a model or milling a piece of wood are processes in which the software calculates the *optimal* or *average* operation to produce the physical manifestation of our ideas. Nonetheless, unlike digital processes that occur inside three-dimensional software, designers do not make according to calculations of optimal data. As Dreyfuss [7] asserts, a machine works according to a constant evaluation of data, while humans apply a more flexible criterion that is related to how we cope with the objects we use to make something and the expectations derived from that inter-action (p. 250). Moreover, according to Radman [8] tools are *negligible* artifacts that remain invisible to us until we attend to, and treat them by handing them (p: 372). Radman asserts that these objects transform for us the space into an environment shaped by motor significations, which inspire most of our motor behaviors (p: 377). In addition, Radman writes, *'what we do with our hands shapes the way things are seen, remembered, imagined, or generally kept in mind'* (p. 378). According to this, and relating the design and make process to digital fabrication, one can say that the limited physical interaction between designer and fabrication machines that the current model offers seems to underestimate the possibilities of the senses and actions of the body in the creative process to handle or cope with different material behaviors, therefore, learning about them and their behavior. This is true if we take into account the idea of the body as a crucial component in the way we think [9] and that as humans we make mistakes, are imprecise, sometimes clumsy, and change our minds about things we see and do that allow us to learn and realize new creative things every time we attend to them.

Taking into account the ubiquity of the digital in the design practice, how to take advantage of the interaction between antithetical worlds of humans and machines in order to make in a 'better way' or just to make 'better things'? How to use of digital fabrication not as a *Making of* process but a *Making for* one as Gürsoy and Özkar [5] state? This paper explores the richness of shape grammars and making grammars as a design paradigm in order to explore computational making as a way to interact and collaborate in real time with digital fabrication tools. It focuses on gestures and the choreography of making as key elements of the process instead of the mere fabrication of an object.

1.1   From Computational Fabrication to Computational Making

Recently, a new area of inquiry emerged inside the Design and Computation Group at MIT known as *Computational Making* seeks to relate design and making under a computational perspective to the design discipline [10]. As opposed to computational fabrication – that is, manufacturing through the use of digital and physical computational automated systems[1]- Computational making understands on the one hand *'making'* as an activity that is time-based, dynamic, improvisational, contingent, situated and embodied, that is tightly interrelated in numerous forms to designing (p. 2). On the other hand, computational making understands computation as the use of mathematical systems, theories, methodologies and so on, along with technologies and tools based on them (p. 3). Moreover, based on the intersection and relation of these two concepts – making and computing- it seeks to understand and formulate new questions and theories about the relationship between abstract computation and embodied making (p. 3) through the affinities and dissensions between them.

One foundational research paper about how computation and making relate to each other is *Making Grammars: From computing with shapes to computing with things* [11] that expands Stiny's computational theory of shapes and the algebra behind them known as shape grammars. This paper proposes a computational theory of making based on the improvisational, perception and action approach of shape grammars (p. 8)

---

[1] As an example, the computational fabrication group at CSAIL MIT (http://cfg.mit.edu) led by professor Wojciech Matusik, is a referent in the field investigating problems in digital manufacturing and computer graphics.

by adapting the computation with shapes grammars to making grammars for the computation with stuff to make things [10]. In this paper, Knight and Stiny [11] inquire into computational making developing implementations that go from drawing (*á la Stiny*), to knotting (*á la Ingold*) to painting with watercolors (*á la Sargent*) in order to frame making as a computational activity –that is, through algebra and rules for its application- by capturing the prominent properties of stuff and things in the making, described computationally (p. 26). Through examples adapted from shape grammar rules and schemas, Knight and Stiny propose a set of time based descriptions for making, classifying the elements involved in each one of the examples. For example, when it comes to knotting, Knight and Stiny extend the computation with lines –an infinite element- to the computation with strings –a finite element- in order to explain how the algebras behind shape grammars apply to the material world. In this example, they describe in a table *Things* (knotted strings in 3D), *Stuff* (strings), *Doing* (knotting by pulling, looping, etc.) and *Sensing* (touching by grasping, focusing attention, repositioning and so on with hands) as the elements involved in the computational making process.

Taking into account the transition from lines as an infinite element -prone to the unique interpretation of the designer through visual perception- to the use of finite physical strings, abstraction is used in order to explicit a step by step computation with knots describing graphically the process of doing and sensing (p. 23) and formalizing an algebraic description of it. Furthermore, when it comes to the last example – painting with watercolors- the authors make a general description about the many possibilities of formalizing Sargent's grammar through the correspondent description of elements involved in the making of the paintings. Nonetheless, as they assert, describing rules for computational making processes that comprise different materials that behave different not only in time but in interaction with other materials is a very complex task that may require further development (p. 25). But in spite of material considerations, also tools and the way the body interact with them - as gestures- are a part of the process that need to be considered when trying to formalize making as a set of rules. Furthermore, in the making process, the richness of shape grammars –and their extension as making grammars- as a methodology for designing by the use of visual perception through observation and embedding, is confronted with the finite nature of physical things. Finally, Knight and Stiny [11] acknowledge the difficulties of trans-lating the properties of shape elements to physical things and the differences and limitations of them when it comes to embedding (p. 21), especially when the com-putation is made with discrete elements such as strings.

1.2   Designing with Discrete Things... Made of Unpredictable Stuff

When it comes to architecture and the work with finite constructive elements, we can consider that if design is a conscious activity of establishing relations between parts to achieve unity [5] and by which -through conscious reasoning- designers establish relations between parts to build up a whole (p. 33), the use of shape and making grammars allow designers not only to understand the emergence of designs but also to externalize it as the application of specific rules. This definition is tightly related to the

German word 'aufbau', that makes reference to the mystic and intuitive nature of the 'art of building' that could be interpreted by three different interrelated concepts: Construction, organization and structure. The last of these concepts is often referred to the action of building, but in specific, it refers to the articulation of the parts that constitute a whole, and the justification of the relations that emerge between them. In the case of making with physical elements, we can argue that although the 'stuff' can have unpredictable behaviors due to its alchemic nature [11], that is very difficult to describe or formalize as a set of universal rules, the computational making approach can deliver some workings to grasp and understand unpredictability as positive aspects of making. Furthermore, because designers and architects work with things made of stuff, they are suitable for description through the use of grammars that describe not only formal operations but also the performance of the elements involved in the heuristic process of design such as tools or body gestures.

Fig. 1. Making Gestures, a personal design and fabrication system (Pinochet, 2015) is an example of new implementations of working with digital fabrication tools in an interactive and perceptual way.

One question that emerges from the discussion is What happens with making in a computational way when digital fabrication tools are used (á la digital fabrication?) and how – taking into account Gürsoy's and Özkar's concept of making for- can we use digital fabrication tools not for representing but also for reasoning about the things we perceived, think and execute as physical objects. How does human can intervene in the process? This paper takes this last example as a starting point to focus on how tools and the gestures that drive the use of them can have a pedagogic role in the making process grasping in a computational way the process of making through digital fabrication tools teaching students about how things are perceived, designed and made (Fig. 1) in original ways.

2 Making and Thinking with Digital Fabrication Tools

According to Idhe [12], the relationship between humans and technology could be explained through the concept of *'intentionality'* and what he calls *'middle ground'* or *'area of interaction'* or *'performance'*. Idhe asserts that the only way to define or understand the relationship between humans and non-humans is through actional situations that happen in a specific time and place. Furthermore, conversely to what Latour asserts, Idhe argues that this relationship is an asymmetrical one. Moreover, this concept of performance talks about real time interaction in which not only humans but also objects -which Idhe and Latour refer as the *'non humans'*- are redefined as a new entity which Latour determine as a *'Sociotechnical Assemblage* [13], derived from this interaction that transforms both human and non human into something else. In this case, Idhe [12] argues that both human and objects enter into a dance of agencies *'as the human with-intentions'* (p. 94) enters into the resistance and accommodation of mechanic agency provided by the object.

The actions and products derived from that interaction are possible neither by the human nor by the object, but by the relationship and actions enacted by their interactions. In relation to this, it is possible to argue that in the design field, specifically in analog design processes, tools become almost invisible to us and act as mediated objects so the designer focuses in the specific action of 'making something'. Clark's (2004) interpretation about the relationship between humans and technologies according to degrees of transparency (p. 37) might be a useful perspective to understand why the problems identified by Pinochet [3] of the *generic, the creative gap,* and *black-box* are relevant for today's design practice through digital technology (p. 38). To Clark [14] the difference between *'opaque'* and *'transparent'* technologies relies on the degrees of transparency according on how well technologies fit our individual characteristics as humans (p. 37).

The more intricate and hard to use the technology is, the opaquer it is in relation to how it deviates the user from the purpose of its use. Suffice it to say that the current model imperative in today's digital design practice is based in pure tool operation neglecting the idea of real time interaction and leaving important parts of cognitive processes of design aside. It is argued that the many intricacies of digital tools -*the black-box*-, lead the designer to engage and focus in the elaboration of plans for representation -*the creative gap* -, that in many cases lead to rely in software to solve a specific design problem -*the generic*- relegating the act of making to an initial effort which is later rationalized by a fixed structure and fabricated –for example- by a 3D printer [3].

According to Schön [15], design is a form of artistry and making, where learning about a specific topic or design emerges through actions -conscious and unconscious- and exploration. The designer learns how to design by knowing and *reflecting in action*, reinterpreting and re-elaborating actions in the particular moment where the act of design takes place, producing new meanings and coherence (p. 29). In addition to this, Ackerman [16] asserts that humans express ideas by making them tangible and shareable *'which, in turn, helps shape and sharpen these ideas... We can only negotiate meaning through tangible forms: our own expressions or existing cultural mediations (language, tools, toys)'* (p. 6). This suggests that every creative process is accompanied with a material representation that is a by-product of a constant interaction with our surrounding objects. Moreover, as Tilley asserts *'material things, unlike words, are not just communicating meaning but actively doing something in the world as mediators of activity'* (as cited in [9]). By interacting with our surrounding objects, we learn and produce meaning and therefore reason. As Robinson [17] argues, reason, that is the power of the mind to think, understand, and form judgments by a process of logic, is actually a proprioceptive circulation of the relationship between mind body and things around us (p. 60).

Digital tools (e.g. the computer, 3D printer, laser cutter, CNC milling machine) are commonly used to perform a task (a set of prescribed rules), which can be coded in an algorithm or defined inside a parametric model as a set of topological relations. In contrast, if design is considered as an activity, moreover, a reasoning one, it can be referred as *'the way people actually realize their tasks on a cognitive level'* [18] by using knowledge, information and tools. Considering this, the problems identified in the previous chapter can be related to the use of digital tools (CAD-CAM) as task performing machines instead of activity performing machines. In other words, we program digital fabrication machines to perform several tasks, however we do not interact with machines to perform an activity in the way Visser claims. In addition, the little interaction between creator and executor -that is, designer and machine- is constrained to an insufficient interface (clicking and typing) to grasp the main qualities of both worlds engaging more creative processes.

In relation to the concept of *'tool,'* a relevant question that emerges is whether the computer is a design tool, a production tool, or it can become a tool to think with. If design and making are considered as creative and cognitive processes that imply the use of artifacts, it is crucial to consider some important aspects related to the use of digital tools in design, and how the dialog between the creator -the human- and the executor -the machine- happen. As stated previously, in digital fabrication processes, while the overall tendency is to follow the current model of interaction with computers through the use of common input devices -such as the mouse or keyboard- it is valid to argue that digital tools can incorporate the ambiguity and the performativity present in analog design processes. This could enable designers to engage creativity in early design stages beyond its use as efficient production and representation tools. If we consider Knight's and Stiny's [11] approach to computational making as a process of sensing and doing with the properties of stuff like alchemy (p. 15), we can argue that current digital fabrication processes do not allow human intervention during the making process, therefore, the opportunity of seeing, discovering and reasoning about new things derived from the alchemic work with materials is lost.

As an example, in analog design processes, the designer uses different tools to create a design such as pencils, rulers, paper, scissors, knives and so on. These tools are part of a repertoire of cognitive, symbolic, and semiotic artifacts by which the designer makes things to solve a specific design problem. Moreover, in this creative process, designers interact with these tools by assimilating and incorporating them as an extension of their bodies [9] in a similar way as Bateson describes: *'Consider a blind man with a stick, Where does the blind man's self begin? At the tip of the stick? At the handle of the stick? Or at some point halfway up the stick?'* (as cited in [9]). According to this example, tactile sensation is projected from the hand to the tool, and through time and practice the tool becomes incorporated and transparent [9] in a similar way to Latour's *Sociotechnical assemblage*. Leder asserts, by his concept of *'phenomenological osmosis,'* the body *'brings within itself novel abilities, its own temporal history, and tools that remain spatially discrete'* (as cited in [9]). The concept of tool embodiment is crucial to analyze and discuss about the use of machines in design - and why this topics should demand the attention of designers - especially because of assumptions about the use of technology in design as a liberating agent of creativity for them.

Through clicking and typing, designers give shapes to different geometries and translate their intentions of the design in a visual way through rendered images, technical drawings or interactive visualizations among other types of representations. Moreover, if the aim of the process is to generate a physical output, digital fabrication techniques enable designers to generate prototypes as design iterations. The one-way visual communication established between human and machine at the different stages of the process (from mind to software, from software to code and from code to material) shows why it seems to be insufficient or at least incomplete in terms of material and tool feedback to reason about the development of different ideas. In visual reasoning – like shape grammars – design becomes externalized as a step by step process in which designers can communicate their ideas. In Addition, we can use Gürsoy and Özkar [5] distinction between *accidental emergence* – derived from the execution of a scripted algorithm- or *anticipated emergence* where shapes and rules are concise and recognizable during the process (p. 33). If digital fabrication tools are prone to be used under a computational making paradigm beyond its representational purpose, the current model of linear operation must transcend to one that allows interaction and human intervention in several parts of the manufacturing process allowing *anticipated emergence* and designer's awareness of the entire process.

In the construal of the embodied mind, an interesting approach is the one made by the Material Engagement Theory. Malafouris [9] argues that action is a form of cognition and that human cognition is not situated in the head but in our entire body (p. 14). Furthermore, an interesting concept introduced by Andy Clark is the 'leaky mind' [19] presented in the Extended Mind Theory (EMT) by which he explains that the local mechanisms of the mind are not exclusively in the head 'cognition leaks out into body and world' (p. xxvii). Likewise, Malafouris [9] explains from an enactive perspective how humans think and learn through things by engaging our surrounding material environment (p. 7) and how the mind extends form the head to the objects we touch and interact with. According to Robinson [17], the EMT *'is the notion that in specific kinds of mind-body-world interaction there emerges an extended mind or extended cognitive system that doesn't just use but incorporates the pencils, paper, computers, and other extra-cranial objects and environments we use to help overcome or work around our brain's Kluge design flaws'* (p. 1). The hand, gestures and the use of tools as mechanisms by which we learn and think is a crucial aspect of why the revision of the process of design through technology is relevant. According to Lakoff [20], *'the very structures on which reason is based emerge from our bodily sensorimotor experiences'* (p. 371).

Ingold [21] asserts that in every creative endeavor *'the role of the artist is not to reproduce a preconceived idea, novel or not, but to join and follow the forces and flows of material that bring the form of the work into being'* (p. 17). Furthermore, is this interaction between mind and tool the one that Robinson [17] denotes as *'Circulation,'* in which tools become externalized mind, and cognition as internalized tools (p. 35). This circulation is crucial to comprehend the role of digital tools -software and hardware- in the creative part of design and to discover the affinities and dissensions that can be established by using tools as *'objects to sense'* and *'objects to think'* with. The mind-tool interface, as Robinson [17] argues, is not a static one, but one that implies a bi-directionality where humans – in this case designers – internalize tools as mind and externalize mind as tools as a *'proprioceptive circulation'* (p. 60). Thus, it can be argued that sense and action as gestures play a crucial role in this negotiation.

Furthermore, the concept of circulation or interaction understood as performance in a constant engagement between humans, tools and environment, has unveiled key factors to formulate how this interaction should happen. At this point, it is argued that this interaction, which is based on action and perception unified, is the base to foster creativity and cognition in the design process. The development of design through technology should focus on real time interaction to grasp through improvisation the real-time contingencies of the world around us (stuff, things, tools, body, and so on). Moreover, considering that design is not a process of making through following pre-structured rules but one of constant discovery -where rules and the actions derived from those rules emerge as new things are seen- the development of interactive systems is imperative in the design practice.

This approach to design is related to Ingold's perspective on creativity [21] in which he refuses the combinatorial approaches to creativity such as Chomky's linguistic vision of 'ruled- governed creativity', as the construction of comprehensible expressions through infinite rearrangements of lexical items (p. 47). To Ingold, creativity is more than a simple re-combinatorial generation of novelty. As he asserts, creativity is a *'movement, or flow, in which every element we might identify is but a moment'* (p. 47).

3 Discrete Heuristics: A Making Grammar Approach to Making Through Digital Tools

The use of shape grammars as an educational paradigm for design offers a broad range of applications in terms of using rules in a perceptual way to create different geometrical designs (Fig. 2). However, when translated to the physical world, these designs are confronted to the material vicissitudes of objects, forcing designers to consider material phenomena as a key aspect of thinking about how we prototype and impress our uniqueness as humans in the physical world. As discussed previously, computational making paradigm set a base to grasp in a computational way the process for designing and making through the development rules and schemas. *'Discrete heuristics'* is a third year design studio that takes visual computation as the base methodology considering design as a reasoning perceptual process by the description and application of geometrical three dimensional rules. On the one hand, students are suggested to study different materials and techniques related to them in order to abstract a process of making developing material and formal rules for further application.

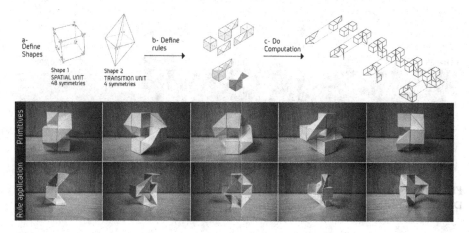

Fig. 2. Study computations of a folding 3D Shape for a house. Diego Pinochet, Visual Computing, MIT 2014.

On the other hand, students are asked to describe the phenomenological characteristics of the process, in order to understand how -by the use of specific tools and unique gestures- these descriptions could bring into being different manifestations of discrete components according to material (Fig. 3). Starting from this concept, the studio invited students to design, reframing the creative act using discrete shapes as things and design heuristics as rules (Fig. 4) grasping the richness of computational making to make explicit a process of thinking. Furthermore, by the development of making grammars and the use of a 7-axis KUKA robot, students were invited to elaborate design methodologies where the robot act as a collaborator or counterpart in the making process. By either working with *stuff* to make discrete components – *things*- or using the KUKA robot as a counterpart for the assembly of designs, students are asked to develop a making process according to shape and material computation using rules to make explicit the making process (Fig. 5).

The methodology applied in the studio took into consideration that in the last decades the design world has been fed from different theoretical and technical approaches in the search of a digital continuity. This has led to constant efforts by which the use of the digital seeks to emulate nature by seeking material continuity of physical designs. Furthermore, 3D printing have emerged as one of the most popular material technologies that have driven design into formal sinuosity, material continuity and formal complexity. Nonetheless, as discussed previously, this produced that by using digital fabrication, the designer is left out of the physical emergence of the object fabricated, and therefore the importunity of learning and discovering new things by these processes is lost. The hylomorphism behind this – the imposition of form over

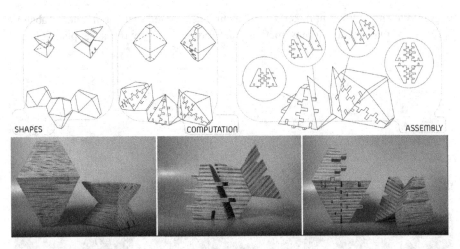

Fig. 3. Computations of different assemblies with plywood components. Alvaro Riquelme, Discrete Heuristics Studio, DesignLab 2016.

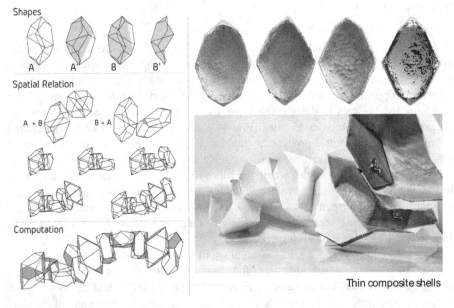

Fig. 4. Material computations of thin composite shells. Francisca Dominguez. Discrete Heuristics Studio, DesignLab UAI 2016.

matter- generates a pause between the ideated and the executed where material behavior, phenomena and feelings involved in the emergent process of making something using perceptual rules are ignored.

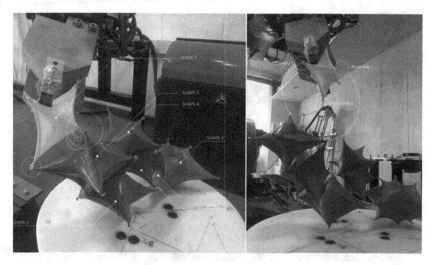

Fig. 5. 'Shaping' Material computations of Elastic Fabric with resins and digital assembly with a 7-axis Kuka Robotic Arm. Lucía Abarca, Discrete Heuristics Studio, DesignLab UAI 2016.

3.1 Designing a Process as a Performance, not a Recipe

As part of the studio requirements, students were asked to design a process of making using visual computation of shapes as a way to describe and therefore learn about the emergence of their designs using 3D shapes. In the first place, students were introduced to shape grammars using different exercises to generate rules computing different designs as an emergent process of design (Fig. 6) in a similar way to Terry Knight's Visual Computation class at MIT[2]. Using discrete elements made out of white paper, students learned about visual computation as a methodology to understand not only their design processes and results but also to analyze other student's designs.

Secondly, students were asked to focus on the assembly between components adding one layer of complexity to the process in order to think about how two or more things stick together beyond the use of double-sided tape (Fig. 7). Students designed not only the rules for aggregation of shapes but the details of the assembly between them. After this stage was completed and students were proficient in designing using visual computation through shapes and rules, the studio added another layer of complexity in which material phenomena was included. This stage consisted in the election of two materials of different characteristics (such as stone and plastic, clay and metal, silicone and wood) in order to describe in a precise way, the technique required to make any shape using these materials. This description comprised on the one hand, the development of knolling pictures identifying tools to be utilized and in the other the *'stuff'* involved in the making as a recipe (Fig. 8).

---

[2] Visual Computing 1 (4.520/4.521)is a class taught by Terry Knight and Theodora Vardouli (TA) at the department of Architecture at the Massachusetts Institute of Technology. Ref. http://stellar.mit.edu/S/course/4/fa14/4.520/.

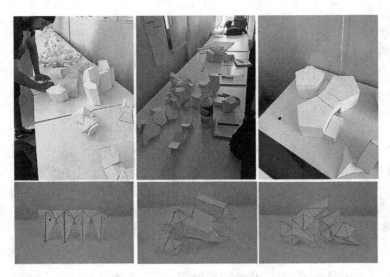

Fig. 6. Shape computations using paper models. Discrete Heuristics Studio, DesignLab UAI 2016.

Fig. 7. Assembly Computation. Students add materiality to their designs and focus on the way shapes assemble to each other in the different stages of computation. Isabel Kovacevic, Discrete Heuristics Studio, DesignLab UAI 2016.

After recognizing the elements and techniques to be utilized, students were asked to describe a step-by-step process by which material stuff is processed focusing on the detailed description body gestures and the phenomenological characteristics emerged from the process of working with materials (Fig. 9). The process of describing tools, quantities of stuff to use and the process of making through gestures, had the objective to teach students to realize about the specific moments where rules and the following of a specific and *'discrete'* recipe proves insufficient if followed strictly.

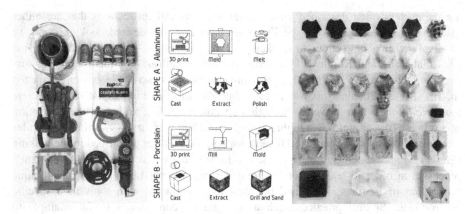

Fig. 8. Knolling pictures of materials and tools to be utilized in the making process. Benito González, Discrete Heuristics studio. DesignLab UAI 2016.

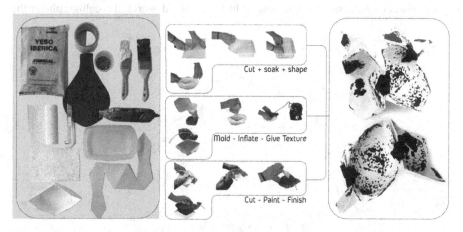

Fig. 9. Knolling and Performance diagrams for making thin composite shells. Francisca Dominguez. Discrete Heuristics Studio, DesignLab UAI 2016.

3.2 Using Discrete Heuristics to Make in the Same Way…Many Different Things

Considering cooking as an analogy, students were asked to understand the process of making by realizing the difference between linear deterministic processes of manufacturing such as 3D printing, and perceptual making processes such as drawing, painting or crafting (Fig. 10). As an example, preparing food, involves a predefined generic structure in the form of a recipe –algorithm- that indicates rules, procedures, and also quantities to be followed. Nonetheless, the act of preparing food involves sensing and acting of the chef by being aware of certain 'moments' impossible to quantify or code beforehand. In a similar way to Stiny's and Knight's alchemic description of Sargent's paintings, thickness, smell, taste, consistency, color, and so on are parameters often described with ambiguous sensorial instructions that are either visual – when meat reaches a specific color according to a desired cooking point- or physical –adding more flour to thicken a sauce preparation. These moments are the ones that Stiny and Knight [11] describe as the *'in between'* moments that are susceptible to be broken up into finer and finer parts, not describable but only enacted (p. 16). The idea behind this was to formulate the act of making as a *deictic 'discrete heuristic'* process that proves to be highly specific according to the partial description of a process (the discrete), yet highly ambiguous when it comes to enacting those rules (the heuristic) according to material behavior and the gestures performed in the making (Fig. 11). Finally, students were invited to imitate, copy and practice other student's processes in order to realize that *'original designs'* emerged because of their unique impression of gestures, ideas and the way they interacted with tools in a specific environment. Skillful practices such as calligraphy constitute a useful example to illustrate deictic forms of creative artistic work using tools. Calligraphy is based upon a model of imitation and learning of precedents as 'models of doing'. Through this process of copying, the artist acquires different skills not to imitate anymore, but to express his/her uniqueness, impressing it to the material world. To calligraphers, the

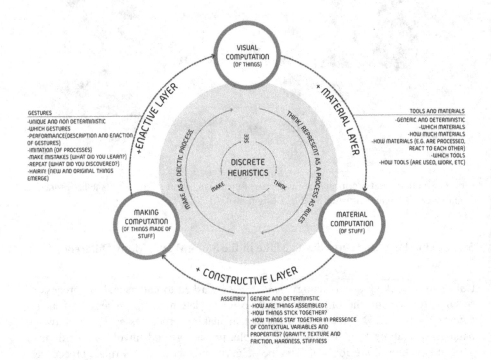

Fig. 10. Discrete Heuristics Studio diagram. Based on Stiny´s and Knight´s Computational Making Paradigm, the studio teaches students about design, material computation and interactive digital fabrication in three stages adding layers of information to the creative process. Diego Pinochet, DesignLab UAI 2016.

practice of 'Rinsho' is considered as the methodical imitation of procedures in order to achieve creative original work through three stages: (1) *'Keirin'*: learning by imitating the mechanics of brush technique. (2) *'Irin'*: reproducing by interpreting intention. (3) *'Hairin'*: reproducing based on memory allowing more freedom. Is the last stage of

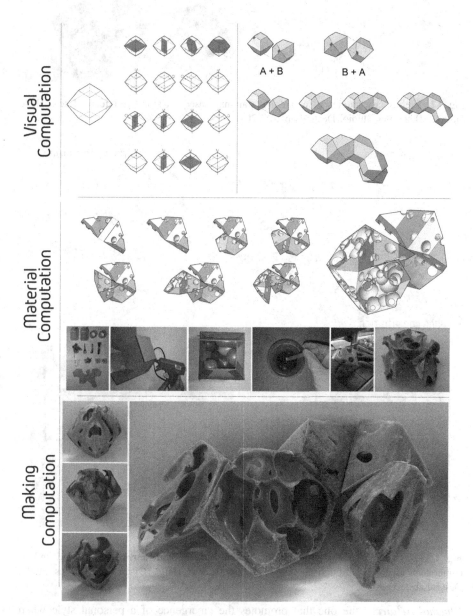

Fig. 11. Discrete Heuristic process for the development of lightweight foam structures. Rosario Yañez.. Discrete Heuristics Studio, DesignLab UAI 2016.

Fig. 12. Preliminary studies of a making grammar based on stone and foam. Lucas Helle, Discrete Heuristics Studio, DesignLab UAI 2016.

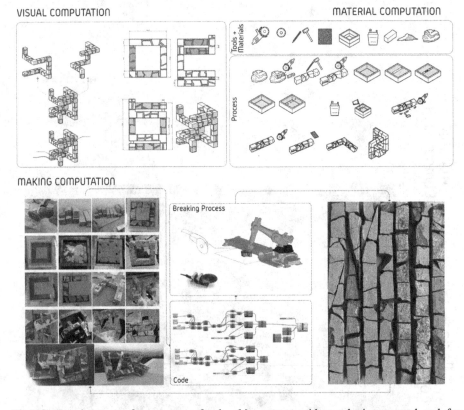

Fig. 13. Development of a grammar for breaking stones with a robotic arm and and for component assembly through molten aluminum. Lucas Helle. Discrete Heuristics Studio, DesignLab UAI 2016.

'Rinsho', 'Hairin', the one that promotes the emergence of a personal style where original and creative work emerges by discarding the act of imitation/reproduction in favor of the expression of the self [22]. Is in the moment of 'Hairin' where the artist, tools and materials enter into a choreography of agencies interacting and producing new types of 'sho', known as the word that describes creative artistic calligraphy.

Taking calligraphy and cooking as examples, students realized that the emergence of the original in their proposals happened not only because of the tension between historical precedents and the contingency of the moment, but also from the tension between human and object as gestures that impressed the uniqueness of the self onto the physical world ad how the materials reacted in the making process (Fig. 12). Programming a robotic arm to break a stone in the work 'Reconciliation' is an example of the discrete heuristics applied in the design studio. In this project, a student worked an entire semester programming a KUKA robot to break -using similar routines- different types of rocks into smaller pieces (Fig. 13). The goal of his proposal was to understand material behavior of the rocks breaking in unpredictable ways and how through the use of metal casting technique, he could reconcile two materials of different natures.

Fig. 14. Emergent stone assemblies through aluminum casting. Lucas Helle. Discrete Heuristics Studio, DesignLab UAI 2016.

The discreteness of the algorithm as a set of fixed rules to break the stone proved to be a rich and fertile creative procedure since the components obtained from that process were always different and demanded a constant re elaboration of new formal rules to work with molten metal to attach the resulting pieces (Fig. 14). Dealing with the imperfections of the rock and working with molten aluminum following fixed procedures but using different gestures resulted in the emergence of a set of different prototypes. The student learned about design describing procedures to generate different geometrical configurations and also to develop 'personalized' routines to work with these two materials.

4   Discussion

This paper starts questioning the role of digital fabrication when used in design beyond its representational potentials. If design is something tightly related to the act of impressing our uniqueness into the material word through drawings, prototypes, mechanisms and so on, this paper questions the use of the linear operational model that lies under the current paradigm of producing through the digital as opposed to creating and designing through the digital. Furthermore, it addresses the question on how in a similar way to analog processes of designing and making, designers can intervene the making process in order to use digital fabrication tools to think and discover new things in the making.

Secondly, this paper takes computational making as the theoretical base to introduce and discuss about working with shape grammars and physical materials as well as using digital fabrication techniques. Through the discussion on Stiny's and Knight's foundational paper on making grammars, this paper elaborates a set of questions about the use of digital tools to make things. Making use of Stiny's and Knight's definition of making as a design endeavor, this paper tries to elaborate further on the discussion about the use of materials, tools and body gestures as key actors in the making process through the elaboration of deictic rules in order to grasp the infinite and unpredictable outcomes emerged from working with physical objects instead of infinite shapes like lines.

Thirdly, this paper elaborates further about the concepts related to tool use and body gestures as promoters of creativity and discovery. Through this discussion, this paper relates these concepts to the current use of digital fabrication for design, identifying the problem of leaving human out of the process due to the creative gap between what is imagined, perceived, and then executed.

This paper presented 'Discrete Heuristics' a design methodology implemented in a third year studio at the design school of Adolfo Ibañez University in Chile that took a computational approach to making teaching students about design and different material techniques through digital fabrication. The studio takes shape grammars -and its extension as computational making grammars- to elaborate a pedagogic methodology in which students do research about 'ways of making'. By elaborating rules, procedures and recipes to design and make as a performance - where the discrete nature of digital fabrication algorithms and the deictic rules that emerged from working intervening in the process of making- resulted in a fertile environment for exploration, creativity and reasoning about other ways of using computers and fabrication machines in a more exploratory way. Furthermore, it was asserted that creativity and originality do not rely on the elaboration of pre-conceived ideas or plans, but on the relationship of perception and action as promoters of creativity and knowledge elicited, in which the concept of real time interaction through body gestures is the key to use digital tools in more creative ways. Finally, the Discrete heuristic studio taught students a methodology to freely explore designs and materials techniques focusing not only in the elaboration of prescriptive rules but also in the analysis and description of sensorial instructions to grasp and understand the unexpected through the heuristic nature of performing with physical objects. By using this methodology, students realized that the emergence of the original in their proposals happened not only because of the tension between historical precedents and the contingency of the moment, but also from the tension between human and object through gestures that impressed the uniqueness of the self onto the physical world ad how the materials reacted in the making process.

References

1. Flusser, V.: Gestures (Roth, N.A., Trans.). University of Minnesota Press, Minneapolis (2014)
2. Perez-Gómez, A.: The historical context of contemporary architectural representation. In: Ayres, P. (ed.) Persistent Modelling: Extending the Role of Architectural Representation, pp. 13–25. Routledge, New York (2012)
3. Pinochet, D.I.: Making gestures: design and fabrication through real time human computer interaction (Master of Science Thesis). Massachusetts Institute of Technology (2015)
4. Pinochet, D.: Making - gestures: continuous design through real time human machine interaction. In: 21st CAADRIA Conference Proceedings, Melbourne, pp. 282–290 (2016)
5. Gürsoy, B., Özkar, M.: Visualizing making in design: shapes, materials and actions. Des. Stud. **41**, 29–50 (2015). ISSN: 0142-694X
6. Goodman, N.: Languages of Art, 2nd edn. Hackett Publishing Company, Inc., Indianapolis (1976)
7. Dreyfus, H.L.: What Computers Still Can't Do: A Critique of Artificial Reason, 1st edn. The MIT Press, Cambridge (1992)
8. Radman, Z. (ed.): The Hand, An Organ of the Mind: What the Manual Tells the Mental. MIT Press, Cambridge (2013)
9. Malafouris, L.: How Things Shape the Mind: A Theory of Material Engagement. MIT Press, Cambridge (2013)
10. Knight, T., Vardouli, T.: Computational making. Des. Stud. **41**, 1–7 (2015). ISSN: 0142-694X
11. Knight, T., Stiny, G.: Making grammars: from computing with shapes to computing with things. Des. Stud. **41**, 8–28 (2015). ISSN: 0142-694X
12. Ihde, D.: Bodies in Technology. University of Minnesota Press, Minneapolis (2002)
13. Latour, B.: On technical mediation - philosophy. Sociol. Geneal. Common Knowl. **3**(2), 29–64 (1994)
14. Clark, A.: Natural-born cyborgs: minds, technologies, and the future of human intelligence, 1st edn. Oxford University Press, New York (2004)

15. Schön, D.A.: Educating the Reflective Practitioner, 1st edn. Jossey-Bass, San Francisco (1987)
16. Ackermann, E.: Constructing knowledge and transforming the world. In: Tokoro, M., Steels, L. (eds.) A Learning Zone of One's Own: Sharing Representations and Flow in Collaborative Learning Environments, pp. 15–37. IOS Press, Amsterdam (2004)
17. Robinson, D.: Feeling Extended: Sociality as Extended Body-Becoming-Mind. MIT Press, Cambridge (2013)
18. Visser, W.: The Cognitive Artifacts of Designing. L. Erlbaum Associates, Mahwah (2006)
19. Clark, A.: Being There Putting Brain, Body, and World Together Again. MIT Press, Cambridge (1997)
20. Lakoff, G.: Women, Fire, and Dangerous Things, 1st edn. University of Chicago Press, Chicago (1987)
21. Ingold, T.: Bringing things back to life: creative entanglements in a world of materials (working paper). Realities/Morgan Centre, University of Manchester (2008). http://www.manchester.ac.uk/realities/publications/workingpapers/. Accessed
22. Nakamura, F.: Creating or performing words? observations on contemporary calligraphy. In: Hallam, E., Ingold, T. (eds.) Creativity and Cultural Improvisation. Bloomsbury Academic, New York (2008)

Shape Studies

EthnoComputation: An Inductive Shape Grammar on Toraja Glyph

Rizal Muslimin[(⊠)]

School of Architecture, Design and Planning,
The University of Sydney, Sydney, Australia
rizal.muslimin@sydney.edu.au

Abstract. This paper aims to highlight the ways in which Shape Grammar inductive reasoning can analyze and represent design knowledge in a tacit environment. Deductive Shape Grammar has effectively examined designs from the past, where access to the artifacts' authors is not possible. However, in a condition where access to the craftsperson and the making process is possible, there is an opportunity to induce design grammar from the evidence on-site. Nevertheless, in such contexts, direct access to the craftsperson does not necessarily mean that access to their design knowledge is straightforward, as reflected in our case study, *Passura*: a Traditional Glyph in Toraja, Indonesia. In this article, the formulation of inductive Shape Grammar is provided, and applications on the tacit environment are discussed.

Keywords: Passura · Inductive reasoning · Shape grammar · Toraja · Ornament · EthnoComputation

1 Introduction

Shape Grammar has been effectively used as a rewriting system to analyze design artifacts from the past, namely for Chinese Ice-Ray lattice windows, Hepplewhite Chairs, the Yingzao Fashi, Mayan ornaments, and the Mughal Gardens [1–5]. By analyzing a series of shapes as design evidence and rewriting them into a new set of design rules, the Shape Grammar method can reproduce similar as well as new emergent designs within the same language.

The deductive aspect of Shape Grammar is useful in situations where access to the artifacts' authors is not possible and needs to be substituted by a deductive approach, hence the adoption of a set of rules. With less attachment to the original context, the deducted rules provide new paths to deduce other artifacts. For instance, the Ice-Ray's subdivision rules have inspired many other designs, including Mughal-Garden, Hepplewhite and Mondrian grammars. Differently, in a situation where the design practice remains active, and access to the craftsperson and the design process are present, there is an opportunity to incorporate evidence not only from the artifact but also from the way in which the craftsperson perceives and produces the shapes. This type of study is imperative in a context where shape, meanings, and production systems simultaneously interconnect to symbolize the multifaceted concepts of culture (e.g. indigenous culture).

© Springer Nature Singapore Pte Ltd. 2017
G. Çağdaş et al. (Eds.): CAAD Futures 2017, CCIS 724, pp. 329–347, 2017.
DOI: 10.1007/978-981-10-5197-5_18

However, in such contexts, direct access to the craftsperson does not necessarily mean that access to their design knowledge is straightforward, as the method might be passed on in a tacit environment. Pure inductive analysis, such as grounded theory or a phenomenological approach, may be effective in capturing the anthropological reflection of the designer or an artifact's appearance [6–8]. Yet, there are limits to representing a mode of design inquiry in textual narratives. Unless the authors artic-ulate their design knowledge explicitly (e.g. via textual, verbal, or visual means), one would need to interpret and rewrite the knowledge comprehensively.

This paper aims to highlight the ways in which the Shape Grammar inductive approach can analyze and represent design knowledge in a tacit environment, where a researcher has access to the designer and the process in situ.

1.1 Case Study and Limits

Our case study is the *'Passura'* engraved ornamentation style, which remains actively practiced in Toraja, Indonesia. The *Passura* ornament serves as a visual narrative (glyph) to address the encoded messages of the house's owner (Fig. 1). While the ornaments have many variations (about 72 to 100 motifs), the style across some motifs is consistent and can be easily recognized in defining the Torajan style [9–11].

Fig. 1. Passura engraved in Toraja's traditional house (Tongkonan)

Ornamentation is integral to local religious principles (*Aluk Todolo*) which govern world-views and ways of life, including the way in which an ornament has to represent an appropriate story about a person's rite of passage [12]. Existing studies on Passura have classified the ornament into four categories for such a passage: *Passura todolo* represents the values for a married person's life until his/her death, *Passura malollek* represents the values for a teenager's journey until his/her marriage, and *Passura pakbarean* symbolizes happiness (possibly representing the values for a person's childhood). The fourth category, *Garontok passura,* represents the main religious principles from which the three Passura categories should pertain. These motifs are engraved in the houses, barns and coffins for the family member to relate to their elders' history and to communicate the ritual messages that are recorded via the Passura glyphs [13, 14]. However, while the *Passura's* glyphs have been properly catalogued, the underlying design method is mostly passed on tacitly from generation to generation within a master-apprentice relationship.

In this paper, our study is limited to the interpretation of Passura's design transformation in its ideation and production. We discuss neither the design semantics nor the underlying cultural significance. For more reference about the semantic and cultural symbolism of Passura see Bagoes, Pakan, Thosibo, Said, and Waterson [13–16] and [17, 18] for previous computational design studies on the visual-semantic aspect of Passuras. Additionally, as Passura design is represented through various crafting techniques, namely engraving and carving, this paper focuses on the phase prerequisite to these processes, i.e., drawing.

2 Methods

For this study, we used Shape Grammar to examine the way in which a Toraja glyph is generated. Our field study included observation of the crafting process in Kete Kesu village, Toraja, Indonesia and an interview with a local engraver to obtain more information about the design principles. The engraver was chosen for his engraving and communication skills. Shape Grammar embedding and generative analysis were used to induce and deduce findings from observation of the crafting process. To navigate and orient this study within the vast Shape Grammar literature, a review of pertinent research is briefly discussed below.

2.1 Precedents

Inductive reasoning has been used to interpret grammar from a set of data in several studies. Talton, et al. [19] automated the induction process using a probabilistic approach (Bayesian Model Merging). In this approach, a design sample was broken-down into a set of elements, along with a series of sample designs to define the space of possible grammars as well as the pertained design parameters/conditions and their structures. Searching for the rules was achieved by merging and optimizing the results with Markov chain Monte Carlo methods. The induced grammars in this experiment were able to reproduce the initial samples as well as generate a possible extended family for the design. Recently, Whiting, et al. [20] proposed methods for automating the induction process from given data sets. A set of data was parsed into sub-datasets by tokens, which were then ranked based on their number of appearances in the data. Through recursive iterations, the sequencing process parsed the sub-datasets into yet smaller subsets and was then formalized into a set of grammar rules. Experiments on one-dimensional (e.g. words) and two-dimensional (e.g. graph data) data-sets from Whiting's case study show the sequencing process was able to induce a set of rules which can regenerate the initial samples. The goal in these two studies was to automate the induction process to produce rules through computer-aided-design.

In relation to the crafting process, perceptual and physical roles have also been examined through previous Shape Grammar studies. The role of material in empowering the design process was explored through the Shape Grammar method, where, for instance, instead of solely relying on the geometry of a shape, rule computation with malleable physical materials allows unprecedented results by embracing the material's mechanical behavior [21]. In this experiment, rules were predefined and calculated physically, from which iteration, the material's uncertainty help to assist novel design. Knight and Stiny [22] highlighted the role of visual perception in drawing and knotting and Muslimin [23] captured the interplay between haptic and visual engagement in weaving. In these studies, Shape Grammar representation signified a two-fold maker-material relationship, such that [9] underlying object transformation in making, there is a constant perceptual coordination across senses that drives the decision for subsequent iteration; and [12] recursive attention on specific part(s) of the object via either visual and/or haptic engagement indicates that some shapes are prerequisite and pivotal in the making process.

Our agenda intersects with the previous inductive grammar experiments in that the goal is to propose a method of producing grammars, rather than analyzing or synthesizing design through a predefined grammar. It also parallels the material approach to discover new possibilities through making on the fly, and the perceptual approach to highlight the hidden shapes not visible from direct observation. However, given the complexity in our data, we neither seek to automate the process nor focus on the perceptual factors that drive the maker's physical process. Instead, we focus on understanding the way in which Shape Grammar principles could serve for inductive reasoning, and whether such an inductive approach could work in tandem with the classical deductive method.

2.2   Formulation

We begin by illustrating the challenges of inducing and deducing the design logic. In a traditional culture, most of which consists of tacitly passed-down traditions, access to an explicit representation of a rule is not always available. For instance, let us assume a hypothetical designer/craftsperson uses rule A → B in Fig. 2a to generate the artifact in Fig. 2b. Later on, if an observer, other than the craftsperson, finds the artifact, either directly or indirectly, it will be challenging for the observer to retrieve the rule. Each of the possible embedded sub-shapes in the craft objects could lead to different rule interpretations because each embedded shape can be used to deduce rules. For instance, based on different observations of the embedded shapes in Fig. 2c, different rules in Fig. 2d (i.e. R2, R3, and R4) can be deduced to interpret how a craftsperson generates the craft object.

In deductive Shape Grammar, the correlation between rule, initial shape, and the computation is less bounded to the original context. Different deduced rules and initial shapes in Fig. 2d and 2e are fine as long as they produce similar artifacts in Fig. 2b. In

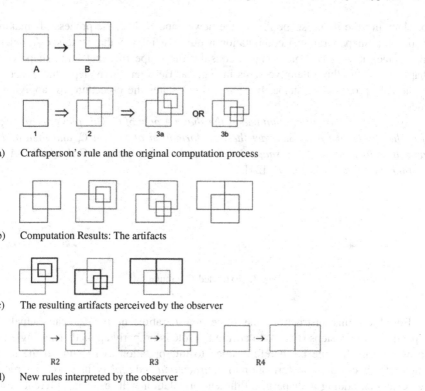

a) Craftsperson's rule and the original computation process

b) Computation Results: The artifacts

c) The resulting artifacts perceived by the observer

d) New rules interpreted by the observer

e) Artifacts produced with interpreted rules

Fig. 2. Computation from unknown rules to deductive rules

contrast, in *in situ* observation, where the making process is accessible, the bound between an initial shape and the making process might be exposed; hence, the number of possible rules could be constrained. By interacting with the maker, we may not only induce the rules, as in Fig. 2a, but also the reason behind them, which could yield a different insight into such rules.

Yet, direct access to the craftsperson's making process could be problematic either because of issues in articulating the rules or that they might inherit different types of rules, as the craftsperson may not be the author of the design rule in Fig. 2a. When such issues occur, deductive reasoning needs to be carefully conducted in tandem with inductive reasoning. Therefore, reconfiguring the arrow's role within the correlation between rule, initial shape and the computation is essential in restructuring the deductive and inductive reasoning in Shape Grammar.

The significant difference between Fig. 2c and a is that there are double-arrows between the shapes in Fig. 2a that signify the making process in producing the artifact. In a rule format A → B, the arrow does not refer to a particular transformation method for changing the initial shape A into the new shape B. Yet, the process of 'making a shape' in a Shape Grammar computation is quite distinctive, that is: to see A, delete A and replace it with B. For example, consider the shape rule that turns shape A into shape B and the three iterative steps in Fig. 2a. Between these steps, more steps are required to produce the shape. In *Shape*, Stiny states the procedure for applying the rules:

'Find a transformation t that makes the shape A part of C. This picks out some part of C that looks like A ... Subtract the transformation of A from C, and then add the same transformation of the shape B. This replaces the part of C that's like A with another part that looks like B' [24].

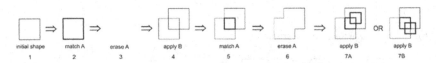

Fig. 3. Extended Computation.

Based on this instruction, the three-step iteration in Fig. 2a can actually be expanded into six steps (Fig. 3) to ensure the rule is properly applied. The single-lined arrow ($\rightarrow$) in the rule is, therefore, open to interpretation as it is up to the user to employ the necessary transformation to *subtract, add* and *replace* in Stiny's instruction. For example, adding a shape in a different orientation will result in different designs (see two possible orientations at step 7A and 7B in Fig. 3).

Double arrows ($\Rightarrow$) in the rule iteration signify the process of applying a rule (r) for a shape (x) in computation (r, x), assuming that rule (r) and shape (x) exist. Yet, when computation (r, x) exists, then observable shapes in the computation can be used to infer the rules (r) and the initial shape (x). This can be obtained by applying inverse computation by assuming the observable making process as the iterative computation to retrieve rule (r) and shape (x).

Figure 4 shows a diagram of inducing rules from a given sequence of making process. Through this diagram, we can record the observable making process to induce shape (x) and rule (r). In the recorded sequence, the earlier shape provides an initial shape for the left-hand side of the rules while the subsequent shapes represent the transformed (or new) shape for the right-hand side of the rule. The inverse process from iterative computation to rule definition is notified by double-arrows that turn into single-arrows. The embedded shape, mentally applied in the rule, is represented with the schema $x \rightarrow x$ to identify the visual embedding process, while the shape transformation in the making process is represented with the schema $x \rightarrow t(x)$, $x \rightarrow y$ or $x \rightarrow x + t(x)$. While the observable process runs in linear time, the relationship between induced embedding (seeing) and transformation (doing) rule is non-linear.

The inductive reasoning will be constrained by the observer's sequencing strategy as to how far the making process is being grouped or separated. Grouping a long process into one step will return a generic process while grouping a short sequence into several steps provides more detailed making processes. Note that just as embedding shapes from the shape rule into shape computation embraces ambiguity, likewise embedding shapes from shape computation into shape rules is also interpretative.

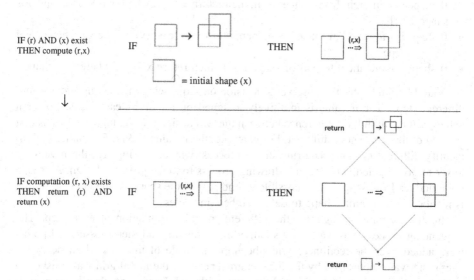

Fig. 4. Inverse-computation from existing computation (top) into inductive rules (bottom): *If* a making process exists (marked with ⇒), *Then* induces the making rules from the visible transformation process x → x + t(x) (top of the lattice), and the implied visual matching process x → x, (bottom of the lattice).

The following experiments are structured in two rounds based on the level of generality and specificity of the Passura design. In each round, the study will alternate between inductive shape grammar, where evidence of the making process is directly observable, and deductive grammar, where evidence is indirectly available.

3   Round 1

3.1   Inductive Shape Grammar

We observed and interviewed the local engraver as he demonstrated the ornamentation process through drawing. The engraver normally draws a Passura motif on a wooden board with a pencil before engraving it. For our analysis, we asked him to draw the motif with pencil on paper. To clarify the visual data, we simplify the engraver's drawing into line drawings and omit the other details (a more detailed analysis will be discussed in a later section). As mentioned earlier, the role of Shape Grammar notation in this observation phase serves as a recording device to represent the iterative process, notated by ⇒ in Fig. 4. At this stage, the drawing sequences are parsed by examining the difference between the spatial compositions in the drawing. Intuitively, steps that show significantly different compositions are separated by the following routines:

For each shape i and shape i + n that appear in the making process, where 'n' indicates the degree of difference between an initial shape and its subsequent appearance during the making process:

- If shape i is different from shape i + n, then return x → y, where x is shape i and y is shape i + 1
- If shape i is repeated in shape i + n, then return x → x + t(x), where x is shape i and t(x) is shape i + 1
- If shape i is identical to part of shape i + 1, then return x → x, where x is shape i

Variable *n* indicates the observer's decision on sequencing the making process into different steps. The n value is intuitively assigned on a case-by-case basis. Lower n values will result in little difference between the two designs, while higher n means that the two designs are more different. For example, the n value in Fig. 5 is rather high to identify different designs occurring in the process, whereas in Fig. 10, the n value is lower to investigate the engraver's drawing process to make just one design. As shape i + n derives from shape i, it is possible to find part of the shape, in the later steps, that is identical to the initial shape to define embedding rules.

In this example, n signifies the different module completion at each step. The sequencing process was started by subdividing a square, and then crosses and points were added over the rectilinear grid (the important role of the crossed shape in the engraving was emphasized by the local engraver). After the initial grid was finished, a new shape (a spiral) was drawn, and then he continued drawing another spiral next to the first one until about four spirals were composed.

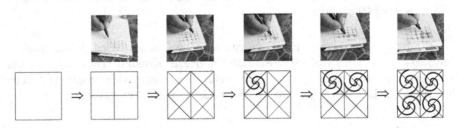

Fig. 5. Observable process from the site. The pictures on the top show the engraver's drawing process. The bottom iteration shows the simplified version of his drawing as a data-sets.

The lattice in Fig. 6 shows a set of nine rules induced from the data-sets, where the rules below the making iteration signify the visual-embedding rules, and the ones above it show the transformation rules. As can be seen, the induced rules appear in a different hierarchy, based on how far the rules can represent the making process in the data-set. Low-level rules are more specific and located closer to the making steps, while higher-level rules are further near the edge of the lattice. The latter is more detailed to highlight the transformation method, while the former is simpler to cover various steps in the data-sets.

The smaller diagrams in Fig. 7 magnify the different hierarchy groups from Fig. 6. For the first group, we incorporate information from the local engravers that the crossed-linear grid is the main template to develop most of the Passura motifs (note: the cross and the blank square is also a motif in itself). Based on this, we induced the rules for making the grid from the first two steps, that is two subdivision rules x → div(x) and one embedding rule x → x (Fig. 7a). The second group is obtained from step four to signify the design process of a newly transformed spiral inside the cross-grid modules which induces an additive-transformative rule, *add a rotated spiral*, and another embedding rule *see a cross-grid* module as to where to add the new spiral (Fig. 7b).

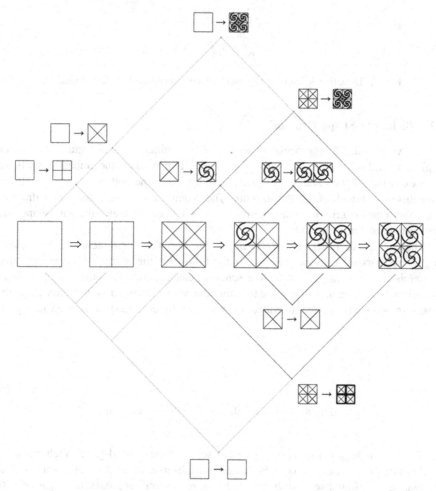

Fig. 6. Inductive Shape Grammar generates rules from the making process

The other two groups indicate the completion of the designs on two different levels. The first level, which is initiated in the third step (the crossed-grid), represent an intention to engrave a chosen motif after the grid is drawn (Fig. 7c) while the second level, initiated much earlier at step one (the blank square), represents the planner's/owner's decision to choose an motif (Fig. 7d).

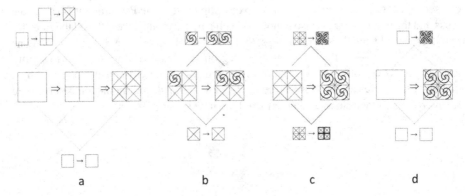

a   b   c   d

Fig. 7. Inductive Reasoning represented separately based on their hierarchy

3.2 Deductive Shape Grammar

The previous inductive process generates a preliminary Passura grammar, which implies several schemas to generalize the process. For instance, the embedding schema x → x can be assigned to embed squares and crosses in the bottom as they are almost prerequisite in transforming the designs. The schema x → x + y applies in drawing new shapes on the grid, and the schema x → x + t(x) encapsulates the way shapes are transformed to finish the motif.

These schemas raised an interesting suggestion that their recurring appearance might also work for the other designs. In the following, the deductive Shape Grammar is exercised to speculate how far the schemas can generate the other motif designs. Starting with the schema x → x for focusing our visual attention on the square and the cross, we deduced several embedded shapes from the crossed-grid, as seen in Fig. 8.

Fig. 8. Embedded shapes from the crossed-grid

There are at least ten squares and six crosses from the crossed-grid, which can serve as placeholders to insert a shape. Following our observation of the motifs surrounding the villages, we found several shapes such as circle, spiral, and stars, to be paired with the embedding schema. Figure 9 shows our deductive iteration to reproduce several ornament types, namely Circular type (A), Stars Type (B) and Meander Type (C). Note that in this deductive reasoning, there are much fewer double-arrows in Fig. 9, compared to Fig. 6. The schema x → x allows different matches for adding new shapes to create the nine sample motifs in Fig. 9. The deduced types are correlated to about 60 ornament designs out of approximately 70 designs.

Within the circular and star types, we also deduce that some motifs could, be a precursor to another one (marked with ⇒ in the diagram) by applying the embedding rule twice for the same additive rule (further deduced association can be inferred between the circle and the star's motif as intersecting circles could eventually produce some of the star's motif). The spatial relationship is also implied in the meander type. Interestingly, while the basic shape for circle and star has a little modification in the addition process, this is not quite the case for the meandering types (Fig. 9c). There are subtle differences between the basic meander module, in which we deduce that there should be low-level rules that vary the meander with schema x → t(x). What follows in the next round is inductive and deductive Shape Grammar to investigate a more refined aspect of the Passura Meander and Spiral design.

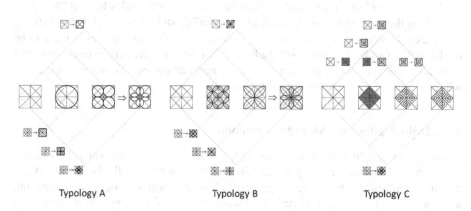

Fig. 9. Deductive rules on synthesizing Ornamental Types

4 Round 2

4.1 Inducing Passura-Meander Grammar

To investigate the meander transformation in Fig. 9c, we asked the engraver to draw one of the meander designs (*paqpapan kandaure*). The induction process is similar to the iteration in Sect. 3.1. However, instead of parsing the making process, based on the ornament design's module, this time we examine the process by parsing the line development within one design, where n (degree of difference) refers to the completion of one maximal line after another.

The engraver first drew a rectilinear 6 × 6 grid, which was much denser than the grid drawn earlier for the spiral (Fig. 10 – top pictures). He then bold the middle lines to subdivide the grid into four 3 × 3 quadrants. In one of the quadrants, he located the quadrant's mid-point, drew an x-y axial line from it, and then drew a square inside the quadrant and subdivided it into four yet smaller squares. It was in this small square that he developed the meander shape (see the diagram in Fig. 10). He started drawing a line from the edge of the square and went from outside to inside. Each time the stroke intersected with the crossing lines, the line turned perpendicularly inward, and this went the same way until meeting the smallest cell in the grid. After the meander in one quadrant was created, he repeated the same process for the other parts.

Figure 10 shows the picture and the simplified drawing. The induction process started with a rectilinear grid as the initial shape and a square for the embedding rule. Each time a line was added, new transformation rules were induced at the top. The process generated several rules with the grid and the line as the left-hand shape. In order to obtain a recursive function, part of the right-hand shape of the rule has to be identical to the left-hand shape. Additionally, the rule needs to have constrained parameters in order to prevent it from becoming too loose and generating outputs that are either out of the corresponding style, or not specific enough so that they do not have the flexibility to cover various designs within a certain style. As seen in Fig. 10, Rule R7 is the first rule that indicates a meander pattern in the steps as the line turns inward. Rules R5 and R6 are too generic as they can easily produce arbitrary L and U shape compositions, whereas Rules R8 and R9 are too specific, as they can only generate an intricate spiraling style. Low-level Rules R10 and R11 inside the diagram can generate the meander with polylines, yet they could also be too loose for analyzing/synthesizing the Passura's meander style, as lines can be matched in multiple orientations. This also means that a new embedding rule to recognize a line will be required (see the lower part of the lattice).

4.2 Deducing Passura Meander Grammar

Instead of adding an extra embedding rule, we deduce a meander using the existing visual embedding rule: *see a square* and incorporate it with Rule R7 in Fig. 10. While the square-embedding holds the visual placeholder, the meander line is completed into a square to make it recursive. Rule R12 mimics the way the engraver develops the meander outside-in from a square or the quadrants (Fig. 11). It starts with a square and then a new inside square is added with an opening on one corner. Mirroring labels by the square's diagonal axis helps to orient the square for recursive iteration to generate a smaller square. A counting variable (i) defines the maximum iteration to end the computation with rule R15 (e.g., when i = 5, it will stop after five steps). Additionally, to include the interlocked meander in the third step of Fig. 9c, a rotation rule R13 is added. Figure 11c shows the rule iteration and design variety that resembles Passura meandering modules, each of which is ready to be contained with the (crossed) grid with the previous deduced rule. Rules to populate the motif on a larger surface are deduced with additive rules that compose the meander modules in a side-by-side spatial-relationship with the reflection-rotation and translation (Fig. 11d).

4.3 Deducing Passura Spiraling Grammar

In the same manner, as the meander is being translated and rotated, the spiral pattern can also be deduced with the law of symmetry. Evidence of symmetrical law has been indicated in a previous study [17, 25]. Linear transformation and additive rules are applied with labels to identify the variation [26, 27]. The initial deductive grammar from observation shows a straightforward process of generating the rectangular grid (Fig. 12).

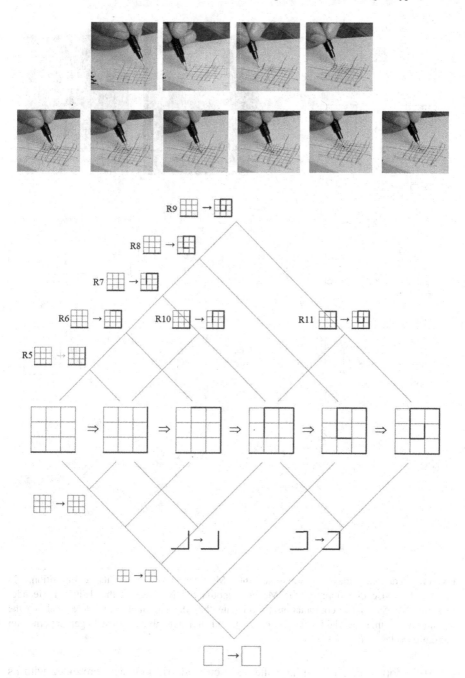

Fig. 10. Pictures of engraver's drawing process (top) and the meander pattern induction rules (bottom)

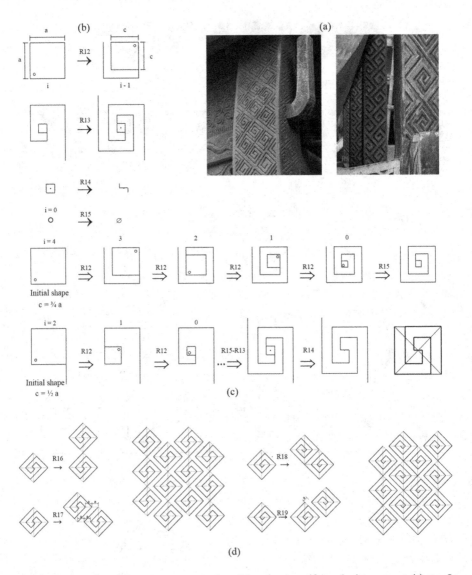

Fig. 11. Deducted rules to compute the Meander motif and its composition. In counter-clockwise direction: (a) the Meander motifs on the site; (b) the deducted Meander rules: R12-R15; (c) the computation to generate the Meander motif's module; and (d) the modules were then overlaid with the crossed grid and assembled into a larger pattern with translation rules R16-R19 (d).

At the top of Fig. 12, we have the basic crossed-grid module represented with its order of symmetry, which implies the crossed grid module has eight different ways of transforming itself to mimic its identity, and when each module is combined, it has n number of shapes times eight spatial relationships. An early suggestion would imply that the possible combination for 2×2 tiling is 32 designs. However, the number of

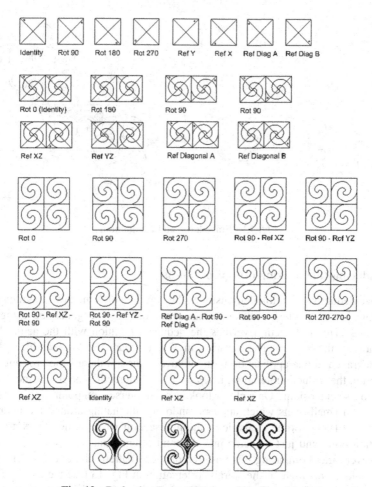

Fig. 12. Deductive Rule of Passura Spiralling Motif

2×2 spiral tilings in Passura is only 14, and only some of them correspond individually to the 32 possible designs. This numbers indicates that the design generation is not based on a one-on-one basis, but rather on a one-to-many or many-to-many. Some designs which have the same tiling configuration need to be perceived visually different to distinguish them (Figure-Ground). For instance, three designs at the lower images in Fig. 12 have the same shape configuration. With different focus, they could be perceived as a different motif (with a different meaning) as one shifts the focus from the figure or the ground shapes, and vice-versa. Sometimes the meaning is symbolized with the shape's boundary (outlines) and sometimes with the shape's plane. This non-zero sum design embraces the role of embedding as functioned in Shape Grammar. These designs become clearer as they are multiplied on a plane. Periodical tiling on a building surface indicates that in resembling the actual object, the spiral tessellation which is a design in itself may also serves as a guidelines to develop the final shape. Figure 13 shows a new emergent shape (stem) embedded from the spiral-composition, rotated and then multiplied along the two-dimensional grid.

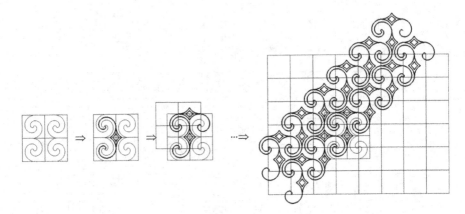

Fig. 13. Embedding and Modulation

4.4 Inducing (the Making of) Spiral Motifs

The above deductive iteration demonstrates the way in which the law of symmetry and embedding helps to interpret how various motif designs are generated using a few simple rules. This last section verifies the deducted iteration with the actual Passura application in the village. The iteration in Fig. 13 managed to resemble a Passura design engraved in one application in the village; although there is no crossing grid as generated in the deductive iteration, instead we found a rectilinear grid coinciding with the rotation's center-point. On a closer look, at each intersection point of this grid, there is an array of small ovals which appears randomly alternating around the intersection points (Fig. 14-left). Some ovals lie at the intersection while some others are off the intersection point and just coincide in a different orientation.

However, after comparing this with the deduced pattern, the ovals' orientation on the site looks comparable to the spirals' orientation in Fig. 13 (see the dots in Fig. 14-right). As these findings come after the interpretation of the design was thought finished, we can infer that the oval might also come after the original design process is finished. In other words, in the past, the ovals may appear later on the grid to aid the drawing process rather than the design process.

To investigate this, we revisited the induction process as shown in Fig. 2 when we asked the engraver to draw the spiral design. While the n value in Fig. 2 was to differentiate the grid and the spiral composition differently, for this case we focused on the relationship between the ovals and the spirals. Additionally, we also asked for information from the engraver about the arrangement of the ovals.

Figure 15 shows the engraver started drawing the grid and then drew an array of oriented ovals (which he called 'the eye') around the grid intersection. Once the 'eye' was drawn, he then extended the ovals' curves out, each from both sides to develop the spirals and then connected them with the other spiraled-curves from the neighboring ovals. We can infer that the designs (including the spiral orientation) have been mentally projected onto the surface and marked by the oval's orientation, which then aids the drawing process (Fig. 15 - second row).

Fig. 14. Spiral orientation on the actual ornament (left) and the deducted version (right)

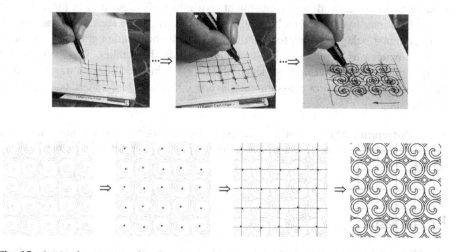

Fig. 15. (top) the engraver's drawing process as observed and (bottom) interpreted design-to-drawing process: (left) intended motif is mentally projected on a surface; (middle) grid is drawn and the motif's eye is placed along the grids intersection, and (right) the intended motifs are drawn.

5 Discussion and Conclusion

This paper has formulated inductive Shape Grammar and exercised the way it alternates hand-in-hand with the classical Shape-Grammar deductive approach, while rendering its application in the tacit environment. As shown in this preliminary study, inductive and deductive rules act in a different manner in analyzing and synthesizing a design, while at the same time contributing to one another. On one hand, the deductive rule is useful for representing the logic behind the mental iteration in generating the design, but it does not always represent the making process. For instance, the additive rules for the spiral and meander patterns may imply stamping or tiling instead of drawing. The deductive Shape Grammar, in this case, should be considered as representing the perception involved in designing the ornament in the first place.

On the other hand, the inductive rule is valuable in recording the making process. However, relying solely on the bottom-up drawing process might not be effective for synthesizing the design logic, especially for culturally restricted designs such as Passura motifs; the use of the induction process is to show more about how to make a design rather than the design process itself. As motif design, and apparently the making process as well, have been well-established, today's ornamentation activities in Kete Kesu are essentially a reproduction of designs that have existed for hundreds of years. It is more analogous to writing than designing, in the sense that in writing, a set of well-known terms is assembled by following a certain consensus to address a message, whereas in designing, either a new term is introduced, or a set of well-known terms are creatively assembled to address a new message.

Nevertheless, both deductive and inductive Shape Grammar have shown promising results in communicating the design and making process more explicitly as well as helping us to understand how ideas might turn into reality. As it is in the nature of Shape Grammar to embrace multiple interpretations, as can be seen in the case of the early grammar being rewritten (e.g., Palladian and Mughal-Garden grammar), we seek to find a better way to represent Passura grammar in further studies. This includes, but is not limited to, interpreting how actual objects are being distilled and translated into Passura designs and how Passura motifs are composed to address cultural/ritual messages.

Acknowledgement. This research is supported by Sydney Southeast Asia Center. The author would like to thank Aleksander Panimba and Ting Ting for their support and contribution during the field study.

References

1. Knight, T.W.: The generation of Hepplewhite-style chair-back designs. Environ. Plan. B Plan. Des. **7**, 227–238 (1980). doi:10.1068/b070227
2. Li, A.I.: A shape grammar for teaching the architectural style of the Yingzao fashi. Unpublished doctoral thesis, Massachusetts Institute of Technology (2001)
3. Müller, P., Vereenooghe, T., Wonka, P., Paap, I, Van Gool, L.J.: Procedural 3D reconstruction of Puuc buildings in Xkipché. In: VAST, pp. 139–146. Citeseer (2006)
4. Stiny, G.: Ice-ray: a note on the generation of Chinese lattice designs. Environ. Plan. B Plan. Des. **4**, 89–98 (1977). doi:10.1068/b040089
5. Stiny, G., Mitchell, W.J.: The grammar of paradise: on the generation of Mughul gardens. Environ. Plan. B Plan. Des. **7**, 209–226 (1980). doi:10.1068/b070209
6. Glaser, B., Strauss, A.: The Discovery of Grounded Theory: Strategies for Qualitative Research. AldineTransaction, London (1967)
7. Heidegger, M.: Being and Time. Blackwell, Hoboken (1927). (Reprinted 1962)
8. Husserl, E.: Introduction to the Logical Investigations: A Draft of a Preface to the Logical Investigations (1913). Springer, Berlin (2012)

9. Adams, K.M.: Art as Politics: Re-crafting Identities, Tourism, and Power in Tana Toraja, Indonesia. University of Hawaii Press, Honolulu (2006)
10. Kis-Jovak, J.I.: Banua Toraja: Changing Patterns in Architecture and Symbolism Among the Sa'dan Toraja, Sulawesi, Indonesia. Royal Tropical Institute, Amsterdam (1988)
11. Waterson, R.: The house and the world: the symbolism of Sa'Dan Toraja house carvings. RES Anthropol. Aesthet. 15(1), 34–60 (1988)
12. Duli, A.: Toraja: Dulu Dan Kini. Pustaka Refleksi, Makassar (2003)
13. Pakan, L.: The Secret of Typical Toraja's Patterns. Ujung Pandang (1961). 2nd edn. (1973)
14. Thosibo, A.: Mengungkap Makna Ornamen Gambar Passuraq pada Arsitektur Vernakular Tongkonan Melalui Persepsi Indra Visual. ITB, Bandung (2005)
15. Said, A.A.: Simbolisme Unsur Visual Rumah Tradisional Toraja Dan Perubahan Aplikasinya Pada Desain Modern. Ombak, Yogyakarta (2004)
16. Waterson, R.: The Living House: An Anthropology of Architecture in South-East Asia. Tuttle Publishing, Clarendon (2010)
17. Muslimin, R.: Decoding Passura'–representing the indigenous visual messages underlying traditional icons with descriptive grammar. In: Stouffs, R., Janssen, P., Roudavski, S., Tunçer, B. (eds.) Open Systems: Proceedings of the 18th International Conference on Computer-Aided Architectural Design Research in Asia (CAADRIA 2013), pp. 781–790. Hong Kong, and Center for Advanced Studies in Architecture (CASA), Department of Architecture-NUS, Singapore (2013)
18. Muslimin, R.: Toraja glyphs: an ethnocomputation study of passura indigenous icons. J Asian Archit. Build. Eng. 16, 39–44 (2017)
19. Talton, J., Yang, L., Kumar, R., Lim, M., Goodman, N., Měch, R.: Learning design patterns with bayesian grammar induction. In: Proceedings of the 25th Annual ACM Symposium User Interface Software Technology, pp. 63–74. ACM (2012)
20. Whiting, M., Cagan, J., LeDuc, P.: Automated induction of general grammars for design. In: Gero, J. (ed.) Design Computing and Cognition, pp. 267–278. Springer, Cham (2017)
21. Gürsoy, B., Özkar, M.: Visualizing making: shapes, materials, and actions. Des. Stud. 41, 29–50 (2015)
22. Knight, T., Stiny, G.: Making grammars: from computing with shapes to computing with things. Des. Stud. 41, 8–28 (2015)
23. Muslimin, R.: EthnoComputation: on weaving grammars for architectural design. Unpublished doctoral thesis, Massachusetts Institute of Technology (2014)
24. Stiny, G.: Shape: Talking about Seeing and Doing. The MIT Press, Cambridge (2006)
25. Oliver, P.: Encyclopedia of Vernacular Architecture of the World, vol. 2. Cambridge University Press, Cambridge (1998)
26. Knight, T.W.: Constructive symmetry. Environ. Plan. B Plan. Des. 22, 419–450 (1995). doi:10.1068/b220419
27. Stiny, G.: Kindergarten grammars: designing with Froebel's building gifts. Environ. Plan. B Plan. Des. 7, 409–462 (1980). doi:10.1068/b070409

Shape Computations Without Compositions

Iestyn Jowers[1($\boxtimes$)], Chris Earl[1], and George Stiny[2]

[1] The Open University, Milton Keynes, UK
iestyn.jowers@open.ac.uk
[2] MIT, Cambridge, MA, USA

Abstract. Parametric CAD supports design explorations through generative methods which compose and transform geometric elements. This paper argues that elementary shape computations do not always correspond to valid compositional shape structures. In many design cases generative rules correspond to compositional structures, but for relatively simple shapes and rules it is not always possible to assign a corresponding compositional structure of parts which account for all operations of the computation. This problem is brought into strong relief when design processes generate multiple compositions according to purpose, such as product structure, assembly, manufacture, etc. Is it possible to specify shape computations which generate just these compositions of parts or are there additional emergent shapes and features? In parallel, combining two compositions would require the associated combined computations to yield a valid composition. Simple examples are presented which throw light on the issues in integrating different product descriptions (i.e. compositions) within parametric CAD.

Keywords: Shape computation · Composition · Embedding · Parametric CAD

1 Introduction

Design is often formalised in a hierarchical process; as Woodbury states *'designers organize their work as...recursive systems of parts with limited interactions between parts'* [1]. Computer-aided design (CAD) replicates this approach, with design representations constructed hierarchically as assemblies of parts, and in parametric CAD the interactions between the parts are made explicit. Instead of defining single instances of a design concept, parametric models define a range of concepts with varying interactions between parts. Using parametric tools, designers dynamically explore these concepts by modifying parameters that control the interactions between parts, either manually or algorithmically [1]. Accordingly, Aish [2] identifies three themes that characterise a parametric approach to design: geometry, composition and algorithmic thought. *Geometry* includes the primitives used to describe a shape, i.e. points, lines, planes, curves, etc., and the relationships between these. *Composition* defines the hierarchical structure of the geometry, so that a concept is organised according to parts and sub-parts. *Algorithmic thought*, or *Logic* for short, is the process by which concepts are derived from a flow of interactions between geometry, within a defined composition.

These three elements, geometry, composition and logic are common generic components of a range of creative processes although articulated differently across

© Springer Nature Singapore Pte Ltd. 2017
G. Çağdaş et al. (Eds.): CAAD Futures 2017, CCIS 724, pp. 348–365, 2017.
DOI: 10.1007/978-981-10-5197-5_19

specific processes. The differences can be exemplified by comparing creative processes in parametric CAD and sketching. The way that design concepts are explored using pencil and paper in sketching is different from parametric CAD [3]. The primary difference lies in composition. When sketching, designers often change composition during exploration of a design concept to accommodate new ways of seeing, and to develop new avenues to explore [4]. Such switches in interpretation during sketching are visually intuitive, but computationally are difficult to achieve. Parametric tools are powerful at changing geometry, perhaps through explicit parameter changes which modify primitives individually, or in transforming the relationships between primitives. However, when compared with sketching, these parametric tools are less adept at changing composition.

The differences between parametric CAD and sketching, however, are not just a matter of degree, in terms of facility with compositions. The informal computations, combining logic and geometry, effected through sketching do not depend on specific compositions while the computations effected by parametric CAD take place within the context of explicit compositions. The former offers the possibility of computation without composition whilst the latter invokes composition as necessary for its computations. For sketching, although compositions are not necessarily required, they are often used to provide context and direction to see-move-see episodes [5].

This paper addresses the middle ground in design processes between the informal sketch and parametric CAD. It uses a model of shape computation based on shape rules [6] which covers characteristics of both sketching operations and the formal generative transformations of parametric CAD [7]. It demonstrates that these types of shape computation do not necessarily depend on compositions. Furthermore, such computations do not necessarily generate compositions. This perspective exemplifies the difference between sketching and parametric CAD. Compositions are defined in terms of geometry and logic which together constrain modifications of composition. This makes selecting a suitable composition an important step in the construction of parametric models, because a model requires an appropriate set of parts to accommodate exploration of design concepts. Subsequently, changing parts by changing compositions, although possible, essentially resets the design process. More significantly, perhaps, the paper demonstrates that changing compositions may just create a more elaborate chimera, monstrous and wildly imaginative but lacking substance or practicality.

This paper explores this problem of shape composition from the perspective of shape computation, where logic is formalised, not as a flow of interactions between geometry, but as a process of applying shape replacement rules. There is a distinction between these two types of logic, most notably in the way that compositions arise, because shape computations generate compositions. Shape computations mimic the sketching process, and rules are used to accommodate new ways of seeing and new ways of exploring [4]. As such, application of a rule changes the structure of a shape according to recognised parts. Figure 1 presents an illustrative example, reproduced from Stiny [6]. The shape rule in Fig. 1a, rotates squares through 45°, and is applied to the shape in Fig. 1b by recognising any of the squares embedded in the shape. Applying the rule gives rise to a network of shapes in a visual shape computation, as illustrated in Fig. 1c. The shape computation is finite, involving only seven distinct shapes, but there are three different compositions of the shape, and these result from how the rule is applied. Applying the rule to the small square gives rise to a different composition than applying it to the large squares, and a third composition results from rotating the two large squares so that line segments overlap.

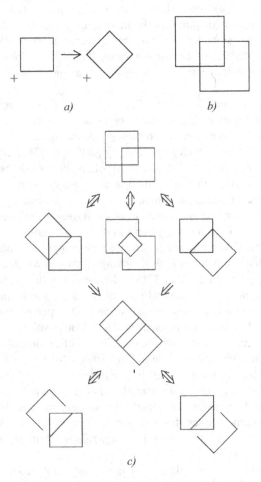

Fig. 1. An elementary shape computation

In shape computation, reinterpretation of compositions is supported by the continuously changing topology of shape [7], however implementing shape computations using parametric CAD is problematic, because changes in composition are difficult to achieve. Instead, it is desirable to identify part structures for shapes that will accommodate all necessary compositions, so that all the parts of interest can be identified and all the shapes in a computation can be derived. This paper explores how such part structures can be identified, and builds on results presented by Stiny [6]. It focuses on the shape computation illustrated in Fig. 1. Stiny showed that this computation gives rise to a part structure where the maximal edges of the shape in Fig. 1b are given by *ababaababa*, where *a* and *b* are both line segments, and $b = a\sqrt{2}$. The paper also considers a slightly more complicated shape computation. To scale the shape computation in Fig. 1, the obvious next step is to add another square to the initial shape, as illustrated in Fig. 2. It might be expected that the addition of the extra small square will result in a part structure that is comparable to that found for the computation in Fig. 1. But, finding a part structure that includes all compositions so that all shapes in the computation can be derived seems to be impossible.

Fig. 2. Three overlapping squares

The reason why this is impossible is not obvious, but is intrinsically linked to the periodic palindromic structure that Stiny identified for the computation in Fig. 1. This structure arises as a result of the embedding relation between line segments as described in [8], and in Sect. 2 key results concerning the part structures that result from embedded lines are reviewed. In Sect. 3 these results are applied to derive the periodic palindromic structure identified by Stiny for the shape computation in Fig. 1, and Sect. 4 uses the same results to show that there is no single structure that will accommodate all compositions necessary to carry out the computation if the shape in Fig. 2 is used as the initial shape. This result has implications with respect to the construction of parametric models, and the selection of composition. It suggests that predicting future manipulations is not the only barrier to identifying the correct composition for a particular parametric exploration. Some explorations are impossible to carry out using a single composition, and it is not necessarily possible to combine compositions in a single hierarchical structure.

2   The Structure of Embedded Lines

The part structures necessary to accommodate lines embedded in lines were explored in detail in [8]. There, the discussion was framed around a simple shape computation involving the recognition of parts of a shape. The identity rule in Fig. 3a, was used to recognise squares embedded in shapes composed of two squares sharing a common edge, an example of which is illustrated in Fig. 3b.

Visually, the computation is trivial because the two squares are easily identified as parts of the shape, as illustrated in Fig. 3c. Here, the compositions that result from recognising either the small or large square are illustrated, but identifying a part structure for the shape that accommodates both these compositions is not trivial. The shared edge of the two squares is the key characteristic of the shape computation, and

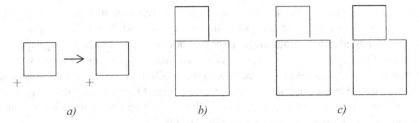

Fig. 3. A trivial shape computation

consequently the problem of identifying a part structure that accommodates both squares is equivalent to identifying part structures that accommodate the elementary operation of embedding a line inside another line, while taking into consideration the reflective symmetry of the lines. Figure 4 illustrates the necessary part structure.

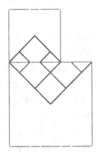

Fig. 4. Part structures resulting from recognition of squares

The triangles are included on the common edge to illustrate part structures while highlighting their symmetry. Each triangle correlates with a line segment embedded in an edge, and these are subdivided into finer structures, representing lines embedded in lines. Embedded lines associated with triangles are symmetrical, and their subdivision into embedded parts is symmetrical; in this sense, the triangles represent the structure of the edges as visual palindromes. The structures of the decomposed line segments are also illustrated in the decomposition of the top edge of the smaller square and the bottom edge of the larger, into line segments. A consequence of this decomposition is that the edges of the larger square and the smaller square have a different part structure, but shape computations that result from applying the rule in Fig. 3a can accommodate this by having two versions of the rule.

The structure illustrated in Fig. 4 is the simplest structure that accommodates the short edge being embedded in the long edge while retaining the symmetric properties of the two squares. Intuitively, it might be expected that embedding a short edge as part of a longer edge would simply result in a decomposition of the longer edge to accommodate the shorter. But this is not what is shown in Fig. 4, and the reason for this becomes apparent in the process for deriving the part structures of the edge. This process is illustrated in Fig. 5, and involves resolving the symmetries of the visual palindromes corresponding to the part structure of the edges.

Figure 5a illustrates the high-level structure of the edges where, to account for the symmetric properties of the squares, each edge is identified as a visual palindrome, represented by a triangle. Figure 5b illustrates the embedding of the shorter edge in the longer; the structure of the longer edge now incorporates an embedded line that is the length of the shorter edge, represented by the triangle highlighted in grey. This new structure breaks the symmetry of the longer edge, which is addressed in Fig. 5c by reflecting the smaller triangle in the illustrated axis of symmetry of the larger triangle. A new triangle is defined by the overlap, and this represents further subdivision of the visual palindrome; it is this emergent form that requires a finer decomposition of the edges than might be intuitively expected. Figure 5d resolves the symmetry of the longer edge by reflecting the emergent triangle in the illustrated axes of symmetry. Finally, in Fig. 5e, the structure of the shorter edge is subdivided according to the structure of the longer edge. The resulting part structure accounts for the symmetric properties of both squares, and allows the edge of the smaller square to be embedded in the edge of the larger square. The result is a periodic palindromic structure where the shorter edge can be described by the string *uvu* and the longer edge can be described by the string *uvuvu*, where *u* and *v* represent line segments of different lengths, determined by the ratio of the lengths of the edges of the squares.

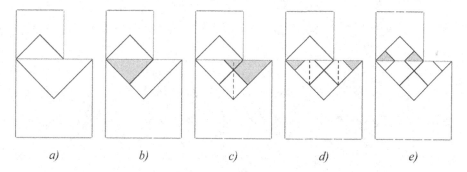

a)   *b)*   *c)*   *d)*   *e)*

Fig. 5. Deriving the part structure of embedded lines by resolving symmetries

Figure 6 explores the part structures that arise when different initial shapes are used in this shape computation. In all of these, the shapes are composed of two squares sharing a common edge, constrained such that the edge of the smaller square is embedded in the larger, with both sharing an end point, and l, the edge length of the larger squares, is kept constant while n, the edge length of the smaller squares, increases from Fig. 6a to h. The shape rule simply recognises the square parts of the shape, and again, triangles are included to illustrate the necessary part structures, whilst highlighting their symmetry. This structure is also reflected in the decomposition of the top edge of the smaller square and the bottom edge of the larger. In Fig. 6a, $n < 1/2l$ and embedding the shorter edge in the longer edge results in the part structure that is

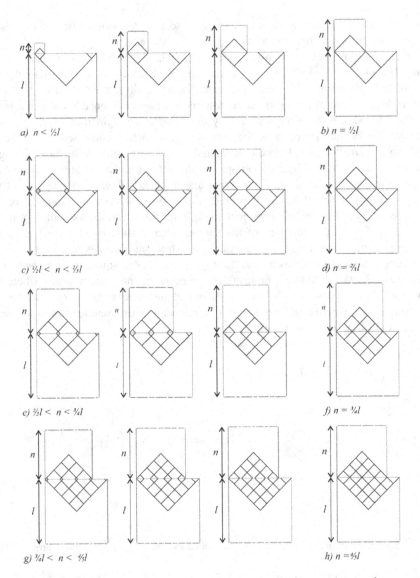

Fig. 6. Part structures resulting from two squares sharing a common edge

intuitively expected: the structure of the shorter edge remains unchanged and the structure of the longer edge includes the shorter edge as an embedded part. As a result, the structure of the shorter edge can be described by the string u, where u represents a line of length of $u = n$, and the structure of the longer edge can be described by the string uvu where v represents a line segment of length $v = l - 2n$. Increasing the edge length of the smaller square results in an increase in the length u, and a decrease in the length v. Specifically, as $n \rightarrow 1/2l, u \rightarrow 1/2l$ and $v \rightarrow 0$, and, in Fig. 6b, when $n = 1/2l$, $v = 0$ and the longer edge can be described by the string uu.

In Figs. 6c–h, $n > 1/2l$ and the embedded shorter edges overlap resulting in the emergence of more complicated structures, similar to Fig. 5. When $n > 1/2l$ embedding the shorter edge in the longer edge results in a decomposition of both edges, and as n increases the symbolic descriptions of the resulting part structures can be categorised according to the following cases:

- In Fig. 6c, $1/2l < n < 2/3l$, the short edge can be described by uvu and the long edge by $uvuvuv$. As $n \to 2/3l, u \to 1/3l$ and $v \to 0$
- In Fig. 6d, $n = 2/3l, u \to 1/3l$ and $v = 0$, the short edge can be described by uu and the long edge by uuu
- In Fig. 6e, $2/3l < n < 3/4l$, the short edge can be described by $uvuvu$ and the long edge by $uvuvuvu$. As $n \to 3/4l, u \to l$ and $v \to 0$
- In Fig. 6f, $n = 3/4l, u = 1/4l$ and $v = 0$, the short edge can be described by uuu and the long edge by $uuuu$
- In Fig. 6g, $3/4l < n < 4/5l$, the short edge can be described by $uvuvuvu$ and the long edge by $uvuvuvuvu$, and as $n \to 4/5l, u \to 1/5l$ and $v \to 0$
- In Fig. 6h, $n = 4/5l, u = 1/5l$ and $v = 0$, the short edge can be described by $uuuu$ and the long edge by $uuuuu$

The pattern identified here continues, tending towards the limiting case where $n = l$ and the two squares are the same size, with the edges of both squares represented by a single line. But, as $n \to l, u \to 0$, and the part structure of the edges gets get finer and finer with the number of line segments increasing. This structure is always defined according to line segments of two alternating lengths, and it can always be described as a periodic palindrome over u and v. In general, the structure of the shorter edge can be described by the string $(uv)^k u$, and the structure of the longer edge can be described by the string $(uv)^{k+1} u$, where u and v represent lines of length u and v, respectively, and k is a positive integer.

To make this explicit, let W represent a line of length l, A represent a line of length m, and B represent a line of length n. Embedding B in W, such that W and B retain their reflective symmetry, gives rise to a palindromic periodic structure, such that

$$A = uv$$
$$B = (uv)^k u$$
$$W = AB = uv(uv)^k u = (uv)^{k+1} u$$

where u is a line of length u, v is a line of length v and k is given by $\lceil n/m \rceil - 1$, where $\lceil \, \rceil$ is the ceiling function. The period of this structure is $u + v = m$, and given that $W = AB = (uv)^{k+1} u$ and $B = (uv)^k u$, the lengths l and n can be written

$$l = (k+2)u + (k+1)v$$
$$n = (k+1)u + kv$$

and it follows that

$$u = (k+1)n - kl$$
$$v = (k+1)l - (k+2)n$$

For example, if $n = 5/8l$, then $m = 3/8l$ and $k = \lceil 5/3 \rceil - 1 = 1$, $u = 1/4l$, $v = 1/8l$. This confirms observations of Fig. 6c, where the edge of the larger square is composed of three line segments of length u and two line segment of length v, so that $l = 3u + 2v$, and the edge of the smaller square is composed of two line segments of length u and one line segment of length v, so that $n = 2u + v$.

3   The Structure of Two Overlapping Squares

Using the results summarised in the previous section, it is possible to derive the palindromic periodic structure identified by Stiny [6] for implementing the computation in Fig. 1. The full computation, including all seven possible shapes, requires three distinct compositions, illustrated in Fig. 7, which result from recognising the small square, the large squares, and from rotating the two large squares so that line segments overlap. To account for these compositions in the part structure of the shape it is necessary that the edges of the large squares include lines of length equal to the edges of the small square and the overlap, as embedded parts. In Fig. 7, these lengths are represented by x, y and p respectively, with $y = 2x$ and $p = (2 - \sqrt{2})x$.

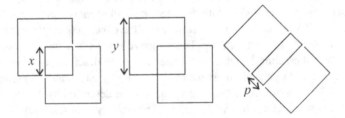

Fig. 7. Compositions necessary to implement the shape computation in Fig. 1

In the previous section it was shown that the structure that results from embedding one line as part of a second line is given by $(uv)^{k+1}u$. For a line of length $x = \frac{1}{2}y$ embedded in a line of length y, k is given by $\lceil x/(y-x) \rceil - 1 = 0$, and the resulting structure is therefore $u_x v_x u_x$, with subscripts used to identify the embedded line. The lengths of line segments u_x and v_x are respectively given by

$$u_x = (k+1)x - ky = x$$
$$v_x = (k+1)y - (k+2)x = y - 2x = 0$$

and the resulting part structure is therefore $u_x u_x$, as illustrated in Fig. 8a. Similarly, for a line of length $p = (2 - \sqrt{2})x$ embedded in a line of length y, k is given by $\lceil p/(y-p) \rceil - 1 = 0$ and the resulting part structure is therefore $u_p v_p u_p$, as illustrated in Fig. 8b. The lengths of line segments u_p and v_p are respectively given by

$$u_p = (k+1)p - ky = p = (2 - \sqrt{2})x$$
$$v_p = (k+1)y - (k+2)p = y - 2p = 2(\sqrt{2} - 1)x$$

The structures in Fig. 8 accommodate the three compositions illustrated in Fig. 7, and in order to implement the full computation in Fig. 1, a structure needs to be identified that incorporates both of these structures.

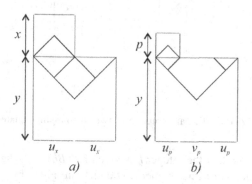

Fig. 8. Part structures resulting from compositions in Fig. 7

Representing the structures symbolically, it is required that

$$u_x u_x = u_p v_p u_p$$

This is shown visually in Fig. 9a, where u_x, u_p and v_p are represented by rectangles. Incorporating $u_x u_x$ in $u_p v_p u_p$ means that the overall part structure includes two distinct but equal parts which can be accommodated by separating v into front and back halves, so that $v_p = v_f v_b$, as illustrated in Fig. 9b.

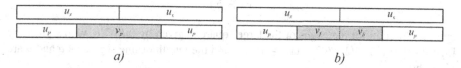

Fig. 9. Combinatorial structure, with lines represented by rectangles

This gives $u_x = u_p v_f$ and $u_x = v_b u_p$, which means that

$$u_p v_f = v_b u_p \tag{1}$$

Here, two structures are equated which share a common part, u_p, which is identified as the prefix of one structure and the suffix of the other. This composition is well understood in the mathematics of combinatorics, and Lyndon and Schützenberger [9] prove the following Lemma:

Lemma 1. If $AB = BC$ and $A \neq \varepsilon$, then $A = UV$, $B = (UV)^k U$ and $C = VU$ for some U, V and some integer $k \geq 0$.

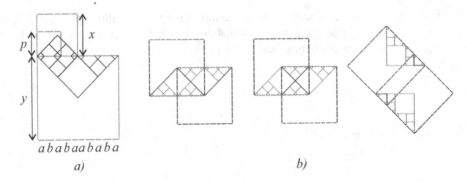

Fig. 10. The part structure of two overlapping squares

In [8] it was shown that the integer k is given by $\lceil B/A \rceil - 1$, where $\lceil \ \rceil$ is the ceiling function, and the lengths of line segments U and V are given by

$$U = (k+1)B - k(A+B)$$
$$V = (k+1)(A+B) - (k+2)B$$

From Lemma 1, the structures $AB = BC$ can be decomposed into a finer structure, $(UV)^{k+1}U$. This is the source of the periodic palindromic line structures identified by Stiny [6] and arises due to the reflective symmetry of the line: lines with identified parts are equal to their mirror images, which themselves contain the same parts. Applying Lemma 1 to Eq. (1) gives

$$v_b = ab$$
$$u_p = (ab)^k a$$
$$v_f = ba$$

and the structure for the edges of the large square is given by $(ab)^{k+1}a$, with k given by $\lceil u_p/v_f \rceil - 1 = \lceil (2 - \sqrt{2})x/(\sqrt{2} - 1)x \rceil - 1 = 1$, and the length of line segments a and b are given by

$$a = (k+1)u_p - ku_x = (3 - 2\sqrt{2})x$$
$$b = (k+1)u_x - (k+2)u_p = (3\sqrt{2} - 4)x$$

The resulting structure is *ababaababa*, with $b = a\sqrt{2}$, confirming the result found by Stiny [6]. This structure is illustrated in Fig. 10, where Fig. 10a shows the structure as it applies to the three lines x, y and p, while Fig. 10b shows the structure applied to the three compositions illustrated in Fig. 7.

4   The Structure of Three Overlapping Squares

Applying the shape rule in Fig. 1a to the shape in Fig. 2 also gives rise to a network of shapes in a visual shape computation, as illustrated in Fig. 11. The shapes produced are stylistically very similar to those in Fig. 1c, but with more squares embedded in the shape there are more opportunities to apply the rule. The resulting computation is again finite, involving only twenty-four distinct shapes, and these require five distinct compositions of the shape, as illustrated in Fig. 12. Applying the rule to the small square gives rise to a different composition than applying it to the medium squares, or the large squares, and further compositions results from rotating the two medium squares or the two large squares, so that line segments overlap.

To account for these compositions in the part structure of the shape it is necessary that the edges of the large squares include as embedded parts, lines of length equal to the edges of the small and medium squares as well as the small and large overlap. In Fig. 12, these lengths are represented by x, y, z, p, and q, with $y = 2x$, $z = 2y = 4x$, $p = (2 - \sqrt{2})x$, and $q = 2p = 2(2 - \sqrt{2})x$. As in the previous section, the part structure necessary to accommodate the full computation can be explored by considering the structures that arise from pair-wise combinations of the line segments, x, y, z, p, and q, with lines embedded as parts of other lines. There are ten different line-in-line combinations to consider, and the resulting part-structures are illustrated in Fig. 13. For the sake of legibility, these are not drawn to scale.

The existence of scaling relations between x, y, z, p, and q means that there is similarity between some of the structures, i.e. they are the same under isotropic scaling. Specifically, Fig. 13a is similar to Fig. 13f and i; Fig. 13b is similar to Fig. 13g; Fig. 13e is similar to Fig. 13j. This is because $z = 2y$, $y = 2x$, and $q = 2p$. Using these relations, it is possible to combine structures to accommodate the merger of the different compositions necessary to implement the computation in Fig. 11. For example, Fig. 14 illustrates two such combinations.

Figure 14a combines compositions that enable recognition of the large and medium squares and the rotation of both large and medium squares. It includes lines of length y, p and q, embedded as parts of the line of length z, but it does not include the line of length x which comes from the composition that enables recognition of the small squares. The resulting structure of z is *abaababababaabababaabababaababababaababa*, with $b = a\sqrt{2}$. Similarly, Fig. 14b combines the compositions that enable recognition of the large, medium and square squares and the rotation of the medium squares. It includes lines of length x, y and q, embedded as parts of the line of length z, but it does not include the line of length p which comes from the composition that enables rotation of the large squares. The resulting structure is *ababaababaababaababa*, with $b = a\sqrt{2}$.

In order to accommodate the full computation in Fig. 11, a part structure needs to be identified that incorporates both structures illustrated in Fig. 14. However, such a merger is impossible because the two structures are incommensurable. This can be shown by attempting to merge the structures illustrated in Fig. 13e and f, which would

Fig. 11. The result of an elementary shape computation

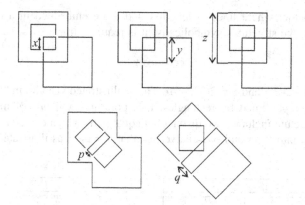

Fig. 12. Compositions necessary to implement the shape computation in Fig. 11

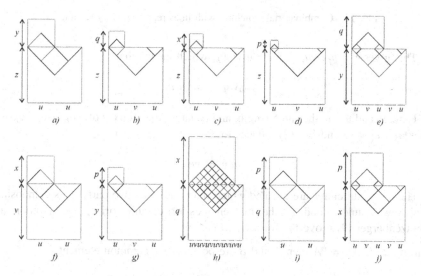

Fig. 13. Part structures resulting from compositions in Fig. 11

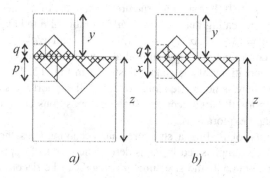

Fig. 14. Example part structures

result in a structure where lines of length x and q are embedded in a line of length y. Representing the structures symbolically, it is required that

$$xx = uvuvu$$

where, $u = 2(3 - 2\sqrt{2})x$ and $v = 2(3\sqrt{2}-4)x$. This is illustrated visually in Fig. 15a where x, u and v are represented by rectangles. Incorporating xx in $uvuvu$ means that the overall part structure includes two distinct but equal parts which can be accommodated by separating u into front and back halves, so that $u = u_f u_b$, as illustrated in Fig. 15b.

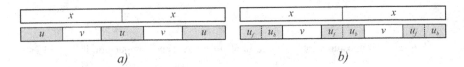

Fig. 15. Combinatorial structure, with lines represented by rectangles

This gives $x = u_f u_b v u_f$ and $x = u_b v u_f u_b$, which means that

$$u_f u_b v u_f = u_b v u_f u_b \tag{2}$$

Here, u_f and u_b are the same length, and equating the prefixes of $u_f u_b v u_f$ and $u_b v u_f u_b$ gives $u_f = u_b = u'$ and Eq. (2) reduces to

$$u'v = vu' \tag{3}$$

Here, two structures are equated which share the same two parts. This composition is also well understood in the mathematics of combinatorics, and Lyndon and Schützenberger [9] prove the following Lemma:

Lemma 2. If $AB = BA$ then A and B are powers of a common element.

Lemma 2 suggests that the structures $u'v = vu'$ can be decomposed into a finer structure defined according to a common element, i.e. $u' = a^i$ and $v = a^j$ for some integers $i \geq 0$ and $j \geq 0$. For such a structure the lengths of u' and v are given by ia and ja respectively, indicating that the ratio v/u' is a rational number j/i. This is clearly not true because $u' = (3 - 2\sqrt{2})x$ and $v = 2(3\sqrt{2} - 4)x$ and $v/u' = 2\sqrt{2}$, which is irrational. There is a contradiction, suggesting that there is no structure that will accommodate all the compositions of the shape illustrated in Fig. 12. This confirms Stiny's [6] suggestion that there is no single structure that will support the shape computation in Fig. 11 and supports the argument that shape compositions cannot be defined prior to carrying out shape explorations.

The impossibility of finding a structure that accommodates the computation in Fig. 11 can be further emphasised by considering the result of applying Lemma 1 to Eq. (3). Applying Lemma 1, the structures $u'v = vu'$ can be decomposed into a finer structure, to give

$$u' = a_1 b_1$$
$$v = (a_1 b_1)^i a_1$$
$$u' = b_1 a_1$$

for some integer i and line segments a_1 and b_1. But here we have $a_1 b_1 = u' = b_1 a_1$, so that

$$a_1 b_1 = b_1 a_1$$

Applying Lemma 1 again, a_1 and b_1 can be decomposed into a finer structure, to give

$$a_1 = a_2 b_2$$
$$b_1 = (a_2 b_2)^j a_2$$
$$a_1 = b_2 a_2$$

for some integer j and line segments a_2 and b_2. But here we have $a_2 b_2 = a_1 = b_2 a_2$, so that

$$a_2 b_2 = b_2 a_2$$

and Lemma 1 can be applied again. The same structure continues to reoccur over and over, as u' and v are decomposed into finer and finer parts in a process that tends towards the infinitesimals of Newtonian calculus. The process can only end when $a_\omega = 0$ or $b_\omega = 0$, for some integer ω. But the lengths of a_ω and b_ω are defined following iteration of

$$a_1 = (i+1)u' - i(u'+v)$$
$$b_1 = (i+1)(u'+v) - (i+2)u'$$

and consequently are linear combinations of u' and v. It follows that $a_\omega = 0$ or $b_\omega = 0$ only when $v = iu'$ or $v = (i+1)u'$, i.e. when the length of v is an integer multiple of the length of u', and u' and v are powers of a common element, as described in Lemma 2. But, this is not the case here, and it can be shown that for each subdivision $b_\omega = a_\omega \sqrt{2}$, and again there is a contradiction.

This argument has explored the possibility that the two part structures in Fig. 14 can be combined in a single composition. The existence of the contradiction proves that this is not possible, and consequently also proves that there is no structure that accommodates all the compositions illustrated in Fig. 12, and supports the shape computation illustrated in Fig. 11. Despite its visual simplicity it is not possible to implement the computation using a static hierarchy of predefined parts.

5 Discussion

Shape computations can be formulated as shape operations analogous to the conventional computations on word strings composed of vocabulary elements. These shape computations can transform shapes in a design process. However, word strings and shapes differ fundamentally. The former have an explicit and well-defined composition of vocabulary elements. The latter lacks an explicit composition. Shapes are not without compositions, however these require construction.

The history of construction of a shape can provide one possible composition [6] which will be familiar in parametric CAD. Other compositions arise from the ways that the shapes themselves are perceived with different views corresponding to different compositions. Both construction and perception provide compositions. Consider the example of the shape computation in Fig. 1. This can be viewed as a set (lattice) of constructions using the rule (Fig. 1a), starting with the shape (Fig. 1b). The constructions in the computation serve to pick out specific parts of the eight maximal lines in the shape. They also create a set of new shapes (Fig. 1c).

A shape can have unlimited possible compositions and one way to consider perceptual views is to equate each perception with a specific composition. Any finite set of parts (covering the whole shape) represents a possible composition and thus a possible perceptual view. However, two issues arise. First, the sets of parts will be augmented by sums, differences and intersections of parts. Second where does each composition come from? Or in other words what is the computation which created that composition? One approach to addressing these issues, especially the second, is to consider the compositions arising from the computations. A question might remain about whether each composition has a generating shape computation. However, more basically – and the focus of this paper – there remains a question about whether generating shape computations necessarily create valid compositions; which among other characteristics will have finite sets of parts. The compositions of a shape are descriptions of that shape in terms of its parts. Multiple descriptions of a design pose significant problems in applications of parametric CAD in several areas of design. In Architectural Design and Construction, BIM models require consistency across different descriptions, for example structural, layout, service and environmental [10]. In Engineering Design two issues emerge. First, generating and coordinating descriptions in different domains for product development; for example, product structures (bill of materials), manufacturing specifications, assembly, supply, service and maintenance; present significant issues for computational support [11, 12]. The second issue is: given two distinct descriptions, is there a consistent minimal 'covering' description?

The shape computation perspective on compositions (and descriptions) in CAD, developed in this paper, has revealed, albeit in simple examples, a critical problem. This is that even elementary shape computations do not necessarily create possible compositions. This has implications for CAD descriptions such as BoMs (Bills of Materials). If such descriptions are constructed ad-hoc for specific projects, then each associated composition can be considered as the result of a shape computation. However, putting two descriptions together may create a shape computation which does not yield a valid composition. In other words, although there may be a description in terms of the computation (and its associated rules), this description will not correspond to a finite set of parts.

The two squares example (Fig. 1) and its successors (Fig. 2, etc.) provide a striking example of scaling and its impossibility in simple, identifiable cases in principle. Common difficulties with scaling are not a question of logical impossibility, as they are for the successors of the two squares example. Difficulties arise because there is a lack of resources – material or time – to carry them out practicably. Merging the structures in Fig. 14 proves to be impossible because they are incompatible in terms of any underlying, finite set of common, non-zero elements. This highlights the special properties of shape computations that puts them beyond standard analytical techniques in CAD that require explicit, finite compositions beforehand – in shape computation, composition is an outcome of calculating, not a prerequisite – and it suggests both the difficulty of shape computation and the importance of re-examining algorithmic approaches to design that go beyond what is common practice today in parametric modelling and BIM. Shape computation presents a host of challenges both for visual design and for calculating beyond composition.

References

1. Woodbury, R.: Elements of Parametric Design. Routledge, London (2010)
2. Aish, R.: From intuition to precision. In: Duarte, J.P., Ducla-Soares, G., Zita, S.A. (eds.) Digital Design: The Quest for New Paradigms, 23rd eCAADe Conference Proceedings, Lisbon, Portugal, pp. 21–24 (2005)
3. Prats, M., Earl, C.F.: Exploration through drawings in the conceptual stages of product design. In: Gero, J. (ed.) Design Computing and Cognition 2006, pp. 83–102. Springer, Dordrecht (2006)
4. Prats, M., Lim, S., Jowers, I., Garner, S., Chase, S.: Transforming shape in design: observations from studies of sketching. Des. Stud. **30**, 503–520 (2009)
5. Schön, D.A., Wiggins, G.: Kinds of seeing and their functions in designing. Des. Stud. **13**, 135–156 (1992)
6. Stiny, G.: Shape: Talking about Seeing and Doing. MIT Press, Cambridge (2006)
7. Stiny, G.: Shape rules: closure, continuity, and emergence. Environ. Plann. B Plann. Des. **21**, 49–78 (1994)
8. Jowers, I., Earl, C.: Structures in shapes: a perspective from rules and embedding. In: Cultural DNA Workshop 2017, KAIST Graduate School of Culture Technology, Republic of Korea (2017)
9. Lyndon, R.C., Schützenberger, M.P.: The equation aM = bNcP in a free group. Mich. Math. J. **9**, 289–298 (1962)
10. Eastman, C., Teicholz, P., Sacks, R., Liston, K.: BIM Handbook: A Guide to Building Information Modeling for Owners, Managers, Designers, Engineers and Contractors. Wiley, New Jersey (2011)
11. McKay, A., Stiny, G.N., de Pennington, A.: Principles of the definition of design structures. Int. J. Comput. Integr. Manuf. **29**, 1–14 (2016)
12. Behera, A.K., McKay, A., Chau, H.H., Robinson, M.A.: Embedding multiple design structures into design definitions: a case study of a collision avoidance robot. In: proceedings of International Design Conference, Dubrovnik, Croatia, pp. 119–128 (2016)

The Marching Shape

Extensions to the Ice-Ray Shape Grammar

Alexandros Tsamis[✉] [iD]

Adolfo Ibanez University, Santiago, Chile
tsamis@gmail.com

Abstract. Contemporary voxel based CAD software uses a predetermined voxel space as a property placeholder for establishing relationships between boundaries and properties (weights). The Marching Shape algorithm, developed as an extension of the Ice Ray Shape Grammar, demonstrate how similar relationships between weights and boundaries can be developed without the fixed structure of Voxels. An extended Ice-Ray is presented that includes rules and schemas for polygons of more than 5 vertices, rules for the manipulation of weights as well as rules that establish relationships between them.

Keywords: Marching · Shape · Ice-Ray · Voxels · Weights

1 Introduction

The recent shift of attention in the architectural/design discourse towards issues of materiality has already put under great scrutiny the workflows of contemporary CAD. Notable examples are the work of [1, 2] and more recently [3, 4]. Through their research projects they all seem to challenge the established hierarchies that exist today in most Boundary Representation (B-Rep) software. One limitation that is being acknowledged is that a B-Rep software does not allow an explicit description of material variability within a volumetric representation, that each volume can only be represented as a discrete homogeneous entity [5] that material - the variation of property in space - is not a manipulable entity within B-Rep CAD [6] or that material compositions in B-Rep are only assigned on a macro level [2].

In an attempt to address issues of materiality and make material properties part of the design process within CAD, Oxman, Tsamis, Payne & Michalatos and Richards & Amos suggest a design model based on Voxels. Unlike B-Rep software that is structured around a Cartesian coordinate system, their work shows how a voxel space can be used as *a property placeholder for calculating with boundaries and properties* [6], as a *multichannel discretized volume that can hold shape and material mixing properties* [5] or as a *material space that can be extended to represent physical and tensor properties* [2]. Especially [6] with his VSpace and [5] with Monolith - now part of Autodesk - have shown how a voxel based representation can be developed to incorporate, various instantiation methods, unary transformation methods as well as binary transformation methods (Fig. 1).

© Springer Nature Singapore Pte Ltd. 2017
G. Çağdaş et al. (Eds.): CAAD Futures 2017, CCIS 724, pp. 366–380, 2017.
DOI: 10.1007/978-981-10-5197-5_20

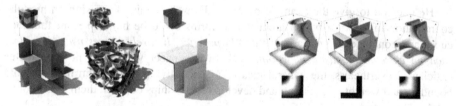

Fig. 1. Boundaries defined in a Voxel Space. *left* VSpace - *right* Monolith

A voxel space is a discrete volume of space that is homogeneously divided using an ordered 3 dimensional array of cubical units (voxels) that is defined by their number, shape, size and location in space. Therefore all of these approaches begin by defining a space - **a canvas** - that although it replaces the Cartesian coordinate system and allows for properties (weights) to be manipulated in space, it nevertheless imposes its unitary structure on any design operation. Similarly to how in a raster based software the image resolution in pixels imposes its structure to the image, the number, size, shape and location of voxels impose their structure to the volumetric representations. Even more specifically, if we look closely at VSpace and Monolith, any form (Fig. 1) is produced as a subset of the voxels in the voxel space (this subset is called a *Property Shape* in the case of VSpace and a *Shape Channel* in the case of Monolith). Therefore at any given point during the design process, with a given number of voxels I x J x K of a voxel space, all possible shapes that can be derived are limited in number to:

$$2^{I \times J \times K} \tag{1}$$

This number can potentially be very big as voxel space resolutions increase but nevertheless the fact still remains that all possible shape designs are countable. In this paper we will demonstrate an alternative approach to space dividing, one that does not predefine and fix subdivisions but instead allows the designer to define the subdivisions of a canvas at the same time as the design process evolves. We have developed the Marching Shape as an extension to the Shape Grammar Ice-Ray in order to define an alternative methodology to building a **canvas** that can still allow properties (weights) to be directly manipulated in space without the limitations of a predefined voxel structure.

2   Background: Voxels and Ice-Rays. The Ice-Ray as a Space Dividing Algorithm

William J. Mitchell suggests in his book "*The Logic of Architecture*", that Voxels first made their appearance as a mode of architectural representation as early as 1936. He writes:

> *In a three-dimensional Cartesian coordinate system, space can be filled, to any desired density, with a cubic array of points. When states are associated with these gridpoints they are known as Voxels-volumetric elements: Voxel (point(x, y, z), **State**) ... In this case the description of state is elaborated to allow representation of spatial distribution of material, thus: Voxel (point (x, y, z), **Material**).*

He goes on to give the example of Albert Farwell Bemis' discussion on modular coordination of 1936 in which architectural forms could be built up from four-inch cubes and concludes by remarking that "*In practice, it rarely proves useful to adopt such an extreme atomistic viewpoint*" [7]. In this paper we adopt and extend this criticism. Nevertheless, the general idea of a space dividing algorithm that can hold boundary and weight information and develop relationships between them is still for us valid.

In 1971, Lionel March and Philip Steadman, demonstrated how voxels - or "cubelets" - can be systematically used to enable a comprehensive description of a type of architectural forms. They describe a computational approach to architectural form using cubelets, in an attempt to link architectural design with the pragmatics of industrial technologies. They generalized this approach by using boolean algebras to provide a precise mathematical description of the cubelet sets. They showed how within a two-dimensional array (grid) of four squares, 16 subsets can be derived as possible combinations. They implemented this algebra to demonstrate how those sets can be used to describe existing plan configurations and just like Bemis did before them, they described the plan of Le Corbusier's Maison Minimum using a "hexadecimal code" [8].

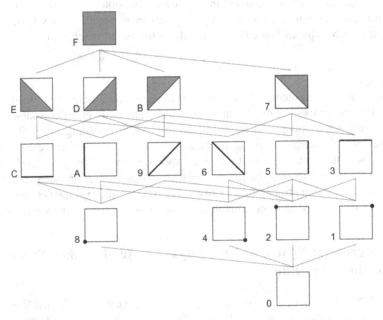

Fig. 2. Lionel March, planes, lines and points from 2d cell (redrawn by author)

With the "Boolean Description of a Class of Built Form", Lionel March extends his previous work with voxels/cubelets and squares [9]. He critiques that his previous descriptive method was limited to forms made from adding rectangular forms together. In this new extension, he describes rectangular and non-rectangular forms by using cells as "scaffolds" upon which boundaries can be drawn using the vertices of a given grid. He shows how for a given 2dimesional cell, there are multiple combinations of planes lines and points that can be drawn (Fig. 2) and he goes on to demonstrate how this Boolean algebra can be implemented also in 3 dimensions (Fig. 3) to describe Mies' Seagram Building or even a "beveled" version of it by using a cube's vertices.

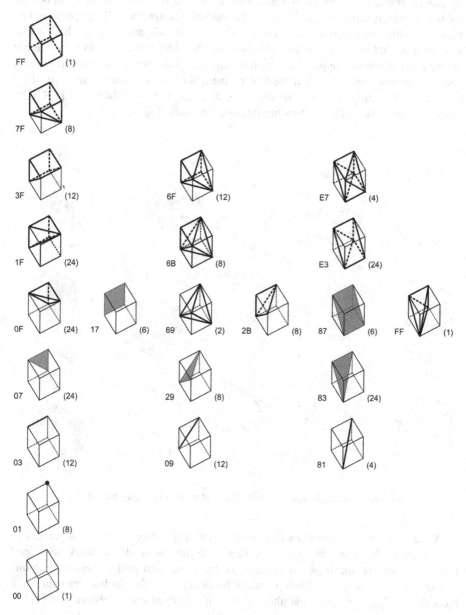

Fig. 3. Lionel March. Solids, planes, lines and points from 3D cell (redrawn by author)

Today, contemporary approaches to Voxel modeling, are direct extensions of the "Boolean Description of a Class of Built Form". Boundaries in software like VSpace and Monolith are visualized by employing what is known as the Marching Cube algorithm. It was first published in the 1987 SIGGRAPH proceedings by William E. Lorensen and Harvey E. Cline and was initially developed for the medical imaging industry for the visualization of data taken from CT and MRI scans. It was basically developed in order to reconstruct 3dimensional surfaces out of Voxel data and is used today extensively among other fields in the medical imaging and 3D graphics industries. The difference between the Lionel March approach and the Marching Cube algorithm is that weights are also attached on the cube vertices. This is what has allowed contemporary approaches to link together boundaries and properties in a common design space. Using a method of interpolation, boundaries are derived by calculating how they intersect voxel edges at a specified weight value [10]. The algorithm uses one of the 15 possible intersection cases (Fig. 4).

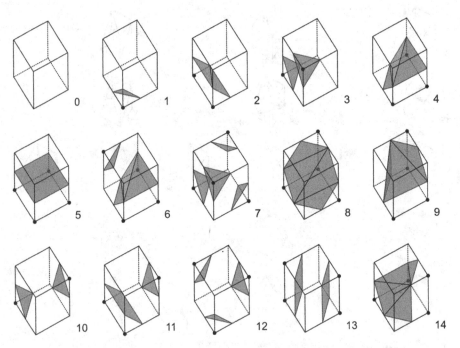

Fig. 4. 15 cases of the Marching Cube algorithm (redrawn by author)

What all of these approaches have in common is that they work with a predefined grid of cubes. From the first works of Bemis, to the computational work developed today with voxels, the imposed structure of the predefined grid is evident. For this reason we have chosen to develop similar boundary - weight algebras by using as a basis the Ice Ray algorithm that altogether dismisses fixed space subdivisions [11].

The Ice-Ray Shape Grammar was first introduced in 1977 in order to show how seemingly irregular patterns observed with Chinese lattice designs can be generated by a set of shape grammar rules (Fig. 5). Although they were originally conceived as a grammar that derives Chinese window frames, it is easy to see that in its most generalized form it can be reinterpreted as an algorithm for dividing space into units that can be defined by the designer during the design process and not beforehand. Indeed Stiny seems to suggest that Ice-Rays can work in various algebras for painting and architecture, and gives the examples of Klee's palm-leaf umbrellas, the paintings of Vantongerloo and Glaner as well as the architecture of Siza, the vernacular architecture in medieval Treviso etc. [12]. If we compare the Ice-Rays to the contemporary approach to Voxel Modeling a few things become evident. Unlike Voxels that have a predetermined number, size, shape and location, with Ice-Rays the same parameters are not fixed in space or time. In other words, the Ice-Ray, proposes an alternative space dividing algorithm, that although includes regular grids as its possible outcome, it opens up the possibility for an infinite amount of polygonal subdivisions that can be dynamically defined as the design process evolves.

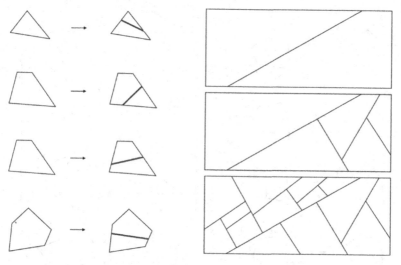

Fig. 5. George Stiny: the Ice-Ray Shape Grammar (redrawn by author)

Taking as a point of departure the algebras of the Chinese lattices, we will demonstrate how the Ice-Ray can be developed further in order to hold and manipulate properties in space without imposing a predetermined structure on the designer during the design process. For the purposed of this demonstration all examples will be shown in a 2D space. Furthermore, all extensions will be expressed in two ways; first as visual right-left type rules and schemas - in traditional shape grammar fashion - and second as a *computer application* structure.[1]

---

[1] It is imperative for the authors to make a distinction between the two modes of representation and discuss essential discrepancies that occur between them in a later publication.

3　Extension 01: Ice-Ray: General Polygon Rules and Schemas

As we saw earlier the original Ice-Ray rules can generate subdivisions of polygons P with 3, 4 or 5 edges, resulting in new triangles, quadrilaterals or pentagonal polygons. By recursively applying these rules to existing polygons, Ice-Rays develop as divided spaces made up of only triangles, quadrilaterals and pentagonal polygons. In the case of its use as a general space dividing algorithm these rules would have to include polygons of higher dimensions N. For example, a pentagonal polygon is divided into a hexagonal polygon and a triangle, a hexagonal polygon into a heptagonal and a triangle and so on. Left - right type rules could be added (Fig. 6). These rules can be infinitely extended and added to the list of rules while the design process is taking place.

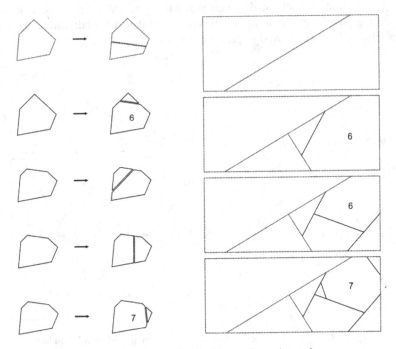

Fig. 6. Added ice ray rules for higher dimension polygons

Two general schemas can describe all possible subdivisions. The first one can describe all general subdivisions:

$$P(X) \rightarrow P(Y) + P(Z) \text{ where:} \tag{2}$$

a. X, Y, Z are positive integers greater or equal to 3
b. $X = (Y + Z) - 4$
c. P is a convex polygon

while a second schema can describe a special case in which polygons are subdivided by connecting two vertices of the same polygon.

$$P(X) \rightarrow P(Y) + P(Z) \text{ where:} \tag{3}$$

a. X, Y, Z are positive integers greater or equal to 3
b. $X = (Y + Z) - 2$
c. P is a convex polygon

For a *computer application* the generalized Ice – Ray can be coded in the following way. Every operation starts with a polygon that has a unique ID and is defined by an ordered (clockwise or counter-clockwise) array of points that correspond to the vertices of the polygon. Any subdivision of a polygon substitutes the original polygon by two new ones by substituting the original array of points with two new ones:

$$\text{Arr}[01]\,(A,B,C,D) \rightarrow \text{Arr}[02]\,(A,B,E,F,D) + \text{Arr}[03]\,(E,C,F) \tag{4}$$

The two new arrays have to maintain the points ordered. In a recursive way original polygon arrays get substituted. In the case that a polygon does not get subdivided but a subdivision point becomes part of one of its edges, that point is added to the corresponding polygon (Fig. 7).

$$\text{Arr}[02]\,(A,B,E,F,D) \rightarrow \text{Arr}[05]\,(H,G,F,D) + \text{Arr}[04]\,(A,B,E,G,H) + \text{Arr}[03]\,(E,C,F,G) \tag{5}$$

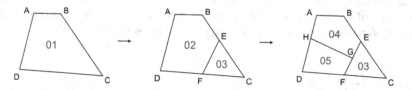

Fig. 7. Point order in Ice Ray computer application

Unlike pixels which are all of the same size and shape and have a predetermined relationship between them, the extend Ice-Ray rules and schema allow the designer to derive a variable unit subdivision of any shape or density during the design process.

4 Extension 02: Ice-Ray: Weights

As we saw earlier, in contemporary approaches, voxels are used to store properties (weights) so that they can also participate the design process. Ice-Ray unit subdivisions like all shapes in shape grammars can have weights associated with them. The Ice-Ray rules can be modified (Fig. 8) so that any property, color, channel etc. can be subdivided to any other.

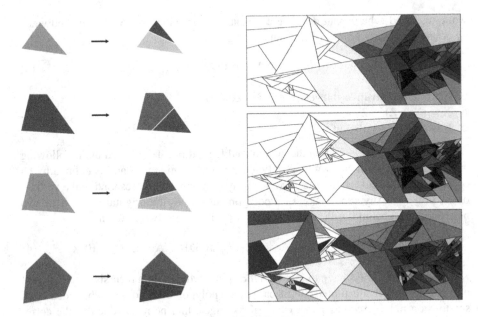

Fig. 8. Weighted Ice-Rays

For a *computer application*, every time a polygon gets subdivided, the weight assigned to it gets associated with all of its vertices. Since many vertices in the resulting Ice Rays belong to more than one polygons, the weight of a particular vertex becomes the average of all the weights of the polygons that the vertex belongs to (Fig. 9). For example, Vertex G, gets the average weight of polygons 05, 04 and 03.

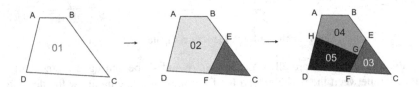

Fig. 9. Weight vertex association

For a *computer application* a special case of weight subdivision may be applied. As a polygon gets subdivided, its weight can also get subdivided into parts proportional to the distance of subdivision. This special case subdivision can be used to average weights between polygons as more subdivisions are added (Fig. 10).

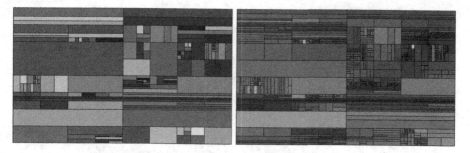

Fig. 10. Weight subdivision. Initial state left - final state right

5 The Marching Shape

In order to associate weights with boundaries (iso-surfaces), as we saw earlier, both VSpace and Monolith use the Marching Cubes algorithm [3, 6]. Its 2dimensional equivalent - the marching square - uses a predetermined set of $2^4 = 16$ possible configurations (Fig. 11) and calculates boundaries at "iso values" by selecting from the list. The cases are determined based on how many vertices of the square are greater or equal to the desired "iso value" that is being calculated. The algorithm then goes through every square in the grid and assigns to it one of the 16 cases. Using symmetry and rotation the cases can be reduced to 4 (Fig. 11).

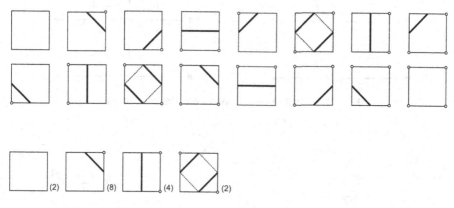

Fig. 11. All marching squares cases above - reduced cases below.

If we were to follow the same approach for an extended Ice-Ray (for triangles, quadrilaterals, pentagonal and hexagonal polygons) we would get a list of cases that could be reduced with symmetry and rotation to the following table (Fig. 12). It becomes quite evident that as the number of vertices in a polygon increases, the number of possible cases also exponentially increases.

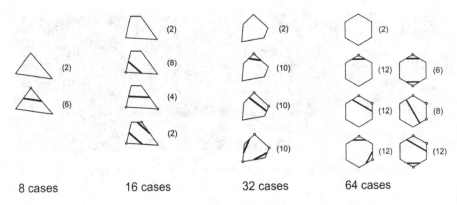

Fig. 12. The Marching Shape as shape grammar rules

Since the extended Ice-Ray does not have a fixed type of unit, and as we saw earlier it can produce polygons with "extra" vertices embedded along its edges, the Marching Shape (Fig. 13) proposes a more generalized approach that could be equally applied to all cases of polygons. In order to calculate boundaries according to the desired "iso-value" the Marching Shape considers each polygon as an "unfolded" poly-line, determines if a point of that poly-line is above or equal to the desired value and uses one of the two following rules to derive boundaries.

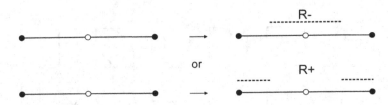

Fig. 13. Visual representation of the Marching Shape

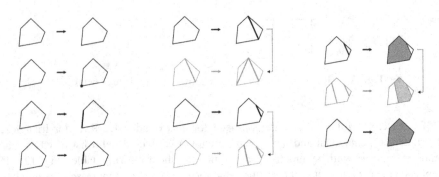

Fig. 14. Points, lines and planes in the Marching Shape for a Pentagon

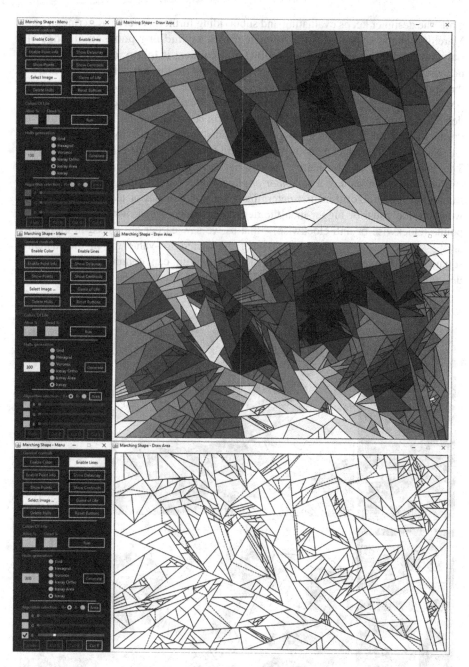

Fig. 15. Workflow of Marching Shape

Each of the two rules can be chosen independently and applied in an Ice Ray regardless of the number of vertices in the definition of the specific polygon. Furthermore, the rule can be applied repeatedly (without breaking the overall topology) while the designer keeps evaluating and subdividing further. A verbal description of the Marching Shape algorithm is the following: **pick or find any point on an edge of a polygon (including start and end point) and connect it to any other point on any other edge of the same polygon.** If we analytically go through all possible results of the application of this rule to a given extended Ice_Ray (Fig. 14) we get to a list of possible shape grammars rules that show how we can derive, points, lines and planes as desired iso-curves. The rules are shown here for a pentagon and in effect mirror the original set of rules of March's boolean algebras without the fixity of a grid.

The Marching Shape, extends the marching square to include all possible polygons. The goal here is to also derive boundaries based on a distribution of properties (weights) on a canvas. For a *computer application* the same verbal rule is applied. The Marching Shape algorithm first determines if a polygon has at least one vertex with weight value equal or bigger than the desired iso-value. Then, it runs through all the points (clockwise or anti-clockwise) - that as we saw earlier are stored in an ordered array - finds the appropriate locations of the deired iso-value (as in the marching square) and connects between them. This algorithm can continuously run as the designer keeps subdividing the canvas (Figs. 15 and 16).

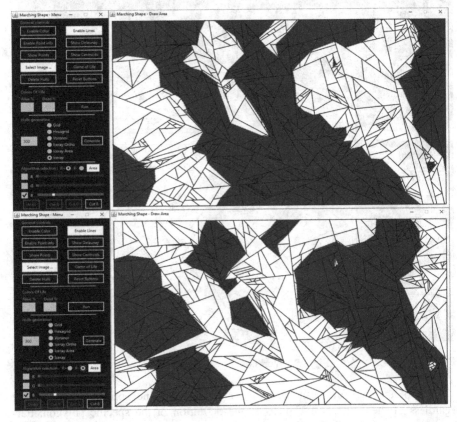

Fig. 16. Application of R − and R + rules in Marching Shape

When considering the Marching Shape in relation to the Marching Square, and interesting consequence emerges as a result of their respective structures. In a Marching Square, the canvas (grid of points) and the iso-curves are two distinct entities that always remain separate (Fig. 17).

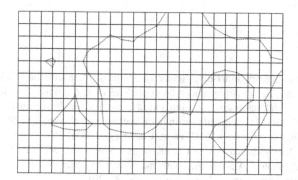

Fig. 17. Iso-curves in Marching Square

On the other hand, with the Marching Shape the current iso curve can be used to literally **cut** the canvas at its specific location (Fig. 18). In other words, in this case the two independently defined entities, Canvas and Iso-Curve, can collapse into one, giving the designer the possibility to use derived boundaries from the canvas to affect the canvas subdivision itself.

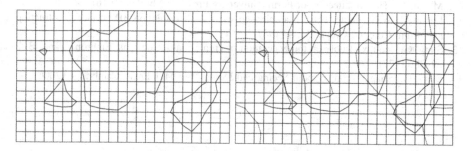

Fig. 18. Iso_curve cut canvas in Marching Shape

6 Conclusion

Although, a "property representation" paradigm seems to complement very well current B-Rep software and has opened up a new direction in the development of computer applications that can deal with the representation of form and materiality through boundaries and properties, we believe that the imposed voxel structure greatly limits the design process by converting it into a combinatorial process. The Marching Shape on the other hand, as an extension of the Ice-Ray can provide an alternative that although maintains the property to boundary relationships and all subsequent operations that are involved in software applications such as VSpace and Monolith, it does not limit the designer with predetermined resolutions and other type of only "zero dimensional calculations" [12].

References

1. Tsamis, A.: Go brown. Inner-disciplinary conjectures. In: Kallipoliti, L. (ed.) Ecoredux: Design Remedies for an Ailing Planet (Architectural Design). Wiley, London (2010)
2. Pinochet, P.D.: Making gestures: design and fabrication through real time human computer interaction. Thesis, Massachusetts Institute of Technology, Cambridge (2015)
3. Noë, A.: Action in Perception. MIT Press, Cambridge (2004)
4. Oxman, N.: Material-based Design Computation. Ph.D. thesis, MIT (2010)
5. Michalatos, P., Payne, A.: Working with multi-scale material distributions. In: ACADIA 2013, Adaptive Architecture, Cambridge, pp. 43–50 (2013)
6. Richards D., Amos M.: Designing with gradients: bio-inspired computation for digital fabrication. In: ACADIA 2014, Design Agency, Los Angeles (2014)
7. Payne, A., Michalatos, P.: Monolith. continuity and differentiation within volumetric models. In: Grigoriadis, K. (ed.) Mixed Matters. A Multi-Material Design Compendium, pp. 30–39. JOVIS Verlag GmbH, Germany (2016)
8. Tsamis, A.: Software Tectonics, Ph. D. thesis, MIT Department of Architecture, Cambridge, MA (2012)
9. Mitchell, W.J.: The Logic of Architecture. MIT Press, Cambridge (1990)
10. March, L., Steadman, P.: The Geometry of Environment. RIBA Publications Limited, London (1971)
11. March, L.: The Architecture of Form. University Press, Cambridge (1976)
12. Lorensen, W.E., Cline, H.E.: Marching cubes: a high resolution 3D surface construction algorithm. Comput. Graph. **21**, 4 (1987)
13. Stiny, G.: Ice-ray: a note on the generation of chinese lattice designs. Environ. Plann. B **4**, 89–98 (1977)
14. Stiny, G.: Shape: Talking about Seeing and Doing. The MIT Press, Cambridge (2006)

Outlining Terragni

A Riddle Reworked

Hayri Dortdivanlioglu[(⊠)] and Athanassios Economou

Georgia Institute of Technology, Atlanta, USA
hayri@gatech.edu

Abstract. Despite his controversial political background, the leading architect of the Italian Rationalist Movement, Giuseppe Terragni, has attracted the attention of a large group of architectural scholars. He has often been acknowledged as an enigmatic architect whose work oscillated between classicism and modernism. This work takes on two of the most emblematic projects by Terragni, the Mambretti Tomb and the Danteum and provides a formal generation of both projects in the form of two parametric shape grammars to inquire on the possibility of a common compositional strategy underlying both projects. A new interpretation of Terragni's work as a non-classical/classical computational model is given in the end.

Keywords: Shape grammars · Generative design · Architectural language · Type and style · Italian rationalism

1 Introduction

In 1991, the Yale exhibition 'Giuseppe Terragni: Two Projects', coupled two unbuilt projects by Terragni, the lesser known Mambretti Tomb and the well-known Danteum in the same architectural setting to foreground the architect's formal language and reflect upon his possible motives and intentions [1]. The two projects shared many commonalities: they were both unbuilt; they were both designed during the later mature career of the architect; they were both amply documented and developed allowing for an in-depth analysis; they both foregrounded a commemorative and symbolically laden program; and significantly, as the curators of the exhibition wrote, both exemplified "a personally imposed agenda which informs, indeed drives, these works" [1]. The two projects are shown in Fig. 1.

This work here takes on the same two unbuilt projects by Terragni to reflect upon the exhibition, test its outcome and claims, offer alternative methods to foreground the principles and the logic upon which such claims can be made, and ultimately suggest a new interpretation of the work. More precisely, the work here provides a formal specification of the Mambretti Tomb and the Danteum in the form of two parametric shape grammars [2] that can be used to reconstruct them. Contrary to the formal analysis of the exhibition that concentrates on the relation between form and symbolism using underlying schemata of specific proportional shapes and spatial relations, this work defines specific visual rules for each project that when taken together

© Springer Nature Singapore Pte Ltd. 2017
G. Çağdaş et al. (Eds.): CAAD Futures 2017, CCIS 724, pp. 381–394, 2017.
DOI: 10.1007/978-981-10-5197-5_21

(a)

(b)

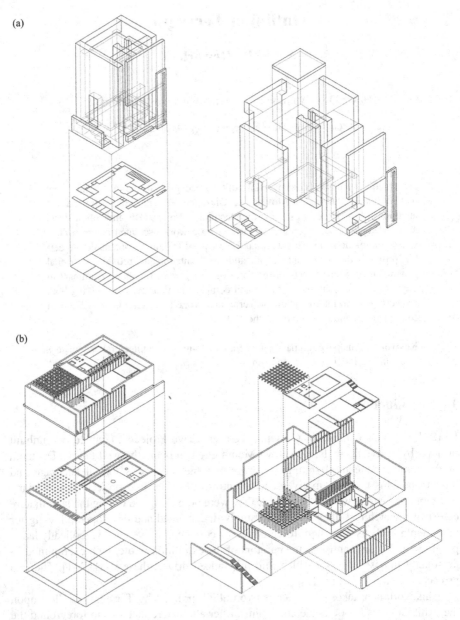

Fig. 1. Composite axonometrics of the two Terragni projects including plan, parti diagram, model and exploded model. (a) The Mambretti Tomb; (b) The Danteum. (Drawing by authors)

foreground explicit similarities and differences between the two projects and suggest logical inferences and constructions between both. More broadly, this work aims at uncovering systematic deep structures behind both projects in order to gain a better insight in the ways formal vocabularies and spatial relations within Terragni's work express the architect's constructive deployment and transformation of compositional principles of neoclassicism and modernism.

The study on the formal generative analysis of the Mambretti Tomb and the Danteum is presented in four parts. The first part presents a brief overview of the current state-of-the art of the critical assessment of Terragni's work and the eluding character of Terragni's architecture that constantly defies ready-made characterizations and conventions. The second part provides a brief description of the two projects along with a schematic analysis of their underlying construction. The third part provides a formal generative description of the two projects in the form of two parametric shape grammars. The last part concludes with a critical discussion on both grammars, their interrelations and products, and the possibilities they offer in helping interpret Terragni's enigmatic motives.

2   The Design of the Mambretti Tomb and the Danteum

The Mambretti Tomb (1937–1938) and the Danteum (1938–1939) were developed roughly at the same time during the later part of Terragni's career. The Mambretti Tomb was commissioned as a funerary monument to be built near Lago Maggiore. The Danteum was commissioned by the director of the Royal Brera Academy in Milan as a museum and library to canonize 'the greatest of Italian poets', Dante Alighieri. Even though they are both unbuilt – as many of Terragni's projects – they are routinely included in critical surveys of the architect's work that contain several significant projects of the Italian modern movement and mid-war twentieth century architecture such as the Novocomum (1929), the Casa del Fascio (1936), the Asilo Sant'Elia (1937), the Casa Giuliani Frigerio (1940) and several others, all designed within a very brief professional career lasting only 15 years. The two projects have attracted a mixed reception from architectural critics over the years. Early historicist and narrative literature on Terragni, unfairly motivated by political conviction, positioned them among other contemporary projects by Italian modernists working under the fascist regime as empty and formulaic [3]. Latter critics were much more sympathetic. Manfredo Tafuri, in his essay "Giuseppe Terragni: Subject and 'Masks'", appraised the abstract nature of Terragni's thoughts and positions these projects and his general work outside the realm of the political sphere of Italian fascism [4]. Thomas Schumacher also appraised both projects seeing them as instances of the wider body of Terragni's work that oscillates between modernism and classicism, abstraction and figuration. For Schumacher, the abstract formal elements of the two projects and especially the Danteum's foregrounded an enigmatic language that reflected the ambiguity of the era in which they were produced: "the polemic of late thirties on abstraction, narration, symbolism, nationalism, and internationalism masked the reality by pronouncements and ambiguity of architectural forms read as political symbols" [5]. More recently, Kanekar has further foregrounded the symbolic characteristics of Terragni's Danteum privileging a much more complex and multifaceted relation to literature [6].

Interestingly, both projects are not prominent in a second prevalent strand of critical scholarship on Terragni's architecture that focuses on the formal analysis of his work, his architectural vocabulary and the formal meaning that can be derived by its manipulations. Paradigmatic in this body of work are Eisenman's studies on the Casa del Fascio and Casa Giuliani-Frigerio [7] and Flemming's grammar for the Casa Frigerio's façade [8]. Still, both projects appear in a more recent work in CAAD analysis by Galli and Mühlhoff where the authors have attempted to digitally reconstruct several unbuilt Terragni projects and critically discuss the conventions used to produce the complete models [9]. More appearances of the two projects can be found in recent scholarship that focuses in the historical documentation of Terragni's prolific output and the systematic survey and description of his projects, both built and unbuilt [10–12].

A significant characteristic that binds both projects together is that they were developed with a heavy narrative program laden with symbolic meaning. Before the 1991 Exhibition at Yale that coupled the Danteum with the Mambretti Tomb, Schumacher pointed out their shared compositional origins: "Formally and constructively, the Mambretti Tomb is the quintessence of Terragni's architecture at the late thirties. Monumental in its form and purpose, yet diminutive in its size, the Tomb shows Terragni wrestling with compositional ideas he will soon develop in a fully orchestrated way in the Danteum project, the ill-fated Dante museum intended for Rome." [3] It is precisely this claim and insight by the Terragni scholar that is taken on here: the quest for the ways these compositional ideas shift, change, and crystallize structuring the formation of the abstract language of the architect.

3   The Geometry of the Mambretti Tomb and the Danteum

The Mambretti Tomb is composed of two distinctive parts: an underground crypto room and a monumental altar above. The altar is based on a square schema: it is composed of a single central volume with two large openings towards the south and the west. These two openings provide entrances to the main volume, the monumental altar, which is connected to the crypto room through vertical circulation. The planar formation of the altar volume provides the distinctive architectural language of the Tomb structure; planes are used in various configurations: squares, rectangles and L-shapes, free standing, superimposed and in reflected and rotated formations, defying gravity and showcasing a definitive change in Terragni's language of funerary works from a manipulation of plastic solids towards a planar, mural composition. A set of three plans, two sections and one elevation of the Mambretti Tomb is given in Fig. 2.

The Danteum is composed of four distinctive parts: a courtyard, a hypostyle hall, and two rooms consisting of undulating floors with horizontal surfaces at various depths. These four rooms are all connected through a continuous circulation from one to another. The circulation starting from the entrance of the courtyard follows an ascending order all the way to the top of the monumental staircase and leads to the ground level again. In the overall design, Terragni uses a limited palette of architectural elements including walls, columns, stairs and platforms all arranged upon a set of overlapping squares and rectangles. The architectural elements are formed through the extrusion of simple, rectangular two-dimensional shapes including squares and rectangles in various proportions. The three-dimensional configuration of the Danteum can be traced as a one-to-one mapping of solid architectural elements on the plan layout. A set of three plans, two sections and one elevation of the Danteum is given in Fig. 2.

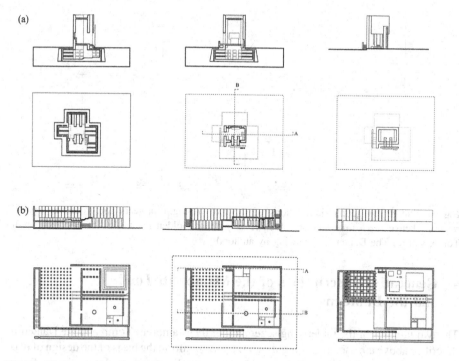

Fig. 2. Plans, sections and elevations of the two Terragni projects. (a) The Mambretti Tomb (b) The Danteum (Drawing by authors).

The geometric constructions and the architectonic expressions of the two projects display great resemblances despite the difference of scale and degree of spatial complexity between them. Both projects exhibit a strong geometric organization characterized by rectangular shapes and spatial relations that elude a straightforward mapping of some alleged programmatic expression. The underlying geometry of both projects based on the construction of golden section and resulting spatial relations between golden rectangles has been discussed in various sources [1, 3, 5]. A series of abstract layout schemata underlying both projects' parti schemas and their affinity to the golden section are constructed here to foreground prevalent spatial relations within the two projects. Each parti diagram emerges from the juxtaposition of a square and a golden rectangle [13]. The generated geometry is divided into proportional sub-geometries by the help of auxiliary lines. Design operations including inserting divisions, shifting and sliding squares are applied according to these sub-geometries. Three alternative constructions including the geometrical construction of the golden rectangle and the partis for the two projects are given in Fig. 3.

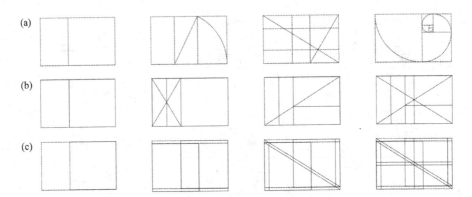

Fig. 3. Underlying geometric relations of the two Terragni projects foregrounding spatial relations between a square and a golden rectangle. (a) Golden rectangle; (b) The Mambretti Tomb; and (c) The Danteum. (Drawing by authors).

4   Generative Descriptions of the Mambretti Tomb and the Danteum

The two families of the underlying schemata for the Mambretti Tomb and the Danteum described above are used in a straightforward way to inform the basis of the design of two parametric shape grammars that provide the formal generative descriptions of the Mambretti Tomb and the Danteum respectively. The shape rules are based on a detailed geometrical analysis of the spatial elements of the underlying schemata and their relations as well as the forms of the architectural elements and their relations to the underlying geometric schemata. Both grammars are defined in three main stages: (a) layout; (b) architectonics; and (c) termination. In the first stage, shape rules for plan layouts are defined to create the interplay of the offset rectangles and their threshold arrangements. In the second stage, labeled shape rules are defined for rooms, porticos, hypostyles, walls, columns, staircases, and so forth to provide a sense of the architectonic quality of the two projects. In the last stage all labels are erased in order to terminate the calculation.

A significant aspect of the design of the two Terragni grammars is that all rules are directly implemented in the online parametric shape grammar interpreter GRAPE [14, 15]. The direct instantiation and testing of the rules in the visual environment of the application provided an immediate visual feedback on the intended function and expressiveness of the rules including the control of their precise geometry, labeling, and the transformations under which they apply. The distinct vocabulary of the architectonic elements of Terragni's language is captured by an extensive usage of labeled shape rules that are readily checked by the automated environment that does not allow incorrect applications of the rules. The generation of the productions in the two grammars strictly follow a two-dimensional geometry to account for the basic parti and the resulting plans of the two projects while the extension to three-dimensional representations including walls, columns, beams, openings, staircases, and so forth is left out for a future development of the project employing the very same labels that specify the two-dimensional elements in the current grammars. Significantly all rules are defined in distinct rule schemata to take advantage of the recent extended formalism of shape grammars to rule schemata [16].

4.1   Stage 1: Parti

In the first stage, two sets of parametric shape rules are defined to generate a specific horizontal section for each project respectively: in the case of the Mambretti Tomb the section goes through the altar and in the case of the Danteum the section goes through the four main rooms at the ground level. The parti grammar for the Mambretti Tomb consists of five shape rules and the parti grammar for the Danteum consists of nine shape rules. The shape rules for both parti schemata are defined by the interplay of squares and rectangles. Both grammars are initiated with the shape rules R_m1 and R_d1 respectively, whereas R_mn denotes a rule for the Mambretti Tomb grammar and R_dn denotes a rule for the Danteum grammar. The shape rules R_m1 and R_d1 create both a square. The shape rules R_m2 and R_d2 copy and shift the square to generate a golden rectangle. The rule R_d3 is defined specifically within the Danteum grammar to translate or slip one of the two squares embedded in the parametric rectangle generated in the previous rule application by R_d2. The shape rules R_m3 and R_d4 divide the square into two rectangles that define the threshold areas in both parti schemata. The rule R_m4 divides a square and the rule R_d4 divides a rectangle. The parametric shape rules R_m5, and R_m6 are defined specifically for replacing the labels for the Mambretti Tomb. The rules R_m5 and R_d6 insert rectangles defining different spatial relations. The Rule R_d6, Rd7 and Rd8 belong uniquely to the Danteum grammar and insert the room division while the rules R_d7 and R_d8 define the room types.

Despite the scale and complexity differences between the Mambretti Tomb and the Danteum, the sets of shape rules of both grammars show a close resemblance both visually and logically too – in terms of the schemata that the rules are defined in [17]. All the shape rules apply under the shape schema $a \rightarrow a + b$ with the exception of the rules R_m1, R_d1 and $R_d2.1$, which apply under the schema $a \rightarrow b$. Moreover, the first three rules are identical rules in both grammars under affinity transformations. These shape rules and the geometric resemblances they produce provide interchangeable components between the two grammars for the parti generation. Significantly, the absence of a unique parametric shape rule in the Mambretti Tomb grammar suggests that the Danteum parti grammar functions as a combination of both parti grammars or alternatively, as an Ur-grammar that can generate hybrid layouts for a cross production of both the Mambretti Tomb and the Danteum. The parti rules for the two Terragni grammars are given in Fig. 4.

4.2   Stage 2: Architectonics

In the second stage two sets of parametric shape rules are defined to generate the distinct architectonic elements and their relations within the two projects. In the case of the Mambretti Tomb grammar the rules capture walls of several kinds, protrusions and extensions of horizontal elements perpendicular to the walls, planar undulations,

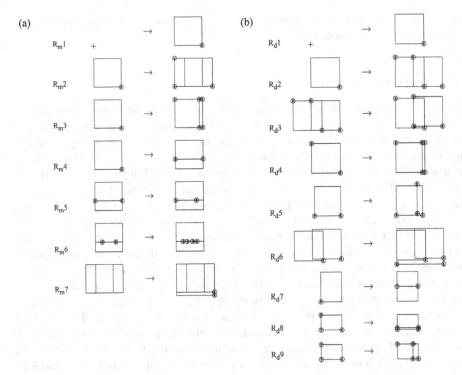

Fig. 4. Shape rules for the parti schemas of the two Terragni grammars. (a) The Mambretti Tomb parti rules (R_m1–7); (b) the Danteum parti rules (R_d1–9).

openings, and so forth, while in the case of the Danteum the rules capture walls, columns, hypostyle configurations, colonnades, openings, and so forth. The architectonic grammar for the Mambretti Tomb is initiated with shape rules defining wall conditions. On the other hand, for the Danteum the architectonic grammar follows a reverse order in which the shape rules defining column and staircase conditions come before the shape rules for the wall conditions. In the Mambretti Tomb grammar the shape rules R_m8 and R_m9 define the solid walls. The rules R_m10, R_m11 and R_m17 define the staircases. The rules R_m12, R_m13 and R_m14 insert niches in the solid walls. The rules R_m15, R_m16 and R_m17 define the openings of doors, windows and the main entrance, respectively. The last shape rule R_m19 inserts the freestanding wall. In the Danteum grammar, the first two shape rules R_d10 and R_d11 define the room types and specify spatial relations for the next rule R_d12 that inserts columns. The shape rules R_d13 to R_d18 define several types of staircases. The shape rule R_d19 eliminates certain lines from the parti schema. Finally the rules R_d20 to R_d26 provide alternative definitions for walls.

The extensive usage of labels in this stage for both grammars specifies the transformations under which the rules apply but mostly define the architectural vocabulary of the two projects. In this sense most of the shape rules in this stage function primarily as terminal replacement rules to substitute geometric elements of parti schemas with

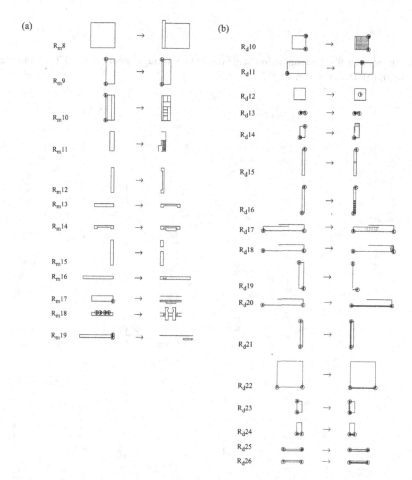

Fig. 5. Shape rules for the architectonic stage of the two Terragni grammars. (a) The Mambretti Tomb architectonic rules (R_m8–19); (b) the Danteum architectonic rules (R_d10–26).

architectonic elements. The architectonics rules for the two Terragni grammars are given in Fig. 5.

4.3   Stage 3: Termination

In the third stage, the termination rules R_mt and R_dt cancel out the remaining labels and end the calculation process. The successive application of these two types of rules erases all labels in the construction and produces designs in the two corresponding Terragni languages. The details for the erasure of each label are here subsumed under a general rule schema given in Fig. 6. The two productions of the original designs of the Mambretti Tomb and the Danteum are given in Fig. 7.

(a) R_{mt} ⊗   →   +   (b) R_{dt} ⊗   →   +

Fig. 6. Shape rules for the termination stage of the two Terragni grammars. (a) The Mambretti Tomb (R_{mt}); (b) The Danteum (R_{dt}).

(a)

(b)

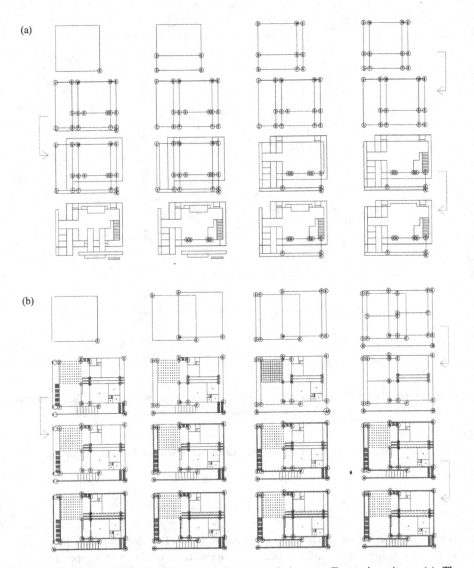

Fig. 7. Automated generation of the ground plan of the two Terragni projects: (a) The Mambretti Tomb; (b) The Danteum.

Significantly the implementation of the two grammars in an automated shape grammar interpreter [15] guarantees that the results of the computation are devoid of errors, flaws or glitches that typically haunt the execution of analog shape rules. This automated encoding of the shape rules and the schemas that describe them provides a seamless environment for the playful testing of the theory about how the two Terragni designs might have been composed. Still, this does not mean that this is a definitive account of the design process that the architect followed. Clearly the design process for making an artifact is complex, iterative, cyclical, it contains dead-ends and all, and nothing is as straightforward as a serial application of rules might imply. ·What is suggested here with the two automated productions above is that potentially complex, iterative, or redundant moves in a design process can be captured and distilled in unique rules that foreground key compositional ideas of the design.

The generation of the two original designs is an important step in this process but not the only one. It is the productions of other designs in the language that demonstrate the constructive understanding of the artifact and the ways the specification of the design resolves geometric, material and programmatic constraints. Two sets of variations based on the designs for the Mambretti Tomb and the Danteum are given in Fig. 8. These architectonic variations are based on parti that are generated in stage one of both grammars and the actual architectonic quality of the designs, the insertion of walls, columns, openings, staircases, and details of all sorts, is conditioned by the straightforward substitution of the shape rules during stage two of the grammar. For every parti there are several solutions based on the substitution of parts of the parti by the corresponding parametric labeled shape rules of stage 2. In this sense these two sets of rules, the parti rules and the architectonic rules can be described as generative rules and parametric rules respectively.

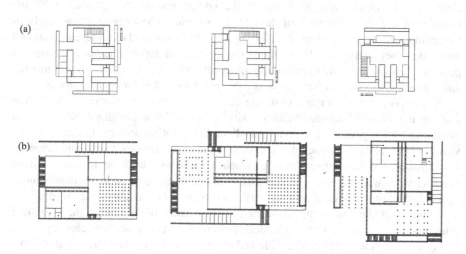

Fig. 8. Automated generation of architectonic plans based on the two Terragni grammars. (a) Variations on the Mambretti Tomb; (b) Variations on the Danteum.

5 Discussion

Schumacher notes that the 1991 Yale exhibition on the Mambretti Tomb and the Danteum illustrates 'the revisionist' character of Terragni mediating between straight classical revival and orthodox modernism. According to Schumacher, the remnants of the neoclassical ideas Terragni inherited from his Italian predecessors allowed him to infuse the abstract formation of modernist notions with figurative motifs and symbolic meanings [1]. Mancini, Mankins, and Yeager, the curators of the Yale exhibition came to the same conclusion through the mapping of contextual, political and historical relations of the two projects with contemporary Italian architectural works of that time. It is precisely this insight by Schumacher and the curators of the Yale exhibition that is reworked here, but the methodology to take it on (and apart) is solely grounded in shape computation and formal analysis and synthesis. This analysis remodels the two projects as two grammars that are predicated upon the visual nature of the shapes used the computation, the desire to constrain these shapes and their relations in specific ways through symbolic labels, and the need for a structured design process to visually explain the construction of the projects by a serial application of parametric shape rules.

These characteristics of visual ambiguity, symbolic clarity, logical structure and the ways they all play out in the two grammars in the design of the shape rules for the parti generation and the shape rules for the architectonic generation recall Knight's and Stiny's schema for classical and non-classical computation [18]. In this schema computation is discussed in terms of two aspects, representation and process, whereas representation deals with the ways the objects in a computation are described and process deals with the ways the rules carry the computation out; and two approaches, classical and non-classical, in terms of the congruence of the approach with the ubiquity of a given framework of thought. Clearly this schema proposes a matrix of four computational models that all differ significantly in the kind of representations and operations they carry out. These models are: classical representation and classical process; classical representation and non-classical process; non-classical representation and classical process; and non-classical representation and non-classical process.

The important pairs for this study are the classical representation/classical process and the non-classical representation/classical process. Most the shape rules in both grammars for the parti stage have a limited number of labels or none; in this sense the visual nature of the unstructured shape in these rules renders the computation as non-classical. On the contrary, most parametric shape rules in the architectonics stage in both grammars feature several types of symbolic labels to provide an unambiguous match of the shape rules and/or a terminal substitution of an underlying geometry with an architectural element; in this sense the symbolic nature of the labeled shape in these rules renders the computation as classical. Moreover, in both cases the rules apply in a highly structured way that can be followed by the user of the grammar, tested to show the possibilities of a rule application within the design, and ultimately used to explain the construction of the design; in this sense, the structured and explanatory nature of the application of the rules in this process renders the computation as classical, while the two models of rules in stages one and two as non-classical/classical and classical/classical.

A nice example of the non-classical/classical model of computation is given here for the calculation of the parti diagrams in both grammars. Figure 9 shows the generation of parti diagrams for both Terragni projects and for new diagrams in their combined languages too. The shape rules for the parti schemas are composed of squares and golden rectangles that function in a similar way in both grammars. The very same shape rules can be merged into a so-called Ur-grammar capable of generating parti diagrams for both projects as well as projects constructed from the union of the compositional rules of both projects. In this sense the Terragni Ur-grammar succeeds at generating a variety of abstract parti diagrams from a limited vocabulary and rules to feature all diagrams from each grammar as well as new ones beyond the productions of either of the two grammars alone.

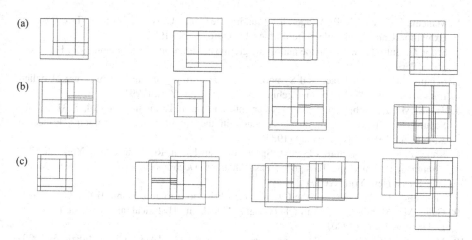

Fig. 9. Automated generation of parti schemata based on the three Terragni grammars. (a) Variations on the Mambretti Tomb; (b) Variations on the Danteum; (c) Variations on the Mambretti/Danteum.

But more than the mere illustration of specific modes of computation and the ways they have been carried out in the two projects, it is suggested here that the characterization of the two stages in both grammars as instances of non-classical/classical and classical/classical computational models casts light on Schumacher's insight on Terragni's architecture. Schumacher claims that Terragni's in-between position mediating straight neoclassicism and orthodox modernism comes from bridging the gap between abstraction and figuration. The architecture of the Mambretti Tomb and the Danteum when cast as formal grammars proves his point by outlining Terragni's design principles in two distinctive generative levels: a non-classical/classical computation of parti generation and a classical/classical computation of architectonic generation. In this sense, the generation of the parti schemas carries out variation and complexity through the interplay of visual shape rules that freely interchange in the design process, while the architectonic generation process is narrowed down to a symbolic substitution of the parti schemas with few architectural elements. Clearly, this conclusion is drawn by the specific way the generative rules are defined in this work. Further studies could evaluate if the shift in the generative process claimed in this study can be traced as a repetitive generative pattern in other works of Terragni as well. The richness of Terragni's architecture still conceals more about his enigmatic characteristics waiting to be revealed by further formal and generative work.

Acknowledgements. We would like to thank Thomas Grasl for his suggestions and technical support in the visual specification of shape rules in GRAPE.

References

1. Mancini, D., Mankins, P., Yeager, R.: Squaring the Circle, Giuseppe Terragni: Two Projects, Exhibition Catalogue, Yale School of Architecture, p. 11 (1991)
2. Stiny, G.: Introduction to shape and shape grammars. Environ. Plann. Plann. Des. B **7**, 343–351 (1980)
3. Schumacher, T.L.: Surface and Symbol: Giuseppe Terragni and the Architecture of Italian Rationalism, p. 138. Princeton Architectural Press, New York (1991)
4. Tafuri, M.: The subject and the mask: an introduction to Terragni. Lotus **20**, 5–31 (1978)
5. Schumacher, T.L.: The Danteum: A Study in the Architecture of Literature. Princeton Architectural Press, New Jersey (1985)
6. Kanekar, A.: Architecture's Pretext: Spaces of Translation. Routledge, New York (2015)
7. Eisenman, P.: Giuseppe Terragni: Transformations, Decomposition, Critiques. The Monacelli Press, New York (2003)
8. Flemming, U.: The secret of the Casa Giuliani Frigerio. Environ. Plann. B **8**, 87–96 (1981)
9. Galli, M., Mühlhoff, C.: Virtual Terragni: CAAD in Historical and Critical Research. Birkhauser, Basel (2000)
10. Marcianò, A.F.: Giuseppe Terragni. Opera Completa 1925–1943, Officina Edizioni (2008)
11. Ciucci, G.: Giuseppe Terragni. Opera Completa. Electa, Milano (1996)
12. Terragni, A., Libeskind, D., Rosselli, P.: The Terragni Atlas: Built Architecture. Skira, New York (2005)
13. Herz-Fischler, R.: A Mathematical History of Division in Extreme and Mean Ratio. Dover, New York (1998)
14. Grasl, T., Economou, A.: Grape: using graph grammar to implement shape grammars. In: Proceeding of SimAUD 2011 Conference, pp. 21–28 (2011)
15. Grasl, T., Economou, A.: From topologies to shapes: parametric shape grammars implemented by graphs. Environ. Plann. B **40**(5), 905–922 (2013)
16. Stiny, G.: Shape: Talking about Seeing and Doing. MIT Press, Cambridge (2006)
17. Economou, A., Kotsopoulos, S.: From shape rules to rule schemata and back. In: Gero, J.S., Hanna, S. (eds.) DCC 2014, pp. 383–399. Springer, Cham (2015). doi:10.1007/978-3-319-14956-1_22
18. Knight, T., Stiny, G.: Classical and non-classical computation. Inf. Technol. **5**(4), 355–372 (2001)

Rectilinear Floor Plans

Krishnendra Shekhawat[1]([⊠]) [iD] and José P. Duarte[2] [iD]

[1] BITS, Pilani Department of Mathematics, Pilani Campus, India
krishnendra.iitd@gmail.com
[2] SCDC, School of Architecture and Landscape Architecture,
The Pennsylvania State University, University Park, PA 16802, USA

Abstract. This work aims at providing a mathematical approach to the problem of allocating given rooms within a given predefined contour shape, while satisfying given adjacency and size constraints. This work is significant with respect to complex building structures, such as hospitals, schools, offices, etc., where we may require floor plans other than rectangular ones and adjacency constraints are defined by the frequency of journeys expected to be made by occupants of the building along different routes. In this paper, we present an algorithmic approach using graph theoretical tools for generating rectilinear floor plan layouts, while satisfying adjacency and size constraints.

Keywords: Adjacency graph · Algorithm · Architectural design · Dual graph · Orthogonal floor plan

1 Introduction

A *floor plan* can be seen as a polygon that is partitioned by straight lines into component polygons called *rooms*. The edges forming the perimeter of each room are called *walls*. Two rooms of any floor plan are *adjacent* if they share a wall or a section of wall; it is not sufficient for them to touch at a point only [1].

Generation of architectural floor plan layout is an elementary activity in building architecture, where architect needs to arrange given spaces (or rooms) in a given floor plan layout (dimensioned or dimensionless geometric schema) such that it satisfies specific requirements or constraints. Two most fundamental constraints are:

i. size constraints, given in terms of room areas with minimum and maximum values in X (horizontal) and Y (vertical) directions,
ii. adjacency constraints, either given by a graph called *adjacency graph* (refer to Roth et al. [2]) or by the number of expected trips between all pair of rooms (refer to Shaviv et al. [3]). These trips can be given in the form of a matrix, called by *weighted adjacency matrix*. Interconnections between rooms and with the exterior, and natural lighting or ventilation into the rooms, are often reasons for such constraints.

Computer-aided architectural design (CAAD) is a broad research area where new computer based algorithmic approaches are presented to facilitate the work of architects

© Springer Nature Singapore Pte Ltd. 2017
G. Çağdaş et al. (Eds.): CAAD Futures 2017, CCIS 724, pp. 395–411, 2017.
DOI: 10.1007/978-981-10-5197-5_22

[4, 5]. There are essentially two well-known approaches to the problem of automated generation of floor plans for buildings: optimization (direct method) [2, 6] and combinatorial (iterative method) [7, 8]. In this paper, using the direct method, we are working over the problem of arranging given rooms (dimensioned) within a given predefined contour shape (dimensionless), while satisfying adjacency constraints, given by a weighted adjacency matrix, and size constraints. Precisely, we present a set of algorithms for generating the required results. The larger aim is to look for a best fit contour shape corresponding to the given constraints.

1.1   History

Throughout the literature, many researchers have worked on the automated generation of floor plans using algorithmic graph-theoretical approaches. This approach was first presented by Levin [9] where a method was proposed for converting the graph into a spatial layout. Then in 1970, Cousin [10] talked about the construction of a rectangular dual of a given graph. In the same year, Grason [11] proposed a dual graph representation of a planar graph for generating a rectangular floor plan. Teaque [12] represented the rectangular spaces by arcs in a network. In 1976, Combes [13] presented very interesting covariants and their relationships to define and categorize different kinds of packings. In 1977, Lynes [14] proposed a solution where each room of the floor plan can have windows overlooking the surroundings. Then in 1980, Hashimshony et al. [15] presented a method for converting non-planar graph into a planar one. In the same year, Baybars and Eastman [6] demonstrated a systematic procedure for obtaining an architectural arrangement (not necessarily rectangular) from a given underlying maximal planar graph. In 1982, Roth et al. [2] presented a method for constructing a dimensioned plan from a given graph. In this method, the given graph is first split into two sub-graphs by a colouring technique [16]; each of these graphs is then converted into a dimensioned graph; the final product of the model is a set of alternative plans where the determination of the envelope's overall size is done by using the PERT algorithm [17]. In the same year, Baybars [18] presented methods of enumerating the circulation spaces within a floor plan. In 1985, Robinson and Janjic [19] showed that, if areas are specified for rooms with a given maximal outer-planar graph, then any convex polygon with the correct area can be divided into convex rooms to satisfy both area and adjacency requirements. In 1987, Rinsma [20] showed that, for any given maximal outerplanar graph with at most four vertices of degree 2, it is not always possible to find a rectangular floor plan satisfying adjacency and area conditions. In 1988, Rinsma [21] provided conditions for the existence of rectangular and orthogonal floor plans for a given tree. In 1997, Irvine et al. [22] presented a graph-theoretical approach for generating orthogonal layouts. In 2000, Recuero et al. [23] demonstrated a heuristic method for checking the realisability of a graph into a rectangular floor plan.

As a recent work in this direction, in 2010, Marson and Musse [24] proposed a technique for the generation of floor plans based on the squarified treemaps algorithm. Treemaps subdivide an area into small pieces to represent the importance of each part in the hierarchy whereas squarified treemaps are treemaps that are used to generate rooms with aspect ratios close to one. In 2011, Alvarez et al. [25] developed a tool for automatic drawing of two dimensional floor plans. In 2012, Regateiro et al. [26] proposed a unique approach called orthogonal compartment placement for architectural layout design problems, which is based on topological algebras and constraint satisfaction techniques. In this work, the authors have proposed 169 ways in which two rectangles or rooms can be adjacent. This gives a new scale to the problem of defining the adjacency relations among the rooms. In 2013, Kotulski and Strug [27] used a particular class of graphs, called hypergraphs, as a means of representing building layouts.

To the extent of our knowledge and in the context of this work, the above mentioned approaches have two limitations in common:

i. The output is restricted to rectangular floor plans only. Only, in a few cases, orthogonal floor plans are constructed from a particular class of graphs, namely, maximal planar graphs [22]. Other than that, in a few approaches, the shape of the layout get evolved which is non-rectangular [6].
ii. The adjacency constraints among the rooms are given by graphs. Clearly, in this case, it is difficult to introduce flexibility in adjacency relations among the rooms.

If we consider the complex building structures, like hospitals, schools, offices, etc., then we may require floor plans other than rectangular ones. Also, in case of complex buildings with large number of rooms, it seems important to consider the distances separating pairs of rooms, and also the frequency of journeys expected to be made by occupants of the building along different routes.

To address the problem of designing of floor plans with a complex nature, in this paper, we use heuristic methods and present a set of algorithms for automated generation of rectilinear shaped floor plans where the adjacency constraints are given by weighted adjacency matrix.

Steps involved in the construction of a rectilinear floor plan are as follows:

i. Partition of given rectilinear polygon into a maximum number of rectangular zones,
ii. Conversion of given weighted adjacency matrix into an adjacency matrix,
iii. Formation of clusters of given rooms (equal to the number of rectangular zones) on the basis of the obtained adjacency matrix,
iv. Construction of a rectangular floor plan corresponding to each cluster,
v. Adjoining of obtained rectangular floor plans to have a rectilinear floor plan.

For smooth reading of the rest of the article, here is the list of notations that are frequently used in the paper:

$A_w(n)$: a weighted adjacency matrix with n rooms,
$R_i : i^{th}$ room
l_i and h_i: length and height of R_i,
$R_S^F(n)$: a spiral-based rectangular floor plan with n rooms,
L_i and H_i: length and height of a $R_S^F(i)$,
$P_S^F(n)$: a spiral-based plus-shaped floor plan with n rooms.

2 Construction of Rectilinear Floor Plans

In this section, we aim at providing a mathematical approach to the problem of allocating given rooms within a given predefined contour shape, while satisfying given adjacency and size constraints. Here, we present a heuristic approach for the construction of rectilinear floor plans, where each step of the process is presented by the following subsections.

2.1 Partition of Given Rectilinear Polygon into Rectangular Zones

The first step is to partition the given rectilinear frame into maximum number of rectangular zones by drawing horizontal and vertical lines within the given frame such that each drawn line must either start or/and end at a corner point of the polygon (at this stage, we are considering the simplest case where drawn horizontal and vertical lines do not cross each other). Dividing the given frame into maximum number of rectangular zones gives us all possibilities of its partition into rectangular zones and creates an option for architects to reduce the number of rectangular zones. For better understanding of the process of partitioning, refer to Fig. 1.

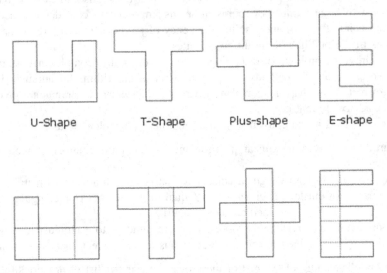

Fig. 1. Dimensionless rectilinear polygons and their partition into the maximum number of rectangular zones

2.2   Converting the Given Weighted Adjacency Matrix into an Adjacency Matrix

Mathematically, a weighted adjacency matrix with n rooms is given as follows:

$$A_W(n) = (a_{ij})_{n \times n} = (a_{ji})_{n \times n} = \begin{cases} k_{ij} \in I^+, & i \neq j \\ 0, & i = j \end{cases}$$

Table 1. A weighted adjacency matrix of order 20

	R_1	R_2	R_3	R_4	R_5	R_6	R_7	R_8	R_9	R_{10}
R_1	0	4	6	6	9	6	3	6	4	5
R_2	4	0	6	9	8	6	9	6	4	5
R_3	6	6	0	8	6	8	6	9	4	4
R_4	6	2	8	0	6	8	6	9	4	4
R_5	9	8	6	6	0	6	9	10	2	2
R_6	6	6	8	8	6	0	10	9	6	2
R_7	3	9	6	6	9	10	0	6	2	2
R_8	6	6	9	9	10	9	6	0	6	6
R_9	4	4	4	4	2	6	2	6	0	8
R_{10}	5	5	4	4	2	2	2	6	8	0
R_{11}	3	3	3	3	2	2	2	4	6	10
R_{12}	2	2	6	4	2	2	2	4	6	4
R_{13}	2	2	6	4	2	2	2	4	6	4
R_{14}	2	2	4	4	2	2	2	4	6	4
R_{15}	8	8	4	4	4	4	4	4	6	6
R_{16}	9	6	7	4	2	3	10	5	10	7
R_{17}	4	8	6	3	2	7	9	8	4	8
R_{18}	3	5	1	10	8	7	4	9	6	7
R_{19}	2	7	5	6	8	5	4	3	8	7
R_{20}	6	1	10	4	9	1	2	3	2	5

	R_{11}	R_{12}	R_{13}	R_{14}	R_{15}	R_{16}	R_{17}	R_{18}	R_{19}	R_{20}
R_1	3	2	2	2	8	9	4	3	2	6
R_2	3	2	2	2	8	6	8	5	7	1
R_3	3	6	6	4	4	7	6	1	5	10
R_4	3	4	4	4	4	4	3	10	6	4
R_5	2	2	2	2	4	2	2	8	8	9
R_6	2	2	2	2	4	3	7	7	5	1
R_7	2	2	2	2	4	10	9	4	4	2
R_8	4	4	4	4	4	5	8	9	3	3
R_9	6	6	6	6	6	10	4	6	8	2
R_{10}	10	4	4	4	6	7	8	7	7	5
R_{11}	0	2	2	2	4	9	9	3	2	3
R_{12}	2	0	8	10	2	3	3	4	4	8
R_{13}	2	8	0	10	2	5	5	6	5	5
R_{14}	2	10	10	0	2	7	6	6	7	3
R_{15}	4	2	2	2	0	2	7	5	5	10
R_{16}	9	3	5	7	2	0	6	6	3	3
R_{17}	9	3	5	6	7	6	0	7	1	5
R_{18}	3	4	6	6	5	6	8	0	1	2
R_{19}	2	4	5	7	5	3	4	5	0	10
R_{20}	3	8	5	3	10	3	4	2	9	0

As an illustration, refer to Table 1, where a weighted adjacency matrix corresponding to 20 given rooms is shown. The data for Table 1 has been taken randomly, i.e., each entry in the Table can have any integer value. To illustrate the result of the paper, we will demonstrate the construction of U-shaped floor plan where the required number of clusters is five (refer to Fig. 1).

To partition the given rooms into the required number of clusters (the required number of clusters is equivalent to the number of obtained rectangular zones), the first step is to convert the given weighted adjacency matrix into an adjacency matrix with entries 0 and 1 only.

Let the number of distinct entries in the $A_W(n)$ be r and denoted by $s_1, s_2, \ldots s_r$ such that $s_1 < s_2 < \ldots < s_r$. The steps of the algorithm for transforming given $A_W(n)$ into an adjacency matrix are as follows:

Algorithm 1

i. Let t = r. Look for the pairs of rooms corresponding to number s_t.
ii. Reduce t by one and look the pairs of rooms corresponding to number s_t. To avoid repetition and to reduce complexity, in each of the coming steps, skip rows corresponding to the rooms covered by the pairs formed in above step/s.
iii. If all the rooms are covered by the formed pair of rooms then terminate the algorithm otherwise go to Step 2.

Corresponding to Table 1, the pair of rooms obtained using Algorithm 1 are as follows:

$(R_1, R_5), (R_1, R_{16}), (R_2, R_4), (R_2, R_7), (R_3, R_{20}), (R_4, R_{18}), (R_5, R_8), (R_7, R_6),$
$(R_9, R_{16}), (R_{10}, R_{11}), (R_{12}, R_{14}), (R_{13}, R_{14}), (R_{15}, R_{20}), (R_{17}, R_7), (R_{17}, R_{11}), (R_{19}, R_{20})$

On the basis of the obtained pairs of rooms, an adjacency matrix is constructed which is illustrated in Table 2.

2.3 Clustering

In this section we will present an algorithm for the formation of clusters of the rooms on the basis of the obtained adjacency matrix in Sect. 2.2.

Algorithm 2

i. Let k_i be the number of 1's in the row A_i of the adjacency matrix obtained in Sect. 2.2, where $1 \leq i \leq k$. M be the maximum of all k_i's.
ii. Look for the rows corresponding to M.
iii. Form a cluster corresponding to each row covered in above steps. The formed cluster corresponding to i^{th} row consists of room R_i and all the rooms adjacent to R_i.
iv. If two clusters have any room/s in common then merge them to form a new cluster.

Table 2. An adjacency matrix derived from the given weighted adjacency matrix in Table 1

	R_1	R_2	R_3	R_4	R_5	R_6	R_7	R_8	R_9	R_{10}
R_1	0	0	0	0	1	0	0	0	0	0
R_2	0	0	0	1	0	0	1	0	0	0
R_3	0	0	0	0	0	0	0		0	0
R_4	0	1	0	0	0	0	0	0	0	0
R_5	1	0	0	0	0	0	0	1	0	0
R_6	0	0	0	0	0	0	1	0	0	0
R_7	0	1	0	0	0	1	0	0	0	0
R_8	0	0	0	0	1	0	0	0	0	0
R_9	0	0	0	0	0	0	0	0	0	0
R_{10}	0	0	0	0	0	0	0	0	0	0
R_{11}	0	0	0	0	0	0	0	0	0	1
R_{12}	0	0	0	0	0	0	0	0	0	0
R_{13}	0	0	0	0	0	0	0	0	0	0
R_{14}	0	0	0	0	0	0	0	0	0	0
R_{15}	0	0	0	0	0	0	0	0	0	0
R_{16}	1	0	0	0	0	0	0	0	1	0
R_{17}	0	0	0	0	0	0	1	0	0	0
R_{18}	0	0	0	1	0	0	0	0	0	0
R_{19}	0	0	0	0	0	0	0	0	0	0
R_{20}	0	0	1	0	0	0	0	0	0	0

	R_{11}	R_{12}	R_{13}	R_{14}	R_{15}	R_{16}	R_{17}	R_{18}	R_{19}	R_{20}
R_1	0	0	0	0	0	1	0	0	0	0
R_2	0	0	0	0	0	0	0	0	0	0
R_3	0	0	0	0	0	0	0	0	0	1
R_4	0	0	0	0	0	0	0	1	0	0
R_5	0	0	0	0	0	0	0	0	0	0
R_6	0	0	0	0	0	0	0	0	0	0
R_7	0	0	0	0	0	0	1	0	0	0
R_8	0	0	0	0	0	0	0	0	0	0
R_9	0	0	0	0	0	1	0	0	0	0
R_{10}	1	0	0	0	0	0	0	0	0	0
R_{11}	0	0	0	0	0	0	1	0	0	0
R_{12}	0	0	0	1	0	0	0	0	0	0
R_{13}	0	0	0	1	0	0	0	0	0	0
R_{14}	0	1	1	0	0	0	0	0	0	0
R_{15}	0	0	0	0	0	0	0	0	0	1
R_{16}	0	0	0	0	0	0	0	0	0	0
R_{17}	1	0	0	0	0	0	0	0	0	0
R_{18}	0	0	0	0	0	0	0	0	0	0
R_{19}	0	0	0	0	0	0	0	0	0	1
R_{20}	0	0	0	0	1	0	0	0	1	0

v. Reduce M by one and look for the rows corresponding to M while skipping the rows corresponding to the rooms already covered in the formed clusters.

vi. If all the rooms are covered by the formed clusters then go to Step 7 otherwise go to Step 3. Corresponding to Table 2, the formed clusters are as follows:

$$\{R_1, R_5, R_8, R_9, R_{16}\}, \{R_2, R_4, R_6, R_7, R_{10}, R_{11}, R_{17}, R_{18}\},$$
$$\{R_3, R_{15}, R_{19}, R_{20}\}, \{R_{12}, R_{13}, R_{14}\}$$

vii. If the number of formed clusters is less than the required number of clusters, then to increase the number of clusters by one, search for the cluster with the maximum number of rooms. Let this cluster be named G. To proceed further, look for a pair of rooms that belongs to G with minimum weight in the weighted adjacency matrix. Let this pair be (R_1, R_2).

viii. Split G into clusters, G_1 and G_2, such that G_1 contains R_1 and G_2 contains R_2. Other rooms of G_1 and G_2 are derived as follows:

ix. If the weight of any room corresponding to R_1 is greater than the weight corresponding to R_2 then this room belongs to G_1 otherwise it belongs to G_2. For example, corresponding to Table 2, the number of formed clusters is four. Here, $G = \{R_2, R_4, R_6, R_7, R_{10}, R_{11}, R_{17}, R_{18}\}$ is the cluster with maximum number of rooms. Two clusters formed by breaking G are $\{R_2, R_4, R_6, R_7\}$ and $\{R_{10}, R_{11}, R_{17}, R_{18}\}$.

x. If the number of formed clusters is greater than the required number of clusters, then to reduce the number of clusters by one, choose two clusters having a minimum number of rooms and adjoin them.

xi. If number of formed clusters is equal to the required number of clusters, then terminates the algorithm otherwise go to Step 7.

2.4 Rectangular Floor Plans

A *rectangular floor plan* is a floor plan in which the plan's boundary and each room are rectangles. Corresponding to every floor plan, there also exist a graph where vertices represent rooms and exterior, and two vertices are joined by an edge whenever corresponding rooms are adjacent. This graph is called dual graph. If in a dual graph, exterior is ignored then it is called weak dual, given by Earl and March [28].

If we restrict ourselves to rectangular floor plans only, then from [13], the maximum number of edges in any dual graph is 3n + 1 and from [29], the maximum number of edges in any weak dual graph is 3n − 7 where n is the number of rooms and n > 3. We say that a rectangular floor plan is best connected if its dual graph and weak dual graph have 3n + 1 and 3n − 7 edges respectively.

Now for each cluster formed in the above section, we need to form a rectangular floor plan. We can see that we were given a weighted adjacency matrix from which clusters were formed. Clearly, for the formed clusters, we do not have any given graph relating their rooms. One way is to drive a graph for each cluster and then construct a rectangular floor plan for each cluster. In this case, it may happen that there may not exist a rectangular floor plan for the corresponding cluster. Therefore, to automate the process, we consider more generalized floor plans, i.e., best connected rectangular floor plans, with maximum connectivity among the rooms, so that we guarantee that appropriate connections can be established at a later stage. The steps of the algorithm, called *spiral-based algorithm*, for constructing best connected rectangular floor plans are as follows (the rectangular floor plans constructed using spiral-based algorithm are called *spiral-based rectangular floor plans*, denoted by R_S^F):

Algorithm 3

Here, we deal with 3 kinds of rectangles where each type is given by its *position* which is the upper left vertex, and its *size*, which consists of its length and height.

At each stage i of the construction process we have the following rectangles:

   i. A new room R_i; with position (x_i, y_i), and size (l_i, h_i).
  ii. An extra space E_i; with position (t_i, u_i) and size (λ_i, μ_i).
 iii. A new rectangular composition $R_S^F(i)$ with position (X_i, Y_i) and size (L_i, H_i).

The process starts with $i = 1$ by placing R_1 to the left of $(0, 0)$. The remaining rooms are placed as follows:

$$i \equiv 1 (\mod 4):$$
$$(x_i, y_i) = (X_{i-1} - l_i, Y_{i-1}), (X_i, Y_i) = (x_i, y_i)$$
$$i \equiv 2 (\mod 4):$$
$$(x_i, y_i) = (X_{i-1}, Y_{i-1} + h_i), (X_i, Y_i) = (x_i, y_i)$$
$$i \equiv 3 (\mod 4):$$
$$(x_i, y_i) = (X_{i-1} + L_{i-1}, Y_{i-1}), (X_i, Y_i) = (X_{i-1}, Y_{i-1})$$
$$i \equiv 0 (\mod 4):$$
$$(x_i, y_i) = (X_{i-1}, Y_{i-1} - H_{i-1}), (X_i, Y_i) = (X_{i-1}, Y_{i-1})$$

If i is odd then

$$(t_i, u_i) = (x_i, y_i + h_i) \text{ and } (\lambda_i, \mu_i) = (l_i, H_{i-1} - h_i) \text{ if } h_i < H_{i-1}$$
$$(t_i, u_i) = (X_{i-1}, Y_{i-1} + H_{i-1}) \text{ and } (\lambda_i, \mu_i) = (L_{i-1}, h_i - H_{i-1}) \text{ if } h_i > H_{i-1}$$

If i is even then

$$(t_i, u_i) = (x_i + l_i, y_i) \text{ and } (\lambda_i, \mu_i) = (L_{i-1} - l_i, h_i) \text{ if } l_i < L_{i-1}$$
$$(t_i, u_i) = (X_{i-1} + L_{i-1}, Y_{i-1}) \text{ and } (\lambda_i, \mu_i) = (l_i - L_{i-1}, h_i) \text{ if } l_i > L_{i-1}$$

For further clarification of the steps of Algorithm 3, refer to the following example.

Example 1

Let us assume that $l_1 = 8, h_1 = 12, l_2 = 12, h_2 = 18, l_3 = 13, h_3 = 20, l_4 = 20, h_4 = 30$. R_S^F is constructed as follows:

i. Place R_1 at a position (x, y) with length l_1 and height h_1 (see Fig. 2(A)).

ii. R_2 is positioned above R_1 with length l_2 and height h_2 as shown in Fig. 2(B). It can be easily verified from Fig. 2(B) that, $l_2 > L_1$, therefore to get a rectangular composition we draw an extra space below R_2 as depicted in Fig. 2(C). It is clear from this step that in the spiral-based algorithm, after positioning each room, aim is to obtain a rectangular composition of all the positioned spaces; and to achieve the rectangular composition, sometimes an extra space is required. This idea of the extra spaces guarantees the generation of a rectangular floor plan irrespective of the size of rooms.

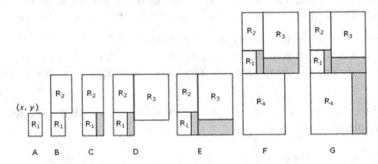

Fig. 2. Construction of a spiral-based rectangular floor plan

iii. Moving in the clockwise direction, we place R_3 to the right of R_1 and R_2 (refer to Fig. 2(D)). Again we can see from Fig. 2(D) that, $H_2 > h_3$, thus we draw an extra space below R_3 as illustrated in Fig. 2(E) to get a rectangular composition.

iv. Now we place R_4 below the obtained rectangular composition (refer to Fig. 2(F)). Since $l_4 < L_3$, we draw an extra space to the right of R_4 as shown in 2(G).

Figure 2(G) gives the required R_S^F for the 4 rooms. If there are more rooms, we keep arranging the rooms in the clockwise direction and add an extra space if required to get a rectangular floor plan for the given rooms.

2.5   Minimum Area Spiral-Based Rectangular Floor Plans

It is clear that if rectangular rooms of different sizes need to be allocated in a frame of a rectangle, then there would be some extra spaces. In this section, we present an optimization technique for reducing the size of extra space in a R_S^F such that the connectivity of the R_S^F remains preserved.

i. Order of allocation

ii. The order in which rooms are arranged to obtain a rectangular floor plan using the spiral-based algorithm is called the order of allocation. Clearly, for n rooms, by considering each order of allocation, $n! R_S^F(n)$ can be obtained and each $R_S^F(n)$ may have a different area because of the presence of different extra spaces.

iii. Swapping of length and height

iv. A room R_i can be positioned either with length l_i and height h_i or with length h_i and height l_i, i.e., we can swap the length and height of each room without changing the area of a room, which in turn produces two R_S^F with different areas. If all the combinations of the rooms whose length and height can be swapped are taken into account then we can obtain $2^n R_S^F(n)$.

v. Using the above two steps, $n! \times 2^n R_S^F(n)$ can be obtained from the spiral-based algorithm. Now, to reduce the areas of extra spaces we can pick the one with minimum area among $n! \times 2^n R_S^F(n)$.

The size constraints corresponding to 20 rooms in Table 1 are given by Table 3. The minimum area R_S^F corresponding to clusters formed in Sect. 2.2 are illustrated in Fig. 3, where R_S^F are constructed using the minimum dimension in X and Y direction given in Table 3.

Table 3. Given size constraints corresponding to 20 rooms in Table 1

	Minimum (X-direction)	Maximum (X-direction)	Minimum (Y-direction)	Maximum (Y-direction)
R_1	80	100	60	80
R_2	80	100	60	80
R_3	80	100	60	80
R_4	75	100	55	80
R_5	60	80	40	60
R_6	65	80	40	60
R_7	35	50	20	40
R_8	40	60	30	50
R_9	120	140	75	90
R_{10}	90	110	70	90
R_{11}	55	70	40	60
R_{12}	80	100	60	80
R_{13}	80	100	60	80
R_{14}	100	120	70	90
R_{15}	100	120	70	90
R_{16}	20	35	30	50
R_{17}	45	60	30	50
R_{18}	60	90	75	90
R_{19}	75	105	50	90
R_{20}	105	120	130	140

The areas of obtained floor plans can be further reduced as follows:

We first consider all rooms with minimum dimension in X and Y directions and compute the area of extra space obtained after allocating the room. Then we consider each room, say R_i, one by one and choose a value for the dimension of R_i in X or Y direction to have an extra space with minimum area. For example, if we draw R_5 with length 50 and height 60 instead of length 40 and height 60 as in Fig. 3, then there won't be any extra space after the allocation of R_5. It should be noted that, to reduce the size of extra space, length and height of R_5 is swapped in Fig. 3, i.e., we consider that its length varies from 40 to 60 instead of 60 to 80. For better understanding, refer to Fig. 4 and Table 4, where we have illustrated the minimum area spiral-based rectangular floor plans and the final length and height of each given room, corresponding to the input of Tables 1 and 3.

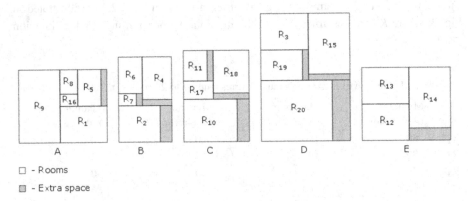

Fig. 3. Spiral-based rectangular floor plans corresponding to clusters formed in Sect. 2.3 with minimum length and height in X and Y directions respectively given in Table 3

Remark. Using the definition of adjacency between rooms via extra spaces, provided in [30] Sect. 2, we can verify that the rectangular floor plans constructed using the spiral-based algorithm are best connected.

2.6   Rectilinear Floor Plans

After constructing a rectangular floor plan for each cluster of rooms (see Fig. 4), a given rectilinear-shaped floor plan can be constructed by adjoining the obtained rectangular floor plans as follows:

i. First the degree of each rectangular zone in the given rectilinear polygon is computed and then arranged in descending order (the degree of a rectangular zone is the number of rectangular zones that are adjacent to it). Let the degrees corresponding to n rectangular zones in descending order be represented as $A_1, A_2, \ldots A_n$.

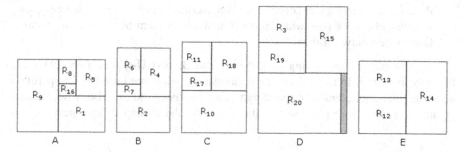

Fig. 4. Minimum area spiral-based rectangular floor plans corresponding to Tables 1 and 3

Table 4. Final length and height of given rooms derived from Table 3 corresponding to the minimum area spiral-based rectangular floor plans, where the length and height of some rooms are swapped and the length or height of some rooms have been extended from minimum dimension to a dimension less than or equal to the maximum dimension given in Table 3

	Length	Height	Swapped	Extended
R_1	80	60	No	No
R_2	95	60	No	Yes
R_3	80	60	No	No
R_4	55	85	Yes	Yes
R_5	50	60	Yes	Yes
R_6	40	65	Yes	No
R_7	40	20	No	Yes
R_8	30	40	Yes	No
R_9	75	120	Yes	No
R_{10}	105	70	No	Yes
R_{11}	45	5	Yes	Yes
R_{12}	80	60	No	No
R_{13}	80	60	No	No
R_{14}	70	120	Yes	Yes
R_{15}	70	110	Yes	Yes
R_{16}	30	20	Yes	No
R_{17}	45	30	No	No
R_{18}	60	85	No	Yes
R_{19}	80	50	No	Yes
R_{20}	140	105	Yes	Yes

ii. Then the degree of each rectangular floor plan is derived and arranged in descending order (the degree of a rectangular floor plan is the number of rooms in the floor plan). Let the degrees corresponding to n rectangular floor plans in descending order be represented as $B_1, B_2, \ldots B_n$.

iii. Replace each rectangular zone in the given rectilinear polygon with degree A_i with a rectangular floor plan with degree B_i and adjoin them by introducing a circulation space between them.

For example, corresponding to Tables 1 and 3, two U-shaped floor plans are illustrated in Fig. 5. In these floor plans, circulation spaces are introduced to partition the rectangular floor plans corresponding to each cluster of rooms. Also, virtual spaces are drawn in these floor plans so that they look like the U-shaped floor plans.

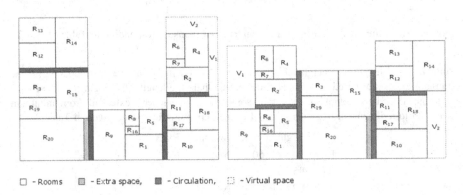

□ – Rooms   ▣ – Extra space,   ▪ – Circulation,   ⸬ – Virtual space

Fig. 5. U-shaped floor plans corresponding to Tables 1 and 3

3   Results

In this paper, we present a set of algorithms for allocating given rooms into a predefined contour shape, while satisfying given adjacency and size constraints, where adjacency constraints are derived by the frequency of journeys expected to be made by occupants of the building along different routes and size constraints composed of length and height of given rooms. Here, the aim is to arrange given rooms in a way that the obtained packing must be confined in a shape similar to the given contour shape and has optimum area and connectivity.

The presented approach comprises of two main steps: the first one is to partition the given contour into a maximum number of rectangular zones and the next is to replace each rectangular zone by a rectangular floor plan, where the rooms of each floor plan are derived on the basis of adjacency constraints.

Using the approach illustrated in Sect. 2, plus-shaped and F-shaped floor plans are illustrated in Fig. 6(A) and (B) respectively. In Fig. 6(A) and (B), the given 20 rooms are partitioned into 5 and 6 clusters respectively on the basis of adjacency constraints given in Table 1. The rectangular floor plans corresponding to each cluster are separated by circulation spaces. Here, size constraints are given in Table 3.

On the basis of the architect's wish, the given contour shape can be partitioned into lesser number of rectangular zones than the maximum number of rectangular zones. For example, refer to Fig. 6(C), where an F-shaped floor plan made up of five rectangular floor plans is illustrated.

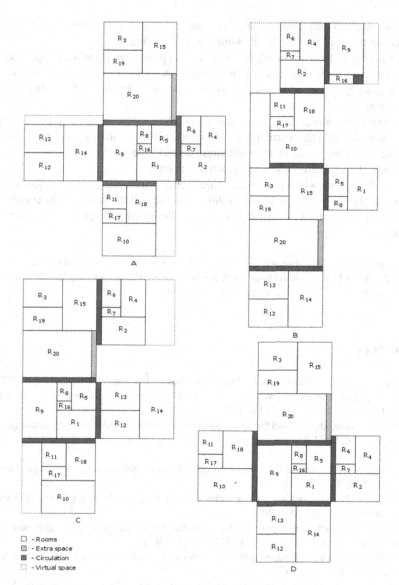

Fig. 6. Plus-shaped and F-shaped floor plans corresponding to Tables 1 and 3

4   Conclusion and Future Work

The work presented here is part of a larger work aimed at exploring exhaustively the use of rectilinear arrangements in the design of layouts. Our ultimate goal is to build a general system for the automatic generation of floor plans, i.e., to provide architects with design aids, that is, algorithms that can generate good candidate solutions, taking size and adjacency requirements into account and that can be further improved and adjusted by them, to provide better solutions to the user.

To the extent of our knowledge, we are first to present an algorithmic approach for the construction of rectilinear floor plans when adjacency constraints are given in terms of the frequency of journeys expected to be made by occupants of the building along different routes.

We know that a multitude of aspects of different nature need to be considered in architectural design. The current work is concerned with the generation of layouts where we are dealing with functional requirements in the strict sense only, i.e., we are considering the adjacency and size requirements only.

In the future, we will try to cover other architectural aspects, e.g., daylight, view etc. To validate the results presented in this paper, we will try to present its comparison with manual space planning developed by some designers with medium to substantial experience.

Acknowledgement. This research has been supported by Research Initiation Grant (Grant number 77), Birla Institute of Technology & Science, Pilani, Pilani Campus, 333031 and by the Stuckeman Center for Design Computing at Penn State.

References

1. Rinsma, I.: Existence theorems for floorplans (thesis). University of Canterbury (1987)
2. Roth, J., Hashimshony, R., Wachman, A.: Turning a graph into a rectangular floor plan. Build. Environ. **17**(3), 163–173 (1982)
3. Shaviv, E., Gali, D.: A model for space allocation in complex buildings: a computer graphics approach. In: Build International, pp. 493–517. Applied Science Publisher Ltd., England (1974)
4. Mitchell, W.: The theoretical foundation of computer-aided architectural design. Environ. Plan. B **2**(2), 127–150 (1975)
5. Kalay, Y.: The impact of information technology on design methods, products and practices. Des. Stud. **27**(3), 357–380 (2006)
6. Baybars, I., Eastman, C.M.: Enumerating architectural arrangements by generating their underlying graphs. Environ. Plan. B **7**, 289–310 (1980)
7. Steadman, J.P.: Graph theoretic representation of architectural arrangement. Architect. Res. Teach. **2**(3), 161–172 (1973)
8. Galle, P.: An algorithm for exhaustive generation of building floor plans. Commun. ACM **24** (12), 813–825 (1981)
9. Levin, P.H.: Use of graphs to decide the optimum layout of buildings. Archit. J. **140**(15), 809–817 (1964)
10. Cousin, J.: Topological organization of architectural spaces. Architectural Des. **40**, 491–493 (1970)
11. Grason, J.: A dual linear representation for space filling location problems of the floorplan type. In: Moore, G.T. (ed.) Emerging Methods of Environmental Design and Planning, pp. 170–178. MIT Press, Cambridge (1970)

12. Teague, L.: Network models of configurations of rectangular parallelepipeds. In: Moore, G. T. (ed.) Emerging Methods in Environmental Design and Planning. MIT Press, Cambridge (1970)
13. Combes, L.: Packing rectangles into rectangular arrangements. Environ. Plan. B **3**, 3–32 (1976)
14. Lynes, J.A.: Windows and floor plans. Environ. Plan. B **4**, 51–55 (1977)
15. Hashimshony, R., Shaviv, E., Wachman, A.: Transforming an adjacency matrix into a planar graph. Build. Environ. **15**, 205–217 (1980)
16. Roth, J., Wachman, A.: A model for optimal compact packing of convex cells in an Orthogonal network. Technion-I.I.T, Faculty of Architecture and Town Planning, Haifa (1978)
17. Radcliffe, P.E., Kawal, D.E., Stephenson, R.J.: Critical Path Method, vol. III. Cahner, Chicago (1967)
18. Baybars, I.: The generation of floor plans with circulation spaces. Environ. Plan. B **9**, 445–456 (1982)
19. Robinson, D.F., Janjic, I.: The constructability of floorplans with certain given outerplanar adjacency graph and room areas. In: Proceedings Xth British Combinatorics Conference, Ars Combinatoria 20B, pp. 133–142 (1985)
20. Rinsma, I.: Nonexistence of a certain rectangular floorplan with specified areas and adjacency. Environ. Plan. **14**, 163–166 (1987)
21. Rinsma, I.: Rectangular and orthogonal floorplans with required room areas and tree adjacency. Environ. Plan. **15**, 111–118 (1988)
22. Irvine, S.A., Rinsma-Melchert, I.: A new approach to the block layout problem. Int. J. Prod. Res. **35**(8), 2359–2376 (1997)
23. Recuero, A., Rio, O., Alvarez, M.: Heuristic method to check the realisability of a graph into a rectangular plan. Adv. Eng. Softw. **31**, 223–231 (2000)
24. Marson F., Musse S.R.: Automatic real-time generation of floor plans based on squarified treemaps algorithm. Int. J. Comput. Games Technol. (2014)
25. Alvarez, M., Rio, O., Recuero, A., Romero, M.S.: AD2D: a tool for a automatic drawing of a-dimensional 2D floor plan. Informes de la Construccion **63**(524), 83–99 (2011)
26. Regateiro, F., Bento, J., Dias, J.: Floor plan design using block algebra and constraint satisfaction. Adv. Eng. Inform. **26**, 361–382 (2012)
27. Kotulski, L., Strug, B.: Supporting communication and cooperation in distributed representation for adaptive design. Adv. Eng. Inform. **27**, 220–229 (2013)
28. Earl, C.F., March, L.J.: Architectural applications of graph theory. In: Wilson, R.J., Beineke, L.W. (eds.) Applications of Graph Theory, pp. 327–355. Academic Press, London (1979)
29. Shekhawat, K.: Why golden rectangle is used so often by architects: a mathematical approach. Alexandria Eng. J. **54**, 213–222 (2015)
30. Shekhawat, K.: Mathematical propositions associated with the connectivity of architectural designs. Ain Shams Eng. J. (2015) (In press). doi:10.1016/j.asej.2015.09.009

Author Index

Adachi, Haruo 60
Aydin, Serdar 231

Basarir, Lale 136
Beirão, José Nuno 42
Bingöl, Cemal Koray 289
Browne, Will N. 151
Buš, Peter 23

Çağdaş, Gülen 121
Çapunaman, Özgüç Bertuğ 289
Çavuşoğlu, Ömer Halil 121
Cichocka, Judyta M. 151

de Klerk, Rui 42
De Luca, Francesco 170
Devadass, Pradeep 273
Donath, Dirk 100
Dortdivanlioglu, Hayri 381
Duarte, José P. 395

Earl, Chris 348
Economou, Athanassios 381
Erdine, Elif 273
Erhan, Halil 81, 191

Fukuda, Tomohiro 60

Genca, Ozgur 136
Gül, Leman Figen 212
Gün, Onur Yüce 252
Gürsoy, Benay 289

Halıcı, Süheyla Müge 212
Hollberg, Alexander 100

Jowers, Iestyn 348

Kallegias, Alexandros 273
Kepczynska-Walczak, Anetta 3
Knecht, Katja 23

Koenig, Reinhard 23
Kolarić, Siniša 81

Mei-Chih, Chang 23
Miao, Yufan 23
Migalska, Agata 151
Moreira, Angel Fernando Lara 273
Motamedi, Ali 60
Muslimin, Rizal 329

Nada, Hideki 60

Pietrzak, Anna 3
Pinochet, Diego 306

Rodriguez, Edgar 151
Ruth, Jürgen 100

Sato, Yusuke 60
Sayah, Iman 231
Schnabel, Marc Aurel 231
Schneider, Sven 100
Shekhawat, Krishnendra 395
Shimizu, Shunta 60
Shireen, Naghmi 191
Stiny, George 348
Sungur, Alican 273

Takei, Chikako 60
Tsamis, Alexandros 366
Tschetwertak, Julia 100

Uzun, Can 212

Vaizoglu, Zeynep 136
Varinlioglu, Guzden 136
Voll, Hendrik 170

Wang, Ivy 191
Woodbury, Robert 81, 191

Yabuki, Nobuyoshi 60

Printed in the United States
By Bookmasters